Trading off Competing Allocation Principles

AF793866

# European University Studies
Europäische Hochschulschriften
Publications Universitaires Européennes

**Series V**
**Economics and Management**

Reihe V Série V
Volks- und Betriebswirtschaft
Sciences économiques, gestion d'entreprise

**Vol./Bd. 3343**

PETER LANG
Frankfurt am Main · Berlin · Bern · Bruxelles · New York · Oxford · Wien

Lars Schwettmann

# Trading off Competing Allocation Principles

## Theoretical Approaches and Empirical Investigations

PETER LANG
Internationaler Verlag der Wissenschaften

**Bibliographic Information published by the Deutsche Nationalbibliothek**
The Deutsche Nationalbibliothek lists this publication in the Deutsche Nationalbibliografie; detailed bibliographic data is available in the internet at <http://www.d-nb.de>.

Zugl.: Osnabrück, Univ., Diss., 2008

D 700
ISSN 0531-7339
ISBN 978-3-631- 58715-7

© Peter Lang GmbH
Internationaler Verlag der Wissenschaften
Frankfurt am Main 2009
All rights reserved.

All parts of this publication are protected by copyright. Any utilisation outside the strict limits of the copyright law, without the permission of the publisher, is forbidden and liable to prosecution. This applies in particular to reproductions, translations, microfilming, and storage and processing in electronic retrieval systems.

www.peterlang.de

# Acknowledgements

I owe a lot of gratitude to my advisor, Prof. Dr. Wulf Gaertner. The present dissertation would have been impossible without his constant support in several ways. Moreover, his probing questions helped me recognise some misunderstandings and made me rethink earlier ideas. Furthermore, the questionnaire investigations presented in chapters two and three are based on joint work with him.

I also acknowledge the kind support of the other members of the board of examiners, Prof. Dr. Ralf Pauly and Prof. Dr. Dirk Standop.

Over the years, my work has benefitted tremendously from numerous discussions with Christian Aumann. Especially his legendary criticism has inspired many thoughts contained in the present book.

I am also indebted to Constanze Binder, Huong Phan, Joanna Jachimowicz, and Dr. Sandra Rodewald for their encouragement and friendship. Moreover, they have provided extensive and valuable comments on various preliminary drafts. Also, the fruitful conversations with Prof. Dr. Frank Westerhoff deserve a special mention.

For three years I was fortunate to be part of an international research project on aspects of distributive justice that was partly financed by the Deutsche Forschungsgemeinschaft (DFG). This project enabled me to receive important academic support from Prof. Dr. Erik Schokkaert, Prof. Dr. Frank Cowell, Prof. Kristof Bosmans, Prof. Xavi Ramos, and Prof. Yoram Amiel.

The administrative support by Brigitte Arnold and the technical help of Dirk Wilmsmann is gratefully acknowledged. Moreover, Ann Bryan has kindly checked the English of the manuscript. All remaining errors have entered the text afterwards. Furthermore, many thanks go to my colleagues and numerous anonymous students who have acted as questionnaire respondents.

Finally, I wish to thank friends and family for their care and support. Especially I could always rely on the help and affection of my parents. Above all, Irina's unconditional love, her warmth and emotionality have given me strength and optimism even in the most hopeless moments during all these years. Hence, I dedicate this work to her.

# Contents

# List of Abbreviations

| | |
|---|---|
| d.f. | degrees of freedom |
| e.g. | for example (abbreviation of Latin 'exempli gratia') |
| i.e. | that is (abbreviation of Latin 'id est') |
| incl. | including |
| LL | Logarithmic Likelihood value |
| LR | Likelihood Ratio |
| ML | Maximum Likelihood |
| p. | page |
| pp. | pages |
| OLS | Ordinary Least Squares |
| QALY(s) | Quality-adjusted Life Year(s) |
| sit. | situation |
| SWF | Social Welfare Function |
| thsd. | thousand |
| viz. | that is (abbreviation of Latin 'videlicet') |

# List of Figures

# List of Tables

# General Introduction

Imagine you were a young researcher in economics starting your studies in the field of distributive justice. From your viewpoint, you certainly possess a well-founded conception of what is just, which is based on numerous everyday experiences starting already from your earliest childhood. Of course, you remember several situations in which your ideas of a fair distribution of goods or burdens conflicted with attitudes or decisions of other people. Obviously, these disagreements not only concerned cases where you or your opponent were directly affected by the consequences of the distribution in question, but included contexts where both of you judged from a detached position. Possibly, you have already realised that sometimes there is a plurality of justice evaluations at least among laymen, and perhaps this is just the reason why you want to learn more about theoretical justice concepts, their explanations for conflicts and their suggested solutions for allocation problems.

But then, when you start to become a member of the community of justice researchers, very soon you are overwhelmed by the mere number of different theoretical conceptions and empirical findings. Regularly, economists only deal with distributive justice. Here, justice principles are defined as normative principles to guide the allocation of benefits or burdens. In social choice theory corresponding axioms then formulate properties that an allocation procedure should possess. Thus, by focusing on outcomes, alternative concepts of procedural justice, which instead concentrate on fair processes to generate these outcomes, are rarely considered.

Hopefully, you do not solely focus on economics but set off to read literature on distributive justice from various fields of research. However, sooner or later you will make two fundamental observations. Firstly, there are two major lines of research on distributive justice. On the one hand, in particular the philosophical and economic literature almost exclusively relies on theoretical discussions and abstract models to determine the appropriateness of different distributive principles. On the other hand, there exist numerous empirical investigations, primarily in the fields of psychology, political science and sociology, that aim at uncovering justice attitudes or allocation behaviours of people outside the scientific community. But probably to your great surprise both lines have developed almost completely disconnected from each other. However, recently some researchers have tried to bring both streams together and have started empirical investigations that are explicitly inspired by theoretical arguments.

The second major observation concerns the fact that in both the theoretical and the empirical literature agreement has neither been reached on one single justice conception nor on the relationship between several distinct allocation principles. Instead, a plurality of different and often conflicting primary principles can be witnessed. In economics, social choice theorists usually identify apparently reasonable axioms whose inclusion or omission determines the acceptance or rejection of certain justice principles. Also, empirical studies regularly reveal heterogeneity of opinions about just distributions.

Thus, you meet again the pluralism of justice concepts among well-trained justice researchers and in profound experiential investigations. Only recently, pluralistic approaches that propose certain orders of conflicting allocation principles have gained momentum in the theoretical literature. Thus, firstly, in the present work we are going to identify situations that provoke trade-offs between allocations selected by different theoretical conceptions. However, secondly, empirical investigations are thought to enrich the ongoing theoretical debate on such conflicts and on possible solutions. More concretely, this work contains three questionnaire studies all of them describing hypothetical situations in which certain distributive principles propose different allocations. They are theoretically grounded in order to make reasonable statements on the acceptance of theoretical ideas being regarded and on possible alternatives in situations described.

Obviously, we do not expect to identify *the* pluralistic concept that prescribes which (combination of) allocation principles to use over others. Moreover, we certainly cannot reject any high-minded theoretical concept on the grounds of judgements of a group of non-experts about resulting allocations. Nevertheless, the ongoing discussion on pluralism of justice conceptions should clearly gain from insights of this kind of empirical investigation. We will see which conflicts between allocation principles may arise, which solutions are proposed in the theoretical literature, and how laymen try to solve these disagreements. By this, the debate among justice researchers should be enriched by new arguments and free from biases and constraints which are likely to appear among rather closed groups of experts.

Consequently, the present work aims at simultaneously informing theoretical and empirical researchers. Therefore, we will introduce both theoretical ideas and empirical methods at some length. Although some of these descriptions may partly seem to be too extensive for the corresponding highly qualified part of the readers, we hope that this approach enables both groups to follow most of the theoretical and statistical elaborations. Hence, we will make use of the possibility to be more detailed in this kind of work compared to the frequently very concise articles that can be found in economic journals.

As already said before, the current text comprises of three empirical investigations. They are closely related to each other in the way that the second and third study contains elements of the corresponding predecessor, but also introduces new facets into the existing structure. Therefore, we frequently refer to several characteristics, methods and results of the other studies.

Nevertheless, we will start this work in chapter 1 by presenting several theoretical conceptions of distributive justice which are important for our investigations. Here, four general allocation principles will be introduced, which prove to be very helpful to bring normative and empirical research together. One usually distinguishes between the principles of equality, efficiency, responsibility and needs. Furthermore, we will describe some theories of justice that make statements on the ordering of these principles. Afterwards, it will be explained in more detail why an empirical approach has been chosen and how the corresponding results may influence theoretical models. The first chapter ends by introducing classifications of studies on distributive justice. Two categories are important with respect to empirical investigations. On the one hand, our studies are descriptive in the way that they identify perceptions of justice held by laymen. It will be explained why artificial contexts instead of real life situations are considered, why attitudes rather than behaviours are regarded, and what effects may result from a small-scale or a large-scale setting of a problem. On the other hand, our studies are explanatory in the sense that they aim at isolating independent factors that either influence or even rationalise the observed perceptions of justice.

One of these independent factors received special attention in several previous examinations. Various studies reveal differences between men and women in social preferences and moral orientation. Therefore, in chapter 2, gender differences with respect to justice evaluations will be considered. We will report extensions and new findings of an existing questionnaire study on the acceptance of an equity axiom from social choice theory that underlies Rawls's difference principle. With respect to hypothetical distribution problems German university students had to decide between helping individuals in need and supporting a successively increasing number of better-off people. We will argue that a persistent choice in favour of the former alternative may confirm the relevance of the needs or equality principle, but the structure of the questions also allows for efficiency arguments as soon as the second alternative is selected. The gender of a respondent plays an important role in two out of four contexts presented. We will relate our findings to several explanations given in the literature. Additionally, verbal comments of participants will enable us to gain insights into decision motives.

The three questionnaire investigations presented are accompanied by advanced statistical examinations. Astonishingly, behaviour observed in carefully and creatively designed economic experiments are not regularly subjected to formal inference. But results could be substantially validated and enriched by adequate econometric modelling. In particular, we apply multivariate models to relate discrete choices to variables based on individual and questionnaire characteristics. However, these analyses are not ends in themselves so that one could certainly carry the statistical examination further.

For example, additionally available tools to improve the power of estimated models are not considered. This is in accordance with common practice in the empirical literature on moral orientations in all social science disciplines, where the overall explanatory power of such models is usually found to be rather low. In contrast, we will focus on the main idea of each study and keep the presentation of statistical results as brief as possible. Nevertheless, the reader will notice that sometimes different approaches are equally appropriate so that a comparison between their results may give further insights into the questions considered. Moreover, since not all readers are necessarily familiar with the applied statistical methods, we will spend some time introducing interpretations of results of these tools. This will be almost completely done in the third section of chapter 2.

In the second questionnaire study, presented in chapter 3, we will focus on the relevance of the principle of responsibility. By reviewing the economic and philosophical literature on this allocation principle, which recently has attracted remarkable attention, its theoretical relevance as well as the lack of consistent empirical results in different social science disciplines will be shown. Two new versions of two situations of the first questionnaire were created by supplementing additional information on the causes of basic needs. Thus, a conflict emerges between the principles of equality and needs on the one side and efficiency and responsibility on the other side. Moreover, the data base has been extended by including further students from Belgium, Germany and Spain. Our findings on the influence of aspects of responsibility on justice attitudes will be a bit of surprise. Here, gender plays again a prominent role in explaining certain evaluations.

In chapter 4, truncated efficiency, which combines the allocation principles of needs and efficiency, will be considered as an alternative distribution procedure. Firstly, we will review the sparse theoretical and the more extensive empirical literature on this idea. Secondly, a new questionnaire will be introduced that contains elements of the two previous studies, but also important modifications. The structure of hypothetical situations allows for more complex trade-offs between several principles. In the discussion of results, we will pay special attention to the importance of the needs principle and the acceptance or non-acceptance of truncated efficiency. This examination will give the deepest insights into the pluralism of allocation principles in the present work.

In the final chapter, we will lead the reader back to theoretical grounds. Here, the structures of all three investigations will be compared by means of graphical presentations. This will allow us to point out explicit or implicit assumptions and restrictions of hypothetical situations, and to detect similarities and differences. Furthermore, our approach enables us to discuss possible motives for some of the choices observed, which were initially hard to understand. The graphs allow for a clear description of findings of the three empirical studies. Moreover, consequences of all four principles considered will be consistently presented. Although this graphical approach is not completely new in the literature, it can shape the discussion and inspire some new thoughts on the relevance and specification of trade-offs between allocation principles.

One of the initial observations in this introduction concerned the fact that theoretical and empirical lines of research on distributive justice have developed almost completely disconnected from each other. However, economists and philosophers have started to bridge this gap, and the present work is another contribution to this growing literature. In contrast, it seems to be likely that future young researchers will continue to stumble over the plurality of different justice principles. Nevertheless, we hope that the questionnaire investigations presented in the following chapters will provide useful insights into this pluralism of justice ideas and lead to a fruitful debate on several aspects being considered.

# 1 Theoretical and Empirical Justice Research

## 1.1 Introduction

In this opening chapter, the basis for the following three empirical investigations of trade-offs between allocation principles will be laid. The aim of these introductory elaborations is twofold. Firstly, concepts of distributive justice provide the general theoretical background of this work. Indeed, over two millennia philosophers have formulated several different notions of theories of justice. Nevertheless, it will be explained that a set of four allocation principles, viz. equality, efficiency, responsibility and needs, underlies these concepts. According to Scott et al. (2001, p. 750), theories of distributive justice can then be classified by which allocation principles they emphasise and, moreover, how they describe the relationship between them. However, resulting allocation proposals often conflict with each other so that trade-offs between principles may be necessary. More specifically, pluralistic justice notions play a crucial role in modern theories of distributive justice. Therefore, they will be introduced and described in some detail. Secondly, the four allocation principles are also important in the empirical literature. Nowadays, various instruments are used in all fields of social sciences to investigate moral judgements held by people without a deeper knowledge of justice theories. Hence, an overview of methods to examine justice evaluations will be offered in this chapter. Here, possible effects, advantages and disadvantages of available instruments are discussed. Furthermore, it will be argued that not only the choice of the empirical methods in general, but also more detailed characteristics of the structure of the investigation, of the context and of the sample may influence observed behaviours or opinions. In particular, differences between male and female justice attitudes are one focal point throughout the present work.

However, let us begin this chapter by introducing a famous example given by Amartya Sen (1984, pp. 290-291), where some justice conceptions are already mentioned, which play a prominent role in the studies being presented. Sen describes a hypothetical situation in which someone is asked by three boys, all of them claiming a flute, to decide which of them should get the instrument. Firstly, Sen regards three separate situations resulting from different information sets. In the first case, the decision-maker only gets to know that one of the boys is much more musical than the other two children.

Thus, he will play the flute much better and will get more happiness. The mediator may follow utilitarian concerns and give the flute to the first boy. In the second case, nothing is known about the abilities of the three boys, but, instead, the arbitrator is told that the second boy is very poorly off in terms of happiness compared to the two other children. Here, as Sen argues, Rawls's difference principle would demand that the flute be given to the deprived child. Thirdly, consider the case where no information on either the abilities or the present happiness of the boys is available. However, the judge gathers that the third child has made the flute by himself from a piece of wood belonging to no one, while the other two boys have not contributed to the production of the instrument. In this case, the decision-maker may want to regard the effort of the third boy and give the flute to him. Moreover, Sen reports that an entitlement structure or a libertarian position may also recommend this allocation.

Each single decision in the three distinct situations seems to be perfectly defensible from a moral point of view. But imagine now that all three information sets, which are consistent with each other, are simultaneously present. Certainly, conceptions such as utilitarianism, the difference principle or entitlement theories still make a clear statement on the allocation decision, but now the formerly unambiguous, single moral claims conflict. Therefore, the arbitrator has to hold some kind of 'meta-principle' on the ordering of the different claims. This example is important for the present work. Hence, we will refer to it on various occasions.

As explained already in the general introduction, the focus of the following material is on distributive justice, which is in line with the general discussion about justice concerns in economic theory. However, despite its traditional relevance in philosophy or, more recently, in economics and other fields of social sciences, up to now there does not exist *the* theory of distributive justice. As Sen's example shows, several prominent justice concepts may demand conflicting solutions. In the second section of this chapter we will introduce the theoretical foundations for a plurality of allocation principles. They mainly come either from (political) philosophy or economics, whereby the latter field is basically represented by social choice theory.

The quintessence of the third section will be that there is need for empirical investigation if theoretical justice conceptions are in conflict with each other. However, this view is not uncontroversial in the literature. In particular, theorists often deny the relevance of empirical findings for the development of distributive justice ideas. Hence, it will be explained to what extent empirical studies may contribute to theoretical discussions, but also limitations of their influence on the solution of theoretical disputes have to be described. It will be argued that empirical studies must be theoretically grounded in order to make relevant statements on the acceptance of certain conceptions.

The corresponding fields of theoretically based empirical research, to which this work intends to contribute, are relatively new. Recently, depending on the theoretical context, respective studies have been subsumed under the designations *empirical social choice* (see e.g. Gaertner, 2006, 2007, for an overview) or *empirical philosophy* (Bar-Hillel and Yaari, 1993).[1] However, alternative laboratory experiments, inspired particularly by game theoretical conceptions, are also regularly used in economics for deriving findings on ethical considerations such as fairness or altruism. In contrast, in the fields of empirical social choice or empirical philosophy, the most common way to elicit equity judgements based on theoretical concepts is by presenting hypothetical situations – similar to Sen's flute example – where different justice principles demand different allocations. Hence, after discussing the general need for empirical investigations, we will classify and characterise empirical approaches in section 1.4. It will be argued that each characteristic which is identified has advantages and disadvantages so that researchers should always justify their choice of the empirical approach. The fifth section presents the conclusions and relates the explanations to the three following empirical studies.

## 1.2 The Pluralism of Allocation Principles

Right from the beginning it should be made clear that we are unable to describe all differences even between the most prominent theories of distributive justice, which are deeply rooted in philosophical and economic thinking. Nevertheless, some important characteristics of these theories and underlying allocation principles should be presented.

In the first subsection we will relate different theoretical conceptions to a smaller number of distinct allocation principles, which can be identified in both the normative and the empirical literature. The flute example in the previous section has already shown that different principles may lead to conflicting distribution proposals in concrete or hypothetical situations. In such cases, it is not clear which allocation procedure should be applied. Results from empirical investigations often show that different allocation principles are regularly weighted by decision-makers. But then the corresponding weighting scheme has to be defined by moral reasoning if it should be relevant for normative ideas. Some of these theoretical conceptions, which explicitly argue either for a certain order or for a combination of principles, will be introduced in the second subsection.

---

1 Note that the former expression more often regards those empirical studies in the field of social choice which focus on issues of distributive justice. Another term could be 'behavioural social choice', which, however, is more regularly used with respect to voting behaviour (see e.g. Regenwetter et al., 2007).

### 1.2.1 Theories of Justice and Allocation Principles

In this subsection, we closely follow the systematisations of Scott et al. (2001), Konow (2003) and Michelbach et al. (2003) who argue that conflicts between theories of distributive justice can mainly be traced to trade-offs between four distinct principles, viz. equality, efficiency, responsibility and needs. We will call them *allocation principles* to distinguish them from distribution principles which are explicitly formulated by theories of distributive justice, although both expressions are used interchangeably in the literature. Following this classification, one example for a distribution principle is Rawls's difference principle, whereas the underlying allocation principle could be the needs principle. Also, those theoretical concepts of distributive justice, which are most important for our investigations, will be presented in some detail. Here, we basically follow the explanations of Gaertner (1994).

In some way, the classification of allocation principles is rather crude so that it is important not only to mention which principles are traded off in each empirical study, but to explain what is specifically meant by the principle in the situations being regarded. Moreover, we will also describe the different temporal aspects of allocation principles to give some more structure to the different approaches.

In general, it is assumed that a certain amount of a well-defined resource has to be distributed among a given number of (groups of) individuals. Probably the most fundamental allocation principle follows from the ideal of equality. But even if this concept is appealing due to the fact that it asks for 'equal treatment of equals', it is particularly vague as long as the appropriate equalisandum, which is not necessarily the given resource, is not defined. Hence, each theoretical approach has to answer Sen's (1980) famous question of "Equality of what?". The respective answers may lead to astonishingly different allocation procedures. For example, the focus could be on equality of initial endowments or equality of outcomes. Other conceptions call for equality of something in between, like rights, opportunities or basic capabilities. According to Birnbacher (2005), these concepts can be traced to the egalitarian idea of human dignity, which should be granted to each individual regardless of merits or prospects. For instance, in the flute example equality of opportunity may be reached by a random allocation device. Certainly, due to the central role of the *principle of equality* it will be of importance for all three empirical studies to be presented.

Birnbacher introduces the temporal dimension to distinguish between further alternative justice principles. One family of principles focuses exclusively on future aspects. Some advocate that those alternatives should be preferred which maximise benefits. The corresponding notion is the *efficiency principle*. Similarly, one could follow Sen (1992, especially pp. 6-8) and define it as a preference for the highest amount of overall goods for the same amount of input. Economists have long since understood that efficiency is an allocation principle that can conflict with the principle of equality.[2] For more than two centuries, one of the most prominent theories has been utilitarianism. Since the work of Hutcheson (1725) and Bentham (1776), the utilitarian justice conception demands that the sum of individual utility, which was originally equated with happiness, should be maximised. Although modern utilitarian approaches include several different brands, three common features can be identified.[3] Firstly, utilitarianism is outcome-oriented in the way that only consequences of allocations have to be evaluated. Secondly, it is welfaristic in the sense that these consequences are evaluated with respect to utility of individuals. Thirdly, distribution mechanisms are evaluated in the light of which one maximises the sum of these individual utilities. With respect to informational requirements, the third feature implies that utility is cardinally measurable and interpersonally comparable.

A modern version of a utilitarian distribution mechanism has been proposed by Harsanyi (1955). He bases the corresponding social welfare function on the Bayesian theory of decision making under uncertainty. Gaertner (1994) explains that the social decision-maker, who may be either a member of society or an ideal observer, has to use his or her empathetic preferences. Then, the aim is to maximise social welfare which solely depends on the utility of the individuals being considered (see e.g. Sen, 1979).

Utilitarian justice is completely unconcerned about interpersonal distributions of utility. Nevertheless, it has to be noted that classical utilitarianism also embodies a concern for equality in the sense that each individual's happiness receives equal weight in the aggregation of utility levels.[4]

However, the strong informational requirements of cardinally measurable and interpersonally comparable utility levels are often regarded as being too demanding (see e.g. Konow, 2001, 2003). Therefore, they may be weakened by combining the *Pareto criterion*, which does not rely on interpersonal comparisons, with a *compensation principle*, whose variations can be traced to Kaldor (1939), Hicks (1940), Scitovsky (1941) or Samuelson (1950).[5] For example, Konow (2001, p. 148) uses a version of Kaldor's definition and states that "[a]n allocation $y$ is preferable to $y'$ if it is potentially Pareto preferred,

2 The principle of efficiency has to be distinguished from the concept of Pareto efficiency that could also be fulfilled by allocations which follow from the principle of equality.

3 See e.g. Smart and Williams (1973) for a comprehensive introduction to utilitarianism and, especially, the texts in Sen and Williams (1982) for a critical discussion.

4 A modified version can be found in Harsanyi (1978) who incorporates weights on individual utility levels in the social preference relation. This idea will be reconsidered in chapter 5.

5 In chapter 3, the reader will meet a completely different 'principle of compensation' that demands to compensate for those bad outcomes for which an agent cannot be held responsible.

that is, if it is hypothetically possible to undertake lump-sum redistribution from $y$ to achieve an allocation that Pareto dominates $y'$".

A very strong focus on the present situation of possible recipients of the allocated resource underlies those criteria which regard the neediness of individuals. They neither consider possible responsibilities for the existence of these needs nor the amount of future benefits. Consequently, the *needs principle* demands to fully regard unsatisfied basic needs of individuals, but of course it also has to be defined what is meant by the expression 'needs'. With respect to income distributions, basic needs are regularly described by a 'social minimum' which is represented by a certain income level. Rawls's (1971) difference principle, which has already been mentioned in the flute example, is usually said to inspire this category. Indeed, the difference principle has been framed by Rawls (1971, p. 277, 1996, pp. 187-190) in terms of needs and a 'social minimum'. In that sense, the needs principle introduces a limit to inequalities.

Let us elaborate a little bit on the difference principle. Unquestionably, the strongest contestant to the utilitarian perspective has been formulated in Rawls's (1971) book *A Theory of Justice.* Building on the theory of *social contract* Rawls proposes a thought experiment where he describes an *original position,* in which future members of society have to agree on a concept of social justice that has to be regarded as "a standard whereby the distributive aspects of the basic structure of society are to be assessed" (p. 9). Here, individuals are assumed to decide behind a *veil of ignorance* so that they are neither aware of their future position in society nor do they know, for example, their talents, preferences, endowments or characteristics. Thus, in the original position equality plays an important role by supposing that individuals are equal with respect to all relevant aspects.

Rawls predicts that in the given situation two justice principles will be chosen unanimously. The first maxim demands equality of basic liberties, while the second principle contains two separate parts: "Social and economic inequalities are to be arranged so that they are both: a) to the greatest benefit of the least advantaged [...], and b) attached to offices and positions open to all under conditions of fair equality of opportunity.", (Rawls, 1971, p. 302). Economic theory almost entirely focuses on the first part of the second principle. This is the *difference principle* which has already been mentioned. It is important to notice that Rawls does not evaluate benefits in terms of utility but through an index of *social primary goods.* Hence, he summarises his general conception by saying that "[a]ll social primary goods – liberty and opportunity, income and wealth, and the bases of self-respect – are to be distributed equally unless an unequal distribution of any or all of these goods is to the advantage of the least favored" (p. 303). Clearly, the Rawlsian concept is means-oriented where primary goods should provide equality of opportunity.

The difference principle is also referred to as the *maximin equity criterion* and is noticeably opposed to the utilitarian approach. In the social choice literature the corresponding allocation procedure has been axiomatically characterised by using Arrow's social choice conditions accompanied by a weak equity axiom as proposed for example by Hammond (1976) or Deschamps and Gevers (1978). If transformed into utility space, information on ordinally measurable and interpersonally comparable utility levels are necessary. In the final chapter we will regard the *utility based maximin* recalled by Sen (1992). The corresponding distribution mechanism recommends maximising the utility of the least advantaged member(s) of society. Thus, it is easy to see that the difference principle does not object to inequalities if they are to the advantage of the worse-off individual. However, in all situations presented in the following three empirical investigations a complete equalisation of utility levels of regarded parties is impossible and, furthermore, external effects are absent so that the maximin principle clearly represents either the equality or the needs principle.

There is a strong conceptual relationship between the principles of needs and equality. The former notion can be interpreted as a special egalitarian concern in the sense of equal fulfilment of basic needs. Nevertheless, the full consideration of everybody's needs may also lead to more unequal allocations (see for example Yaari and Bar-Hillel, 1984, or Miller, 1999). Moreover, there are some reasons for a distinction between both principles.[6] Firstly, the existence of unsatisfied needs of all individuals being regarded could give reason for unequal allocations. For example, Tungodden (2000) describes a situation where a certain amount of a resource has to be distributed between two individuals, both of them living below the poverty line. Tungodden argues that in this case one should try alleviating as much suffering as possible even if this means giving the total amount to one person. Secondly, if equality is considered in absolute terms, it is quite obvious that the needs principle may demand rather unequal distributions of the additional resource in order to alleviate the situation of the least well-off people. Thirdly, especially in empirical studies on income distributions the recognition of a poverty line is regularly found to be independent from other equality concerns (see the literature summarised in Michelbach et al., 2003). We will come back to the distinction between the principles of equality and needs in chapter 4. Nevertheless, it should already be noted that in the present work the term 'needs principle' explicitly regards the complete fulfilment of basic needs. If only one considered group of individuals has unsatisfied basic needs, the principle surely demands an unequal distribution of the resource, but the aim is to

6 In the literature, reviewed in Mitchell et al. (1993), Scott et al. (2001) or Michelbach et al. (2003), a separation of the two principles has also been proposed, while Konow (2001, 2003) subsumes egalitarian ideas and Rawls's difference principle into one single justice principle.

equalise the fulfilment of needs. In this sense, we follow Birnbacher's (2005) line of argument and interpret Rawls's difference principle as one variant of this principle.

In the first two studies there will be no difference between allocations following either from the needs or from the equality principle. Here, individuals in need are also said to be worse off than their counterparts and neither a full equalisation of individual welfare nor a split of the additional resource is possible. However, in the third investigation we will follow the suggestion by Scott et al. (2001) and consider needs in absolute terms by introducing a poverty line. Furthermore, this 'social minimum' can fully be regarded with the available amount of resources which can be split up in a continuous fashion. Hence, this additional setting allows for a separation of equality and needs arguments.

A fourth group of allocation principles focuses on the past. More specifically, we will call the corresponding notion *responsibility principle*, but besides aspects of responsibility it also summarises other prominent conceptions such as desert, merit, Aristotle's famous proportional solution, which has been axiomatically characterised by Kalai (1977), or effort, as in Sen's flute example. According to this principle individuals have to carry the consequences only of those variables for which they are said to be responsible. Certainly, if, for example, the degree of responsibility or effort varies between individuals regarded, the principle of responsibility also demands a departure from an equal distribution (see e.g. Fleurbaey, 1995a).[7] In contrast to political philosophy, the consideration of aspects of responsibility is rather new in social choice theory, where responsibility-sensitive egalitarianism plays a prominent role.[8] At least three theoretical approaches can be distinguished, namely equality of resources as advocated, for example, by Rawls (1971, 1982) and Dworkin (1981a), equality of opportunity, which has been introduced by Arneson (1989, 1990) and Cohen (1989, 1993), and equality of selected functionings, which has been proposed by Fleurbaey (1995b, 1998, 2001). In our second and third empirical investigation worse-off people are said to be responsible for their fate. Hence, the first part of chapter 3 contains a more detailed review and classification of the relevant literature.

Obviously, other justice concepts have been equally enthusiastically defended in the literature, but they are not considered in the present work. Prominent examples are theories of *envy-freeness*, as proposed by Tinbergen

7 Notice that by honouring or punishing past behaviour, the decision-maker may also focus on the future in the way that the behaviour of possible recipients should be influenced. In this way, aspects of 'reciprocity' or incentive considerations are introduced.

8 For a comprehensive overview see Fleurbaey (2008).

(1946) or Foley (1967) [9], concepts of *cooperative bargaining theory*, which can be traced back to the seminal works by Nash (1950) and Kalai and Smorodinsky (1975)[10], or the principle of *reciprocity*, as discussed by Rabin (1993).[11]

For the moment, notice that a certain set of different allocation principles exists. All of them are justified and intuitively plausible on moral grounds, as shown in the discussion on the flute example. Therefore, decisions in accordance to each principle should be unambiguous. However, as Sen also suggests, it seems to be quite plausible to ask what happens if these principles are simultaneously relevant and recommend conflicting allocations.

### 1.2.2 Trade-offs between Allocation Principles

A good starting point to explain what is meant by 'plurality of allocation principles' are the elaborations by Scott et al. (2001). As already said, they argue that philosophical dispute about what is 'just' can be reduced to a discussion about four distinct allocation principles, viz. "equality, merit, need, and efficiency" (p. 750). The authors claim that, apparently, there seems to be a consensus in theoretical and empirical research on the existence of these principles, but they also write that "theories of distributive justice can be categorized by which allocation principle they emphasize and how they conceptualize the relationship among them" (p. 750). Indeed, while Rawls (1971) proposes a lexicographical order of principles, Miller (1999) concludes from reviewing several empirical studies and relating them to theoretical approaches that individuals use different principles simultaneously and make trade-offs between them. In the economic literature, this idea is also followed by Konow (2001, 2003), who moreover argues that the weighting of allocation principles is context-dependent. In contrast to Scott et al. (2001), he derives these principles from empirical studies.

Walzer (1983) also acknowledges the existence of different allocation principles. However, he argues that their relevance depends on the considered 'sphere of justice'. According to Walzer, people are members of different spheres, including for example the family, the place of work or the political

9 Discussions can be found in Thomson and Varian (1985) or Moulin (1995, chapter 4). Notice that Roemer (1996, p. 10 and pp. 317-322) is very sceptical that the theory of envy-freeness is a compelling theory of justice at all. See his elaborations for further details.

10 For a comprehensive discussion of corresponding axiomatic characterisations see Roemer (1996, chapter 2). Note that Konow (2003, p. 1201, footnote 11) explicitly separates theories of justice from bargaining theories.

11 Konow (2003) argues that reciprocity – similarly to self-interest or altruism – may confound distributive preferences and should be separated.

community. In each sphere, different allocation principles may dominate.[12] Partly, the approach of Walzer will be covered in the present work by regarding similar decision problems in different contexts.

Finally, it has to be mentioned that heterogeneities of opinions about just allocations are also often called 'pluralism of fairness ideals' (see e.g. Cappelen et al., 2007). However, this is a purely empirical conception of pluralism without a theoretical foundation in the first place. In contrast, what we have in mind is a morally sound relationship among different principles.

Thus, in the present subsection the focus will be on a closer investigation of possible conflicts between allocation principles and on some theoretical approaches that argue for a specific relationship among them. Later on, the contradictions described will serve as the basis for our empirical investigations.

Now, let us take a closer look at the trade-off between the principles of equality and efficiency. Rawls (1971, p. 36) has termed this tension the "aggregative-distributive dichotomy". In fact, some important arguments to depart from equality towards efficient allocations have already been stated. As explained above, the underlying concept of classical utilitarianism gives equal weight to members of society and redeploys the scarce resource to those alternatives which generate the highest overall welfare or utility gains. Another argument in favour of efficiency arises from the fact that individuals have some influence over their own outcomes. Consequently, egalitarian solutions especially with respect to outcomes could yield big efficiency losses. Furthermore, in the context of income distributions, Sen (1984, p. 291) explains that unequal allocations may have an "instrumental justification" in the way that they serve some other goal, for example, produce more income and create incentives if production is regarded. Thus, in his profound discussion on competing justice principles Sen (1992, p. 92) concedes that "equality would typically be one consideration among many, and this could be combined with *aggregative* considerations including *efficiency*".

However, concepts based on the principle of efficiency are regularly denied to be an appropriate justice principle. With respect to utilitarian theories Sen (1973, p. 16) objects that they are "supremely unconcerned with the interpersonal distribution of [the] sum [of utilities]". Hence, it is argued that the influence of utilitarian concerns on allocation decisions should be limited.

Nevertheless, the question arises how much inequality, caused by efficiency considerations, is acceptable. For example, Hochschild (1981) explains after analysing numerous opinion polls, that allocations resulting from different principles of justice could be placed on a continuum limited by the principle of absolute equality and a principle of differentiation, i.e. proportional equity

12 However, as Birnbacher (2005) points out, it is quite possible to observe conflicting principles even in one single sphere. To give an example, he refers to the ongoing discussion about the health care system. According to Birnbacher, it is still controversial whether the allocation of health services should follow aspects of needs, the principle of desert or market principles.

in her case. Thus, in our concept, all degrees of inequality on a scale, bounded by solutions following either from efficiency or absolute equality, are potential candidates to be accepted by participants of our studies if further normative guidance on the exact location is missing. Indeed, in Hochschild's work justifications for resulting compromises are purely empirical. In the economic literature it has been suggested to represent the equality-efficiency trade-off by an isoelastic social welfare function containing a term that reflects a certain degree of inequality aversion. This function will be presented and discussed in chapter 5.

Clearly, the basic idea of this degree of inequality aversion is that the principles of equality and efficiency should be followed at the same time. It is important to notice that Rawls (1971) does not deny at all the existence of several different allocation principles. However, he claims that this *intuitionism* "holds that in our judgments of social justice we must eventually reach a plurality of first principles in regard to which we can only say that it seems to us more correct to balance them this way rather than that" (p. 39). In this case, as mentioned already above, a morally sound decision on the appropriate weights given to the various principles is needed. Consequently, Rawls remarks that "[i]f we cannot explain how these weights are to be determined by reasonable ethical criteria, the means of rational discussion have come to an end" (p. 41). Undeniably, philosophers – but also normative economists – are far away from reaching agreement on a sufficient and morally acceptable weighting scheme for a given set of allocation principles. In the next section, it will be argued that in this search for an adequate concept, empirical investigations may have a certain – albeit limited – role to play.

A related approach that regards certain relationships between different principles is also rejected by Rawls (1971, pp. 315-325). *Mixed conceptions* demand "substituting the standard of utility and other criteria for [Rawls's] second principle of justice" (Rawls, 1971, pp. 315-316). He admits the possible relevance of especially two mixed concepts of justice principles, namely the maximisation of average utility subject to either a social minimum or a certain proportion of the standard deviation of the resulting income distribution. However, he rejects both alternatives by virtue of his more general criticism on 'intuitionist doctrines'. Here, Rawls makes the case that the relevant values, i.e. the floor level or the multiplier of the standard deviation, are not constituted by any fundamental justice principle. Also, he mentions the "absence of a procedure for assigning the appropriate weights (or parameters)" and argues that "mixed conceptions may resort to [intuitive] judgements too soon and fail to define a clear alternative to the difference principle" (p. 320). Moreover, he explains that the reappearance of utilitarianism beyond the social minimum provokes further concerns. The discussion on both intuitionism and mixed conceptions will be continued in chapters 4 and 5.

In contrast to both approaches just described, Rawls suggests deriving a lexicographical order of first principles in the sense that allocation principles do not have to be balanced but, instead, "those earlier in the ordering have an absolute weight, so to speak, with respect to later ones, and hold without exceptions" (p. 42). Throughout his book, Rawls explains that individuals, placed in the original position behind the veil of ignorance, would choose the justice concept that has already been described in subsection 1.2.1. With respect to the present question about a plurality of principles, he states that his "second principle of justice is lexically prior to the principle of efficiency and to that of maximising the sum of advantages" (p. 302).

Coming back to the notion of different allocation principles, we have already argued that the difference principle shows a concern for aspects of needs. Hence, the trade-off described by Rawls regards a conflict between the notions of needs and efficiency. The priority of the former has been confirmed by several authors. For example, in the realm of political science, Boulding (1962) demands that society should fulfil the basic needs of all its' members despite aspects of just deserts. We will come back to this idea in chapter 4.

However, Rawls's difference principle was criticised immediately after publishing *A Theory of Justice.* Most importantly for the present work, Harsanyi (1975) argues that the unconditional support for worse-off individuals may lead to 'counterintuitive' allocation decisions. By giving several examples, he explains that this might be the case if an incremental utility gain for a single worse-off person is confronted with the possibility of inducing a significantly higher utility gain for a large number of better-off individuals. Harsanyi declares that "both utilitarian theory and common sense" would support the solution which achieves "much more good", i.e. the assistance for the better offs (p. 596). Therefore, to put it differently, Harsanyi questions the absolute priority of the needs principle over efficiency concerns. Nowadays, this criticism is well-known in the literature. For example, the demand to unconditionally support worse-off individuals and, by this, to disregard possibly enormous alternative benefits has been called the 'bottomless pit problem' by Brighouse (2001). The structure of the situations that have been presented in our first and second questionnaire exactly reflect the case which has been described by Harsanyi. Thus, we will also be able to evaluate the acceptance of the solution suggested by him.

Several arguments for and against both the needs and the efficiency principle exist. Perhaps the most illustrative description comes from Elster (1995, p. 93) who writes that "if there is a choice between wastefulness and unfairness, it is not clear to [him] that people would overwhelmingly favour the former". Certainly, wastefulness refers to the difference principle, whereas unfairness is attributed to utilitarian theory, but it must be noted that scholars of both directions would strongly oppose these characterisations. Thus, we should try to learn more about the 'true' opinions of people and their common sense conception of justice.

Finally, let us briefly comment on theoretical work on trade-offs including the principle of responsibility. A more extensive discussion will follow in chapter 3. Aspects of responsibility, or of one of the related ideas that have been mentioned in subsection 1.2.1, are potentially in conflict with the principle of equality if previous individual contributions to the present distribution situation differ. One example is the case of the third boy in Sen's flute story who has produced the instrument. Interestingly, as Fleurbaey (1995a) argues, equality would unduly relieve individuals from carrying the consequences of their actions and choices. However, Fleurbaey also agrees that one may depart from the principle of responsibility because "it may sometimes be incompatible with other values one may want to promote. Efficiency is an example." (p. 685). The needs principle may be another case. Here, Fleurbaey (1995b, 2008) claims that the principle of responsibility should not justify all unequal outcomes no matter how disastrous they are. While the conflict between the principles of efficiency and responsibility is not regarded in the present work, the effect of responsibility concerns on the needs-efficiency trade-off is explicitly considered in the second and in the third questionnaire study.

In different fields of social sciences, there exists by now a great number of empirical studies on the pluralism of justice concepts. Elster (1995, p. 98) also uses a lexicographical order of several principles to describe a "commonsense conception of welfare", in which poverty and deprivation play a superior role. Furthermore, Forsé and Parodi (2006) show with the help of the 'European Values Survey' that people in all European countries lexically prefer the needs principle to equality or merit concerns. In contrast, Konow (2001, 2003) finds that "people entertain several principles contemporaneously [whereby] preferences over principles [...] reflect trade-offs" rather than lexicographical orders (2003, p. 1234). Moreover, social psychologists regularly reveal that participants in various different types of studies behave in a pluralistic manner.[13]

Obviously, theorists recognise the possibility of pluralism of justice concepts or, at least, the existence of different allocation principles. The equality-efficiency trade-off is the most prominent example. Clearly, empirical studies also show that pluralistic concepts are frequently followed. Nevertheless, part of the relevant literature in psychology or sociology is too detached from normative discussions to be valuable for theoretical consideration. Hence, the general question about the usefulness of empirical work for theoretical approaches – and vice versa – immediately arises and will be considered in the following section.

## 1.3 The Need for Empirical Investigations

In this section arguments for the application of empirical investigations in the realm of distributive justice research will be collected. Above, it has been shown that different justice principles, which are sound from a moral point

13 See e.g. Törnblom (1992) for a comprehensive review.

of view, may, nevertheless, lead to conflicting allocation decisions. Thus, the implementation of empirical studies could give more insights into the acceptance of incompatible allocation principles and possible weighting schemes applied by participants in such studies. However, there is disagreement about the general role that empirical investigations should play when different normative concepts are considered. Therefore, it is important to discuss possible applications – but also limitations – of these studies.

The existence of two almost completely separated directions in the literature on distributive justice is often acknowledged. According to the first direction, theoretical work, mainly in the realms of philosophy or economic theory, is characterised by the conviction that "[e]ssential ingredients of a debate over normative issues are critical reflection and thorough assessment of the arguments being used" (Bossert, 1998, p. 283). And Miller (1994, p. 178) explains that this conception is in line with a *Platonic position* which claims "that, by special method of reasoning accessible only to the philosopher, true knowledge can be attained". Therefore, especially the view that empirical research can 'test' the appropriateness of different theoretical concepts is often vehemently rejected since "intuitions, existing in a given society, may be completely inconsistent" (Schokkaert and Overlaet, 1989, p. 22).

This point of view particularly excludes investigations from the second direction of justice research. Here, empirical studies, primarily in the fields of psychology and sociology, investigate attitudes and behaviours of *laymen* when facing interpersonal allocation problems. These investigations are usually informal and descriptive. As a typical example for this direction, Törnblom (1992, pp. 177-178) rejects the compatibility of empirical results and theoretical concepts and states "that it is likely that there is no true or essential justice beyond its socially constructed meanings".

Thus, the two branches seem to be clearly separated. However, in recent years several studies on distributive justice have demonstrated that there might be a fruitful cooperation between both directions if empirical studies are theoretically grounded. Some of this work has been summarised by Miller (1992, 1999), Schokkaert (1999) or Gaertner (2007). The following three questionnaire studies are also intended to contribute to this 'intermediate' way between purely theoretical and purely empirical approaches. Hence, let us now explain the role that this approach can play for theoretical discussions.

One fundamental reason for a fruitful relationship between both branches originates from the supposition that each theory is finally intended to be put into practice.[14] At least at this point the normative theorist needs to convince the general public about the suitability of his or her theoretical concept. Thus, empirical studies offer the opportunity to get insights into possible difficulties, misunderstandings or even rejections on the side of uninformed and untrained laymen when facing consequences of proposals by theorists.

14 See e.g. Bossert (1998) for this line of argument.

However, it is possible that theorists can learn more from empirical studies. If there is a debate about different distributive concepts, opinions expressed by non-expert samples may enrich the theoretical discussion. For example, Elster (1995, p. 94) explains that although empirical studies "cannot substitute for argument, they can shape the structure and focus of argument". Furthermore, he reports that there are enormous disparities between "moral intuitions, even among well-informed and thoughtful observers" (p. 93). For instance, as explained in the previous subsection, both Elster and Harsanyi claim that their concepts result from 'common-sense'. One possible reason might be that convictions held by normative theorists are biased by influences reaching from self-interest to social background characteristics of the individual researcher. This point will play a major role in the first study presented in the second chapter, where the focus is on gender differences in justice evaluations. Moreover, disparities between women and men are also regarded in the second and third study. In general, empirical investigations can help to detect possible sources of some theoretical disputes and ensure that the theorist is free from individual biases.

Additionally Schokkaert (1999) identifies two further possible biases. Firstly, there exist 'typical cases' that theorists like to discuss in order to explain the motivation of their concepts. The story of shipwrecked Robinson is one example. But if justice evaluations are assumed to be context-dependent – a point that will be further elaborated in the next section – then the theorist may also be influenced by the context of regularly used examples in his research community. Secondly, mathematically demanding structures are usually applied to formulate justice concepts in social choice theory. However, the availability of methods also introduces constraints to the allocation procedures being considered. Again, these constraints may be detected by presenting allocation problems to laymen.

So far, the arguments mentioned admit that empirical investigations have a rather moderate role in developing theoretical justice concepts. But let us now elaborate on an undoubtedly more ambitious role of empirical studies. Some authors, like Miller (1994), are convinced that a complementary relationship between the empirical and the theoretical branch of distributive justice research could be established. In fact, Miller contrasts this approach with the aforementioned Platonic position and, correspondingly, calls it *Aristotelian position.* It is very close to Rawls's (1971, pp. 48-51) idea of a *reflective equilibrium* and is carefully described by Yaari and Bar-Hillel (1984) as a process of self-correction in the field of social choice. The latter authors start by describing the method of model-building with the help of axioms, which formulate properties that an allocation procedure should possess. If the resulting procedure is not unique, additional characteristics have to be identified. But they should be incorporated into the axiomatically described model only if they are found to be 'tenable'. Now, it is this *tenability* which should be the object of empirical investigation. In a later paper, the authors put it even more directly. Usually, normative theories of justice rely on personal intuitions of the theorist, whereas in the empirical investigations to be considered "the size of the sample of introspectors" is increased (Bar-Hillel and Yaari, 1993, p. 58). It is important to notice that this process is explicitly based on theoretical formulations. By corrections and self-corrections a stable equilibrium should finally be reached.

In comparison to the two previous aims of empirical studies, viz. informing the theorist either about possible difficulties when putting his concept into practice or about potential biases, this third objective is clearly more demanding. Nevertheless, Schokkaert (1999) argues that the process which has been described was already fruitful in the field of social choice. He explains that several new approaches depart from traditional welfare economics and move towards a position held by *Mr. Fairmind*, an imaginary person who is supposed to be representative for the general public opinion.[15] But most importantly for the present work, Schokkaert also notes that Mr. Fairmind has a pluralistic concept of distributive justice. Therefore, in the words of Schokkaert and Overlaet (1989), there may be a potential for empirical studies to play a 'constructive role' for theoretical concepts during their development.

Let us reconsider the basic question which will be investigated in the present work. Various conflicting notional approaches with regard to different justice values and corresponding weighting schemes have already been presented. On the one hand, the almost single focus of utilitarian concepts on the principle of efficiency has been rejected because of the missing concern for interpersonal distributions. On the other hand, Rawls's lexicographical order of the maximin criterion over the principle of efficiency has been countered by utilitarians. This conflict will be regarded in the second chapter by investigating the acceptance of an equity axiom that underlies Rawls's difference principle. Furthermore, aspects of responsibility may justify a rejection of the equality principle, while some theorists deny the relevance of the responsibility principle if basic needs are regarded. This conflict will be the starting point for the second questionnaire study. Moreover, intuitionism and mixed conceptions have been criticised by Rawls for the absence of moral foundations of proposed weights or threshold values. Besides the previously investigated trade-offs, the role of mixed conceptions will also be examined in the third study. Thus, obviously, there is potential for theoretically grounded empirical investigations to inspire future theoretical research on the pluralism of allocation principles.

From our point of view, all three arguments in favour of empirical research in the realm of distributive justice are sensible. Finally, it is also important to state again what empirical studies should not be used for. With regard to the objectives of these investigations, which have just been described, it is obvious that empirical studies are not a feasible substitute for moral reason-

15 In chapter 2, the reader will meet Mr. Fairmind – and his wife – again.

ing. Thus, again Elster (1995, p. 95) emphasises that "these procedures are external to the theory itself" while Schokkaert (1999, p. 22) clarifies "that a simple vote over different options will not do". Consequently, the theoretical foundation of empirical investigations is the core element of this branch of research. Nevertheless, it is important to describe and discuss possible methods of empirical justice research. This will be done in the next section. Moreover, we will cite several empirical studies from all fields of research throughout the present work which are not necessarily theoretically grounded.

## 1.4 Characterisation of Empirical Studies

In order to characterise and distinguish several empirical approaches on justice evaluations, the classifications proposed by Elster (1995) will prove to be very helpful. He identifies three categories of studies on distributive justice. Firstly, *descriptive* studies are applied to identify perceptions of justice held or accepted by subjects. Secondly, *explanatory* studies aim to isolate independent factors that either influence or even rationalise the findings of the first category. Thirdly, *normative* studies ought to identify valid and defensible conceptions of justice. At least to some degree studies that belong to the last category have already been discussed in the preceding sections. Furthermore, in the last subsection we have argued that both descriptive and explanatory studies should be theoretically grounded in order to be of relevance for theoretical discussions.

Nevertheless, the first two categories describe very important characteristics of empirical investigations in the realm of distributive justice. Researchers should give good reasons for the chosen empirical method and, moreover, be aware of possible difficulties and shortcomings of the selected approach. Therefore, our three questionnaire investigations will be characterised with respect to the available classifications. Furthermore, the identification of influencing – or one could also say explaining or biasing – factors will help to separate an unbiased concept of justice. First, elements of descriptive studies are considered. Then, explanatory studies will be characterised.

### 1.4.1 Descriptive Studies

According to Elster (1995) there are at least three distinct dimensions to structure descriptive studies on distributive justice.[16] Our three investigations consider artificial contexts, examine attitudes and usually present either large- or small-scale settings. In this subsection, these aspects will be discussed in turn and, moreover, respective alternatives will be described.

16 Miller (1992) also regards two different dimensions that are similar to the second and third aspect presented here.

As a first distinction, we regard artificial contexts instead of real life settings. In fact, studies with respect to the latter possibility are rare. One example is the determination of wages or taxes that has been analysed by Walzer (1983) or Elster (1992). Another prominent case is the system for allocating kidneys (see e.g. Young, 1994). However, the great majority of investigations, especially in the realm of economics, belongs to the first group and includes both laboratory and survey studies. Besides fewer difficulties in gathering appropriate data, artificial contexts are also said to contain less confounding details with regard to the underlying decision problem, whereas in real life settings, the researcher may not even be aware of all unwanted influences. Additionally, the manipulation of significant information is regularly more straightforward in artificial settings. Nevertheless, an important warning comes from Levitt and List (2007). They focus on social preferences that have been uncovered in various game theoretical experiments, and compare them with observations from field experiments. The authors find that results from the laboratory are usually influenced by several other factors besides intended monetary calculations: Moral considerations, non-anonymity of subjects, the context of presented situations, self-selection of participants and different stakes in the outcome are found to have an impact on findings. However, in the field of empirical social choice especially moral considerations, which have also been mentioned, are of greatest importance. Most of the other influential factors will be considered in the next subsection. Moreover, Levitt and List ask whether all these aspects have the same effect in real world settings and deny this hypothesis for many investigated cases. Hence, one should be aware of unwanted influences and control for them as much as possible.

Let us turn now to the second dimension to classify descriptive studies. In the realm of artificial settings, the main distinction is between studies that consider behaviours – most often in laboratory experiments – and investigations that focus on attitudes, opinions or beliefs – regularly with the help of questionnaires. We applied the second method, but both approaches have advantages and disadvantages so that the researcher should be well aware of them. In modern behavioural economics, game theoretical experiments play a leading role. They permit a strict control of the experimental setting, which is particularly important with respect to the information set and the underlying context. Furthermore, Dickinson and Tiefenthaler (2002) reason that commonly incorporated payments allow reflecting intended incentive schemes and showing participants that they make meaningful choices.

However, one of the given strengths of these experiments is also a major disadvantage with respect to justice evaluations. The potential monetary benefit for players in these games is likely to introduce a self-serving bias. For example, Gaertner (2007, p. 2) writes that probands are perhaps "not so much interested in the underlying issues which the experimenter wishes to study, but primarily in the sum of money they can bring home". The possibly confounding factor of self-interest motivated Konow (2000) and Dickinson and Tiefenthaler (2002) to construct modified payment structures in experiments, where the decision-maker only receives a 'show-up fee', but has to allocate real monetary units on two other parties.[17] Konow calls this setting a *benevolent dictator experiment*. For the same reason, Rubinstein (1999) concludes his report and reflections on experiences in teaching courses in game theory by saying that he still prefers to use survey studies where respondents have to reflect on hypothetical scenarios. The relevance of self-serving biases will be discussed in more detail in the next subsection.

An additionally important disadvantage of experimental studies with respect to the present question about pluralism of allocation principles has to be noted. It seems to be particularly difficult to investigate the acceptance of the needs principle in experimental studies. In what way can a laboratory situation be created where one participant has unsatisfied basic needs? And how should a context be constructed that reflects Rawls's original position and requests subjects to make far-reaching decisions about the structure of future society?[18]

In general, questionnaire studies on opinions about alternative distributions in hypothetical scenarios are viewed as being closer to the normative literature on distributive justice. For example, Schokkaert (1999) uses this argument with respect to empirical examinations on social choice theory. Regularly, investigations from this branch of empirical studies are said to be contextually richer, make it easier for respondents to imagine a real life situation and are better able to incorporate basic needs. Furthermore, due to both the absence of payment schemes and the anonymity of answers they face less problems to put respondents in an impartial spectator position.[19] Probably the most vivid defence of questionnaire studies focusing on attitudes in the realm of social choice comes from Bar-Hillel and Yaari (1993). They believe "that 'justice' can usefully be studied via 'judgments of justice,' and that these judgments can justifiedly be elicited to hypothetical questions", because "the focus of this research is precisely the ethical notions in people's minds – not their actual behavior" (pp. 58-59).

Nevertheless, survey studies also suffer from crucial shortcomings. One counterargument is the suspicion that respondents may state their "Sunday-best beliefs" (Miller, 1992, p. 557) and report those moral views, which the

17 See Konow (2005) for a more general review of various empirical studies on the relevance of 'impartiality'.

18 Herne and Suojanen (2004, p. 191) reach a similar conclusion and comment on their income distribution experiment that "participants might not be as risk averse as Rawls assumes they would be in an experimental setting, where they know that they are not choosing principles of income distributions for the rest of their lives".

19 See e.g. Demuijnck and Le Clainche (2007) and Konow (2009) for some of these arguments.

experimenter or other participants may expect from the respondent. Furthermore, Williams and Cookson (2000) point out that context and other framing effects may have a stronger influence in hypothetical questions. Economists usually tend to present highly simplified situations that could lead to unanticipated interpretations by laymen. Clearly, there is a trade-off between presenting rather uncomplicated contexts and giving more detailed information, which carries a higher risk of biasing responses or even boring participants. Interestingly, this point has been taken up by Faravelli (2007). He confirms that there is indeed a certain lack of information in many studies. But it can be supposed that respondents fill these gaps in accordance to their attitudes and their personal background. Therefore, another argument in favour of controlling for individual characteristics is identified. Overall, there seem to be more advantages than disadvantages of studies on justice attitudes over experiments focusing on behaviour.

Empirical studies may be divided along a third dimension, which could also be observed in the discussion previously mentioned between Harsanyi and Rawls. As we said above, Harsanyi (1975) describes several hypothetical allocation problems among different individuals to show the 'counterintuitive' consequences of Rawls's difference principle. But Rawls (1974a) rejects Harsanyi's examples by pointing out that the difference principle concerns the general structure of society but not every small-scale situation. Hence, this argument relates to the distinction between 'micro- and macro-justice'. One could either consider small-scale contexts, i.e. allocations among single individuals or groups, or regard large-scale contexts, where distributions among the whole society are concerned. Our questionnaires describe mainly, but not entirely, micro-justice situations.

A closer examination of comments on this characteristic in the literature reveals that the importance given to this dimension strongly differs among authors. According to a first position scope-aspects are interpreted as important contextual effects. Hence, they may be used as an additional possibility to classify empirical studies.[20] Assuming such a moderate role of this distinction, Miller (1992) discusses both groups of studies. He explains that small-scale settings enable the researcher to present a great variety of different contexts. But the question may arise as to whether results of micro-justice studies are relevant for large-scale problems. In contrast, macro-justice investigations introduce a great deal of contextual constraints to possible answers. For example, if a participant is asked about a fair income distribution in a hypothetical society, the current income distribution of the subject's home country may guide the answer. Similarly, present welfare practices could influence opinions on the demanded extent of help for people in need. However, to some degree this aspect may also be relevant for micro-justice contexts. Here, some illuminating examples with respect to health expenditures will be

20 One example for this opinion is Konow (2003).

presented in chapter 3. Harsanyi objects to Rawls's defence mentioned above by pointing out that "the basic principles of morality should [not] take different forms for large-scale and small-scale situations" (Harsanyi, 1975, p. 605).

A second position goes beyond the simple context effect and infers that people may apply different justice principles with respect to different scopes of the allocation problem being presented. This position can mainly be found in the social-psychology and sociology literature. For example, Brickman et al. (1981, p. 178) offer a classification of distributive principles and explain that micro-justice concepts, such as needs or merit, always regard "qualifying attributes of individuals", whereas macro-justice principles, for example a minimum income or a maximised average income, concern the appropriate order of society.[21]

Indeed, several authors have used this distinction to develop more advanced characterisations of justice concepts. The taxonomy proposed by Sabbagh (2001) is a nice example. She argues that there are different justice principles in micro- and macro-justice contexts. But these concepts could be multidimensional in the way that they combine several principles from both contexts.

One may greatly appreciate the possibility of distinguishing justice principles with respect to an easily observable measure such as the scale of the underlying allocation problem. However, some concerns remain. Let us briefly reconsider the dispute between Harsanyi and Rawls about the appropriateness of counterexamples to the difference principle. While Rawls (1971, p. 142) pointed out that "Maximin is a macro not a micro principle.", Harsanyi (1975) claims that his examples – similar to basic principles of morality – are independent of the regarded scale. Also, he somewhat provocatively asks where the exact number of concerned people lies that separates large-scale from small-scale problems.

To summarise the discussion on micro- and macro-justice, one should clearly pay attention to the scale of an allocation problem. Therefore, corresponding information should be treated as a framing effect. However, a distinction of justice principles with respect to the dimension of the considered situation is more controversial. Several of the hypothetical contexts in the following investigations regard small-scale problems. Nevertheless, we are convinced that they can shed some more light on trade-offs between the four allocation principles which have been introduced.

---

21 Probably one of the most famous examples in this area is the so-called 'Bakke case' reviewed by Jemmott and Tebbets (1980). Here, a student named Bakke applied for a medical school. Obviously, due to his results in the entrance examination, his previous career, and his voluntary social work he clearly deserved to be admitted on micro-justice grounds. However, an affirmative-action program focusing on discriminated minorities allowed members of such groups to go to this school even though they had poorer results in the tests. This lead to a rejection of Bakke. The decision was reasoned by the macro-justice argument that society would gain from additional minority doctors.

In the present subsection, we have discussed the choice of our empirical method. It has been explained why we consider artificial contexts instead of real life settings and for what reason we examine attitudes rather than behaviour. Furthermore, the context of a situation may have an influence on observed decisions.

### 1.4.2 Explanatory Studies

In the previous subsection it has already been argued that micro- and macro-justice contexts often affect justice evaluations. Moreover, personal attitudes and social background of respondents may bias the way in which information gaps are filled. More generally, it is often shown that the individual usage of different allocation principles is influenced by a larger number of effects, which may then in turn serve as explanatory factors for heterogeneities that are regularly observed in empirical studies. Moreover, in section 1.3 it has been argued that even the theorist may be biased by certain influencing factors. The present subsection aims at systematically describing some of these aspects. Clearly, "causally oriented approaches to justice" (Elster, 1995, p. 85) are further away from theoretically grounded empirical studies. However, the proposed classifications make it possible to describe several empirical settings and explain differing results. Furthermore, relevant effects point towards potential biases of observed behaviours or stated opinions. Clearly, empirical researchers should be aware of them.

Consequently, influencing factors on empirical findings should be controlled for in order to identify unbiased attitudes. Konow (2001, p. 139) argues that we need to "isolate unbiased justice" to understand the relations between self-concerned and ethical factors that influence behaviours.[22] In each of the three studies in this work we try to identify and control for a greater number of possible effects. In particular, the first investigation aims at examining gender differences in justice evaluations.

To begin with, one approach to explain different individual attitudes or behaviours focuses on self-interest. It has already been described above, that especially experimental studies on aspects of game theory often induce self-concern by introducing payment schemes that also affect payoffs of the decision-maker. Certainly, this is not accidental since traditional economic theory, which serves as the basis for these investigations, predicts that individuals will follow their own interests and maximise benefits or utility gains. However, the additional aspects of fairness and altruism, revealed in ultimatum or dictator games, have enriched economic theories.[23] In this case, as

22 See Michelbach et al. (2003, especially p. 524) for a similar line of argument.

23 Camerer (2003) reviews various experimental studies with respect to fairness concerns. Messick and Sentis (1979) show that a self-serving bias even exists if payments are hypothetical.

especially Fehr and Schmidt (1999) and Bolton and Ockenfels (2000) propose, theoretical models should introduce a concern for other people's payoffs into individual utility functions and, thus, allow for altruism and inequality aversion. Yet, Faravelli (2005) points out that modified utility functions are not able to cover different contexts such as needs. Even though questionnaire studies regularly regard hypothetical situations, they are, of course, also able to provoke either self-interest or a strong identification of respondents with the individuals or groups which are described.

However, it is important to recognise that self-interest is a strong bias of justice evaluations. Dana, Weber and Kuang (2007) call it 'moral wiggling' if respondents follow their own self-interest at the expense of fairness. One very helpful example is the experiment by Konow (2000) mentioned in the previous subsection. He uses a benevolent dictator setting to reveal the influence of personal stakes of the decision-maker in the outcome. In the theoretical literature, the importance of impartial judgements is well-known. However, it has been formulated in rather different ways. Three notions are most prominent in economic theory.[24] Firstly, Rawls's original position behind a veil of ignorance that has been described in subsection 1.2.1 intends to provoke both impartiality of free and rational individuals in this hypothetical situation and unanimous agreement on the justice principles for the structure of society. However, subjects are supposed to be members of society later on so that, in a way, they are still 'self-interested'. Secondly, Harsanyi has proposed two different versions of an *impartial observer* approach. Both of them are formulated in terms of lotteries with cardinal von Neumann-Morgenstern utility functions. While a more complete comparison – and especially an empirical examination – of both variants can be found in Amiel, Cowell and Gaertner (2009), only the basic ideas will be sketched in this paragraph.[25] In his first model, Harsanyi (1953, 1955, 1977, 1978) proposes imagining an observer who regards both the objective circumstances and the individual characteristics of each member of society and imagines he or she could be each of these individuals with equal probability. In contrast, in a second model, Harsanyi (1978) assumes that the evaluator could be an outside observer, who has internalised moral preferences expressed by a utility function that fulfils the conditions mentioned. Furthermore, it serves as a social welfare function to be maximised. In both models, Harsanyi predicts that utilitarian ethics should be followed.

However, most questionnaire studies in the realm of empirical social choice apply a kind of 'strict' impartial spectator approach which is closest to the second model of Harsanyi. Here, the description of hypothetical situations

24 See Konow (2009) for a discussion on the relevance of these notions for empirical studies.

25 Another empirical investigation of different types of impartiality has been conducted by Traub et al. (2005). All of their examples regard lotteries and vary information sets and future positions of respondents in the income distribution.

either completely removes all personal stakes or incorporates a rather abstract kind of self-interest. In the three studies presented in the current work both alternatives will be considered by varying information sets.

A second group of approaches to explain individual justice attitudes or behaviours, and, thus, to distinguish empirical studies, may be summarised under the very general expression of *contextual effects*. If context is understood in a narrow sense, one could follow Deutsch (1975), who claims that contexts like professional or family relations are probably governed by different justice principles. In many instances, this definition is used in the present work. We will control for these contextual effects by describing decision problems that are similarly structured in different contexts.

However, Törnblom (1992) finds that it is well-known that the evaluation of justice principles is context-specific. Consequently, "[i]t is now time to move ahead in the direction of specifying the most important and powerful contextual factors" (p. 203). Hence, if context is interpreted in a broader sense, one may follow Konow (2003, p. 1215), who counts "the group of individuals being compared, the type of goods being distributed and the framing of information" as the context.[26]

The first element in this broader sense refers to (hypothetical) people and their individual characteristics in the situation being presented. It is possible that, for instance, information about gender, profession or the social position of an individual may influence the decision of an outside observer. For example, participants in questionnaire studies may be more willing to support their own sex or members of their own (perceived) 'social class'. In our studies we will also regard these effects and control for socio-demographic characteristics of respondents in multivariate regression models.

Next, the kind of goods to be distributed may have an effect on the applied allocation principle. In a hypothetical situation presented by Yaari and Bar-Hillel (1984), preferences over fruits are determined either by their content of vitamins or by their taste. However, these different characteristics of the goods displayed a crucial influence on preferred distributions. In a second example, Walzer's (1983) spheres of justice are also defined by the goods to be distributed.

Usually, the goods in question are said to be scarce in order to create a distribution conflict. Moreover, at least in the situations presented in the following studies, income – or a substitute – is considered to be available without costs. Cappelen et al. (2007) call such resources 'manna from heaven'. Clearly, the nature of the distributed good may vary between empirical studies and, thus, influence the corresponding results. Furthermore, at least in the field of empirical social choice, many studies have employed discrete choice formats so

26 Remember that Konow defines aspects of context as an additional element of justice, whereby justice principles are "interpreted, weighted and applied in a manner that depends on the context" (Konow, 2003, p. 1235).

that goods are regarded as non-divisible. This is also the case in the first two investigations to be presented in chapters 2 and 3. However, as Konow (2009) explains, the consideration of a continuous split offers several new distribution alternatives, although, admittedly, the cognitive task is more advanced. The third study will include this modification which is also discussed in chapter 5.

Another contextual effect concerns the framing of a situation, i.e. the way in which a problem is presented. At least since the work of Tversky and Kahneman (1981) it is well-known that the framing of a situation or question has a strong biasing impact on empirical results. With respect to justice evaluations, Gamliel and Peer (2006) show that the description of consequences either in positive or in negative terms leads to different choices of allocation rules.

A final contextual aspect, which is closely related to framing effects, regards the phrasing of the question. Let us concentrate on a very explicit point that is considered by Konow (2001, 2003). He discusses the question whether participants in survey studies should be asked about 'fair' or 'just' distributions or, instead, what 'should' be chosen or what they 'prefer'. Then, Konow reports findings of a study by Ordóñez and Mellers (1993). The two authors presented different income distributions for a society and asked subjects in one version to name the 'more fair society' and in a second version to state where they 'prefer to live'. Regarding the results, 'preferred' distributions corresponded to higher minimum or mean incomes, while 'fairness' was concerned with the contribution of a subject to the outcome. Konow (2001, p. 156) summarises these and some of his own findings by declaring that "[e]fficiency and needs exist as distributional goals distinct from justice, whereas accountability represents the distinguishing feature of justice".

So, what to ask exactly in questionnaires on distributive justice? For the following reasons, in the present questionnaires it is asked 'What should be done?'. Firstly, there are experiments on attitudes about income distributions by Frohlich and Oppenheimer (1992) who directly mentioned distributive justice as one goal in their initial version. However, then they worried that this "might skew subjects' responses and choices" and that respondents may "desire to please the researcher" (p. 46). Thus, the two authors used a second version without any reference to justice but could not detect any significantly different results. Secondly, Pharo (2001) reports that different social groups attain different meanings to the words 'justice' and 'equity'. Therefore, these expressions may even bias answers due to these different understandings. And thirdly, Amiel et al. (2008) argue that they purposely asked respondents what they would 'decide' in order to explicitly capture social choice elements.

It seems to be quite plausible that different people hold different interpretations of the expression 'fair allocations' so that they already differ with respect to their understanding of their task. Moreover, indeed, social choice is about the generic idea of choices.

Let us regard a third group of confounding influences on justice attitudes besides self-interest and different contextual aspects. These factors relate to individual attributes of the evaluating person. In the field of empirical social choice, student samples are most often used, although it is regularly criticised that this may create biased results. However, the advantages are obvious. Students are easy to access by researchers at universities, their participation is often cheap, and they are intelligent and have, therefore, fewer problems to understand even more advanced distribution problems presented in questionnaires. Usually, students are motivated to participate and, finally, comparisons between subjects from different countries are easier, because several of their characteristics are rather similar. The latter advantage is particularly important in the second investigation to be presented.

There are only a few studies that compare results of student samples with samples being representative for the total population. Ball and Cech (1996) summarise several laboratory experiments and conclude that results from student samples do not significantly differ from other groups considered. With respect to questions on distributive justice, Schokkaert and Capéau (1991) report that the choice of principles was similar among university students and a representative sample of the population in Belgium. Thus, student samples may lead to reliable results, although findings should be carefully interpreted.

Furthermore, in all investigations we asked students at economics departments to complete our questionnaires. However, the subject of study could also have a confounding effect on attitudes and behaviours of participants in empirical investigations. Carter and Irons (1991) formulate both a selection and a learning hypothesis to explain why economists may behave or answer differently from non-economists. Jungeilges and Theisen (2005) and Faravelli (2007) review several economic experiments and summarise that results are not conclusive with respect to both hypotheses but depend on the setting. In contrast, both papers present questionnaire studies which revealed some differences between equity evaluations of first-year and third-year economics students. Additionally, Faravelli (2007) found disparities between economists and sociologists which were stronger among third-year students. Hence, we should keep in mind that self-selection effects may be of relevance in our study, while the learning hypothesis is not important due to the fact that only undergraduate students answered our questions.

However, further confounding effects resulting from attributes of the decision-maker may occur. Especially psychological studies, like those reported by Major and Deaux (1982) or Engle (1990), show that the personality, characteristics and values of the allocating subject are important for the choice of several individual principles. In the present work, the focus will be especially on possible gender differences. Hence, in chapter 2, the relevant literature will be reviewed in much more detail.

Additionally, Rubinstein (2001) points out the importance of repeating empirical investigations in order to evaluate the robustness of results. Consequently, we used the questionnaires in different years. Furthermore, the second study was also repeated at different places.

To summarise, justice attitudes are likely to be biased by several aspects. Therefore, researchers should identify as many confounding factors as possible and control for them to observe unbiased justice attitudes.

## 1.5 Conclusions

Let us conclude this introductory chapter by summarising the main statements and, based on them, pointing out the resulting structure of the subsequent chapters. In fact, the preceding overview considered two main lines of research that have been developed almost completely separated from each other until recently. Firstly, theoretical work on distributive justice has been outlined. Several attempts to organise the numerous theories of justice can be found in the literature. Nevertheless, a rather simplifying but, perhaps especially because of this characteristic, often applied systematic identifies four allocation principles that are supposed to be inherent in various justice concepts. While the equality principle is the most fundamental idea, the principles of efficiency and responsibility usually recommend departures from equal split. Moreover, this is sometimes even the case for the principle of needs. Another way to characterise these principles is the consideration of corresponding temporal dimensions. Indeed, today many theorists acknowledge the existence of these or other allocation principles, but disagreement remains about the relationship between them if their distribution proposals conflict. This leads to the claim that a pluralistic conception is needed in the sense that different concepts exist simultaneously and may be fulfilled to some degree by corresponding justice theories. One possibility is intuitionism, which regards compromises between aspects of equality and efficiency. While there is some empirical evidence on the importance of such balancing, the moral foundation of an arbitrarily chosen weight is supposed to be rather weak. A related idea are mixed conceptions which define a concrete relationship between two or more allocation principles. In contrast, Rawls demands a lexicographical order of his difference principle, which inspired the needs principle, over the principle of efficiency. However, the relevance and importance of the other allocation principles is equally often defended.

Secondly, possible methods and characteristics of empirical studies have been summarised. A first group of empirical investigations aims at identifying justice perceptions and can be separated at least along three dimensions. All three studies to be presented in chapters 2 to 4 use artificial contexts rather than real life settings. However, biases may result from both approaches. In all cases, justice attitudes instead of just behaviours are regarded. In this respect, it has extensively been argued in this chapter that this focusing on attitudes might be better able to reveal normative conceptions held by respondents, whereas several important factors, in particular a possible self-interest, may confound behaviours in experiments. Interestingly, the question of impartiality is one of the rare occasions where a close connection between empirical and theoretical justice research can be observed. Finally, the studies regard both small-scale and large-scale settings. This characteristic is supposed to be an important contextual effect.

A second group of empirical work aims at identifying causes for observed justice attitudes or behaviours. Besides self-interest, contextual effects and attributes of the decision-maker have been discussed. All three groups of causes also play vital roles in the following questionnaire studies. Clearly, they may bias judgements so that their influence should be separated. This will especially be done by multivariate statistical tools. Also, further insights into justice evaluations can be received from analysing possible causes for observed equity evaluations. Particularly, it will be argued that the gender of a respondent may have a strong influence on observed decisions.

Both of the just described directions of justice research have been brought together in section 1.3. Still, the role that empirical research can play in theoretical concepts of justice is a controversial point. Three arguments in favour of a more central function have been identified in this respect. Firstly, the theorist could get information about problems that he may face if he wants to put his ideas into practice. Secondly, and closely related to the description of the two groups of empirical studies, theoretical concepts may be biased by attributes of the theorist, by the examples used in the scientific community, or by specific methods applied by theorists to develop their models. In all cases, empirical studies could identify these biases. Thirdly, the most active and also most controversial function of empirical studies is the constructive role that they may play if they are theoretically grounded. In this sense, empirical investigations can display a stronger influence on theoretical developments. This is especially the case if new theoretical disputes need inspiration from outside. The above described discussion on the appropriate system of conflicting allocation principles offers a predestine case for a fruitful debate between both branches of distributive justice research.

Often, empirical investigations reveal that laymen hold a pluralistic justice concept. The following three chapters contain clear statements on the underlying theoretical conflicts. Moreover, the empirical research on the considered trade-offs between allocation principles is reviewed and described on the basis of theoretical concepts. In the first study, a trade-off between the needs principle and possible efficiency considerations is regarded.[27] In the second study, the aspect of responsibility is additionally incorporated in the first setting and contrasted with the needs principle. The third investigation examines

27 Alternatively, as already explained several times, according to Yaari and Bar-Hillel (1984), the settings could be described as creating conflicts between aspects of equality and efficiency in the context of basic needs.

the acceptance of a mixed principle that has been called 'truncated utilitarianism' in the literature. Furthermore, allocations based on intuitionism are available.

This fifth chapter leads the empirical work back to theoretical grounds and offers a new perspective on the trade-offs which have been considered. Thereby, all studies are finally reconsidered from a theoretical point of view. With the help of graphical presentations, observed behaviours are interpreted and compared.

# 2 Gender Differences in Justice Evaluations

## 2.1 Introduction

Are women more likely than men to support people in need instead of backing an offered alternative? Can we observe gender disparities if the latter alternative becomes more and more attractive? And do females and males give similar reasons for their allocations? The present study will offer some empirical answers to these questions from questionnaires distributed among students, although, initially, this study was not explicitly intended to control for gender differences. However, beforehand, let us come back to some elaborations in the first chapter. In the domain of social choice theory, Schokkaert (1999) argues that current post-welfarist developments may be interpreted as a convergence towards justice conceptions held by Mr. Fairmind, an imaginary person who is supposed to be representative for the general public opinion. In turn, and in order to facilitate this process, the attitudes of Mr. Fairmind should be carefully determined by theoretically inspired questionnaire examinations. Nevertheless, as Elster (1995) remarks, besides the mere description of possible differences in justice evaluations of respondents, empirical investigations could also provide further insights into the causes of these disparities. Here, independent variables, which are presumed to bias justice evaluations and, thus, generate part of the observed variations among individual assessments, can be identified. But certainly, as Schokkaert (1999) warns, the theorist is also likely to differ from Mr. Fairmind, e.g. with respect to social background or possible self-interest, so that such prejudices could even be of relevance to his or her theoretical justice conception.

But why should we observe gender disparities in our contexts? And if any exist, in what direction are women and men supposed to differ? An interdisciplinary perspective seems to be a promising way to regard these questions. Starting with findings from psychological research, probably the best-known work that recognises gender differences in moral reasoning is Gilligan's (1982) claim that women are more likely to follow a *care perspective* and relate hypothetical scenarios to real life problems, whereas men tend to be more oriented towards a *justice perspective* and apply an abstract, consistent and often hierarchical ordering of ethical principles.[1] However, for example Miller (1992) criticises the evidential basis of Gilligan's conclusion, and especially Jaffee and Hyde (2000) could not deduce from their meta-analysis that either of the two perspectives is used significantly more often by one sex. Nevertheless, Gilligan's claim frequently serves as a starting point for many studies on gender disparities. Eagly (1995) reviews various psychological studies and finds gender differences to be strong, stable, non-artificial, and consistent. Women are found to be more socially oriented and men to be more individually oriented (see Eckel and Grossman, 1998); females more often support politics like public protection (Shapiro and Mahajan, 1986) and are better able to take on the perspective of others (Davis, 1983, and Eisenberg and Lennon, 1983). Furthermore, Gilligan (1982) argues that women's and men's moral development may proceed along different lines. She identifies different moral stages, passed through by young adults, which depend on age but also seem to be gender-specific.

With regard to views of justice, the previously mentioned classifications of empirical studies proposed by Miller (1992) or Elster (1995) prove to be useful again, although not all of the considered studies are theoretically grounded. As before, we will distinguish between distributive behaviour and beliefs about justice and also between small-scale and large-scale settings. It has been explained in chapter 1 that surveys are viewed to be better able to detect unbiased preferences, particularly, because distributive behaviour of participants in experiments is regularly influenced by self-interest due to introduced payment schemes. Therefore, Konow (2000) proposes the use of a benevolent dictator setting in experiments. To the best of our knowledge, there are only two studies that applied this approach and also commented on gender differences. Firstly, in experiments by Dickinson and Tiefenthaler (2002) probands had to divide a certain amount of tokens between two other players who differed in their ability to transform the resource into real money. Here, men were found to be more frequently concerned about efficiency, whereas women were more likely to prefer equal outcomes. In a second study, Traub et al. (2005) explicitly examined different concepts of justice in an income-distribution setting including real monetary payoffs. However, in one situation participants acted as external judges. The authors did not find any gender differences, but it should be mentioned that their sample included only 61 participants, and nothing is said about the proportions of both sexes.

Interestingly, lack of impartiality particularly confounds gender differences. For example, Major and Deaux (1982) concluded that gender disparities are often observable when decision-makers are affected by their own choices in the

1 With respect to the possible gender bias of the theorist, Lévy-Garboua, Meidinger and Rapoport (2004, p. 33) review Gilligan's work by arguing "that, because most of the theory of morality has been formulated by males, the morality of care, supposed to be mainly present among females, has not received enough attention".

way that females distribute less to themselves compared to male allocators. Nevertheless, besides biases from self-interest, economic experiments identify further environmental aspects to have an impact on behavioural gender differences. Therefore, they may also be of relevance for justice views. Eckel and Grossman (2000) and Croson and Gneezy (2008) reviewed several studies and found that, in general, women tended to be significantly more risk-averse than men. Moreover, the latter authors confirmed the persistence of such disparities between different cultures.

Similar to our review in chapter 1, Croson and Gneezy also stress the importance of 'framing effects', i.e. differences in the setting of an experiment – even the previously mentioned variations in the phrasing, which are found to have stronger effects on females compared to males. Additionally, gender disparities seem to be influenced by costs of behaviour. Eckel and Grossman (1996) used a 'third-party punishment game' and discovered women to punish unfair behaviour of the other party towards somebody else more often than men only if costs were low, but less frequently when costs were high. The authors conclude that men more often make allocation decisions on principle. In contrast, in a dictator experiment by Andreoni and Vesterlund (2001) women acted more altruistically than men if giving was costly, but men were kinder if giving was cheaper. Hence, they concluded that men were found to be more sensitive to price changes. Finally, by using field studies – instead of artificial settings – on altruism, Rooney et al. (2005) analysed charitable giving of American households and found important differences in donating by gender in the way that females tended to donate both more frequently and higher amounts. In contrast, Frey and Meier (2005) discovered that women were less likely to voluntarily contribute to university funds.

Concerning surveys in macro-justice settings, there are some illuminating studies from other social science disciplines. In the investigation by Michelbach et al. (2003) on the fairness of income distributions, results on gender differences have been particularly clear. Firstly, the authors confirmed findings from several earlier studies in the way that women were significantly more sensitive to needs than men. This observation is important for all three studies in the present work. Secondly, women obviously tended to prefer the equality principle, whereas men were more likely to consider aspects of efficiency. This finding has also relevance for the equality-efficiency trade-off being regarded in all of our investigations. Furthermore, in addition to their earlier work, i.e. Scott et al. (2001), they could corroborate that gender differences depended in turn on the degree of inequality. If inequalities concerned the existence of unsatisfied basic needs, women tended to follow the needs principle, whereas men still focused on merit aspects which demand to distribute goods in proportion to contributions that are thought to deserve reward. This finding is important for our second and third study.

A review of questionnaire investigations on different allocation principles which use micro-scale settings shows that individual characteristics are rarely considered. One exception to be mentioned here is the previously presented study by Schokkaert and Capéau (1991). Among other groups, they used a representative sample of adult Belgians in order to analyse attitudes towards fair salaries in several hypothetical situations. Thus, they also considered aspects of accountability, and found gender differences in one single case, in which men were more likely to reward education.

To summarise this rather extensive review, gender played a role in several investigations not only of justice views but also of social preferences and behaviour. Often, the influence of sex is confounded by other factors. Obviously, in most of the studies females allocated more to their opponents than males, but only as long as neither self-interest nor risk was involved. However, results appear to be influenced by the framing of the investigation. Furthermore, altruism of women seems to depend on related costs, while surveys on large-scale problems showed women to be more concerned about people in need. Two findings are particularly important for the concept of pluralism of allocation principles. On the one hand, females admitted absolute priority to the needs principle, while males regarded merit considerations even if hypothetical individuals live below the poverty line. On the other hand, Gilligan (1982) explains that males try to follow a hierarchical order of principles, while female decisions are more often influenced by contextual effects.

Overall, it seems to be possible that we will observe at least some gender differences in justice attitudes and with respect to the weighting of allocation principles, but what would be the consequences? Firstly, such results may certainly contribute to the growing literature on various gender disparities. Secondly, gender may be found to be one significant cause for various heterogeneities in justice attitudes. Thirdly, and probably most ambitiously, it is of major interest whether there are distinct female and male justice concepts. Is it likely that female decision-makers allocate differently from their male colleagues? Can we then still rely on the concept of Mr. Fairmind? Or do we also have to introduce *Mrs. Fairmind*? These questions will reappear in all three empirical investigations.

The present chapter is organised as follows. Section 2.2 gives information on the theoretical background of the study, introduces the questionnaire and formulates research questions. In section 2.3, several statistical tools are introduced. These instruments will be used throughout this work. The sample will be presented in section 2.4, while in section 2.5 answers of respondents are analysed. Moreover, some additional verbal comments of participants of the questionnaire study are presented to gain insights into underlying decision motives. In the concluding section, results are related to several explanations for gender differences in the literature.

## 2.2 Theoretical Background

It has already been stated that empirical examinations should be thoroughly directed by theoretical concepts. As the aim of the present study is to evaluate gender differences with regard to the trade-off between the equality or needs principle and the principle of efficiency, the theoretical background of the investigation should be explained in some more detail. We will focus on the acceptance of an equity axiom from social choice theory that underlies Rawls's (1971) difference principle. The equity axiom to be presented is essential for many mathematical characterisations of the difference principle (see e.g. Hammond, 1976, or Deschamps and Gevers, 1978). However, for the present purpose it may be sufficient to state only the intention of the axiom. Consider a society where only two members, individuals 1 and 2, are affected by a policy change from alternative $x$ to $y$, whereas all other individuals in society are either not affected or equally well off under both options. Suppose that person 1 prefers $x$ to $y$, while person 2 prefers $y$ over $x$. Furthermore, person 2 is assumed to be unambiguously always better off than person 1, no matter which alternative is realised. For the situation being described, the axiom states that $x$ should be socially preferred to $y$.

But how can we evaluate whether individuals – namely women and men – act in accordance with the considered axiom? Gaertner (1992) makes the suggestion to consider a two-person profile of so-called extended orderings $\tilde{R}_i, i \in \{1,2\}$, that shall be denoted by $E^1$:

$$\tilde{R}_1 : (y,2)(x,2)(x,1)(y,1),$$
$$\tilde{R}_2 : (y,2)(x,2)(x,1)(y,1).$$

This has to be interpreted in the following way. Individuals 1 and 2 agree that in the given situation it is best to be person 2 under alternative $y$. Moreover, both of them prefer to be person 2 under $x$ than being person 1 under $x$, which again is deemed better than being person 1 under $y$. Clearly, this profile reflects the structure described by the equity axiom. Therefore, if our questionnaire situations also follow this construction, we may deduce from the choices of respondents whether there are gender differences with respect to the fulfilment of the axiom.

However, having established this basic structure, it is possible to extend the profile $E^1$ by successively adding extended orderings of further better-off people. They are assumed to have the same preferences as person 2 and are also unambiguously always better off than person 1. For example, the corresponding three-person profile of extended orderings, which may be denoted by $E^2$, reads:

$$\tilde{R}_1 : (y,3)(x,3)(y,2)(x,2)(x,1)(y,1),$$
$$\tilde{R}_2 : (y,3)(x,3)(y,2)(x,2)(x,1)(y,1),$$
$$\tilde{R}_3 : (y,3)(x,3)(y,2)(x,2)(x,1)(y,1).$$

It is important to notice that this extension goes beyond the statement of the considered equity axiom. Nevertheless, a choice of alternative $x$ instead of $y$ will be interpreted as being in the *spirit* of the axiom. However, it is also possible that a consecutively increasing number of better-off individuals causes more and more support of this group, since the principle of efficiency may gain successively more momentum. Clearly, utilitarian concerns cannot completely be separated in this setting since no information about utility gains of all people under both alternatives is given. Nevertheless, it is likely that the efficiency principle plays an important role if a switch from alternative $x$ towards option $y$ occurs.

In the questionnaire study, several hypothetical situations are presented all of them reflecting the described structure of the equity axiom. A within-subject design was used so that each participant received the initial case with two (groups of) individuals, but also three enlargements of the better-off group in each context.[2] Participants always faced either-or decisions so that a split up of the given resource was not possible. In the first situation, a certain amount of money should be used either to help a handicapped person learning some very basic things (alternative $x$) or to further the education of one, two, three or four intelligent children (alternative $y$). The second situation requires allocating money to starving people in Africa ($x$) or to environmental programs in the home country of the respondent ($y$). The third situation describes a poor country that could purchase either dialysis machines for kidney patients ($x$) or vitamins and fruit to support some groups of the population, namely pregnant women, children, teenagers and workers ($y$). In the final context, the issue at stake is whether an economically run-down country should fully restore workers' rights and, as a result, accept a slower economic recovery ($x$) or take up a favourable loan that serves an increasing number of economic groups but is conditioned on a longer curtailment of workers' rights ($y$).

Some clarifications seem to be necessary. It should be stated that the worse-off people in all situations have basic needs that are not completely satisfied. Although we do not offer a precise definition of basic needs, the situations of the handicapped person, the starving Africans and the kidney patients seem to be uncontroversial. Moreover, the relevance of the case of human rights in situation 4 has been extensively discussed in Gaertner and Schwettmann (2007). Hence, these contexts obviously regard the needs principle described in the first chapter. Moreover, the equality principle also demands to support the worse-off individuals in all cases. It is assumed that all participants in the study agreed on the fact that one hypothetical person or group is always worse

2 The questionnaires can be found in Appendix 2.7.1. All in all, there have been six different situations in the first three years of the investigation, but two of them were only incorporated in order to evaluate the consistency of the students' answers. Hence, they are omitted in the present text.

off. However, even a constant choice of alternative $x$ in all three extensions of an initial situation cannot 'prove' the absolute priority of the needs principle. Therefore, we also asked respective students to explain whether they would *ever* be willing to switch from $x$ to $y$.

Certainly, this study does not aim at 'testing' Rawls's theory of justice, but instead intends to examine whether laymen satisfy the described equity axiom. Moreover, it cannot be claimed that in all situations a veil of ignorance has been erected. In fact, as the discussion of the results will show, contextual influences are of some importance and provoke certain gender differences. Furthermore, in contrast to Rawls's theory most of the following situations consider small-scale settings in the way that allocations among (smaller groups of) individuals are regarded instead of overall distributions of a resource for a given society. However, as also discussed in the first chapter, this contextual effect is not expected to lead to the acceptance of completely different allocation principles.

In the following investigation, we firstly ask for gender differences with respect to the fulfilment of the equity axiom. Secondly, we want to see whether women and men stick equally often to their initial choice of alternative $x$ even when additional better-off people are introduced. Alternatively, respondents could 'switch' towards alternative $y$ at some point. It might be possible that gender differences with regard to the location of this 'switching point' can be detected. Thirdly, the examination of verbal answers of men and women should reveal whether both sexes use different arguments for their decisions.

But what do we expect to observe? Clearly, the structure of all situations could be interpreted as creating an increasing conflict between the principles of equality or needs and efficiency (see Konow, 2003, for this interpretation of the given structure). However, as is known from the literature reviewed, women often tend to recognise needs more frequently than men. Furthermore, if faced with an equality-efficiency trade-off, men, compared to women, are more likely to decide in accordance with the efficiency principle. Thus, both the fulfilment of the equity axiom and the 'switching' decision just described may be affected by the sex of a respondent. This prediction could gain further backing if the refused support of the better offs is interpreted as opportunity costs of a decision in favour of alternative $x$. When the number of better-off people goes up, these costs also increase. Hence, results can be compared with experiments on giving and altruism, where costs also varied and gender differences occurred.

The position of the decision-maker could be another reason for different answer patterns. In situation 2, the groups who are benefitting from environmental programs are inhabitants of the home country of the respondent. Moreover, the first group that is affected by alternative $y$ in situation 3 consists of pregnant women. Certainly, this information may tackle stronger feelings among female respondents. Compared to these two contexts, situations 1 and 4 are supposed to be farther away from the everyday life of our students. Hence, all situations may be interpreted as displaying different degrees of identification of respondents with hypothetical groups. However, this degree could differ among sexes.

Additionally, women seem to relate their decisions more closely to the framing of the given context. Therefore, we may find stronger variations of decision patterns between the four situations among females compared to their male counterparts. This aspect will be reconsidered in the final section.

## 2.3 Empirical Methods

In the following section, those statistical methods are introduced, which will be applied in order to answer the questions just stated. Our approach closely follows Manski's (2002) suggestion that behaviour in economic experiments should be investigated by adequate econometric analysis. In the present work, we will basically focus on the interpretation of results of different regression models that relate observed choices to a set of variables based on individual and questionnaire characteristics. At several occasions in all three chapters on empirical investigations, we will come back to the more general parts of these methods.

### 2.3.1 Descriptive Comparisons

In chapters 2 to 4, descriptive comparisons will be considered first. While in the third investigation answer patterns are rather diverse, in the first two studies all possible decision patterns are represented by four-digit sequences. Here, a choice of alternative $x$ is coded as 0, whereas a decision in favour of $y$ is reflected by 1. The first number of each sequence corresponds to the selection in the initial case of the situation to be considered and, therefore, reflects the possible fulfilment of the equity axiom. The relative frequencies of corresponding respondents will also be given in the respective tables on the descriptive data. The next three digits of a sequence represent decisions in each successive extension. Hence, there are 16 possible answer sequences. We will use them to denominate and distinguish different decision patterns. Here, the sequence 0000 represents those students who choose alternative $x$ in all cases, i.e. in the base situation and in all its variants. They not only fulfil the equity axiom, but always stick to this decision in favour of the worse-off person or group. Furthermore, the sequences 0001, 0011 and 0111 correspond to verdicts of those respondents who initially decided in terms of the equity axiom, but revised their choice later on. These patterns reflect a *sensible switch* from $x$ to $y$, and the proportion of individuals following this behaviour is also stated in the result section. In contrast, although sequences such as 0101 or 1100 also display an alteration of the initial decision, they are rather difficult to interpret; they could be called *unintelligible*.

In most of the following analysis, respondents are divided into two respective samples. In the present chapter, females and males are separated, whereas in the following investigation an additional distinction between probands facing either a *responsibility version* or a *no-responsibility version* of the questionnaire is found to be appropriate. The third study utilises similar divisions. Hence, one possible nonparametric statistical tool to compare results from different groups is to apply $\chi^2$ tests for independent samples.[3] In general, these tests investigate the hypothesis $H_0$ that the relative frequency, with which members of both regarded groups g=1,2 fall into one of the $m$ considered discrete answer categories, is identical between the two samples. In other words, the null hypothesis states that both groups come from the same population. This is tested by calculating the $\chi^2$ test statistic

$$\chi^2 = \sum_{g=1}^{2} \sum_{h=1}^{m} \frac{(n_{gh} - E_{gh})^2}{E_{gh}}, \tag{2.1}$$

where $n_{gh}$ represents the observed absolute frequency of choices in group $g$ reflected by the $h$-th category, while $E_{gh}$ denotes the expected number of respondents in sample $g$ to answer in accordance with category $h$ if hypothesis $H_0$ holds. For example, for group g=1 the latter value is derived from

$$E_{1h} = \frac{n_1(n_{1h} - n_{2h})}{n_1 + n_2}, \tag{2.2}$$

where $n_1$ and $n_2$ are the corresponding numbers of respondents in samples 1 and 2. The calculated $\chi^2$ values are asymptotically distributed as $\chi^2_{(m-1)}$. $H_0$ is rejected if this value exceeds $\chi^2_{(m-1),(1-\alpha)}$. Usually, in order to avoid undefined equations, standard statistical computer programs, such as the applied SPSS software package, consider only those categories where either $n_{1h}$ or $n_{2h}$ is positive. Consequently, this eventually reduces $m$, and, thus, adjusts the degrees of freedom. More concretely, in the following two investigations, $\chi^2$ tests will be applied either for $m \times 2$ contingency tables, with $m \leq 16$ if the relative frequencies for all possible decision patterns are concerned, or for $2 \times 2$ contingency tables if differences with respect to single sequences or certain behaviours, such as the fulfilment of the equity axiom, are considered. Similar tests are used with respect to the third study, but here $m$ takes on different values.

### 2.3.2 Binary Response Model

The just described $\chi^2$ tests are an appropriate tool to investigate differences, for example, between female and male samples. However, due to their one-

3 See e.g. Siegel and Castellan (1988) for a more complete description of the following tests.

dimensional character they are not able to simultaneously incorporate influences of additionally available individual attributes of respondents or questionnaire characteristics. Therefore, these tests could lead to invalid inference. For example, if women and men differ with respect to some of these additional attributes, and if these attributes are supposed to display a significant influence on regarded decisions, we should also control for these effects in order to separate the influence of the gender variable and, furthermore, to identify reasons for possible gender differences. Hence, multivariate regression models have to be considered. Clearly, in the questionnaire previously described participants are asked to make choices between two alternatives in the initial case, but also in three extensions. Thus, the discrete nature of the resulting dependent variables suggests the application of discrete choice models, so that the influence of independent variables on the probability of observing certain behaviours can be evaluated. Here, relevant choices might be described either as a binary decision, for example if the fulfilment of the equity axiom is considered, or as ordered or multinomial responses if the regarded subject has to decide between more than two discrete alternatives, for instance by choosing in accordance with one out of five sensible sequences. In the next two subsections, regression methods for both interpretations are introduced.

In the case of binary responses, a logit model will be utilised. Suppose we are interested in gender differences with respect to the fulfilment of the equity axiom described in section 2.2. Let

$$z_i^{B*} = x_i'\beta + \varepsilon_i \tag{2.3}$$

be the latent regression. Here, according e.g. to Heij et al. (2004, pp. 440-442), $z_i^{B*}$ can be interpreted as an unobserved continuous variable that represents the positive or negative latent utility that person $i$, with $i = 1, ..., n$, receives, for example, from choosing alternative $x$ over $y$ in the initial case. It is supposed that we have available information on $k$ different characteristics for each individual $i$. The model includes a constant term, whereby $x_{i0}$=1 for all individuals $i$. Thus, the values of $(k + 1)$ independent variables are represented by the $(k + 1) \times 1$ vector $x_i$ so that the linear index function $x_i'\beta$ reflects the systematic utility gain. Moreover, the terms $\varepsilon_i$ denote the individual-specific effects. In the logit model, they are assumed to be independently and identically logistically distributed, hence

$$Pr(\varepsilon_i < t) = \frac{exp(t)}{1 + exp(t)}, \tag{2.4}$$

where $t$ is an expression that will be replaced in due course. The alternatively available probit model assumes these effects to be independently and normally distributed. Nevertheless, for example Lee (1983) already shows that both approaches give extremely similar results, which mainly differ with respect to the scale of estimated coefficients for explanatory variables. But the structure of a logit model offers the possibility to interpret these coefficients with the help of so-called 'odds' that will be introduced and explained below.

Instead of the continuous variable $z_i^{B*}$ the discrete choice $z_i^B$ is observed, which is supposed to be related to the latent model in the way that

$$z_i^B = \begin{cases} 1 & \text{if } z_i^{B*} \geq 0, \\ 0 & \text{if } z_i^{B*} < 0. \end{cases} \tag{2.5}$$

It follows that

$$\begin{aligned} Pr(z_i^B = 1|x_i) &= Pr(-x_i'\beta \leq \varepsilon_i|x_i) \\ &= 1 - \frac{exp(-x_i'\beta)}{1 + exp(-x_i'\beta)} = \frac{exp(x_i'\beta)}{1 + exp(x_i'\beta)} = \Lambda(x_i'\beta). \end{aligned} \tag{2.6}$$

Thus, the conditional probability of observing a choice of $z_i^B$=1 (support of the worse-off individual), given the regressors, equals the cumulative density function of the standard logistic distribution denoted by $\Lambda$.[4]

The parameters $\beta$ can be estimated by the method of maximum likelihood.[5] Standard statistical computer packages, such as SPSS, which has been applied to produce all statistical results in the present text, routinely run these regressions. However, instead of describing the well-known method of maximum likelihood, which can be found in all modern textbooks, we will focus on the interpretation of results.

Two possible interpretations of coefficients are applied. Firstly, the marginal probability effect of the $l$-th regressor is given by

$$\frac{\partial Pr(z_i^B = 1|x_i)}{\partial x_{il}} = \frac{\partial \Lambda(x_i'\beta)}{\partial(x_i\beta)} \frac{\partial x_i'\beta}{\partial x_{il}} = \lambda(x_i'\beta)\beta_l, \tag{2.7}$$

where $\lambda(x_i'\beta) = \Lambda(x_i'\beta)[1 - \Lambda(x_i'\beta)]$ represents the first derivative of $\Lambda(x_i'\beta)$ and, therefore, denotes the probability density function of the logistic distribution. Equation (2.7) shows that marginal effects differ among individuals so that we would have to determine the mean marginal probability effect for the $l$-th regressor by estimating

$$\frac{1}{n}\sum_{i=1}^{n} \frac{\partial Pr(z_i^B = 1|x_i)}{\partial x_{il}} = \beta_l \frac{1}{n}\sum_{i=1}^{n} \lambda(x_i'\beta). \tag{2.8}$$

Indeed, in our interpretations we are basically interested in the direction of the influence of a change in the considered explanatory variable on the probability

4 See e.g. Winkelmann and Boes (2006) for an elaboration of this and the following two models in this section.

5 For clearness reasons we do not use a further index for the betas to indicate the model regarded.

of observing $z_i^B$=1. But, as can be seen from equation (2.8), the sign of the marginal effect is equal to the sign of $\beta_l$. Also, note that by using marginal effects we only approximate, inter alia, a discrete change in the probabilities associated with a discrete change in a dummy variable from zero to one.[6]

Secondly, the specific structure of the logit model also allows us to interpret the estimated coefficients with the help of odds, which are usually given by

$$\frac{Pr(z_i^B = 1|x_i)}{Pr(z_i^B = 0|x_i)} = \frac{\Lambda(x_i'\beta)}{1 - \Lambda(x_i'\beta)} = exp(x_i'\beta). \tag{2.9}$$

Consider a factor change in the odds caused by a one unit increase in $x_{il}$, i.e. $\Delta x_{il}$=1. An example is a change from '0' (female) to '1' (male) in the gender dummy variable. In this case the resulting odds ratio is given by

$$\frac{exp(x_i'\beta + \Delta x_{il}\beta_l)}{exp(x_i'\beta)} = exp(\beta_l). \tag{2.10}$$

Thus, according to equation (2.10) the odds ratio, viz. the odds for males divided by the odds for females, is given by the exponent of the estimated coefficient for the gender dummy variable. Here, a value of 1.0 indicates the absence of differences caused by the increase in the explanatory variable. The deviation of the odds ratio from the value 1.0 will be evaluated by using corresponding confidence intervals for the exponents of the logistic coefficients.

Certainly one may argue that one-sided tests are more appropriate from a statistical point of view. However, since the direction of influences of the factors investigated in the following chapters is not clear a priori, the application of two-sided tests seems to be a reasonable approach. Furthermore, we will mainly focus on predicted odds rather than on predicted probabilities. Here it could be objected that the transformation due to the application of predicted odds usually leads to an overestimation of the effect being analysed. Moreover, their relation to the descriptive data is less obvious compared to (means of) individual predicted probabilities. Clearly, odds allow for statements with regard to ratios of probabilities. Nevertheless, the questions being regarded in our investigations basically consider binary comparisons, for example between men and women or between different questionnaire versions. Hence, odds seem to be sufficient. Moreover, Jaccard (2001, p. 3) reports that "[most] researchers who use logistic regression rely on the concept of odds to impose theoretical meaning on the results of the analysis". He explains that "the intuitive appeal of odds and odds ratios results in the vast majority of social science research being reported in these terms" (p. 11). In particular, this is the case with regard to interaction effects that will be explained below. Nevertheless, according to equation (2.4) an odds can easily be converted to a probability. We will give an example in Table 2.11.

6 See Winkelmann and Boes (2006, p. 105) for a clarification.

### 2.3.3 Ordered and Multinomial Response Model

In this subsection, two statistical methods to analyse sequential enlargements of the better-off group will be presented and compared. They will only be used in the first and second study since possible variations of allocations are too complex in the third case. Both approaches, the ordered and the multinomial logit model, are commonly applied in those empirical studies where multinomial responses are observed. However, while the first approach possibly better reflects the previously described structure of situations, it implicitly uses an assumption that is not necessarily fulfilled by the available data. Thus, the ordered logit model and its inherent critical assumption will be introduced first. Afterwards, the alternative multinomial logit model is presented. Finally, some decision guidance is given, although in most of the following cases outcomes from both methods are considered in the results sections.

It is known that a respondent who decides in accordance with sequence 1111 rejects the equity axiom right away, whereas answers reflected, for example, by the sequence 0011 represent a 'later' reconsideration of the initial choice of alternative $x$. This could be interpreted in the way that the second respondent displays a higher *closeness* to the spirit of the equity axiom. Therefore, the focus is on those strings, which denote either an unconditional support for one alternative, i.e. sequences 0000 and 1111, or a sensible switch from $x$ to $y$, viz. sequences $0001, 0011$ and 0111, whereas other possible decision patterns are ignored in these analyses. It should be mentioned that this reduction is in contrast to the binary response model where all 16 sequences are used and distinguished only by their first digit. Hence, compared to the binary model sample sizes are probably smaller if ordered or multinomial models are applied so that we loose some information.

Thus, the five sensible sequences can be ordered with respect to the previously mentioned closeness that is lowest for the sequence 1111 and highest for 0000. An appropriate way to represent this interpretation statistically is to apply an ordered logit model. This can be done by considering the latent regression

$$z_i^{O*} = x_i'\beta + \varepsilon_i, \tag{2.11}$$

where $z_i^{O*}$ denotes a latent continuous variable, while $x_i'\beta$ is the linear index of regressors. Furthermore, the random term $\varepsilon_i$ is supposed to be independently and identically logistically distributed.[7] Here, the value of $z_i^{O*}$ reflects the utility that person $i$ derives from choosing alternative $x$. In contrast, supporting alternative $y$ yields an expected utility of $\mu_s$, where $s = 1, 2, 3, 4$ may be an ordinal indicator for the size of the better-off group. It is rather intuitive to assume that $\mu$ increases with $s$ so that $\mu_1 < ... < \mu_4$. As be-

7 Greene (2003) explains that the assumption of normally distributed disturbance terms makes no difference.

fore, $z_i^{O*}$ cannot be detected, but now we observe $z_i^O$ with five discrete values $z_i^O = 1, \ldots, 5$. Accounting for the ordering information in $z_i^O$ it is assumed that

$$z_i^O = \begin{cases} 1 & \text{if } z_i^{O*} \leq \mu_1, \\ s & \text{if } \mu_{s-1} < z_i^{O*} \leq \mu_s \text{ with } s = 2,3,4, \\ 5 & \text{if } \mu_4 < z_i^{O*}. \end{cases} \tag{2.12}$$

Consider for example situation 1 in the first questionnaire. From observing $z_i^O$=5 it can be deduced that even in the case of $s$=4 intelligent children, participant $i$ is not willing to switch from alternative $x$ to $y$, hence sequence 0000 is observed. Therefore, the (unobserved) utility from choosing $x$ is supposed to be higher than the corresponding benefit from supporting four better-off individuals. In contrast, for $z_i^O$=3 the probability that respondent $i$ switches, if the number of intelligent children is increased from two to three (this is sequence 0011), is equal to the probability that the unobserved variable $z_i^{O*}$ is between $\mu_2$ and $\mu_3$.

Similar to equation (2.6), the following probabilities are obtained:

$$\begin{aligned} Pr(z_i^O = 1|x_i) =& Pr(z_i^{O*} \leq \mu_1) = \frac{exp(\mu_1 - x_i'\beta)}{1 + exp(\mu_1 - x_i'\beta)} = \Lambda(\mu_1 - x_i'\beta), \\ Pr(z_i^O = s|x_i) =& \Lambda(\mu_s - x_i'\beta) - \Lambda(\mu_{s-1} - x_i'\beta) \quad for \quad s = 2,3,4, \\ Pr(z_i^O = 5|x_i) =& 1 - Pr(z_i^{O*} \leq \mu_4) = 1 - \Lambda(\mu_4 - x_i'\beta). \end{aligned} \tag{2.13}$$

The threshold values $\mu_s$ are estimated along with the $\beta$ coefficients by means of the method of maximum likelihood. Here, the intercept term is usually not included in the model in order to identify the $\mu$ parameters. Nevertheless, while some programs exclude a constant term from all ordered logit estimations, the SPSS software package offers the opportunity to incorporate a 'multinomial constant term' for calculating comparable log likelihood values in both models. Borooah (2002, p. 10) explains the consequences of including a constant term. He shows that both approaches essentially lead to identical results except for the estimated coefficients for the threshold values; however, these are not important for our interpretations. Moreover, we also observed very small differences with respect to some standard errors. Nevertheless, we will report estimated ordered logit models, which implicitly include this constant term for calculating the log likelihood values, since they are necessary to perform the 'suggestive' likelihood-ratio test described at the end of this subsection to evaluate the appropriateness of the ordered logit model.

However, it is also possible to motivate an ordered logit model by considering odds. In this case, they are commonly defined as the following fraction:

$\frac{Pr(z_i^O \leq s|x_i)}{Pr(z_i^O > s|x_i)}$, $s = 1, ..., 4$. Consequently, from equations (2.13) it can be seen that equation (2.9) in the binary logit model now corresponds to

$$\begin{aligned}\frac{Pr(z_i^O \leq s|x_i)}{Pr(z_i^O > s|x_i)} &= exp(\mu_s - x_i'\beta) \\ &= exp(\mu_s)exp(-x_i'\beta) \quad for \quad s = 1, ..., 4.\end{aligned} \tag{2.14}$$

Clearly, for each possible odds there exists a specific intercept term $\mu_s$ that is supposed to be ordered as before.

Nevertheless, according to Winkelmann and Boes (2006), it is much more natural to interpret estimated coefficients in ordered logit models as discrete or marginal probability effects. Thus, the corresponding marginal effect of the $l$-th element in $x_i$ can be calculated from equations (2.13) by taking first derivatives:

$$\begin{aligned}\frac{\partial Pr(z_i^O = 1|x_i)}{\partial x_{il}} &= \lambda(\mu_1 - x_i'\beta)(-\beta_l), \\ \frac{\partial Pr(z_i^O = s|x_i)}{\partial x_{il}} &= [\lambda(\mu_{s-1} - x_i'\beta) - \lambda(\mu_s - x_i'\beta)]\beta_l \quad for \quad s = 2, 3, 4, \\ \frac{\partial Pr(z_i^O = 5|x_i)}{\partial x_{il}} &= \lambda(\mu_4 - x_i'\beta)(\beta_l).\end{aligned} \tag{2.15}$$

From equations (2.15) it becomes obvious that for a positive coefficient $\beta_l$ the probability for $z_i^O$=1 decreases with a growing independent variable $x_{il}$, while it increases for $z_i^O$=5. The effects on the other three possible outcomes are not unambiguous. Therefore, marginal effects of selected variables for each probability are also calculated. Two different procedures are utilised. Firstly, for continuous variables, like the age of a respondent, the suggestion by Winkelmann and Boes (2006, p. 182) is followed. They explain that in equations (2.15) $\beta$ has to be substituted by its ML estimates $\hat{\beta}$ before taking the mean value in order to obtain average marginal probability effects. Secondly, with respect to dummy variables, for instance the gender indicator, the alternative and perhaps more intuitive method described by Borooah (2002, pp. 33-36) is applied. Here, the probabilities of person $i$ being at levels $z_i^O = 1, ..., 5$ are calculated ceteris paribus from $\sum_{l=1}^{k} \hat{\beta}_l x_{il}$ with $x_{i,Male}$=1 and, afterwards, with $x_{i,Male}$=0. Hence, for each person in the sample the differences between both probabilities in each outcome category are entirely due to the gender effect. In the following studies, the mean of these individual marginal effects will be interpreted.

The ordered response model has the property of using a single index function. Although this is a positive attribute especially in terms of number of estimated coefficients (see e.g. Heij et al., 2004, p. 475), Winkelmann and Boes (2006) illustrate the immanent limitation: If we calculate marginal probability effects, we face the "single crossing property" (p. 187), which means that as we move from $z_i^O$=1 to $z_i^O$=5 the marginal effects can change their sign only once. Clearly, this is not necessarily the case for our questionnaire results. For example, it might be possible that male respondents are more likely than their female counterparts to choose in accordance with either sequence 0000 or sequence 1111. But this cannot be reflected by a single estimated coefficient for the gender dummy variable. Hence, if the researcher has any doubt concerning this implicit supposition, Borooah (2002, p. 15) recommends applying a multinomial logit model, "notwithstanding the fact that the dependent variable is clearly ordinal".[8]

The multinomial logit model to be considered is a repeated application of the binary logit model. The five observed outcomes, $z_{ij}^M$, i.e. sequences in the present case, are *arbitrarily* indexed by $j = 1, ..., 5$. Consider the latent regression

$$z_{ij}^{M*} = x_i'\beta_j + \varepsilon_i. \tag{2.16}$$

We can interpret the latent variable $z_{ij}^{M*}$ in equation (2.16) as the unobserved utility that person $i$ receives from choosing sequence $j$. But now, a higher value for $j$ does not necessarily corresponds to a higher supposed utility level, because they are not ordered. Again, the linear index $x_i'\beta_j$ contains the vector of individual characteristics $x_i$, but also outcome-specific vectors $\beta_j$ with (k+1) elements. In contrast to the ordered logit model, the latter vectors are allowed to differ between the five outcome probabilities. The probability of observing $z_i^M = j$ is given by

$$Pr(z_i^M = j|x_i) = \frac{exp(x_i'\beta_j)}{\sum_{r=1}^{5} exp(x_i'\beta_r)} \quad j = 1, ..., 5, \tag{2.17}$$

but because all probabilities sum to 1, equation (2.17) is indeterminate. Hence, for example, the parameters of the fifth alternative, $\beta_5$, are set equal to zero and, by this, the fifth outcome is defined as the *base sequence.* Due to this normalisation we get

$$\begin{aligned} Pr(z_i^M = s|x_i) =& \frac{exp(x_i'\beta_s)}{1 + \sum_{r=1}^{4} exp(x_i'\beta_r)}, \quad s = 1, ..., 4, \\ Pr(z_i^M = 5|x_i) =& \frac{1}{1 + \sum_{r=1}^{4} exp(x_i'\beta_r)}. \end{aligned} \tag{2.18}$$

As before, $s$ is defined as the number of better-off (groups of) people considered in the chosen sequence. However, the probability of observing sequence 0000 serves as the baseline. Again, odds are utilised to interpret the

8 Borooah proposes a 'suggestive' likelihood-ratio test to compare the appropriateness of both models. This test will be described after introducing the multinomial logit model.

parameters. From equations (2.18) the odds of outcome $s$ versus the base sequence are given by

$$\frac{Pr(z_i^M = s|x_i)}{Pr(z_i^M = 5|x_i)} = exp(x_i'\beta_s) \quad s = 1, ..., 4. \tag{2.19}$$

Similar to the binary logit model, the term $exp(\beta_{sl})$ denotes the odds ratio of the $l$-th independent variable. For example, an estimated positive value $\widehat{\beta}_{3,Male}$ implies that the odds ratio is larger than one and, thus, a change in the gender dummy from $Male$=0 to $Male$=1 raises the probability to observe sequence 0011 relative to the probability to find the base sequence 0000. Again, ML estimations are applied by using the SPSS software package.

To summarise, on the one hand, in a multinomial logit model $(k+1)\times s$ parameters have to be estimated compared to only $k+s$ parameters in the ordered logit model. This is due to the fact that the latter model uses a single index function. Therefore, the model estimates a single impact of the considered predictor variable on the ordered outcomes. On the other hand, the multinomial logit approach allows us to estimate outcome-specific coefficients for the gender dummy. Certainly, this feature is superior if the previously described implicit single crossing assumption is violated. Such a violation is not easy to detect and, as far as we know, a clear decision rule is not proposed in the literature. An inspection of descriptive data may serve as a first possibility to see whether there is any reason to doubt this crucial supposition. Moreover, Borooah (2002, p. 15) proposes a 'suggestive' likelihood-ratio test. Here, the likelihood values $L_M$ from the multinomial and $L_O$ from the ordered logit model have to be calculated. Then, the term $2(L_M - L_O)$ is compared with $\chi^2_{k(5-2)}$, where $k$ represents the number of estimated coefficients for independent regressors in the ordered logit model and 5 denotes the number of outcomes. Accordingly, 'very high' $\chi^2$ values would suggest the application of the multinomial logit method even though the outcome variable is clearly ordered. This test will also be employed in the following two empirical investigations to evaluate both proposed models. Nevertheless, it should be mentioned that the test just described compares the multinomial and the ordered logit model only at an overall level but not for each variable separately. Moreover, Borooah (p. 15) notes that "this is not strictly a likelihood-ratio test because the ordered logit model is not nested within the multinomial logit model". Hence, this test is only 'suggestive'. Thus, as a third but least accurate test, results for each of the variables regarded will also be critically examined with respect to the marginal effects estimated in the ordered model. In any case, estimations of the multinomial logit models will also be presented in each chapter, which seems to be necessary to allow for both a comparison of results of the two models and a more complete investigation of supposed influential factors on answer patterns.

### 2.3.4 Interaction Effects

The previously described multivariate models are applied to separate the effect of the variable we are focusing on from other confounding individual and questionnaire attributes. However, this approach assumes these factors to bias decisions of distinguished groups, e.g. women and men in the present chapter, in the same direction. But if we want to allow for gender specific influences of such characteristics, we have to control for *interaction effects*. A respective test is usually modelled by incorporating a product term of $x_{Male}$, the *focal variable*, and $x_{Mod}$, a so-called *moderator variable*, in the single estimated model. Hence, for example, the right hand side of equation (2.9) reads

$$exp(\beta_0 + \beta_{Male}x_{i,Male} + \beta_{Mod}x_{i,Mod} + \beta_{Prod}x_{i,Male}x_{i,Mod} + \cdots + \varepsilon_i), \quad (2.20)$$

where $\beta_{Prod}$ represents the coefficient of the interaction term. As equation (2.20) shows, the introduction of a product term establishes the possibility of a relationship between two independent variables.

In order to evaluate the relevance of interaction effects in logistic regressions, Jaccard (2001, p. 18) suggests to determine "whether the product terms significantly improve model fit over and above the case where no product terms are included in the model". Thus, depending on the set of possible interaction effects, we will apply two different methods in our regression models. Firstly, with respect to combinations of the focal variable, e.g. the gender dummy, and other individual or questionnaire attributes stepwise backward elimination of interaction terms based on likelihood-ratio tests is employed; the critical p-value is set at 0.05. This standard procedure is offered by the SPSS software package. Secondly, in chapter 3 we will also incorporate sets of product terms and assess the corresponding change in the log-likelihood compared to the model without interaction terms by standard likelihood-ratio tests (see e.g. Winkelmann and Boes, 2006, pp. 83-86, for some elaborations). In most cases it will be observed that interaction effects are not statistically significant.

However, interpretation of the coefficient $\beta_{Product}$ in non-linear models is complex. Unfortunately, the literature lacks a consensus about the most appropriate way to do this.[9] Ai and Norton (2003) report that most applied economists falsely calculate marginal effects of interaction terms. The authors show that there are several difficulties with interpreting such marginal effects and signs of coefficients. Nevertheless, in the present studies – instead of using rather advanced statistical tools to determine marginal effects in binary and multinomial logit models – it seems to be sufficient to construe interaction by means of *ratios of odds ratios*. Thus, we follow the work of Jaccard (2001), Agresti (2002) or Borooah (2002).

---

9 See e.g. Berry and Berry (1991), Nagler (1994), Berry (1999), Jaccard (2001) and Ai and Norton (2003).

The underlying idea is that the influence of the focal variable, viz. gender, on the outcome concerned may in turn depend on the value of the moderator variable. Firstly, consider a binary logit model. For each value of the moderator variable an odds ratio for the focal variable could be calculated. Thus, we have to consider what Agresti (2002) calls 'conditional odds ratios'. Furthermore, a ratio of predicted odds ratios can be calculated for each two categories of the moderator variable. If this ratio takes on the value 1.0, then there is no interaction effect noticeable. In contrast, numbers that are significantly different from 1.0 imply an influence of the moderator variable on the effect of the gender dummy variable on the considered binary outcome when we hold the other predictors constant. If the moderator variable is coded as a dummy, Jaccard (2001) explains that the exponent of the coefficient $\beta_{Product}$ equals this ratio of predicted odds ratios. Also, in the case of a continuous moderator variable the corresponding exponent denotes the multiplicative factor by which this ratio varies due to an increase of the moderator variable by one unit. We will use 95% confidence intervals for the exponents to provide an appreciation for sampling errors for the ratios of predicted odds ratios. Furthermore, in Table 2.11 on page 82 a simplified example is presented.

Secondly, since the multinomial logit model is a (j-1)-fold application of a binary logit model, the respective interpretation of product terms remains the same. However, thirdly, in ordered logit models the focus is on marginal effects of interacted variables – but not of the interaction term, as Ai and Norton (2003) warn. Thus, for example Borooah (2002, p. 37) explains that in this case $\beta_{Product}$ simply measures the 'strength' of the interaction effect.

A general remark is necessary. As Jaccard (2001) explicitly pronounces, the estimated values of the non-product coefficients of interacted variables are conditional on the other product component(s) being zero. The important consequences of this fact will become apparent in due course.

In order to reduce the usually high covariance between the product term and its components, continuous variables in the model are centred about their mean value.[10] Hence, their effects are evaluated at the sample means. A centred variable will be marked by a subscript $c$. This is most often the case for the variable $AGE_c$. However, the centring has no effect on the variables that are not interacted.

Furthermore, in anticipation of the analysis of the second empirical study, it should already be mentioned that the no-responsibility and the responsibility samples will be pooled, and the additional dummy variable RES will be introduced to indicate the respective version. Then, in order to investigate gender differences the statistical models are extended by incorporating an additional product term consisting of RES, which is now the focal variable, and the gender dummy. Furthermore, since we have available samples from different

10 See e.g. Jaccard, Turrisi and Wan (1990) or Aiken and West (1991) for a discussion of this procedure.

places, two interaction terms are introduced that allow us to control for local effects on the influence of the variable RES on decisions. In addition, local differences of the influence of gender effects on responsibility considerations are also controlled for. This is done by using three-way interaction terms, where place dummies are introduced as *second-order moderator variables.* In this case, as Kleinbaum and Klein (2002) explain, the model has to comprise all lower-order components in order to be hierarchically well-formulated.

### 2.3.5 Treatment of Missing Data

Finally, let us comment on our treatment of missing data, which are part of almost all empirical investigations in the literature. For a variety of reasons data on dependent or independent variables could be unavailable. Here, the term *item non-response* refers to the fact that respondents leave single items blank on questionnaires. The problem is that data gaps could either be random or depend on the context of the study. In the latter case, reasons for *missingness* would carry information that may be important for the researcher.

With respect to dependent variables, regression models are often applied to fill missing values. But Greene (2003, p. 60) warns that "in a single-equation regression context" these methods lead "to biases in the estimator which are difficult to quantify". Instead, he proposes to employ sample selection models. This approach uses a two-step procedure and includes the estimation of the selection mechanism (see Heckman, 1976, 1979). However, since the specification of both the selection equation and the model equation has to be exact, the reliability of this approach is frequently questioned.[11] Furthermore, one has to identify a variable that is significant for the selection mechanism but external to the research design. Therefore, in each of our three investigations we have decided to omit all cases where data on at least one dependent variable is missing. This problem is more apparent in the first and second study. Here, the approach is similar to the procedure applied in preliminary investigations on this questionnaire so that we are able to compare our results with earlier findings.[12] A refusal to consider one or more contexts is interpreted either as displaying difficulties to understand the decision problem being described or as expressing unease with the given hypothetical situation. Indeed, some students wrote that they felt they were unable to decide in favour of one of the hypothetical groups.

In the following paragraphs we will focus on missing data on independent variables. According to the classification proposed by Rubin (1976), three different 'missingness mechanisms' can be distinguished: Firstly, *missing com-*

11 See e.g. Stolzenberg and Relles (1997), Allison (2002) or Schnell, Hill and Esser (2005).

12 See Gaertner, Jungeilges and Neck (2001), Gaertner and Jungeilges (2002) and Gaertner and Schwettmann (2007).

*pletely at random (MCAR)* is a condition that exists when missing values are randomly distributed across all subjects. Secondly, *missing at random (MAR)* exists when the missing of data on one variable can be explained by other variables.[13] For example, the probability of missing data on the variable 'future income expectation' may depend on the gender of a respondent, but for each sex this probability is not conditional on 'real' future income expectations – which are certainly unobservable if the case is missing. The last comment points towards the most problematic form, where the probability of missingness depends on the 'real' value of the missing data. For example, respondents could be more likely to reject to answer the question on their future income expectations if they expect to receive a low income. This third mechanism is called *missing not at random (MNAR)*. It is impossible to detect MNAR, and only sample selection models mentioned above are able to treat this form.

Several further methods to deal with the problem of missing data are proposed in the literature. However, we will only briefly mention some of them.[14] The classical and most common approach is *listwise deletion*. Here, cases are omitted if they do not contain data on all variables. The number of deleted cases determines the corresponding loss of statistical power. Moreover, if missing values are not MCAR, estimates may be biased.

*Imputation methods* represent another way to treat missing data. In this case, numbers are fed into a procedure, which then treats the imputed values as 'real data'. Classical methods, such as mean substitution or regression imputation, are no longer recommended. Instead, modern approaches either rely on maximum likelihood solutions or involve *multiple imputation*. Unfortunately, the former method tends to estimate individual cases that are close to regression imputation. Therefore, the latter approach is more often advocated today. Here, several completed data sets are simultaneously created and analysed.

Nevertheless, according to Göthlich (2007, pp. 131-132) severe doubts remain. On the one hand, modern solutions suggest an accuracy that does not exist at all. On the other hand, especially the method of multiple imputation is costly in terms of time and effort, and it is not implemented in many statistical software packages. Furthermore, if missing values are MNAR, which is the most likely case, all approaches proposed are insufficient. Hence, it is small wonder that Göthlich (p. 129) reports that no case exists where the application of a modern approach lead to a revision of results which have been obtained by traditional methods.

---

13 The phraseology is a little bit awkward. Missing at random means that missingness does not depend on the 'true' value of the considered variable after controlling for another variable.

14 Reviews can be found in Allison (2002), Little and Rubin (2002) or Göthlich (2007).

Consequently, we will choose a much less ambitious procedure. Although data on each of our independent variables in all three studies are almost always incomplete, we regularly decide to delete respective cases from the sample due to their rather small frequencies. It is often criticised that in most empirical studies comments on the extent of missing values and their treatment are completely absent. Therefore, we will describe all sample reductions in detail. Nevertheless, in the first and in the second study one variable, viz. 'future income expectation', causes some problems. We will report results of binary logit models which reveal that missing values are not MCAR. Also, relatively low $R^2$ values will prevent the application of sample selection models for independent variables. Thus, we decided to produce two samples in each of the two chapters. The smaller samples include only complete cases and allow us to control for all independent variables. However, the larger samples also contain those cases, in which only the answer on the 'future income' question is missing. Hence, the estimated models exclude the corresponding variable. Regression results will show that a sample selection bias may exist. Consequently, in chapter 2 results of both samples are presented in detail, while in chapter 3 only results from the larger sample are presented at full length due to the detected sample selection bias. Nevertheless, results with respect to the influence of either gender in both chapters and or aspects of responsibility in chapter 3 are very robust. Hence, we omit more demanding methods to treat missing data.

At the end of this section two less technical comments seem to be advisable. Firstly, throughout the present work, a 5% significance level will be applied. We are convinced that this value is better able to detect probably meaningful influences than the more generous 10% level, which is more often used in other empirical investigations. Nevertheless, there are exceptions. With respect to the 'suggestive' likelihood-ratio test the applied 10% level is more critical with respect to the appropriateness of an ordered logit model. Moreover, occasionally only rather small sub-samples are available. Thus, the consideration of the 10% level seems to be helpful to get at least an impression of possible effects.

Secondly, the main purpose of the applied multivariate models is to examine the effects of focal variables such as the gender or the responsibility dummy variable while controlling for other possibly confounding factors. Thus, we are not primarily interested in identifying the model that best predicts choices of respondents being observed. In particular, the statistical power of the analyses could be increased by eliminating predictors that are statistically nonsignificant. However, usually variables introduced are theoretically meaningful so that this strategy may introduce bias. Hence, Jaccard (2001, p. 67) argues that "the trivial gain in power by saving a few degrees of freedom does not outweigh the potentially serious problems that can derive from model specification". In general, almost all empirical studies, which are reviewed in the present work, reported equally low values with respect to the used measures of model fit.

In the following investigation, the statistical tools introduced will be applied in order to answer the questions stated at the end of the last section.

## 2.4 The Sample

In this section, the implementation of the study is presented first. Moreover, besides the previously introduced hypothetical situations, questions on individual characteristics are included in the questionnaire. They are introduced in the second subsection. Afterwards, some necessary sample reductions are described, which lead to different working samples for situations 1 and 4 on the one hand and for situations 2 and 3 on the other hand. Finally, demographic characteristics of the reduced samples are reported.

### 2.4.1 Questionnaire Implementation

In section 2.2 the four different situations have been described in some detail. The study was carried out with undergraduate students at the Department of Economics in Osnabrück (Germany) in the years 1989, 1990, 1993 and 2002; in the year 2003 only situations 1 and 4 have been presented to the students.[15] Following a within-subject design each respondent faced all designated contexts whereby the order of questions remained the same between students and over the years. However, in the first three years, two different versions of the questionnaire have been used, a technical one, which incorporates the extended orderings presented above, and a non-technical version, giving a longer verbal explanation, instead. The latter text can be found in Appendix 2.7.1. Using $\chi^2$ test statistics for all four situations, we could not detect any differences at the 5% significance level between answers resulting from these two versions for every single year and for all three years together. Furthermore, we incorporated a product term of the gender dummy and the variable indicating the questionnaire version in several regression models for these earlier years, but could not find any significant influence. Hence, samples from both versions of the questionnaire are pooled. In the year 2002, some participants received modified descriptions of the four situations, but in the present investigation only those respondents are included who faced the initial version. Finally, in 2003 further variations have been introduced, which mainly concerned aspects of responsibility; they will be analysed in chapter 3. Here, only situations 1 and 4 have been used. While the description of the fourth context remained unchanged in one version so that the incorporation

15 Additionally, the questionnaire has also been used in the year 1994. However, demographic characteristics of respondents are not available so that this sample is excluded from the following investigations.

of corresponding respondents is unproblematic, the version of the first situation being regarded in the present study involved a short additional note saying that the handicap exists since birth. Results from this slightly modified version are also considered to be comparable to those of earlier years. In Gaertner and Schwettmann (2007) it has been shown that results from the years 2002 and 2003 are almost identical.

As we said already above, in each situation respondents were also asked to give some verbal explanations for their decisions. Moreover, those participants who supported alternative $x$ in all extensions of the initial situation being regarded should state whether they would *ever* be willing to switch towards option $y$. These additional verbal comments serve advantages that will be discussed in subsection 2.5.3.

With regard to experimental studies, it is worth mentioning that students were not paid for their participation. Instead they voluntarily completed the questionnaires during tutorials. These are held by graduates for groups of about 10 to 40 students as a supplement to lectures. The high overall response rate and the earnestness, with which many respondents reasoned their decisions in verbal comments, lead to the impression that most of the subjects could not have been better motivated to participate, for example, by receiving a kind of show-up fee. Not least, due to the intended avoidance of a self-serving bias, which has been extensively discussed in the first chapter, other monetary incentives do not seem to be reasonable in the given setting of the investigation.

Following the recommendations of good survey design, tutors were carefully briefed before the application of the questionnaires. For this, the instructions reproduced in Appendix 2.7.3 were discussed with them. Hence, even in simultaneously held tutorials a consistent implementation of the study was possible.

### 2.4.2 Modelling of Demographic Variables

Besides the previously described hypothetical situations, the sheets also contained socio-demographic questions. They are also included in the questionnaires given in Appendix 2.7.1. However, in 2003 we experimented with some modified or even new questions that are given in Appendix 2.7.2. In order to indicate the resulting variables, the questions in the questionnaires, which are reported in the Appendix, are supplemented by variable names in brackets. They correspond to variables reported in the first two columns of Table 2.1.

To start with, the sex of a respondent is the focal individual attribute in the present chapter. The respective dummy variable MALE takes on the value 1 if the student is male, and 0 otherwise. The consideration of the age of a participant is also common in empirical investigations. Certainly, using a student sample there is no great variation in the age of probands.

Table 2.1: Variable descriptions - Female and male samples

| Variable code | Description | Situations 1 and 4: Females (n=231) | Situations 1 and 4: Males (n=410) | Situations 2 and 3: Females (n=184) | Situations 2 and 3: Males (n=358) |
|---|---|---|---|---|---|
| AGE | Age of proband (in years) | 22.34<br>(1.69) | 23.09<br>(1.76) | 22.48<br>(1.72) | 23.11<br>(1.72) |
| BA | B.A. student: 0=No, 1=Yes | 0.89<br>(0.32) | 0.83<br>(0.37) | 0.90<br>(0.31) | 0.83<br>(0.38) |
| JOB | Work experience: 0=No, 1=Yes | 0.41<br>(0.49) | 0.38<br>(0.49) | 0.45<br>(0.50) | 0.40<br>(0.49) |
| MALE | Proband is male: 0=No, 1=Yes | 0.00<br>(—) | 1.00<br>(—) | 0.00<br>(—) | 1.00<br>(—) |
| TIME | Number of semesters, starting in 1989 | 12.87<br>(12.05) | 10.01<br>(10.29) | 8.75<br>(9.93) | 7.26<br>(7.82) |
| FUTURE dummy variables: Proportion of the citizens expected by the proband to earn less than the proband in 10 years' time: | | | | | |
| $FUT_1$ | Less than 50% | 0.15<br>(0.36) | 0.11<br>(0.31) | 0.13<br>(0.33) | 0.09<br>(0.28) |
| $FUT_2$ | 50% | 0.49<br>(0.50) | 0.41<br>(0.49) | 0.56<br>(0.50) | 0.45<br>(0.50) |
| $FUT_3$ | More than 50% | 0.36<br>(0.48) | 0.48<br>(0.50) | 0.32<br>(0.47) | 0.46<br>(0.50) |
| PARENT dummy variables: Profession of the main earner of the family in which the proband grew up: | | | | | |
| $PAR_1$ | Worker, craftsman | 0.15<br>(0.36) | 0.17<br>(0.38) | 0.15<br>(0.36) | 0.18<br>(0.38) |
| $PAR_2$ | Employee/civil servant in the public sector | 0.29<br>(0.45) | 0.28<br>(0.45) | 0.30<br>(0.46) | 0.28<br>(0.45) |
| $PAR_3$ | Employee in the private sector | 0.27<br>(0.45) | 0.28<br>(0.45) | 0.27<br>(0.45) | 0.28<br>(0.45) |
| $PAR_4$ | Self-employed | 0.29<br>(0.46) | 0.27<br>(0.45) | 0.28<br>(0.45) | 0.26<br>(0.44) |

Note: The reported numbers are mean values. Standard deviations are given in parentheses.

However, the incorporation of this variable allows for the separation of possible influences from other variables, especially work experience.[16]

Next, the parental background may also have an impact on justice evaluations. As Miller (1992) reports, in sociological studies the social background – or more generally the social environment – of an individual is supposed to be one of the major influences on justice attitudes. In the present case, it is assumed that the profession of the main earner of the family, in which the student grew up, imprinted his or her moral judgements. In the initial questionnaire six different professional classes were offered, whereas in the 2003 version of the demographic questions we experimented with even more discriminating categories. However, finally separating four groups, which will be represented by the four dummy variables $PAR_1$, $PAR_2$, $PAR_3$ and $PAR_4$, proved to be sufficient to build larger groups and to create substantially meaningful differences.[17]

Furthermore, respondents can be distinguished with respect to the subject they study. Since participants were recruited from an undergraduate course in microeconomics, there is no strong telling variation in the stated subjects. The resulting variable BA takes on the value 1 if the person is registered as a business administration student, and equals 0 if the corresponding subject is economics (as the first or subsidiary course).

A further influence on equity judgements may result from existing work experience. In situation 1, experiences of young men during civilian service can enhance support for the handicapped person, while in situation 4, students with work experience may either support the rights of workers or back economic growth in order to create more jobs. Unfortunately, we are only able to model a single dummy variable, because further information on the character of these experiences, being it part- or full-time jobs, vocational training or compulsory military or civilian service, are not available. This was the reason for reformulating the respective question in the year 2003, and, thereby, explicitly focusing on professional training. As a result, the relative frequency of respondents affirming the fourth question declines in the respective year. Nevertheless, women and men are supposed to be almost equally affected by this slight reformulation as could be deduced from the corresponding percentage numbers.

Students were also asked about their expected position in societal income distribution in ten years' time. While in the first years respondents had to choose a value out of five proposed answers, in the year 2003 a continuous variable was introduced. Thus, participants had to state a number on their

16 See e.g. Jungeilges and Theisen (2005) for a similar argument.

17 In the questionnaires in the Appendix, the classification of single professional groups into the four final classes are represented by the given numbers in brackets. In the 2003 version, some problems may arise by the last group 'others', but it does not occur in the final sample.

own. This caused unexpected problems that will be explained in the next subsection. From the corresponding answers, three dummy variables ($FUT_1$, $FUT_2$ and $FUT_3$) are modelled and represent pessimistic, neutral and optimistic prospects, respectively; the initial categories '5%' and '95%' were rarely chosen. In the first chapter it was pronounced that participants should evaluate hypothetical situation from an impartial viewpoint in order to avoid self-serving biases. Nevertheless, it might be possible that respondents display more empathy with 'their' social class. For example, if a student expects to belong to the lower income class in the future, he or she may want to create more jobs at the expense of human rights in situation 4. In contrast, individuals who expect their own income to be above average could prefer a society, in which efficiency arguments are more important than the concern for worse-off groups.

Table 2.1 includes one further variable. In Gaertner and Schwettmann (2007) the importance of allowing for developments over time is demonstrated. Also, possibly, the temporal distance between two investigations is of additional importance. Thus, instead of creating dummy variables for the different years of the investigation, a continuous variable is modelled. It is measured in the number of academic semesters since the first study.[18]

As shown in Appendix 2.7.2, the socio-demographic questionnaire in the year 2003 included modified and additional questions. Firstly, three items, viz. questions number 3, 4 and 5, have been shaped to get clearer statements of possible reasons for detected influences on analysed decisions. Secondly, some new questions should allow for further insights into possibly relevant individual differences. Item number 7 consisted of three different questions aiming at identifying students from abroad. Moreover, German respondents with migrational background should also be recognised. The latter aspect especially concerns either immigrants from Russia with German origins or people with other nationalities who adopted the German citizenship. Unfortunately, the numbers of these groups are too small to make reasonable statements on the effects of these supplementary individual attributes.

### 2.4.3 Sample Reductions

Overall, 786 students participated in the present investigation. The corresponding numbers for the five different years are 184 subjects in the year 1989, 179 in 1990, 182 in 1993, 98 in 2002 and 143 in 2003. It has to be remembered that situations 2 and 3 were not presented to respondents in the last year. However, it has already been argued in subsection 2.3.5 that similar to the procedure applied in preliminary investigations on the questionnaire, only those respondents are included who provided answers to all given sit-

18 Nevertheless, we also modelled dummy variables for each single year and reran several regressions. All results reported in the next section remained unaffected.

uations. Thus, in total 60 subjects (or 7.6% of all respondents) had to be excluded from the sample on these grounds. Out of these people, 52 stated their sex; there were 18 women and 34 men. A $\chi^2$ test showed that gender differences with respect to rejecting to consider one or more situation(s) are not statistically significant (p=0.610).[19]

Moreover, out of the remaining 726 students, 681 subjects also answered the gender question, which is a natural precondition to be incorporated in a study on gender differences. Interestingly, the other 45 individuals did not answer any demographic question. From the 681 people, 153 completed the questionnaire in the year 1989, 159 in 1990, 160 in 1993, 82 in 2002 and 127 in 2003.

Now, another 40 students refused to answer at least one remaining demographic question. Astonishingly, 34 of them only skipped the question about their expected future income. The break up with respect to the years of the investigation reveals the reason. In the year 1989, three respondents, in 1990 five subjects, in 1993 none, in 2002 two participants and in the last year 24 interviewees left out only the income question. Even more surprisingly, 25 out of these 34 students are female. The probability for women to reject only the income question was significantly higher at the 1% level compared to the corresponding likelihood for men.

Thus, obviously the necessity to state a clear number on the income question is mainly responsible for the inclusion of the majority of students into this group. Certainly, the task to state a concrete number rather than choosing from five different alternatives is already more advanced. Furthermore, women seem to display stronger difficulties than men. Maybe, they are more uncertain about their income. This could be a realistic point of view if one thinks of gender differences in income levels (see Croson and Gneezy, 2008) or of the possibility of having a child in the future and receiving no personal income at all. Hence, especially females could have been tempted to omit this particular question. But this would clearly point towards a kind of sample selection.

In subsection 2.3.5, several alternative methods to deal with missing data have been discussed. Also, it has been argued that we will focus on the remaining 675 cases with either no missing values or only missing data on the variable 'future income expectation'. In order to test whether the mechanism behind missingness is MCAR, the dichotomous variable MISSING has been modelled which equals 0 in the former and 1 in the latter case. Then,we estimated a binary logit model including all variables presented in the previous

19 In the present work sample sizes differ from earlier investigations mainly for two reasons. Firstly, the inclusion of the technical questionnaire version significantly extended the number of observations compared to the study by Gaertner and Schwettmann (2007). Secondly, the procedure to reduce the sample, which will be presented in the following paragraphs, has been modified due to some new socio-demographic questions in the year 2003.

subsection (except the dummy variables indicating future income expectations). The results show that the variables AGE, JOB, MALE and TIME have a statistically significant influence at the 5% level on the probability of observing missing data. Hence, the mechanism is not MCAR. Correspondingly, McFadden's $R^2$ amounts to 0.204, indicating that the fit of the model is not very high. Furthermore, the identified significant factors are also supposed to have a strong effect on the behaviour in question. Thus, a two-step procedure inspired by Heckman's method seems to be inappropriate. However, other approaches to treat missing data also have drawbacks.

In the literature, the item non-response problem is especially well-known for income and wealth questions.[20] Hence, the question arises whether to exclude such cases from the sample, which allows for analysing all variables of interest but introduces the possibility of a sample selection bias, or to include all available answers of these subjects on other items, which would extend the sample size by 34 probands but eliminates the possibility of investigating the influence of future income expectations.

Preliminary $\chi^2$ tests reveal that only in situation 1 some differences in equity judgements between these 34 students and the remaining 641 individuals are apparent. The smaller group was significantly more likely to fulfil the equity axiom ($p=0.025$).[21] Nevertheless, the result indicates the existence of a sample selection bias.

Thus, what can be done? Certainly – as described already in the previous paragraphs – neither the gain from the inclusion of the income variable nor the benefit from extending the sample by at least 34 students comes without some costs. In the present chapter, the main focus is on gender differences. As will be seen in the following subsection, there are notable gender differences with respect to future income prospects. Therefore, it is of greater interest whether possible differences between distributive judgements of women and men hold if disparities with respect to income expectations are controlled for. This consideration is supposed to be more important than including 34 additional cases, let alone other partly unanswered items. Nevertheless, some regression results for situations 1 and 4 using the larger sample and omitting the FUTURE dummy variables will be provided in the Appendix of this chapter. Finally, comments on regressions using the reduced sample but leaving out the income variables will be added in section 2.5 on the results.

### 2.4.4 Sample Characteristics

In Table 2.1 the sample means of constructed variables are summarised for the reduced samples. The distributions of the attributes just described for the

20 See for example the studies cited by Riphan and Serfling (2005).

21 Note that differences in situations 2 and 3 are not investigated here since these two contexts have not been presented in the most problematic year 2003.

female and male sub-samples reveal some important differences and, therefore, give reason for applying multivariate statistical models.

To start with, there are clearly more males than females in both samples. Obviously, in general studying either economics or business administration in Osnabrück was more popular among young men. Furthermore, females more often decide to study the latter subject, while males are more likely than females to be registered in economics courses. Using a two-sample $t$-test to evaluate the corresponding mean values, we find statistically significant differences at the 5% level for the sample concerning situations 2 and 3. Nevertheless, from the variable TIME it can be seen that the overall proportion of women has increased remarkably in more recent years. Consequently, if time matters, this effect should be controlled for in the following regression models in order to separate gender differences.

Certainly, using a student sample there is no great variation in the age of participants. But, as can also be seen from the sample means of all sub-samples, male students are clearly older than females even at the 1% significance level. Primarily, this disparity can be explained by compulsory military or civilian service that young men have to complete in Germany. Furthermore, there are apparently no gender differences with respect to work experience or parental background. Thus, despite the compulsory military or civilian service, the proportion of male students with work experience is not higher than the corresponding percentage of females.

Finally, as already mentioned in the previous subsection, male respondents are significantly more optimistic about their income in ten years' time. This observation is very much in line with assumptions in the literature about the self-perceived socio-economic status of women (see e.g. Croson and Gneezy, 2008, for a literature review). And again, if future income expectations are supposed to have an influence on justice evaluations, one has to control for this variable in order to separate gender effects.

To conclude, Table 2.2 presents Pearson correlation coefficients for all individual variables in both samples. Besides usually high coefficients for dummy variables, especially the variable AGE is positively correlated with JOB and MALE. This has already been explained above. Additionally, AGE is highly correlated with the PLACE dummies in the third investigation. Hence, one may argue that the variable AGE should be excluded from the following regressions.

In the statistical literature there does not exist any specific value for a correlation coefficient that denotes critical outcomes. Studenmund (2001, p. 256) reports that an arbitrary number of 0.80 is often picked, which is higher than the values presented. From our point of view, three further arguments in favour of an inclusion are important. Firstly, as already explained in the introduction, Gilligan (1982) found that the moral development of young females and males proceeded along different lines and at different rates. Thus, the age of a respondent might be an important confounding factor with re-

Table 2.2: Correlation matrix for individual characteristics

| | Situations 1 and 4 (n=641) | | | | | | | | | | | |
|---|---|---|---|---|---|---|---|---|---|---|---|---|
| | $AGE$ | $BA$ | $JOB$ | $MALE$ | $TIME$ | $FUT_1$ | $FUT_2$ | $FUT_3$ | $PAR_1$ | $PAR_2$ | $PAR_3$ | $PAR_4$ |
| $AGE$ | 1.000 | 0.092 | 0.575 | 0.205 | −0.117 | 0.033 | −0.005 | −0.021 | 0.036 | 0.028 | −0.021 | −0.037 |
| $BA$ | | 1.000 | 0.142 | −0.072 | −0.037 | 0.019 | −0.075 | 0.062 | 0.018 | −0.057 | 0.021 | 0.021 |
| $JOB$ | | | 1.000 | −0.026 | −0.126 | 0.015 | −0.015 | 0.001 | 0.014 | 0.058 | −0.046 | −0.024 |
| $MALE$ | | | | 1.000 | −0.124 | −0.059 | −0.072 | 0.108 | 0.028 | −0.011 | 0.008 | −0.021 |
| $TIME$ | | | | | 1.000 | 0.072 | −0.160 | 0.108 | −0.003 | −0.057 | 0.001 | 0.058 |
| $FUT_1$ | | | | | | 1.000 | −0.331 | −0.327 | 0.053 | −0.008 | 0.004 | −0.039 |
| $FUT_2$ | | | | | | | 1.000 | −0.781 | 0.103 | 0.007 | −0.053 | −0.039 |
| $FUT_3$ | | | | | | | | 1.000 | −0.137 | 0.001 | 0.053 | 0.060 |
| $PAR_1$ | | | | | | | | | 1.000 | −0.277 | −0.276 | −0.276 |
| $PAR_2$ | | | | | | | | | | 1.000 | −0.386 | −0.386 |
| $PAR_3$ | | | | | | | | | | | 1.000 | −0.384 |
| | Situations 2 and 3 (n=542) | | | | | | | | | | | |
| | $AGE$ | $BA$ | $JOB$ | $MALE$ | $TIME$ | $FUT_1$ | $FUT_2$ | $FUT_3$ | $PAR_1$ | $PAR_2$ | $PAR_3$ | $PAR_4$ |
| $AGE$ | 1.000 | 0.121 | 0.563 | 0.172 | −0.073 | 0.020 | −0.026 | 0.009 | 0.047 | 0.027 | −0.040 | −0.026 |
| $BA$ | | 1.000 | 0.171 | −0.090 | −0.062 | 0.034 | −0.061 | 0.040 | 0.004 | −0.055 | 0.015 | 0.038 |
| $JOB$ | | | 1.000 | −0.044 | −0.063 | 0.045 | −0.030 | −0.001 | 0.016 | 0.056 | −0.047 | −0.024 |
| $MALE$ | | | | 1.000 | −0.082 | −0.061 | −0.102 | 0.138 | 0.037 | −0.015 | 0.011 | −0.027 |
| $TIME$ | | | | | 1.000 | −0.062 | −0.007 | 0.037 | 0.001 | −0.028 | 0.006 | 0.022 |
| $FUT_1$ | | | | | | 1.000 | −0.325 | −0.277 | 0.017 | −0.009 | 0.013 | −0.019 |
| $FUT_2$ | | | | | | | 1.000 | −0.815 | 0.119 | −0.006 | −0.064 | −0.028 |
| $FUT_3$ | | | | | | | | 1.000 | −0.130 | 0.014 | 0.060 | 0.034 |
| $PAR_1$ | | | | | | | | | 1.000 | −0.285 | −0.277 | −0.268 |
| $PAR_2$ | | | | | | | | | | 1.000 | −0.397 | −0.384 |
| $PAR_3$ | | | | | | | | | | | 1.000 | −0.374 |

Note: The given numbers are Pearson correlation coefficients (Pearson's $r$).

spect to justice evaluations, which should be controlled for. By this, we will confirm Gilligan's hypothesis in the present chapter. Secondly, Studenmund (2001, p. 259) argues that a remedy for possible multicollinearity should be considered only if the consequences produce insignificant or ambiguous estimated coefficients. In our third study we will observe significant place effects despite the inclusion of the variable AGE. Thirdly, the author warns that the exclusion of a multicollinear variable could lead either to specification bias or to "accidentally significant regression results" (p. 260). For these reasons, we decided to include the variable AGE in the presented models. Nevertheless, all models have also been estimated without incorporating this variable, but most of the significant results remained unchanged.

To summarise, several reductions resulted in two final samples. Moreover, we will regard an additional larger sample for situations 1 and 4. With respect to gender differences, it cannot be ruled out that women and men display different life courses, which are partly covered by individual attributes. The present data set enables us to analyse such characteristics and incorporate them in multivariate regression models. Of course, these variables can only be a very rough measure for assumed disparities. But if these factors have a significant influence on moral decisions in general, they should be controlled for in order to get more valid results on gender differences.

## 2.5 Results

In the following section, the questions initially stated will be answered in turn. Firstly, descriptive results are presented. Afterwards, binary, multinomial and ordered logit models are applied to control for several individual and questionnaire characteristics. Finally, additional verbal comments of respondents will be reviewed.

### 2.5.1 Descriptive Results

Descriptive results for the four situations considered – separated with respect to gender – are summarised in Table 2.3. As explained above, all 16 possible decision patterns are represented by four-digit sequences in the first column. Here, a decision in favour of alternative $x$ is coded as 0, whereas a choice of alternative $y$ is denoted by 1. In the table, relative frequencies are given.

In general, with respect to comparisons between the four situations many similar results for both men and women are visible. The highest fulfilment of the equity axiom and, correspondingly, the lowest relative frequency of sequence 1111 can be observed in situation 1. In contrast, in situation 2, where alternative $y$ concerns the home country of respondents, least support for the worse-off individuals is detected. This finding concerns the sequences 0000 and 1111, but also the fulfilment of the equity axiom. The results for

Table 2.3: Relative frequencies - All possible decision patterns

| Sequence | Situation 1 | | Situation 2 | | Situation 3 | | Situation 4 | |
|---|---|---|---|---|---|---|---|---|
| | Females (n=231) | Males (n=410) | Females (n=184) | Males (n=358) | Females (n=184) | Males (n=358) | Females (n=231) | Males (n=410) |
| 0 0 0 0 | 0.528 | 0.515 | 0.380 | 0.385 | 0.446 | 0.433 | 0.532 | 0.534 |
| 0 0 0 1 | 0.095 | 0.046 | 0.033 | 0.036 | 0.033 | 0.042 | 0.091 | 0.085 |
| 0 0 1 0 | 0.0 | 0.0 | 0.0 | 0.0 | 0.0 | 0.0 | 0.0 | 0.0 |
| 0 0 1 1 | 0.182 | 0.156 | 0.065 | 0.089 | 0.082 | 0.081 | 0.091 | 0.061 |
| 0 1 0 0 | 0.0 | 0.0 | 0.0 | 0.003 | 0.011 | 0.006 | 0.0 | 0.0 |
| 0 1 0 1 | 0.004 | 0.002 | 0.005 | 0.0 | 0.0 | 0.0 | 0.0 | 0.002 |
| 0 1 1 0 | 0.004 | 0.0 | 0.005 | 0.008 | 0.011 | 0.006 | 0.0 | 0.002 |
| 0 1 1 1 | 0.121 | 0.144 | 0.120 | 0.087 | 0.185 | 0.168 | 0.095 | 0.066 |
| 1 0 0 0 | 0.0 | 0.002 | 0.016 | 0.014 | 0.011 | 0.003 | 0.004 | 0.002 |
| 1 0 0 1 | 0.0 | 0.005 | 0.0 | 0.003 | 0.0 | 0.0 | 0.0 | 0.0 |
| 1 0 1 0 | 0.0 | 0.0 | 0.005 | 0.008 | 0.0 | 0.0 | 0.0 | 0.002 |
| 1 0 1 1 | 0.004 | 0.005 | 0.016 | 0.008 | 0.005 | 0.0 | 0.0 | 0.0 |
| 1 1 0 0 | 0.013 | 0.002 | 0.016 | 0.011 | 0.022 | 0.011 | 0.004 | 0.010 |
| 1 1 0 1 | 0.0 | 0.0 | 0.0 | 0.0 | 0.0 | 0.003 | 0.0 | 0.0 |
| 1 1 1 0 | 0.0 | 0.0 | 0.076 | 0.070 | 0.011 | 0.003 | 0.004 | 0.002 |
| 1 1 1 1 | 0.048 | 0.122 | 0.261 | 0.277 | 0.185 | 0.246 | 0.177 | 0.232 |
| % Switch | 39.8 | 34.6 | 21.7 | 21.2 | 29.9 | 29.1 | 27.7 | 21.2 |
| % Fulfilment of equity axiom | 93.5 | 86.3 | 60.8 | 60.8 | 76.6 | 73.5 | 81.0 | 75.1 |

Note: A choice of alternative x is coded as 0, a decision in favour of y is coded as 1.

situations 3 and 4 are 'somewhere in the middle'. However, in situation 4, the relative frequencies of sequence 0000 are comparable to the corresponding values in situation 1. The similarity between these two situations has already been noted by Gaertner and Jungeilges (2002) for another sample.

Now, consider women and men separately. Although the proportion of respondents who fulfil the equity axiom is rather high for both sexes, in neither situation does the respective value for males exceed the corresponding number for females. Moreover, differences are statistically significant at the 1% level in situation 1 and at the 10% level in situation 4; the p-value of a $\chi^2$ test for $2 \times 2$ tables equals 0.006 for the first and 0.091 for the last case. In contrast, if the better-off group is successively enlarged, the unconditional support of the least advantaged – expressed by sequence 0000 – is almost the same for both samples in each situation. Interestingly, apart from situation 2, gender plays a role among those students who decided in favour of alternative $y$ either immediately or when additional better-off individuals are introduced. Among these subjects, men were more frequently willing to support the better-off people right from the beginning (corresponding p-values of $\chi^2$ tests for $2 \times 2$ tables are 0.002 for situation 1, 0.037 for situation 3 and 0.107 for situation 4), while women were more likely to reconsider their initial decision in favour of alternative $x$ later on and switched more often towards $y$.

Nevertheless, only in situation 1 can evidence be generated against the hypothesis $H_0$ that the distribution of responses on the 16 possible sequences is similar between both samples ($\chi^2_{10} = 21.58$, p-value $= 0.017$).

A brief look at descriptive results in situations 1 and 4 from the larger sample, which have been summarised in Table 2.13 in Appendix 2.7.4, reveals that results are almost completely unaffected by incorporating answers of the 34 additional individuals who did not answer the question on future income expectations. This observation concerns all relevant sequences.

To summarise the descriptive results, women were more likely to fulfil the equity axiom in situation 1. Moreover, differences are significant at the 10% level in situation 4. Among those respondents who opted at some point for alternative $y$, females tended to switch later than males especially in situations 1 and 3. Thus, particularly situation 1 provoked some stronger gender differences, while in situation 2 least disparities are observable.

### 2.5.2 Multivariate Regression Models

Next, multivariate regressions are employed in order to get further insights into the statistical relevance of observed similarities and disparities. Therefore, regression models incorporate all individual and questionnaire attributes presented in the previous section. Certainly, the main interest will be on the gender dummy variable. As explained above, the two reduced samples, which only contain those respondents who completed all questions, will be used. Nevertheless, some results from the larger samples are presented in Appendix 2.7.4 and allow for investigating possible sample selection effects.

For all three regression approaches we distinguished between 'single effects' models and 'interactive' models. As explained in subsection 2.3.4, included interaction effects allow us to display different effects on the dependent variable for males and females. Single effects of explanatory variables are considered first, while results of 'interactive' models will be summarised later on.

First, the focus will be on the fulfilment of the equity axiom, which is modelled as a dichotomous variable. Maximum likelihood estimates of binary logit models are summarised in Table 2.4. As can be seen from the LR statistics, which test whether the respective model significantly improves model fit compared to a model that includes only a constant term, and from the $R^2$ values in all estimated equations, the explanatory power of each model is rather weak. However, the aim is not to identify an optimal model, but to investigate possible gender differences. For this reason, all non-significant factors also remain in the model in order to separate the gender effect instead of improving the explanatory power.[22]

Note that non-significant variables are omitted in this presentation, although they are included in the models. Despite the gender dummy variable, only the year of the investigation is found to have a significant influence on the initial choice in more than one situation. Over the period of time covered, our students clearly less often fulfilled the equity axiom in the last context, but more often in situation 2. Moreover, in the first situation the corresponding p-value of the estimated negative coefficient for TIME equals 0.084. The results of the larger sample, which are reported in Table 2.14 in Appendix 2.7.4, confirm these findings. Interestingly, the influence of the variable TIME in the 'single effects' model of situation 1 is even stronger than in the smaller sample. This effect is not due to the inclusion of the FUTURE dummy variables, as could be deduced from regression results using the reduced sample but excluding the corresponding two dummy variables.[23] Thus, two effects are possible. On the one hand, we may observe consequences of a sample selection bias. On the other hand, if there is a trend over time, this effect should be more significant when regarding larger samples in the very early or very late years of the investigation. Hence, even with this considerably larger sample the earlier findings on intertemporal effects reported in Gaertner and Schwettmann (2007) are confirmed.

The results on the gender dummy variable support only some of the preliminary observations. Clearly, men have been significantly less likely to fulfil the equity axiom in situation 1, but also in the fourth context. The latter observation is in some contrast to the one-dimensional descriptive analysis. Thus, leaving aside the unintelligible sequences, there also seemed to be con-

22 Certainly, $R^2$ values would be even lower with less variables in the models.

23 These regression results are not presented here.

Table 2.4: ML estimates of binary logit models
Dependent variable: Fulfilment of Equity Axiom

| | Situation 1 | | Situation 2 | Situation 3 | Situation 4 | |
|---|---|---|---|---|---|---|
| Independent variables | Single effects | Inter-active | Single effects | Single effects | Single effects | Inter-active |
| *Constant* | 3.192** | 3.141** | 0.808* | 1.014* | 2.154** | 2.065** |
| | (0.572) | (0.574) | (0.365) | (0.394) | (0.414) | (0.414) |
| $AGE_c$ | 0.010 | −0.410** | 0.020 | −0.003 | 0.091 | −0.156 |
| | (0.093) | (0.158) | (0.064) | (0.071) | (0.071) | (0.110) |
| $JOB$ | 0.189 | 0.216 | −0.113 | 0.127 | −0.423 | −0.398 |
| | (0.334) | (0.338) | (0.223) | (0.251) | (0.248) | (0.249) |
| $MALE$ | −0.891** | −0.826* | 0.021 | −0.173 | −0.523* | −0.462* |
| | (0.321) | (0.322) | (0.197) | (0.223) | (0.218) | (0.216) |
| $TIME_c$ | −0.020 | −0.024* | 0.025* | −0.009 | −0.022* | −0.025** |
| | (0.011) | (0.012) | (0.011) | (0.011) | (0.009) | (0.009) |
| $MALE{*}AGE_c$ | | 0.546** | | | | 0.350** |
| | | (0.174) | | | | (0.122) |
| Log likelihood | −215.03 | −210.17 | −357.45 | −304.80 | −336.64 | −332.54 |
| LR statistic | 16.22 | 25.93** | 10.56 | 5.40 | 14.60 | 22.80* |
| McFadden $R^2$ | 0.036 | 0.058 | 0.015 | 0.009 | 0.021 | 0.033 |
| Mean dependent variable | 0.889 | 0.889 | 0.609 | 0.745 | 0.772 | 0.772 |

Note: Values are logistic coefficients (betas). Asymptotic standard errors are reported in parentheses. Level of significance: $^{*}0.01 \leq p < 0.05$, $^{**}p < 0.01$. All models also include the dummy variables $BA, FUT_1, FUT_3, PAR_2, PAR_3$ and $PAR_4$, which are not significant at the 5% level in any model.

siderable gender differences with respect to the probabilities for choosing in accordance with sequence 1111 with men being more likely to display this answer pattern.

As explained in section 2.3.3, predicted odds ratios can be obtained from the estimated logistic coefficients $\widehat{\beta}_{Male}$. Therefore, we get $exp(-0.891) = 0.410$ for situation 1 and $exp(-0.523) = 0.593$ in situation 4. These results state, for example, that in the first context the predicted odds of fulfilling the equity axiom for males are 0.410 times the corresponding value of the predicted odds for females.[24] Hence, although the probability of observing an initial choice of alternative $x$ is rather high for both groups, there are significant differences.

In contrast, neither in the case of environmental programs in the home country in the second context nor in situation 3, where children and pregnant women are the beneficiaries of alternative $y$, can any remarkable gender disparities be detected.

Next, successive extensions of the better-off groups will be considered. It has been argued already in section 2.3.3 that either an ordered logit model or a multinomial logit model seems to be the appropriate way to reflect and investigate the underlying decision problems. However, as also explained above, the choice of the suitable model is not unequivocal. Certainly, overall evaluations, like the presented 'suggestive' likelihood-ratio test for the single crossing assumptions, are easy to apply in order to evaluate the appropriateness of the ordered logit model. Nevertheless, results may be misleading if special effects are of interest, for example the influence of gender on the distribution decision being regarded. Thus, the data should be carefully analysed with the help of the tools described.

First of all, both available regression models will only focus on the five sensible answer patterns. However, 13 students in situation 1, 71 in situation 2, 24 in situation 3, and 12 subjects in situation 4 did not state reasonable answer patterns.[25] Therefore, these respondents have to be eliminated from the corresponding samples.[26] The corrected relative frequencies for the remaining decision patterns are summarised in Table 2.5 for the smaller samples and in Table 2.15 in the Appendix for the larger sample. Also, an additional variable is introduced in these two tables. The index $z$ represents the sequences being regarded in the ordered logit models by a single number. To recapitulate our explanations in subsection 2.3.3, the higher $z$ is, the closer the respective answer pattern is to the spirit of the equity axiom. Hence, as we move from $z$=1 to $z$=5 the single crossing assumption, which is inherent in the ordered

24 The 95% confidence intervals for the two values are [0.219; 0.770] and [0.386; 0.909], respectively, and, consequently, do not contain the value 1.0.

25 Note that the higher rate of refusal in situation 2 has already been observed for other samples. See Gaertner, Jungeilges and Neck (2001) and Gaertner and Jungeilges (2002).

26 With respect to the larger sample presented in the Appendix, 16 participants in the first and 13 subjects in the fourth context have to be excluded.

logit model, demands that the difference between the relative frequencies for both compared groups changes its sign only once.

As can be seen from differences between relative frequencies of women and men in Table 2.5, this assumption is fulfilled only in situation 1. Let us take situation 4 as an example. The relative frequencies for females are lower for the sequences 0000 and 1111 but higher for the remaining three relevant decision patterns. Hence, in three contexts the application of the ordered logit model may be problematic. This observation also holds for the relative frequencies for situations 1 and 4 in the larger sample, as can be observed from the results in Table 2.15.

Nevertheless, as already explained in subsection 2.3.3, there are two additional assessing tools that require estimating the two models before evaluating their results. However, before we further evaluate the two available regression methods, a technical remark should be repeated. All multinomial logit models include a constant term. Since this model is a repeated application of a binary model, this approach naturally follows from the implementation of the latter method. Though, as also explained in subsection 2.3.3, the ordered logit model is commonly stated without including a constant term. But this would lead to inaccurate log likelihood values with respect to a suitable comparison between the two models. Hence, the results reported in the following tables are calculated by including this constant term.

Now, consider the results of $\chi^2$ tests for the single crossing assumption that are summarised in Table 2.6. In subsection 2.3.3 it has been explained that large differences between respective log likelihood values should give reason for some reservations about the application of the ordered logit model. Surprisingly, in the present investigation this is the case only in both models of situation 1 at the 10% level. However, it should be mentioned again that this test only gives an overall measure for the suitability of the applied method, whereas the focus should be on the influence of gender.

A third and even more vague test is available. It demands to evaluate the algebraic signs of both estimated marginal effects of the ordered logit model and estimated coefficients from the multinomial logit model. However, in contrast to the next chapter, we will not follow this suggestion immediately, since the appropriateness of the ordered logit approach is already doubted. In three contexts, the single crossing assumption is violated with respect to the descriptive data, while for the remaining context the 'suggestive' likelihood-ratio test reveals possible problems. Hence, the recommendation of Borooah (2002) is followed and a multinomial logit model is applied even though the dependent variable is clearly ordered. Nevertheless, and basically for the sake of completeness, estimates of ordered logit models will be supplementarily presented. There, it will become obvious that the estimated marginal effects of this model are found to indicate some inappropriateness of the ordered logit approach in the present case.

Table 2.5: Relative frequencies - All sensible decision patterns

| | | Situation 1 | | Situation 2 | | Situation 3 | | Situation 4 | |
|---|---|---|---|---|---|---|---|---|---|
| Sequence | $z$ | Females (n=225) | Males (n=403) | Females (n=158) | Males (n=313) | Females (n=171) | Males (n=347) | Females (n=228) | Males (n=401) |
| 0 0 0 0 | 5 | 0.542 | 0.524 | 0.443 | 0.441 | 0.480 | 0.447 | 0.539 | 0.546 |
| 0 0 0 1 | 4 | 0.098 | 0.047 | 0.038 | 0.042 | 0.035 | 0.043 | 0.092 | 0.087 |
| 0 0 1 1 | 3 | 0.187 | 0.159 | 0.076 | 0.102 | 0.088 | 0.084 | 0.092 | 0.062 |
| 0 1 1 1 | 2 | 0.124 | 0.146 | 0.139 | 0.099 | 0.199 | 0.173 | 0.096 | 0.067 |
| 1 1 1 1 | 1 | 0.049 | 0.124 | 0.304 | 0.316 | 0.199 | 0.254 | 0.180 | 0.237 |

Note: A choice of alternative x is coded as 0, a decision in favour of y is coded as 1. The variable $z$ represents the corresponding sequence in the ordered logit model.

Table 2.6: Suggestive likelihood-ratio test for single crossing assumption

| Effects | Ordered $L_O$ | Multinomial $L_M$ | $\chi^2$ value: $2(L_M$-$L_O)$ | $k$ | $\chi^2_{k(5-2)}$, 5% level | $\chi^2_{k(5-2)}$, 10% level |
|---|---|---|---|---|---|---|
| Situation 1: | | | | | | |
| Single | −724.34 | −703.46 | 41.77$^\dagger$ | 10 | 43.77 | 40.26 |
| Interactive | −721.92 | −698.61 | 46.61$^\dagger$ | 11 | 47.40 | 43.72 |
| Situation 2: | | | | | | |
| Single | −557.48 | −539.08 | 36.80 | 10 | 43.77 | 40.26 |
| Situation 3: | | | | | | |
| Single | −618.84 | −604.22 | 29.24 | 10 | 43.77 | 40.26 |
| Interactive | −615.62 | −596.48 | 38.27 | 11 | 47.40 | 43.72 |
| Situation 4: | | | | | | |
| Single | −712.16 | −695.05 | 34.23 | 10 | 43.77 | 40.26 |

Note: $L_O$ and $L_M$ are log likelihood values. Level of significance: $^\dagger 0.05 \leq p < 0.10$, $^* p < 0.05$. $k$ = number of estimated coefficients in the ordered logit model.

In Tables 2.7 and 2.8 results from multinomial logit models are presented. The proportions of those students who supported the worse-off individuals in every extension were almost equal for both samples in each situation. Hence, it seems to be obvious to choose sequence 0000 as the base sequence for the comparison of odds of other decision patterns. Again, the 'single effects' models will be regarded first, whereas results of 'interactive' models are summarised afterwards for all different regression models.

The estimated coefficients confirm the previously detected developments over time in situations 1, 2 and 4. Moreover, in situation 3 we can observe differences over time which are similar to the developments in the first and in the last context. In all three cases, the probability of choosing in accordance with sequence 0000 has declined with respect to several other sensible sequences. In contrast, in situation 2 this probability has increased compared to the corresponding value for sequence 1111.

Moreover, future income expectations have some influence in situations 3 and 4, but the results seem to be somewhat arbitrary and are, therefore, difficult to interpret. Nevertheless, the significance of the estimated coefficients justify the inclusion of this additional information. Other independent variables have no considerable influence in more than one situation.

More importantly, again there are no significant gender effects in situations 2 and 3, where the differences detected by $\chi^2$ tests disappeared, while the predicted odds ratios hint at some differences in the other two contexts. In situation 1, men, compared to women, were more likely to choose in accor-

Table 2.7: Multinomial logit estimates - Situations 1 and 2

| Situation | Model | Variables | Sequence 1111 | | Sequence 0111 | | Sequence 0011 | | Sequence 0001 | |
|---|---|---|---|---|---|---|---|---|---|---|
| Sit. 1: | Single effects: (n=628) | $AGE_c$ | −0.102 | (0.105) | −0.249* | (0.100) | −0.036 | (0.082) | −0.029 | (0.121) |
| | | $MALE$ | 1.243** | (0.380) | 0.738* | (0.295) | 0.054 | (0.253) | −0.709* | (0.356) |
| | | $TIME_c$ | 0.051** | (0.013) | 0.071** | (0.012) | 0.042** | (0.011) | 0.000 | (0.017) |
| | | | Log likelihood: −703.45, LR test: 96.35**, McFadden $R^2$: 0.058 | | | | | | | |
| | Interactive: (n=628) | $AGE_c$ | 0.366 | (0.184) | −0.205 | (0.165) | 0.067 | (0.124) | −0.093 | (0.168) |
| | | $MALE$ | 1.174** | (0.380) | 0.748* | (0.316) | 0.032 | (0.253) | −0.689 | (0.370) |
| | | $AGE_c{*}MALE$ | −0.586** | (0.200) | −0.069 | (0.175) | −0.152 | (0.138) | 0.134 | (0.199) |
| | | | Log likelihood: −698.61, LR test: 106.04**, McFadden $R^2$: 0.064 | | | | | | | |
| Sit. 2: | Single effects: (n=417) | $MALE$ | 0.025 | (0.244) | −0.473 | (0.340) | 0.281 | (0.394) | 0.297 | (0.560) |
| | | $TIME_c$ | −0.031* | (0.014) | 0.013 | (0.017) | 0.004 | (0.019) | 0.013 | (0.026) |
| | | | Log likelihood: −539.08, LR test: 46.64, McFadden $R^2$: 0.037 | | | | | | | |

Note: Sequence 0000 is the base sequence. Values are logistic coefficients (betas). Asymptotic standard errors are given in parentheses. Level of significance: $^{*}0.01 \leq p < 0.05$, $^{**}p < 0.01$. 'Single effects' models include all variables. However, only those parameters are reported, which proved to be significant at the 5% level for at least one category. For 'interactive' models only interacted variables are given.

Table 2.8: Multinomial logit estimates - Situations 3 and 4

| Situation | Model | Variables | Sequence 1111 | | Sequence 0111 | | Sequence 0011 | | Sequence 0001 | |
|---|---|---|---|---|---|---|---|---|---|---|
| Sit. 3: | Single effects: (n=518) | $MALE$ | 0.368 | (0.260) | 0.089 | (0.273) | 0.063 | (0.373) | 0.350 | (0.541) |
| | | $TIME_c$ | 0.029* | (0.013) | 0.026 | (0.014) | 0.042* | (0.018) | 0.044 | (0.026) |
| | | $FUT_1$ | −0.220 | (0.386) | −1.494* | (0.633) | −0.297 | (0.592) | −1.321 | (1.063) |
| | | $FUT_3$ | −0.076 | (0.244) | −0.166 | (0.260) | −0.062 | (0.357) | −1.139* | (0.546) |
| | | | Log likelihood: −604.22, LR test: 44.08, McFadden $R^2$: 0.032 | | | | | | | |
| | Interactive: (n=518) | $AGE_c$ | −0.123 | (0.093) | −0.226* | (0.110) | −0.240 | (0.148) | 0.080 | (0.178) |
| | | $MALE$ | 0.309 | (0.263) | 0.028 | (0.277) | 0.019 | (0.378) | 0.353 | (0.564) |
| | | $AGE_c{*}MALE$ | −0.315* | (0.150) | −0.295 | (0.161) | −0.747** | (0.210) | −0.095 | (0.311) |
| | | | Log likelihood: −596.48, LR test: 59.57, McFadden $R^2$: 0.043 | | | | | | | |
| Sit. 4: | Single effects: (n=629) | $JOB$ | 0.519 | (0.266) | 0.872* | (0.412) | 0.293 | (0.426) | 0.149 | (0.376) |
| | | $MALE$ | 0.504* | (0.236) | −0.063 | (0.345) | −0.094 | (0.344) | 0.091 | (0.320) |
| | | $TIME_c$ | 0.030** | (0.010) | 0.063** | (0.015) | 0.016 | (0.015) | 0.014 | (0.014) |
| | | $FUT_1$ | 0.302 | (0.333) | −0.179 | (0.552) | 0.316 | (0.456) | 0.526 | (0.425) |
| | | $FUT_3$ | −0.138 | (0.227) | −0.153 | (0.346) | −0.817* | (0.372) | −0.222 | (0.329) |
| | | $PAR_2$ | 0.131 | (0.325) | 1.291* | (0.587) | 0.850 | (0.602) | −0.381 | (0.418) |
| | | $PAR_3$ | 0.228 | (0.321) | 0.817 | (0.610) | 0.945 | (0.598) | −0.463 | (0.425) |
| | | $PAR_4$ | 0.060 | (0.324) | 0.591 | (0.615) | 0.949 | (0.594) | −0.368 | (0.413) |
| | | | Log likelihood: -695.05, LR test: 61.61*, McFadden $R^2$: 0.039 | | | | | | | |

Note: Sequence 0000 is the base sequence. Values are logistic coefficients (betas). Asymptotic standard errors are given in parentheses. Level of significance: $^{*}0.01 \leq p < 0.05$, $^{**}p < 0.01$. 'Single effects' models include all variables. However, only those parameters are reported, which proved to be significant at the 5% level for at least one category. For 'interactive' models only interacted variables are given.

dance with sequence 1111 in relation to sequence 0000. The corresponding multiplicative factor is $exp(1.243) = 3.466$; the 95% confidence interval is 1.645 to 7.302 and does not contain the value 1.0. Furthermore, in this context males seem to switch remarkably earlier from alternative $x$ to $y$ than their female counterparts. This can be seen from the significant estimated coefficients of the gender dummy variable for the sequences 0111 and 0001, which is positive in the first and negative in the second case. In situation 4, significant differences with respect to the probability for an unconditional support of the better-off individuals compared to the corresponding value for the worse offs can be observed. Here, the corresponding 95% confidence interval is [1.042; 2.631].

Compared to these findings, the corresponding results for the larger sample, which are summarised in Table 2.16 in the Appendix, show only minor differences. In situation 1, the previously described gender differences with respect to sequence 0111 are now significant at the 1% level, while the respective effects on the observation of sequence 0001 are significant at the 10% level. Similarly, in situation 4 the differences mentioned with regard to sequence 1111 are now significant at the 10% level. In order to see whether these changes are due to the incorporation of additional subjects or the omission of FUTURE dummy variables, we reran the regressions using the reduced sample but excluded the income dummies. Results were more similar to the estimated models for the smaller sample including the FUTURE dummies so that we possibly observed a sample selection bias. However, overall there are only some minor changes, although results for situation 4 are somewhat weaker.

Next, the alternative ordered logit model should briefly be regarded. The underlying calculations follow the procedures described in the statistical part in subsection 2.3.3. Remember that this model has the advantageous property of applying a single index function, which enables us to estimate only one coefficient for each explanatory variable. However, it implicitly uses the single crossing assumption that might be violated in the present data set, as discussed above. The results are summarised in Table 2.9. As before, consider only the 'single effects' models. Similar to results of the multinomial logit models, in more recent years, students were less in favour of the spirit of the equity axiom in situations 1, 3 and 4. This can be seen from the estimated negative coefficients for the variable TIME. Hence, the previously discovered trend over time can clearly be confirmed in these three contexts. Moreover, interestingly, the existence of work experience lead to less support for workers' rights in situation 4. Thus, it might be possible that students are more concerned about the creation of jobs when they have already worked outside the university. Effects of other explanatory variables are of minor importance again; they basically confirm results of the multinomial logit models.

Coming back to the main question of this chapter, the gender of a respondent is of particular relevance in situation 1. From the negative and highly

Table 2.9: ML estimates of ordered logit models
Dependent variable: 5 Ordered Sequences

| | Situation 1 (n=628) | | Situation 2 (n=471) | Situation 3 (n=518) | | Situation 4 (n=629) |
|---|---|---|---|---|---|---|
| Independent variables | Single effects | Interactive | Single effects | Single effects | Interactive | Single effects |
| $AGE_c$ | 0.103 | −0.052 | 0.020 | 0.044 | −0.128 | 0.084 |
| | (0.056) | (0.088) | (0.063) | (0.059) | (0.093) | (0.056) |
| $BA$ | −0.024 | −0.010 | −0.156 | −0.031 | −0.042 | −0.421 |
| | (0.217) | (0.217) | (0.246) | (0.231) | (0.232) | (0.230) |
| $JOB$ | −0.206 | −0.170 | 0.139 | 0.008 | 0.020 | −0.459* |
| | (0.201) | (0.201) | (0.215) | (0.208) | (0.208) | (0.199) |
| $MALE$ | −0.552** | −0.476** | 0.036 | −0.237 | −0.190 | −0.294 |
| | (0.175) | (0.175) | (0.191) | (0.184) | (0.185) | (0.172) |
| $TIME$ | −0.047** | −0.050** | 0.019 | −0.022* | −0.026** | −0.030** |
| | (0.007) | (0.007) | (0.010) | (0.009) | (0.010) | (0.007) |
| $FUT_1$ | −0.050 | −0.040 | 0.192 | 0.425 | 0.401 | −0.183 |
| | (0.250) | (0.250) | (0.344) | (0.300) | (0.300) | (0.246) |
| $FUT_3$ | 0.015 | 0.007 | −0.180 | 0.072 | 0.044 | 0.204 |
| | (0.168) | (0.169) | (0.182) | (0.175) | (0.175) | (0.170) |
| $PAR_2$ | 0.089 | 0.091 | −0.077 | −0.187 | −0.226 | −0.291 |
| | (0.240) | (0.240) | (0.266) | (0.253) | (0.254) | (0.243) |
| $PAR_3$ | −0.056 | −0.067 | −0.339 | −0.104 | −0.108 | −0.296 |
| | (0.239) | (0.239) | (0.266) | (0.255) | (0.256) | (0.244) |
| $PAR_4$ | −0.024 | −0.025 | 0.073 | 0.286 | 0.258 | −0.139 |
| | (0.239) | (0.239) | (0.271) | (0.261) | (0.262) | (0.245) |
| $MALE*$ $AGE_c$ | — | 0.217* | — | — | 0.259* | — |
| | | (0.097) | | | (0.104) | |
| $\mu_1$ | −3.347** | −3.275** | −0.864* | −1.502** | −1.521** | −2.526** |
| | (0.357) | (0.356) | (0.363) | (0.355) | (0.355) | (0.350) |
| $\mu_2$ | −2.237** | −2.158** | −0.368 | −0.647 | −0.662 | −2.101** |
| | (0.339) | (0.338) | (0.361) | (0.349) | (0.350) | (0.345) |
| $\mu_3$ | −1.374** | −1.290** | 0.013 | −0.296 | −0.307 | −1.754** |
| | (0.331) | (0.330) | (0.360) | (0.348) | (0.349) | (0.342) |
| $\mu_4$ | −1.087** | −1.001** | 0.178 | −0.128 | −0.136 | −1.369** |
| | (0.329) | (0.329) | (0.360) | (0.348) | (0.349) | (0.339) |
| LL | -724.34 | -721.91 | -557.48 | -618.84 | -615.62 | -712.16 |
| LR statistic | 54.57** | 59.43** | 9.85 | 14.84 | 21.29* | 27.38** |
| (Pseudo-)$R^2$ | 0.033 | 0.036 | 0.008 | 0.011 | 0.015 | 0.017 |

Note: Given are logistic coefficients (betas). Standard errors are reported in parentheses. Level of significance: $^*0.01 \leq p < 0.05$, $^{**}p < 0.01$.

Table 2.10: Ordered logit models - Selected marginal probabilities

| Variable | $\frac{\partial Pr(z_i=1)}{\partial x_{il}}$ | $\frac{\partial Pr(z_i=2)}{\partial x_{il}}$ | $\frac{\partial Pr(z_i=3)}{\partial x_{il}}$ | $\frac{\partial Pr(z_i=4)}{\partial x_{il}}$ | $\frac{\partial Pr(z_i=5)}{\partial x_{il}}$ |
|---|---|---|---|---|---|
| | | | Situation 1 | | |
| *MALE* | 0.044 | 0.046 | 0.032 | 0.005 | −0.127 |
| *TIME* | 0.004 | 0.004 | 0.003 | 0.000 | −0.011 |
| | | | Situation 2 | | |
| *MALE* | −0.008 | −0.001 | −0.000 | 0.000 | 0.009 |
| *TIME* | −0.004 | −0.001 | −0.000 | 0.000 | 0.005 |
| | | | Situation 3 | | |
| *MALE* | 0.041 | 0.015 | 0.002 | −0.000 | −0.058 |
| *TIME* | 0.004 | 0.001 | 0.000 | −0.000 | −0.005 |
| | | | Situation 4 | | |
| *MALE* | 0.047 | 0.011 | 0.007 | 0.005 | −0.070 |
| *TIME* | 0.005 | 0.001 | 0.001 | 0.000 | −0.007 |

Note: Only 'single effects' models are considered. Sums of marginal probabilities in each row do not always equal zero due to rounding.

significant estimated coefficient it can be seen that male students were less often inclined to the spirit of the equity axiom compared to their female counterparts. This effect seems to be less clear in the fourth context, where the estimated coefficient for the dummy variable MALE is significant only at the 10% level.

However, remember that the suitability of this approach is doubted. Additional insights are offered by the marginal probabilities that have been calculated for selected variables, following again the previously described algebraic procedures. Corresponding values are reported in Table 2.10. For example, according to the given estimated effects, the probability of observing sequence 0000 ($z_i$=5) in situation 1 decreases by 12.7% if males instead of females are regarded. Moreover, these marginal effects could be used for making further statements about effects of variables on the probabilities for 'intermediate' sequences (i.e. $z_i$=2,3,4). But particularly the results stated in the table can be utilised for the third test to evaluate the appropriateness of the ordered logit approach. Consider, for example, the estimated effects in situation 4. We know from the descriptive results in Table 2.5 that the relative frequencies are higher for males in the two unconditional cases 0000 and 1111, with almost equal values for both groups in the first case. However, the estimated marginal probabilities firstly indicate that the difference is highest for the sequence 0000 with a lower frequency for males. Secondly, the prob-

Table 2.11: Interpretation of interaction effects
Example: Situation 1, MALE∗AGE

| | AGE of Proband | | | Ratio of OR |
|---|---|---|---|---|
| | Mean-1 | Mean=22.82 | Mean+1 | Factor |
| | | Predicted Odds | | |
| Males | 5.264 | 6.227 | 7.366 | |
| Females | 19.259 | 14.064 | 10.269 | |
| | | Predicted Probabilities | | |
| Males | 0.840 | 0.862 | 0.880 | |
| Females | 0.951 | 0.934 | 0.911 | |
| | | Odds Ratios | | |
| Males/Females | 0.273 | 0.443 | 0.717 | 1.623 |

Note: The dependent variable is 'Fulfilment of Equity Axiom'. The estimated coefficients of the initial binary logit model, using a mean value of 22.82 for AGE, are $\beta_0 = 2.644^{**}$ (0.275), $\beta_{Male} = -0.815^{**}$ (0.310), $\beta_{Age_c} = -0.314^{*}$ (0.146), $\beta_{Male*Age_c} = 0.482^{**}$ (0.171). Asymptotic standard errors are reported in parentheses.

ability is higher for males with respect to the other four decision patterns. Similar contradictions can also be found for other contexts. Thus, in general the results from the ordered logit approach seem to be rather critical in the present investigation.

Finally, let us consider interaction effects. By applying the stepwise backward elimination procedure based on likelihood-ratio tests which have been mentioned in subsection 2.3.4, one significant interaction term has been identified in all models. The age of respondents proves to be the most prominent variable that displays a major influence on the effect of gender on equity judgements. Firstly, reconsider the binary logit models summarised in Table 2.4. Additional likelihood-ratio tests show that the product term significantly improves model fit ( $\chi^2_1 = 9.72$, p-value $= 0.002$, in situation 1 and $\chi^2_1 = 8.20$, p-value $= 0.004$, in situation 4).

To give an impression of the interpretation of these results, we estimated a further binary logit model that only included a constant term, the independent variables MALE and $\text{AGE}_c$, and the product term MALE$*\text{AGE}_c$. The estimated coefficients are given below Table 2.11.

Here, the exponent of the intercept term of the binary logit model is the predicted odds when all predictors equal zero. Thus, it reflects the odds for females at the sample mean of the variable AGE, because we have centred this continuous variable about the mean value. Since this is only a simplified example, we renounce to give more meaningful interpretations. Then, we followed the suggestion by Jaccard (2001) to respecify the gender dummy and received the corresponding predicted odds for males. The first important observation is that the resulting odds ratio (0.443) is also given by the exponent of the estimated coefficient associated with gender. Next, we repeated our calculations and generated predicted odds and odds ratios when the moderator variable AGE is centred about the values 'mean-1' and 'mean+1', respectively. Now, from our results in Table 2.11 it can be seen that the exponent of the estimated coefficient for the product term indicates the multiplicative factor by which the odds ratio changes given a one-year increase in AGE.[27] Also, to illustrate the relationship between odds and probabilities we state predicted probabilities that are calculated from predicted odds by using equation (2.4). The probabilities equal the corresponding proportions of those students who fulfil the equity axiom stated in table 2.3 if the sample mean of the variable AGE equals 22.82.

Now, it can be demonstrated that in situations 1 and 4 younger women were much more likely to support the worse-off individual(s) initially compared to men of the same age. However, the positive signs of predicted coefficients show that this disparity declines if respondents grow older (corresponding 95% confidence intervals are well above the value 1.0). Especially for situation 1 in Table 2.4, this can also be seen from the exponent of the estimated coefficient for $AGE_c$ which is significantly lower than 1.0. Since this effect is now conditional on MALE=0, it reveals that women are less likely to fulfil the equity axiom when they grow older. Secondly, the 'interactive' multinomial logit models in Tables 2.7 and 2.8 reveal additional differences.[28] Obviously, younger women were less likely to choose in accordance with sequence 1111 in situations 1 and 3. This is also confirmed by results of the ordered logit models. It is important to notice that this effect is separated from other influences, especially work experience. Furthermore, the observations described also hold for the larger samples as can be seen from the regression models presented in the Appendix. We will come back to this age effect in our conclusions.

Other individual characteristics of respondents had no significant influence on the effect of gender on justice evaluations. Especially the interaction term of gender and time is not found to be significant. Thus, the results on gender differences have been stable over the period of time covered.

To summarise, in two situations strong gender differences have been discovered for the initial fulfilment of the equity axiom. Moreover, these differences also concerned the switching decision in situation 1, when the better-off group is enlarged. In contrast, no disparities in situation 2 and only minor differ-

27 It should be remarked that the estimated coefficient for the product term is very close to the corresponding value reported in Table 2.4, although predicted odds are certainly different. However, basically for didactic reasons we have chosen this simplified model.

28 Results of corresponding likelihood-ratio tests are $\chi^2_4 = 9.68$, p-value $= 0.046$, in situation 1 and $\chi^2_4 = 15.48$, p-value $= 0.004$, in situation 3.

ences in situation 3 could be observed. Surprisingly, an equal share of both groups in each situation followed the intention of the axiom unconditionally. With respect to confounding factors, the age of a respondent had a remarkable influence on the effect of gender on the hypothetical allocation decision. Finally, for the given data set, the multinomial logit model proved to be more appropriate compared to the ordered logit model, although the latter approach confirmed most of the results.

### 2.5.3 Verbal Answers

In the final part of this section, some more light should be shed on possible decision motives of respondents. In the questionnaires, subjects should give additional verbal explanations on their choices. Moreover, students who decided in accordance with sequence 0000 were also asked whether they would switch towards alternative $y$ if the better-off group were further extended.

Thus, the aim is to examine which arguments are used by theoretically uninformed women and men in order to justify their decisions. Following the reasoning in the first chapter, possible disagreements of laymen with theoretical proposals have already been discovered. Also, this procedure seems to be appropriate if we want to evoke a reconsideration of theoretical concepts and also to uncover possible sources of gender disparities. Moreover, offering participants the possibility to give verbal explanations served three additional advantages. Firstly, it seems as if students thought more deeply about the underlying decision problems in each situation. This can be observed from both the relatively high proportion of students who gave verbal comments and the effort many of the participants spent on these answers. Secondly, in conversations with students who completed the questionnaire it became obvious that they appreciated the possibility to explain their choices. They considered that either-or decisions were preceded by stronger concerns. For these subjects, a single choice of one alternative without any comment would have been a too stark moral statement. Thirdly, somewhat surprisingly most survey investigations and game theoretical experiments abstain from the opportunity to look behind simple choices or answers. Hence, we have the almost unique opportunity to get further insights into decision motives of participants.

Certainly, the analysis and interpretation of verbal answers is afflicted with many problems. Presumably, although it might be unintended by them, respondents usually neither state all underlying motives nor do all participants reveal their 'true' intentions. Moreover, it is also possible that some of them try to disguise their motivation and, instead, attempt to fulfil suspected external expectations. But more frequently, it seems as if students do not get their underlying motives straight. This impression basically results from several incoherent comments. Additionally, many arguments of subjects are difficult to distinguish; often statements consider only the first or the later decisions of a situation or even contain arguments in favour of both alternatives offered at the same time. Furthermore, it is not straightforward to build more general answer categories from regularly vague verbal comments. Therefore, as the coding of verbal answers in Appendix 2.7.5 shows, more diverse arguments have been formulated in order to cover the comments more closely. Only thereafter, they are further summarised.

There is no doubt that the categorisation of verbal answers is necessarily subjective and depends on interpretations made by the researcher. Nevertheless, the examination of underlying decision motives clearly goes beyond existing studies and should at least be seen as a supplementing device to better understand observed choices. More precisely, it should be investigated, which reasons play a role and how often they have been considered. This concerns in particular motives that are in line with three allocation principles, viz. equality, efficiency and needs. In addition, we are able to examine whether the rank ordering of possible motivations is identical between women and men; differences in relative frequencies could help identifying typical female or male answers. On the one hand, we are able to detect reasons for gender differences with respect to distinct decision patterns. On the other hand, it might also be possible that females and males are indeed equally likely to display a certain answer pattern – but for different reasons.

Probably, some general observations are of interest. In all situations men more often refused to give a verbal answer. Also, women tended to give more sophisticated answers while men focused more often on a single reason. Therefore, on average women stated 1.41, 1.09, 1.15 and 0.97 different arguments in situations 1 to 4, whereas the respective numbers for men are 1.19, 0.99, 1.05 and 0.89. Additionally, the specific context described in situation 3 may have affected female students stronger than males, so that they dealt more thoroughly with this choice situation. Overall, it is possible that women are more likely than men to use *all* arguments, but typical male motives also exist.

Concerning situation 1, four general categories have been generated (see the overview in Appendix 2.7.5). In the first part of Figure 2.1, the corresponding relative frequencies for women and men are depicted. Additionally, $\chi^2$ tests for $2 \times 2$ tables have been employed to evaluate the differences between proportions of these answer categories in both samples. Respective p-values are also given. The relevance of basic needs has been mentioned by 43.3% of female respondents but only by 33.9% of male students. This difference is statistically significant. Furthermore, it is also interesting to regard certain answer classes, which have been distinguished in previous sections. Among those students who fulfilled the equity axiom, 45.8% of the women and 39.3% of the men referred to the importance of basic needs (p=0.123). The corresponding values for participants acting in accordance with sequence 0000 are 63.1% and 58.8% (p=0.435). Obviously, for these groups gender differences are not remarkable. However, this might be due to the smaller sample sizes.

Figure 2.1: Verbal answers of females (F) and males (M)

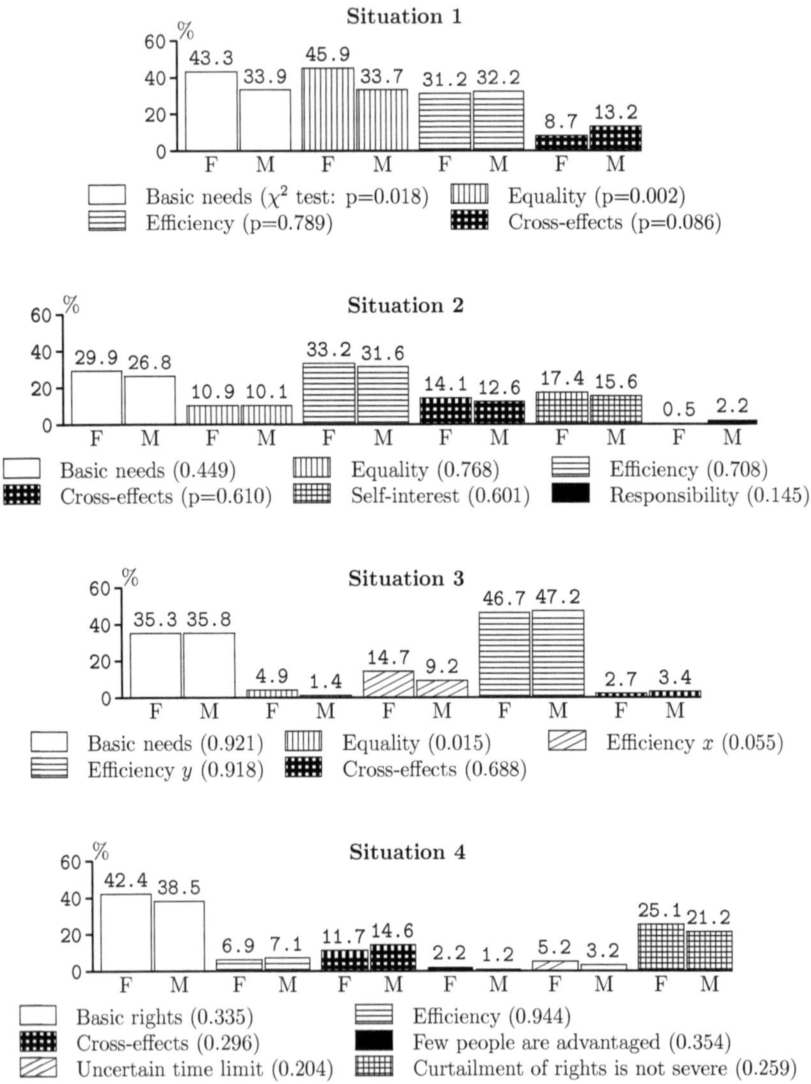

In general, women were also considerably more likely to mention equality aspects. These remarkable gender differences can also be found among those respondents who answered in accordance with sequence 0000 (72.1% of the females but only 57.3% of the males stated equality arguments) and with the fulfilment of the equity axiom (49.1% of the women and 39.0% of the men). Furthermore, with respect to the three single arguments summarised in this category, we find that especially the better situation of the intelligent children was significantly more often mentioned by females. Thus, equality considerations seemed to be a typical female motive in the given context.

Next, different efficiency arguments are summarised. Although men somewhat more often stated these reasons, no gender differences can be observed even if we take into account single answer classes like the sequence 1111. The hope for cross-effects, i.e. to help both parties, has more frequently been expressed by male respondents (p=0.086). Such arguments probably reflect the wish to split up the given resource.

Obviously, gender differences concerning the stated motivations are apparent, with females considering basic needs and especially equality arguments more frequently than their male counterparts. The four general answer categories in situation 1 are also of relevance in the other three contexts. In situation 2, basic needs and efficiency arguments were again important for women and men, although the first motive was less often mentioned compared to situation 1. A similar decline is even more apparent for equality arguments, while the proportion of cross-effect motivations are almost the same. In general, no gender differences can be detected in the second situation. This observation also holds for two additional context-specific motives. Neither arguments driven by self-interest, which pronounce the possible support for the home country of the respondents, nor responsibility considerations show any gender disparities. With respect to the similarities that have previously been found for this situation, these results are not surprising.

In situation 3, there are two prominent motives, which, however, do not display gender disparities. Firstly, basic needs have been mentioned by more than one third of both groups. Secondly, the efficiency of alternative $y$ was admitted by almost 50% of the respondents. Nevertheless, a new efficiency argument in favour of alternative $x$ has been used by some subjects in this situation. They reasoned that the utility gain for kidney patients is higher, and also questioned the usefulness of vitamins. This observation will be reconsidered in the presentation of possible decision motives in chapter 5. Interestingly, 14.7% of the women but only 9.2% of the men adopted this line of argument (p=0.055). Moreover, considering only those individuals who decided in accordance with sequence 0000, it is found that 31.7% of the females but only 20.0% of the males (p=0.045) ascribed a higher marginal utility to alternative $x$. Similar results can be found for the group of respondents who fulfilled the equity axiom. Hence, although at a low level, female students more frequently doubted the usefulness of vitamins for pregnant women.

Moreover, relatively more females than males argued in terms of equality motives and noted that pregnant women are already better off. Nevertheless, the corresponding frequencies are rather small.

As already described above, situation 4 somewhat differs from the other three situations. Here, basic rights are considered and, furthermore, procedural aspects are incorporated. This contextual change is also reflected by a variety of new arguments. Nevertheless, the importance of human rights clearly constitutes the most prominent reason for those respondents who supported alternative $x$, while the severeness of the curtailment of these rights has been played down by those students, who instead decided in favour of alternative $y$. All other motives are of no greater importance, although again a certain proportion of each group wanted to reach both targets at the same time. Surprisingly, in this situation there are no gender differences observable, although men have been found to fulfil the equity axiom considerably less frequently in previous subsections. Maybe some respondents thought that their distributive principles were already clear from their earlier answers.

Finally, in all situations students were also asked whether they would switch from alternative $x$ towards alternative $y$ later on if they had so far decided in favour of the worse-off individual(s). An almost equally high proportion of respondents in both groups is identified, who also denied a later reconsideration of their initial choice. Usually, the proportion was well above 85%. These results confirm earlier observations saying that an unconditional support for alternative $x$ is equally popular among both sexes. In chapters 3 and 4, we will argue that there seems to be a certain number of students who give absolute priority to the needs principle independent from aspects of efficiency and responsibility.

Certainly, as explained at the beginning of this subsection, the examination of verbal answers is afflicted with many problems. Thus, the present study only allows for limited insights into distinct decision motives. However, if we want to understand the motivation of women and men and, thereby, expose possible reasons for observed gender differences, we have to use all the available information at our disposal. In the final section, some of our findings will be discussed and related to the existing literature.

## 2.6 Conclusions

At the starting point there were findings from surveys on macro-justice and benevolent dictator experiments, which revealed gender differences with regard to the trade-off between the principles of efficiency and equality, but also with respect to the consideration of basic needs. In two out of four of the hypothetical situations presented, female respondents fulfilled the equity axiom significantly more often than males. This observation could also be related to the previously mentioned experimental findings that women act more socially oriented when no risk for the decision-maker is involved. But what makes them choose more in accordance with the equity axiom? Again, findings from different social science disciplines may be helpful. One possible explanation comes from the psychological literature. Females are said to be better able to take on the perspective of others and, thus, exhibit effective empathy. According to Eisenberg and Lennon (1983), this plays an essential role in social and moral life. Also, Gilligan's (1982) claim that women more often follow a care perspective, while men tend to adopt a justice perspective more frequently, may be of importance for our observations. However, the underlying reason for such behaviour is not obvious. Eagly (1995) reports that in the psychological *social role theory* it is assumed that women are expected – and expect themselves – to behave in a warm and friendly way. Certainly, such stereotypes may also be of relevance in the current survey. Interestingly, especially in the first context women were more likely to mention both basic needs and equality arguments. Hence, underlying reasons seem to be interdependent and, therefore, rather complex.

Next, the better-off groups were successively enlarged. Certainly, higher relative frequencies of the sequence 1111 for males in all situations can be ascribed to differences with respect to the fulfilment of the equity axiom. However, in each questionnaire situation the proportion of those students who unconditionally supported alternative $x$, was astonishingly similar between women and men. Furthermore, at least in situations 1 and 4, women seemed to be more likely to revise their initial decision in favour of the least advantaged individuals. Hence, overall men more frequently supported the better-off individual(s) right from the beginning, whereas women turned to alternative $y$ if the better-off groups were enlarged. But what changes occur when the number of better-off individuals is raised? One possible interpretation is that opportunity costs increase. Thus, it becomes more and more expensive to support the least advantaged individuals in the way that subjects simultaneously had to reject the help for an increasing number of individuals. Women seemed to be more effected by this expansion. This observation especially contradicts findings by Andreoni and Vesterlund (2001) who concluded from their dictator experiment that women are more altruistic than men if giving is more expensive.

Another observation is also remarkable. In two out of four contexts in the questionnaire, only minor gender disparities could be identified. As argued already above, the hypothetical situations may have provoked different degrees of identification or, more indirectly, self-projection between both sexes. While situations 1 and 4 can be interpreted as being rather far away from the lives of our students, situation 2 presents a context, in which the respondents are assumed to belong to the group of beneficiaries of alternative $y$. Moreover, situation 3 could be interpreted as being less gender-neutral, since female probands probably identify more with the hypothetical group of pregnant women. Nevertheless, it is known from several studies in experimental economics that such identification even with a hypothetical group confound decisions, while e.g. Dickinson and Tiefenthaler (2002) detect remarkable gender differences in an explicitly abstract setting. Surprisingly, in the third context more women than men argued that pregnant women are better off, but clearly, females were also more likely to opt for alternative $y$ than in situations 1 and 4. Obviously, in the study disparities between women and men disappeared in these less 'neutral' contexts.

In connection with contextual effects, observations by Croson and Gneezy (2008) are of interest. They confirm Gilligan's (1982) suggestion of men deciding less context-specific than women, but more in compliance with abstract rules. They argue that females more often derive distinct social clues even from small differences in the experimental setting and react more strongly to them. Initially, the questionnaires presented were not intended to test for gender differences and, therefore, did not conduct any systematic variations in the hypothetical context. Nevertheless, if Gilligan's claim is right, we would expect women to regard each situation separately, whereas men try to uncover a common structure of the different contexts considered and probably decide more similarly between the situations. Thus, we compared individual answer patterns between different situations. Simple $t$-tests have been performed to find evidence against the hypothesis $H_0$ that women and men are equally likely to display completely identical answer patterns in respective situations. Results are reported in Table 2.12.

It can be seen that in situations 1, 2 and 3 men have significantly more often chosen identical decision patterns. This can be interpreted as a confirmation for the supposed gender difference. However, no disparities can be observed in comparisons with situation 4. One reason might be that two additional situations between the third and fourth reported context have been used – but not presented here – in the first three years. In order to test for consistency of answers support for well-off individuals has been described as buying them expensive wines while the other alternative concerned again people in need. It can be supposed that almost all individuals would choose the latter alternative in these two contexts. Hence, students trying to follow a principle that supports better offs at some point could have been biased by this modification.

Finally, the incorporation of additional individual attributes shows that the age of a proband displayed a remarkable influence on gender differences. Younger women were more likely to fulfil the equity axiom in all situations compared to men of the same age – but also in relation to older women. Furthermore, they acted more often in the spirit of the equity axiom. One possible explanation comes from Gilligan's (1982) suggestion of different stages of moral development, which has been described in the introduction.

The present study regards a well established equity axiom and, therefore, is theoretically grounded. The main focus was on the acceptance of the needs or equality principle, since all four contexts regarded different aspects of the two

Table 2.12: Equal answers in different situations

| Equal answers in situations | Females | Males | t-statistic (p-value) |
|---|---|---|---|
| 1 and 2 | 25.54% | 38.83% | −3.106** (0.002) |
| 2 and 3 | 26.09% | 37.43% | −2.660** (0.008) |
| 1 and 3 | 36.41% | 39.39% | −0.673 (0.501) |
| 1 and 4 | 37.66% | 41.46% | −0.942 (0.347) |
| 2 and 4 | 29.89% | 28.17% | −0.066 (0.947) |
| 3 and 4 | 37.50% | 32.68% | 1.118 (0.264) |
| 1, 2 and 3 | 14.13% | 21.51% | −2.078* (0.038) |
| 1, 2 and 4 | 17.93% | 20.11% | −0.606 (0.545) |
| 1, 3 and 4 | 24.46% | 22.07% | 0.626 (0.531) |
| 2, 3 and 4 | 16.28% | 15.36% | 0.285 (0.776) |
| 1, 2, 3 and 4 | 13.59% | 12.01% | 0.524 (0.601) |

Note: 540 d.f. in all comparisons but "1 and 4" (639 d.f.). Level of significance: *$0.01 \leq p < 0.05$, **$p < 0.01$, two-tailed test.

principles. However, due to the enlargement of the better-off groups efficiency considerations have been introduced. Thus, we could make statements on the trade-off between equality or needs and efficiency. Here, similarities – but equally often disparities – between women and men have been discovered. They seem to depend on the degree of identification with hypothetical groups and the age of the respondent. Overall, the gender of a subject may be an important confounding factor for equity judgements. In the following chapter, we will detect even stronger gender differences and, thereby, clearly confirm the observations of the present study.

Certainly, it is rather speculative to give deeper reasons for the occurrence of such differences even if verbal comments are available. Obviously, findings from the domains of psychology and sociology could help economic researchers when interpreting empirical results. An interdisciplinary perspective may be a promising way to better understand gender differences with respect to social and economic behaviours. Clearly, only a very limited extract of distributive justice has been considered, which needs to be extended by future work; and of course, we are currently far away from separating female and male justice theories. Nevertheless, apparently there are some indications for gender-specific justice concepts. Hence, to pick up Schokkaert's notion, Mrs. Fairmind may exist, but she does not always disagree with her husband.

As we argued already in chapter 1, characteristics of decision-makers may bias allocation behaviour. The gender of a respondent is one of the most often investigated attributes. In the present chapter, we have concentrated on gender differences with respect to solutions to the equality-efficiency trade-off in the context of basic needs. Some remarkable gender differences have been revealed. These results should inform empirical researchers to pay attention to the structure of their samples and to routinely control for gender influences. In the next two investigations, we will take these findings into consideration. Regarding the consequences of our empirical results for theoretical conceptions, theorists may be encouraged by the high acceptance of the equity axiom, but at the same time somewhat disappointed due to the low general acceptance of the *spirit* of the axiom when the better-off groups are successively enlarged. In the next chapter, we will additionally introduce the principle of responsibility. Again, gender differences will play an important role.

## 2.7 Appendices

### 2.7.1 Appendix A: The Questionnaire

**Situation 1:**

(o) A small society has received a certain amount of money which can be used either to provide some help and assistance for a handicapped person or to further the education of an intelligent child. The child could receive a good education in languages and in natural sciences, let's say. Let the retarded person be person 1; if the sum of money were used for her support (alternative $x$), she would be able to learn some very basic things, so that at least in certain areas of daily life she would no longer be totally dependent on the assistance from other people. Let the intelligent child be person 2; the investment into its education represents alternative $y$. It is not possible to split up the given amount.

Which alternative should be realized in your view, $x$ or $y$?

(a) Imagine that the sum of money which could be used to help the handicapped person, is so large that, on the other hand, this amount would suffice for the education of not only person 2 but also a second child (person 3) who is even somewhat more intelligent than person 2. Person 3 would, therefore, benefit even a bit more from the education than person 2. Let $y$ be the investment into the education of the two children and let $x$ again stand for the support of the handicapped person.

Would you choose $x$ or $y$ under these conditions?

(b) Imagine that if the money were used to finance alternative $y$ it would be possible to educate still another child (person 4). The reason may simply be "economies of scale" or the fact that a talented teacher will be able to provide a good education for several children simultanously. Let us assume that all the other characteristics of the situation remain as before.

Which alternative should be picked in your view, $x$ or $y$?

(c) Add another child to the situation (person 5), who could also receive an instruction in languages and the natural sciences out of the given budget. Everything else remains the same.

Would you want $x$ or $y$ to be realized?

($d_1$) If up to this point you have always decided in favor of alternative $x$, could you imagine a situation, in which you would choose $y$ after all (from the 5th, 6th, 7th, ... intelligent child onward? Or even later?), or would you always decide in favor of the handicapped person, i.e. alternative $x$?

($d_2$) On which criteria did you base your decision? Give a brief explanation.

**Situation 2:**

(o) Imagine that due to an unexpectedly large profit of the Federal Reserve (or an unexpectedly large budgetary surplus, if you prefer), Government has the possibility to spend several billion euros either on environmental protection within its own territory (alternative $y$) or to spend that amount of money to finance an aid program against hunger in various countries of Subsaharan Africa (alternative $x$). Given the available amount of money, the environmental program would aim at improving the current situation of the North Sea. This would primarily benefit the fishing industry and, perhaps to a somewhat lesser degree, the people who spend their vacation along the North Sea. Henceforth, these two groups are called "person 2". Those who suffer from famine in Subsaharan Africa are "person 1". Undoubtedly, both the fishermen and the vacationers in this country are, in terms of welfare, better off than the starving people in Africa, independent of whether alternative $x$ or alternative $y$ will be realized. We want to assume that either only $x$ or only $y$ can be realized, not both.

Which alternative should be chosen according to your view, $x$ or $y$?

(a) Imagine now that the profit of the Federal Reserve (or the budgetary surplus) has turned out to be higher than anticipated originally. On the one hand, the fight against hunger could now be intensified, on the other the environmental program could be extended. The proposal is to improve the quality of the air in the neighbourhood of coal power plants. The group benefiting from this measure will be called "person 3". We shall assume that this group will always be better off than groups 2 and 1 with respect to alternative $y$, and be definitely better off than group 1 with respect to alternative $x$. Alternative $y$ again stands for environmental protection and $x$ stands for relief of hunger (both programs would, of course, now be larger due to the higher level of financial resources).

Which alternative should be realized according to your view, $x$ or $y$?

(b) Assume that it has become clear that "economies of scale" would occur in the environmental program, once alternative $y$ should be realized. We postulate that a program for cleaner water in rivers should also be feasible which would benefit primarily those citizens of the country (group 4) who live close to the rivers (it seems obvious that cleaner water in rivers would, among other things, increase the stock of fish). In other words, not only would groups 2 and 3 benefit from the environmental program but also an additional group. Alternative $y$ again stands for the environmental program and $x$ stands for the aid program for Subsaharan Africa.

Which program should be chosen now, $x$ or $y$?

(c) Imagine that, given the financial resources, a further enlargement of the environmental program appears realistic. It has, for example, been found out that an additional program aiming at a reduction of traffic noise along the highways would be financially feasible. Through this investment, still another group of people (group 5) would experience an increase in its living conditions. We assume that group 5 is better off than all the other groups under alternative $y$ and that it is at least better off than group 1 under alternative $x$.

Which alternative should now be realized according to your view, $x$ or $y$?

($d_1$) If up to this point you have always made a decision in favour of alternative $x$, could you imagine a situation, in which you would choose $y$ after all? And how should $y$ look like in your view, or would you always take a decision in favour of the aid program against hunger?

($d_2$) On which criteria did you base your decision? Please give a brief explanation.

**Situation 3:**

(o) Imagine a country that has a severe shortage of western currencies. The governing body of this country has the possibility to purchase on the world market either a certain number of badly needed dialysis machines (alternative $x$) that cannot be produced within the country, or a certain quantity of vitamin pills as well as tropical fruit (alternative $y$). This quantity would only be enough to satisfy the urgent needs of a relatively small group of people. The realization of both alternatives together or a combination of both alternatives to some extent is assumed to be infeasible. The group of people suffering from kidney problems is group 1, the group of people benefiting from the import of vitamins and fruits is group 2. There is unanimous agreement in the country that all pregnant women should make up group 2. It is also unanimously agreed that the individuals with kidney trouble are clearly worse off than the expectant mothers.

Which alternative should be realized in your view, $x$ or $y$?

(a) Imagine now that the world market price for vitamin pills and tropical fruit has fallen. If alternative $y$ were realized it would be possible to provide not only the expectant mothers, but also all the country's babies and toddlers (group 3) with the needed vitamins. The price of dialysis machines is assumed to rest unchanged, however. The welfare levels of groups 2 and 3 are clearly higher than the level of group 1 both under $y$ and under $x$.

Would you choose alternative $x$ or alternative $y$?

(b) Let us imagine that there is a further decline in the world market price for vitamin pills and tropical fruit so that it turns out that under the given amount of western currencies the country's adolescents (group 4) could also be provided with vitamins if alternative $y$ were chosen.

Which alternative should be chosen, $x$ or $y$?

(c) The world market price of vitamin pills and tropical fruit declines once more so that under alternative $y$ the given amount of western currencies would now suffice to provide those workers of the country who are engaged in physical labour (group 5) with the needed vitamins. Clearly, these workers are better off, no matter whether they receive the vitamins or not, than the group of people who suffer from kidney problems.

Which of the two alternatives, $x$ or $y$, should now be chosen?

($d_1$) If up to this point you have always made a decision in favour of alternative $x$, could you imagine a situation, in which you would choose $y$ after all? And how should $y$ look like in your view, or would you always take a decision in favour of $x$?

($d_2$) On which criteria did you base your decision? Please give a brief explanation.

**Situation 4:**

(o) Imagine a country which had been totally run down economically by a long-lasting dictatorship. Finally, the country could get rid of this dictatorship. Furthermore, imagine that an international bank group is offering a rather large loan (under very favourable conditions of repayment) to this country for economic reconstruction (alternative $y$). However, the consortium declares that the prerequisite for this loan should be that the employees in the country be granted neither a right to strike nor the free choice of occupation. This precondition would remain valid for the foreseeable future. If the new Government were unwilling to enforce this curtailment of individual rights, no loan would be offered, and, therefore, the country would have to pull itself up by its bootstraps (alternative $x$). In that case, the country would, of course, have the option to reinstall the right to strike and other basic rights, a measure which had been promised to the citizens of the country after the fall of the dictatorship. If the bank loan were granted, the large enterprises (group 2) would be the first to experience an economic recovery. The workers and employees in the firms (group 1) would be hard hit by the restriction of basic rights. Also, their economic situation would be worse than that of the people in charge of the large enterprises.

What should the country do in your view, should it decide in favour of $y$ or $x$?

(a) Imagine that the initial situation were to undergo the following modification: The loan which is offered would have such a large volume that an additional group of the population, the self-employed persons with a small or middle-sized business activity, let's say, would benefit from the financial aid (group 3). Let this alternative again be denoted by $y$. Alternative $x$ remains as before.

Should the country choose $x$ or $y$?

(b) Imagine again a change of the initial situation: The bank loan offered is so large that under alternative $y$ still another group of the population, the civil servants, let's say, would realize larger economic benefits (group 4). Alternative $x$ remains unchanged.

Which alternative should now be picked by the country?

(c) A further variation: we shall assume that still another group within the population, the retired members of society (group 5), would experience an improvement of their economic situation under alternative $y$. Alternative $x$ remains unchanged.

Which alternative should now be chosen according to your view, $x$ or $y$?

($d_1$) If up to this point you have always made a decision in favour of alternative $x$, could you imagine a situation, in which you would choose $y$ after all? And how should $y$ look like in your view, or would you always take a decision in favour of $x$?

($d_2$) If right from the beginning or "fairly quickly" you took a decision in favour of $y$, what kind of reasons or motives could have moved you to decide in favour of $x$? A further confinement of basic rights such as a law against founding political parties, the introduction of censorship of the press, TV etc. or a confinement of religious freedom? Or something else? Please give a brief explanation.

**Demographic Characteristics:**

(1) Sex: (1=female, 2=male) [*MALE*]

(2) Age: [*AGE*]

(3) Which of the following categories describes best the professional status of the family in which you grew up? [*PARENT*]

1=unskilled worker, 2=skilled worker, 3=craftsman, [1]
4=employee or civil servant in the public sector, [2]
5=employee in the private sector, [3]
6=self–employed) [4]

(4) Subject of study: (1=business administration, 2=mathematics, 3=economics, 4=other) [*BA*]

(5) Were you employed before starting with your studies? [*JOB*]

(1=yes, 2=no)

(6) How many percent of the citizens of your country do you expect to have, in the year 2012, a net–income lower than your own? [*FUTURE*]

(1=5%, 2=25%, 3=50%, 4=75%, 5=95%)

### 2.7.2 Appendix B: Demographic Characteristics (2003)

(1) Sex: (1 = female, 2 = male) [*MALE*]

(2) Age: [*AGE*]

(3) Subject of study: (1 = business administration (diploma), 2 = economics (diploma), 3 = other) [*BA*]

(4) Have you already completed a professional training? [*JOB*]

(1 = yes, 2 = no)

(5) Which of the following categories describes best the professional status of the main earner of the family in which you grew up? [*PARENT*]

(a) self-employed farmer [4]
(b) freelance academic person [4]
(c) self-employed (except farmer) [4]
(d) worker [1]
(e) skilled worker [1]
(f) public servant (no executive position) [2]
(g) executive public servant [2]
(h) employee - public sector (no executive position) [2]
(i) executive employee - public sector [2]
(j) employee (no executive position) [3]
(k) executive employee - private sector [3]
(l) others

(6) How many percent of the citizens of your country do you expect to have, in the year 2013, a net–income lower than your own? [*FUTURE*]

(7) a) Do you possess the German citizenship?

(1 = yes, 2 = no)

b) How many years have you been living outside of Germany?

c) If you have ever lived outside of Germany, in which country have you been living for the longest time?

### 2.7.3 Appendix C: Instructions for Tutors

- The present questionnaire is part of a larger research project on distributive justice. It is NOT an exam.
- The questionnaires are anonymous. They serve only scientific purposes.
- The questions are not related to topics of the lecture. The knowledge of certain parts of the lecture is not necessary for answering the questionnaires.
- There are neither right nor wrong answers. Students are asked to express their opinions.
- Each proband should complete the questionnaire just once. This is especially important if someone visits more than one tutorial.
- There are different versions of the questionnaire. They should be given to the students in alternating order. Thus, compared to his or her neighbour, each student receives a different questionnaire. It is important to inform the students about this procedure. This should prevent students from copying the answers from their neighbours. (This information was only given in the years 2002 and 2003.)
- The numbers of the questionnaires are intended to reflect the seating arrangements of the students. Please try to give consecutive questionnaire numbers to side by side sitting students.
- Please ask the students to write as clearly as possible. Sometimes, written x and y are difficult to distinguish.
- The answers should reflect the opinions of the students. Please prevent discussions and other influences from outside.
- The answering of the questionnaires will take about 30 minutes.
- Distributed but incomplete questionnaires should also be collected. Do not use them again during another tutorial.

**Thank you very much for your cooperation!**

### 2.7.4 Appendix D: Results from the Larger Sample

Table 2.13: Relative frequencies - All possible decision patterns (larger sample)

| | Situation 1 | | Situation 4 | |
|---|---|---|---|---|
| Sequence | Females (n=256) | Males (n=419) | Females (n=256) | Males (n=419) |
| 0 0 0 0 | 0.531 | 0.511 | 0.512 | 0.535 |
| 0 0 0 1 | 0.090 | 0.045 | 0.102 | 0.084 |
| 0 0 1 0 | 0.0 | 0.0 | 0.0 | 0.0 |
| 0 0 1 1 | 0.164 | 0.155 | 0.094 | 0.064 |
| 0 1 0 0 | 0.0 | 0.0 | 0.0 | 0.0 |
| 0 1 0 1 | 0.004 | 0.002 | 0.004 | 0.002 |
| 0 1 1 0 | 0.004 | 0.0 | 0.0 | 0.002 |
| 0 1 1 1 | 0.125 | 0.148 | 0.094 | 0.064 |
| 1 0 0 0 | 0.0 | 0.002 | 0.004 | 0.002 |
| 1 0 0 1 | 0.0 | 0.005 | 0.0 | 0.0 |
| 1 0 1 0 | 0.0 | 0.0 | 0.0 | 0.002 |
| 1 0 1 1 | 0.008 | 0.005 | 0.0 | 0.0 |
| 1 1 0 0 | 0.016 | 0.002 | 0.004 | 0.010 |
| 1 1 0 1 | 0.0 | 0.0 | 0.0 | 0.0 |
| 1 1 1 0 | 0.0 | 0.002 | 0.004 | 0.002 |
| 1 1 1 1 | 0.059 | 0.122 | 0.184 | 0.232 |
| % Switch | 37.5 | 34.8 | 29.0 | 21.2 |
| % Fulfilment of equity axiom | 91.8 | 86.2 | 80.5 | 75.2 |

Note: A choice of alternative x is coded as 0, a decision in favour of y is coded as 1.

Table 2.14: ML estimates of binary logit models (larger sample)
Dependent variable: Fulfilment of Equity Axiom (n=675)

| | Situation 1 | | Situation 4 | |
|---|---|---|---|---|
| Independent variables | Single effects | Inter-active | Single effects | Inter-active |
| *Constant* | 2.742* | 2.696** | 1.916* | 1.848** |
| | (0.502) | (0.501) | (0.377) | (0.377) |
| $AGE_c$ | −0.049 | −0.401** | 0.065 | −0.167 |
| | (0.084) | (0.141) | (0.067) | (0.105) |
| *JOB* | 0.359 | 0.401 | −0.344 | −0.318 |
| | (0.319) | (0.323) | (0.240) | (0.241) |
| *MALE* | −0.688* | −0.644* | −0.466* | −0.419* |
| | (0.285) | (0.282) | (0.207) | (0.204) |
| $TIME_c$ | −0.029** | −0.033** | −0.023** | −0.027** |
| | (0.011) | (0.011) | (0.008) | (0.008) |
| $MALE{*}AGE_c$ | — | 0.473** | — | 0.334** |
| | | (0.156) | | (0.177) |
| Log likelihood | −235.53 | −230.97 | −355.96 | −351.88 |
| LR statistic | 16.26* | 25.39** | 13.08 | 21.24* |
| McFadden $R^2$ | 0.033 | 0.052 | 0.018 | 0.029 |
| Mean dependent var. | 0.883 | 0.883 | 0.772 | 0.772 |

Note: Values are logistic coefficients (betas). Asymptotic standard errors are reported in parentheses. Level of significance: $^{*}0.01 \leq p < 0.05$, $^{**}p < 0.01$. All models also include the dummy variables $BA, PAR_2, PAR_3$ and $PAR_4$, which are not significant at the 5% level in any model.

Table 2.15: Relative frequencies - All sensible decision patterns (larger sample)

| | | Situation 1 | | Situation 4 | |
|---|---|---|---|---|---|
| | | Females | Males | Females | Males |
| Sequence | $z$ | (n=248) | (n=411) | (n=252) | (n=410) |
| 0 0 0 0 | 5 | 0.548 | 0.521 | 0.520 | 0.546 |
| 0 0 0 1 | 4 | 0.093 | 0.046 | 0.103 | 0.085 |
| 0 0 1 1 | 3 | 0.169 | 0.158 | 0.095 | 0.066 |
| 0 1 1 1 | 2 | 0.129 | 0.151 | 0.095 | 0.066 |
| 1 1 1 1 | 1 | 0.060 | 0.124 | 0.187 | 0.237 |

Note: A choice of alternative x is coded as 0, a decision in favour of y is coded as 1. The variable $z$ represents the corresponding sequence in the ordered logit model.

Table 2.16: Multinomial logit estimates (larger sample)

| Situation | Model | Variables | Sequence 1111 | | Sequence 0111 | | Sequence 0011 | | Sequence 0001 | |
|---|---|---|---|---|---|---|---|---|---|---|
| Sit. 1: | Single effects: (n=659) | $AGE_c$ | −0.069 | (0.099) | −0.216* | (0.095) | −0.043 | (0.081) | −0.027 | (0.120) |
| | | $MALE$ | 1.105** | (0.341) | 0.763** | (0.279) | 0.174 | (0.246) | −0.652 | (0.347) |
| | | $TIME_c$ | 0.056** | (0.012) | 0.073** | (0.011) | 0.037** | (0.010) | −0.002 | (0.016) |
| | | | Log likelihood: −650.34, LR test: 92.31**, McFadden $R^2$: 0.053 | | | | | | | |
| | Interactive: (n=659) | $AGE_c$ | 0.340* | (0.167) | −0.182 | (0.154) | 0.054 | (0.123) | −0.067 | (0.163) |
| | | $MALE$ | 1.053** | (0.337) | 0.781** | (0.295) | 0.156 | (0.246) | −0.647 | (0.357) |
| | | $AGE_c{*}MALE$ | −0.532** | (0.183) | −0.057 | (0.164) | −0.144 | (0.137) | 0.090 | (0.195) |
| | | | Log likelihood: −645.69, LR test: 101.62**, McFadden $R^2$: 0.059 | | | | | | | |
| Sit. 4: | Single effects: (n=662) | $JOB$ | 0.425 | (0.258) | 0.867* | (0.402) | 0.271 | (0.400) | 0.121 | (0.362) |
| | | $MALE$ | 0.386 | (0.224) | −0.125 | (0.332) | −0.237 | (0.322) | −0.106 | (0.298) |
| | | $TIME_c$ | 0.033** | (0.009) | 0.062** | (0.014) | 0.015 | (0.014) | 0.018 | (0.013) |
| | | $PAR_2$ | 0.143 | (0.311) | 1.425* | (0.583) | 0.779 | (0.597) | −0.319 | (0.397) |
| | | $PAR_3$ | 0.140 | (0.309) | 0.877 | (0.606) | 0.947 | (0.584) | −0.498 | (0.408) |
| | | $PAR_4$ | 0.063 | (0.309) | 0.745 | (0.605) | 1.014 | (0.578) | −0.413 | (0.396) |
| | | | Log likelihood: -652.06, LR test: 56.37**, McFadden $R^2$: 0.033 | | | | | | | |

Note: Sequence 0000 is the base sequence. Values are logistic coefficients (betas). Asymptotic standard errors are given in parentheses. Level of significance: $^{*}0.01 \leq p < 0.05$, $^{**}p < 0.01$. 'Single effects' models include all variables. However, only those parameters are reported, which proved to be significant at the 5% level for at least one category. For the 'interactive' model only interacted variables are given.

### 2.7.5 Appendix E: Coding of Verbal Answers

| General category | Single arguments | Some typical comments |
|---|---|---|
| | **Situation 1** | |
| Basic needs | (1) Basic needs | "The disabled person depends on help", "it is a question of human dignity". |
| Equality | (2) Intelligent children are advantaged anyway | "Intelligent people are able to help themselves", "there is already enough help for the intelligent in our society". |
| | (3) Improving opportunities of the handicapped person | "Equalising opportunities", "help for the weaker person", "integration of disabled", "reduction of disadvantages". |
| Efficiency | (4) Higher number of benefiting people | "2 individuals are more than one person", "one single person should not blockade many others". |
| | (5) Higher utility gain for society from education | "Common welfare will be increased", "investing in the future of the country". |
| | (6) Higher marginal utility for intelligent children | "The high potential of children should be considered", "children will gain more", "help for handicapped person is useless and a waste of money". |
| Cross-effects | (7) Talented children may help the handicapped person | "Higher taxes of intelligent people may finance the care for disabled", "the intelligent can do research and, by this, help the handicapped". |
| | **Situation 2** | |
| Basic needs | (1) Basic needs | "Hunger threatens lives", "hunger is the more urgent problem". |
| Equality | (2) Environmental problems are less important | "Environment protection is luxury", "Africans can do more with the money", "there is already enough environment protection in Germany". |
| | (3) Improving opportunities for Africans | "Equalising life conditions", "Africans are least advantaged in the world", "global injustice". |

Continuation: Coding of verbal answers

| General category | Single arguments | Some typical comments |
|---|---|---|
| | **Situation 2 (continued)** | |
| Efficiency | (4) Higher marginal utility for Germany | "Aid for Africa only helps for a short time and is a drop in the ocean", "environmental programs concern our future", "more sustainable help would be necessary". |
| | (5) Success in Africa is unclear | "Success of project against hunger is uncertain, but the utility gain for Germany is certain". |
| Cross-effects | (6) Aid for Africa also helps Germany | "Help for Africa also helps us because our companies receive more orders". |
| | (7) Programs in Germany also help Africa | "Environmental problems are global problems". |
| Self-interest | (8) Self-interest | "Own problems should be solved, first", "Germany is also in a bad condition", "hunger is a global problem, which can't be solved by one country". |
| Responsibility | (9) Germans are responsible for pollution | "Pollution is caused by Germans", "polluters should carry the costs". |
| | **Situation 3** | |
| Basic needs | (1) Basic needs | "Kidney patients are in a life-threatening state, they die without help". |
| Equality | (2) Pregnant women are better off | "Pregnant women are already better off". |
| | (3) Equalising quality of life | "Kidney patients should also enjoy a reasonable quality of life". |
| Efficiency $x$ | (4) Higher utility gain for kidney patients | "Vitamins do not have any effect", "dialysis machines have a long-term benefit". |
| | (5) Substitutes | "Other sources of vitamins are available". |
| | (6) Higher number of benefiting people | "We should help the bigger group", "increasing number of important groups". |
| | (7) Higher utility gain for society from $y$ | "The benefiting groups are more important for the country". |

Continuation: Coding of verbal answers

| General category | Single arguments | Some typical comments |
|---|---|---|
| | **Situation 3 (continued)** | |
| Efficiency $x$ | (8) Higher marginal utility for women and children | "Help for children is long-lasting, kidney patients will go on suffering", "children are important, the future is theirs". |
| Cross-effects | (9) Buying vitamins can help kidney patients | "Good health leads to economic growth, which also helps kidney patients". |
| | **Situation 4** | |
| Basic rights | (1) Absolute priority to human rights | "Human rights are always most important", "human rights are necessary for a democracy", "economic recovery is valueless without freedom". |
| | (2) No new dictatorship | "People fought for these rights", "these rights have been promised to the people", "the curtailment of these rights is a new dictatorship". |
| Efficiency | (3) Higher number of benefiting people | "The welfare of more people is more important", "at some point, almost all people gain from the economic program". |
| Cross-effects | (4) Human rights bring about economic recovery | "First human rights and then economic recovery", "people are willing to work harder if they enjoy freedom". |
| | (5) Economic recovery brings about human rights | "From a secure existence human rights will follow automatically". |
| Few people advantaged | (6) Few people are better off at the expense of others | "We should not support the enrichment of few groups at the expense of other people", "the benefiting groups are already better off". |
| Uncertain time limit | (7) Time limit is uncertain | "The limitation of the curtailment is not clear enough". |
| Curtailment of rights is not severe | (8) Curtailment of human rights is limited and not severe | "The limitations are not that severe", "they are temporally limited", "the concerned rights are not important". |

# 3 Needs and Responsibility

## 3.1 Introduction

In the previously presented questionnaire study, the principles of needs and efficiency were contrasted. It was discovered that allocations in accordance with the needs principle initially dominated answers of respondents, but participants often tended to switch to the alternative solution if the benefits from supporting the better-off group were increased. In two different contexts, this trade-off was significantly affected by the gender of the impartial spectator in the way that women more often supported the hypothetically worse-off individuals and, thus, followed the needs principle over aspects of efficiency. These results are in agreement with many findings in the literature.

In the first chapter, it was also argued that the compliance with the needs principle should be interpreted as focusing on the unfortunate situation of people in need. However, our hypothetical contexts have been constructed in the way that the principles of needs and equality propose the same allocations. This structure will be used again in the present questionnaire.

The consideration of aspects of efficiency can be understood as comparing future benefits that may result from spending the available resource on either of the two alternatives offered. If benefits are unequal, the principle of efficiency demands unequal distributions. In the following chapter, we will introduce a further argument in favour of a possible deviation from the equality principle. Here, the focus is on past behaviour – or the omission of certain behaviour – of hypothetical recipients being regarded. However, the incorporation of such considerations leads to even more complex distribution problems. In fact, we are leaving now situations that Yaari and Bar Hillel (1984, p. 8) describe as "simple fixed-bundle-and-no-prior-claims" problems. These authors refer to philosophical writings and argue that differences with respect to contribution, effort or productivity could justify 'prior claims' leading to unequal allocations of the given resource.

For example, the concept of *merit* is a prominent candidate to justify departures from equality especially in income (re)distribution problems. In general, this allocation principle demands that "goods be distributed in proportion to contribution where that contribution is due to qualities or activities thought to 'deserve' reward" (Scott et al., 2001, p. 751). Advocates of the merit concept explicitly name ability, effort and performance as relevant aspects of contribution which deserves reward (see e.g. Miller, 1999, pp. 63-73). But, in particular, effort is one of the most prominent examples for regarding aspects of responsibility. Nevertheless, it has to be mentioned that some theorists question the moral relevance of merit based on effort. For example, Rawls (1971, p. 74) claims that the distribution of income should be regarded "arbitrary from a moral perspective", because it is "determined by the natural distribution of abilities and talents". Moreover, "[even] the willingness to make an effort, to try, and so to be deserving in the ordinary sense is itself dependent upon [...] social circumstances".[1] However, in the next section it will be shown that Rawls introduces the concept of individual responsibility instead.

A closely related principle is the concept of *accountability* mentioned in the work of James Konow (2000, 2001, 2003). Konow (2000, p. 1075) defines accountability in the way that "the entitlement varies in direct proportion to the value of the subject's relevant discretionary variables, ignoring other variables, but does not hold a subject accountable for the differences in the values of exogenous variables". In this version, Konow explicitly integrates his principle into a production context. Consequently, he defines 'discretionary variables' as those influencing factors on the production process that can be manipulated by the individual, whereas 'exogenous variables' also influence the output but cannot be influenced by the individual. In other cases, Konow (2001, 2003) applies this principle to a larger number of contexts.

In the literature on theories of distributive justice, several of these aspects are covered by the notion of *responsibility*. More precisely the term 'responsibility' is regularly employed to denote a more general idea that underlies other concepts such as effort or merit. Hence, a clear definition of what is meant by 'responsibility' is necessary. However, in the theoretical literature on theories of distributive justice two major questions have to be answered by a theoretical concept that aims at incorporating aspects of responsibility. Firstly, a theory has to distinguish between compensation- and responsibility-variables. While the first group summarises individual characteristics for which people should be compensated, the second set of variables comprises attributes for which individuals are to be held responsible. This partitioning of individual characteristics is known as defining the *responsibility cut* (see e.g. Schokkaert and Devooght, 2003). Nevertheless, secondly, even if such a distinction is available, one still has to decide on the concrete allocation procedure that takes this information into account. In section 3.2, some relevant theories will be reviewed. However, note that this overview can only offer a small glimpse at some very deeply rooted philosophical approaches. On various occasions reference will be given to more complete presentations of general ideas and possible extensions.

Afterwards, in section 3.3, several empirical investigations on the influence of aspects of responsibility are reviewed. Moreover, the links to the previously explained theoretical concepts are described. Nevertheless, only few studies

1 Similar ideas are stated, for example, by Nozick (1974) and Hayek (1976).

combine the needs principle with responsibility considerations. But these studies are most important for our investigation, which intends to empirically analyse the allocation consequences of the fact that individuals are supposed to be responsible for the existence of their unsatisfied basic needs.

The two relevant situations in this chapter are presented and discussed in section 3.4. They are extensions of the contexts described in the preceding questionnaire study so that actually the influence of aspects of responsibility on the trade-off between the principles of needs or equality and the principle of efficiency is regarded. Thus, we are considering a more complex situation: The needs principle is simultaneously confronted with the principles of efficiency and responsibility. Therefore, the influence of aspects of responsibility can be interpreted as moderating the needs-efficiency trade-off. Apparently, the present study can only make a small contribution to the questions described. Nevertheless, theoretical interpretations of possible outcomes will show the relevance of this work.

The sample structure will be presented in some detail in section 3.5. Again, some socio-demographic characteristics of respondents are available. Also, sample reductions are necessary. It will become apparent that the consequences of these reductions will be much stronger than before. In section 3.6, the previously introduced statistical tools are applied to shed some more light on the influence of aspects of responsibility. As before, an important additional question concerns the existence of gender differences. The seventh section presents the conclusions.

## 3.2 Responsibility in Theories of Justice

Inspired by various empirical investigations, sociologists and social psychologists have long since been aware that responsibility concerns, and related concepts, are independent allocation ideas that justify departures from the equality principle. In contrast, theoretical approaches in the realm of economics have ignored such aspects until recently and focused instead on efficiency arguments as the main contestant for egalitarian solutions. However, especially since the writings of Dworkin (1981a, 1981b) and his explicit focus on responsibility, economists have also begun to identify this aspect as another major allocation principle. Earlier contributions came from Rawls (1971), who emphasised individual responsibility for preferences after the distribution of rights and resources, and Sen (1980), who instead regarded functionings and the still open question of "Equality of what?". Here, it is important to note that Rawls formulated his concept of individual responsibility as an explicit egalitarian objection to classical utilitarianism. Before this change of view, egalitarian ideas were formulated in terms of welfare and demanded the equalisation of individual levels. Modern theoretical concepts are usually summarised as responsibility-sensitive egalitarianism (see Fleurbaey, 2008, for an overview). In subsection 3.2.2 we will describe some helpful definitions to distinguish theoretical approaches and briefly review some of the main concepts in subsection 3.2.3. However, before that a completely different approach will be presented, which has less often been considered in the present context. It is formulated in the realm of utilitarianism.

### 3.2.1 Act and Rule Utilitarianism

One proposal to extend the principle of subjective individual welfare maximisation comes from Harsanyi (1977). Clearly, his suggestion of a 'critical rule utilitarianism' does not explicitly consider the incorporation of aspects of responsibility, but regards the more general question of how to assess the moral value of individual actions. His argument is based on the insight that the maximisation of the sum of individual utilities does not necessarily coincide with the welfare of society. In order to clarify this claim, Harsanyi distinguishes between 'act utilitarianism' and 'rule utilitarianism'. The former criterion of moral value focuses on individual acts and is evaluated by individual utility. Consequently, each individual action will be regarded as 'morally right' if it maximises the value of the individual 'consequences' of this particular act. But this *act utilitarianism* may have undesired consequences. Harsanyi uses the example of a person who has borrowed some money and signed a contract about the repayment. The lender is supposed to be much richer than the borrower. Thus, it could be possible that marginal utility from the amount of money regarded is higher for the poorer individual compared to the richer one. But then, repaying the debt would decrease the value of the sum of individual utilities which is 'morally wrong' from the view of act utilitarianism. Hence, the question arises as to why complying with contractual obligations in such a way is usually judged as socially desirable.

Harsanyi argues that individual behaviour should not only be evaluated in a particular situation but from a societal point of view. Hence, those general moral rules have to be accepted that best serve social interest. They should be identified by determining the value of the overall 'consequences' if a particular rule is followed by all members of society. Since this view concentrates on alternative rules instead of alternative individual actions, it is called *rule utilitarianism*. In Harsanyi's example, it can be supposed that society is better off if debts are always repaid, because this has positive effects on expectations of and incentives for members of the society. Following this line of argument, individual actions cannot be freely chosen in order to maximise the sum of individual utilities following from this situation, but are constrained not to violate existing social obligations towards other people. Harsanyi points out that this approach follows the utilitarian tradition, but uses social utility to evaluate different moral rules instead of individual actions.

Finally, the author proposes to correct consequences of "antisocial attitudes" (p. 64).[2] If we transfer this idea to situations involving aspects of responsibility, similar lines of reasoning are possible, although they are not explicitly mentioned by Harsanyi. Indeed, in various of the empirical studies summarised in section 3.3, the case is made that respondents want to punish misbehaviour that has led to the present existence of unsatisfied basic needs. The authors often reason that either the worse-off individuals or other members of society should *learn* from this punishment. Furthermore, participants want to see that they live in a society where 'antisocial' behaviour has negative consequences. We will come back to this argumentation in due course. However, at least the last argument may also point towards an opposite motive. It is plausible that individuals want to be sure that they live in a society where people in need receive help independently from the causes of their miserable situation.

### 3.2.2 The Concept of Responsibility and Two Principles

Since the first theoretical works on individual responsibility by Rawls (1971) and Sen (1980), political philosophy and economic theory have witnessed an impressive evolution of different concepts over time. It has already been noted in the introduction of this section that responsibility is a difficult notion. Therefore, in a series of papers Bossert (1995), Bossert and Fleurbaey (1996) and Fleurbaey (1995a, 1995b, 1998) propose some characteristics to organise different arguments especially in the vastly growing literature on responsibility-sensitive egalitarianism, on which we will focus. Firstly, in order to define the location of the responsibility cut they distinguish between 'responsibility by control' and 'responsibility by delegation'. Secondly, responsibility can be construed either as a 'responsibility over factors' or as a 'responsibility over outcomes'. Thirdly, two intuitions with respect to responsibility-sensitive egalitarianism can be distinguished, i.e. the 'principle of natural reward' and the 'principle of compensation'. All three distinctions are briefly introduced in this subsection, before some important theoretical approaches will be sketched in subsection 3.2.3.

The first distinction concerns the divide between responsibility- and compensation-variables. Schokkaert and Devooght (2003, p. 208) call this the "problem of locating the responsibility cut". It regards the basis, on which responsibility is attributed. Here, the term *variable* denotes individual characteristics or outcomes. If responsibility is assigned by *control*, the agent is supposed

2 Harsanyi proposes to 'censor' individual utility functions. He calls this view *critical rule utilitarianism* because – in contrast to rule utilitarianism – it does not stop at individual utility functions as they are. While rule utilitarianism would accept the utility functions of individuals without any qualification, critical rule utilitarianism even 'corrects' people's probably erroneous functions. However, this distinction of different terms is not important for the present work.

to be responsible for the value of the considered variable if he or she has full control over this value. Consequently, individuals are only held responsible for those variables whose values are (fully) determined by voluntary choices of the person, while all remaining variables should cause compensation. Also, Fleurbaey (2007) argues that in this case responsibility is related to 'free will' and, therefore, is subject to limits and difficulties entailed in this notion.[3]

In contrast, if responsibility is assigned by *delegation*, society should only provide "good conditions of choice" (Fleurbaey, 2007, p. 31) and let the agent choose or decide in accordance with his or her preferences. Individuals may be held responsible for variables that are not under their control, but for which they *feel* responsible. Thus, influences of undesirable factors on the framework of the decision of the actor should be neutralised, but it does not matter whether the agent actually controls the value of the variable being regarded. Hence, the choice or decision is delegated to the agent. Certainly, this concept faces the problem that the notion of 'good conditions of choice' has to be characterised and, also, that individual preferences, which serve as the main example for responsibility variables in the literature, are not always sound.

The second division is between *responsibility over factors* and *responsibility over outcomes*. According to the former concept, agents are held responsible for the value of a certain factor, which then determines the outcome. For example, a person may not be deemed responsible for his or her well-being, but for the development of some factors which influence this individual outcome. Instead, the latter notion focuses on the outcome obtained by an agent and, therefore, does not regard factors that lead to this outcome. We will see in the following paragraphs that especially Fleurbaey's (1998) idea of 'equality of selected functionings' follows this conception.

While responsibility by control is usually assigned over factors, because individuals can rarely entirely determine the outcome, responsibility by delegation could be given either over factors or over outcomes.

Based on these first two distinctions, a classification of variables is possible. They can either justify compensation of individuals or they can have the effect that people are held responsible for the value of the factor or the outcome. In the literature the discussion about the location of this responsibility cut is not settled. Hence, we will also elaborate this question with respect to the situations presented in our questionnaire.

But even if one would agree on such a portioning proposed by a theoretical conception, it is not clear what the preferred operationalisation of responsibility-sensitive egalitarianism should be. Fleurbaey (1994, 1995a, 1995b, 1998) has demonstrated that the two following basic principles are logically independent and, therefore, conflict with each other at least to some

3 See e.g. Cohen (1989) and Devooght (2003) for a more detailed discussion on problems related to the concept of 'free will'.

extent. The principles have slightly different implications for responsibility over factors compared to responsibility over outcomes. Let us firstly regard the former case. Here, the *principle of natural reward* asks the social planner to let individuals perform their responsibility over factors and carry the consequences of such exercise. However, if agents differ only with respect to previously defined responsibility characteristics, but not with regard to corresponding compensation variables, their final outcome should reflect these differences.

In contrast, the *principle of compensation* demands equal outcomes for those individuals whose responsibility characteristics are similar.[4] Therefore, possible differences with respect to compensation variables should not prevent people from obtaining equal outcomes.

In the case of responsibility over outcomes the principle of natural reward is satisfied by the fact itself, if this outcome is not an argument for social objectives, while the principle of compensation demands equality of non-responsible outcomes.

Because the two principles cannot be fully regarded simultaneously, several different allocation rules exist at the border of this trade-off.[5] Fleurbaey (2001) argues that the principle of natural reward introduces the idea of responsibility into egalitarian theory, while the principle of compensation would even be satisfied in the case of full equality of outcomes. However, when there is a conflict between both principles, Fleurbaey recommends weakening the first notion without fully abandoning it in order to retain some responsibility-sensitivity, but this is not the only possible solution.

Now, we are prepared to compare some theoretical concepts as briefly as possible. In the present work, they are needed to explain how aspects of responsibility are modelled in our needs-responsibility trade-off.

### 3.2.3 Responsibility-sensitive Egalitarianism in a Nutshell

Before aspects of responsibility have been introduced into theories of distributive justice, equalising subjective welfare was the prevailing concept. This was challenged by the utilitarian dictum to maximise the sum of individual utility. In a way, Rawls (1971, 1982) criticises both concepts for their uncritical acceptance of individual preferences. Since this may lead to counterintuitive results, he suggests to hold people responsible for these preferences. Hence, with respect to the temporal dimension he wants to consider not only future gains from different alternatives but also past behaviour. In order to clarify

4 It is important to note that this principle of compensation, which will only appear in the present chapter, should not be confused with the compensation principle that has been introduced above with respect to the principle of efficiency.

5 Summaries can be found in the work by Fleurbaey being already mentioned, but also in the contribution by Fleurbaey and Maniquet (2005).

his argument, Rawls mentions offensive preferences as one example, where the focusing on individual welfare may have a negative effect on other people. For instance, 'sadistic' preferences would demand letting other individuals suffer.

Thus, Rawls proposes that each individual should get an equal share of rights and resources. Here, the concept of primary goods serves as the corresponding equalisandum. Consequently, agents are said to be responsible for their personal goals and individual conceptions of a good life that they want to adopt based on the allotted rights and resources. Clearly, in this concept responsibility is by delegation so that differences with respect to resulting outcomes do not justify compensation. Moreover, as Fleurbaey (1998) explains, responsibility is over factors, while responsibility over outcome, which is defined as well-being in the present case, does not play a role.

Rawls's notion of individual responsibility is restricted to individual preferences and mainly intends to depart from the utilitarian tradition. The theory introduced by Dworkin (1981b) also follows this idea. Again, responsibility is by delegation so that agents are held responsible for their preferences, tastes and ambitions which they identify with. The remaining individual characteristics are regarded as internal resources, which should be equalised. Consequently, respective approaches are said to promote *equality of resources*. Furthermore, in order to distinguish between responsibility- and compensation-variables Dworkin suggests a distinction between *brute luck* and *option luck*. Here, brute luck happens to an individual who faces the effects of risk-taking behaviour that he or she neither anticipated nor could avoid. Hence, it does not result from free choices of the agent. In contrast, option luck exists if consequences follow from a voluntary choice by the individual out of conscious options. This distinction will be important in the next questionnaire study.

Based on this conception, several rather different theories have been summarised under the label of *luck egalitarianism*.[6] These theoretical concepts admit that inequalities are justified only if they result from option luck. At least with respect to the present *resourcist* point of view, this term seems to be misleading, because the equalisandum is not luck or uncertainty but resources when facing luck or uncertainty.

Furthermore, Dworkin (1981b) explains that brute luck declines if the possibility of insuring against the consequences of any kind of bad luck is introduced. In this case, the individual who abstains from such insurance agrees to enter a gamble and, therefore, faces option luck. We will come back to this idea in the next section on relevant empirical investigations.

6 See e.g. Anderson (1999) for a more general criticism of this concept and, for example, Arneson (2004) for a clear defence of the indeed quite distinct approaches. Nevertheless, this discussion is not the focal point of the present work so that it will not be considered in more detail here.

To summarise, from Dworkin's point of view agents should carry the costs for the good life they are willing to adopt so that brute luck, but not consequences of optional misfortunes, should be compensated.

Fleurbaey (1995a, 1998) explains that resourcist views regularly satisfy the principle of natural reward but often fail to fulfil the principle of compensation to a reasonable degree. He contrasts these theories of justice with the concept of *equality of opportunities.* Probably a good way to approach this second group of theories is by analysing the respectively regarded equalisandum. Concepts that ask for some kind of equality of opportunity regularly promote the equalisation of something in between individual welfare and resources. The first author who has to be mentioned here is Sen (1985, 1987) and his concept of *functionings*. "A functioning is an achievement of a person: what he or she manages to do or to be. It reflects, as it were, a part of the 'state' of that person. It has to be distinguished from the commodities which are applied to achieve those functionings.", (Sen, 1985, p. 10). And he goes on to explain that the "totality of all the alternative functioning vectors the person can choose from [...] reflects the person's capabilities, i.e., the various alternative functioning bundles he or she can achieve through choice.", (p. 27). Hence, equality of basic capabilities is requested to guarantee equal opportunities. It must be noticed that Sen's notion of equality of opportunities intends to promote positive freedom but not to punish the waste of opportunities. Therefore, one may instead call this concept 'equality of positive freedom'.[7]

Opportunity-egalitarianism has been promoted by Arneson (1989, 1990), who argues in favour of a kind of 'equality of opportunities for welfare', and by Cohen (1989, 1993). The latter author explains that the relevant equalisandum should be 'equal access to advantages'. "It is 'posterior' to 'having goods' and 'prior' to 'having utility'.", (Cohen, 1989, p. 943). In contrast to Sen's concept, these authors explicitly refer to personal responsibility. On the one hand, equal opportunities have to be assured for all agents but individuals should be held responsible for the consequences of their voluntary choices on the relevant characteristics they control. On the other hand, it is supposed to be unfair "if some are worse off through no fault or choice of their own" (Temkin, 1993, p. 13). Hence, Fleurbaey (1995a, 1998) characterises these theories as endorsing responsibility by control over factors. Finally, Roemer (1993) also promotes a concept of equality of opportunity but argues that the location of the responsibility cut is likely to be culture-dependent. This idea will reappear in the next section.

Nevertheless, there exists by now a third proposal to incorporate aspects of responsibility into egalitarian theories of distributive justice. The main representative is Fleurbaey (see especially 1995b, 1998, 2001) who demands that

7 See Fleurbaey (1995b, 1998) for a discussion of the relevance of Sen's idea for responsibility-sensitive egalitarianism.

people be held responsible by delegation over outcomes. This view, which will be explained in more detail in the next paragraph, could be derived from three possible shortcomings of equality of opportunities and the principle of natural reward. Firstly, Fleurbaey argues that concepts of responsibility over factors may be too unforgiving. Someone who once made a mistake has to carry the consequences for the rest of his or her life. Moreover, secondly, as soon as an individual is supposed to be responsible, the concept of equal opportunity legitimates all unequal outcomes no matter how disastrous they may be. But Fleurbaey (1995b, pp. 40-41) objects that "also the amount of welfare loss [that the responsible person] is about to suffer following his mistake" ought to be of relevance since it is "obviously a matter of egalitarian distributive justice that the satisfaction of basic needs should be given priority". The reader will notice that here the conflict between the principles of needs and responsibility is explicitly mentioned, while the previously presented theoretical concepts seemed to give absolute priority to the responsibility principle.[8] Therefore, this point is most important for our study. Thirdly, the distinction between option luck and brute luck is questioned by some authors. Lippert-Rasmussen (2001) states that even inequalities resulting from gambles that a subject voluntarily accepted could demand (partial) compensation, if society has a priori failed to create good conditions of choice. He explains this by an example of a person who has been brought up in a slum. Even if such a worse-off subject could be held responsible for his or her own fate because of declining certain actions that would have improved the situation, the state may have a priori influenced the level of this option luck by not preventing the existence of the slum. Similarly, Fleurbaey (2001) pronounces that it is often unclear whether risks are completely or only partially avoidable. Thus, opportunity sets should only contain clear cases of option luck. We will see that this point is important for our second context.

Based on these criticisms, Fleurbaey derives a dichotomous concept that he calls *equality of selected functionings* (Fleurbaey, 1998, p. 229). On the one hand, society should select a set of functionings, which form an index that should be equalised over individuals independently of responsibility concerns. This point is made more explicit in Fleurbaey (2008).[9] Here he argues that, no matter what, individuals who fall below a certain threshold, which comprises human rights and the status of citizen, should receive help. Hence, "there are certain basic equalities that cannot be rendered contingent by the operation of personal responsibility" (p. 267).

On the other hand, beyond these basic functionings, compensation will be suppressed without regarding the actual degree of responsibility of agents for the corresponding outcomes. Thus, we have responsibility by delegation.

---

8 In chapter 1, it has already been argued that humanitarian concerns could also justify the priority of needs. This important point will be discussed again in chapter 4.

9 See especially subsection 10.6 and the references cited therein.

While the first part of this approach is derived from the possible harshness of equality of opportunity, Fleurbaey defends the second part on the grounds of granting agents a private sphere, where they can try to realise their individual plans for a good life. This idea is closely related to Rawls's concept of individual responsibility. However, Fleurbaey (2008, p. 270) criticises this part of his idea due to problems that arise "when it comes to determining what the private sphere consists of".

Clearly, we may interpret Fleurbaey's approach in the way that the first part acknowledges the priority of the needs principle. Correspondingly, basic needs are completely regarded if the previously defined index is equalised over all individuals. If basic needs are equally fulfilled, the responsibility principle may unfold. Following the concept of 'truncated efficiency' that will be considered in the next chapter, we could call this approach 'truncated responsibility'.

Theories of responsibility-sensitive egalitarianism play a major role in today's philosophical and economic discussions. Clearly, the previous illustrations could only be a small abstract of well formulated and thoroughly stated theories. Nevertheless, they are important for the present investigation for two reasons. Firstly, statements on the location of the responsibility cut are necessary and will be considered with respect to the two situations in our questionnaire. Secondly, we create conflicts between the principles of needs and equality on the one side and efficiency and responsibility on the other side. Thus, even if the location of the responsibility cut is well-defined, various theoretical approaches propose different allocation behaviour. In the next section, empirical investigations of some aspects of theories previously described are reviewed.

## 3.3 Some Empirical Studies on Responsibility

Especially in the economic literature, the introduction of aspects of responsibility into empirical studies on distributive justice has recently gained momentum. This development may be due to new theoretical approaches that have been described in the previous section. Some of these investigations will be presented in the first subsection. Nevertheless, related questionnaire experiments in the fields of political science and social psychology have focused already on the influence of merit concerns on justice evaluations of income distribution. Some of these studies are briefly presented in the second subsection. They also allow for trade-offs between different allocation principles. In the present questionnaire, the previously investigated trade-off between the principles of needs and efficiency is supplemented by aspects of responsibility on the side of the needy individual(s). Hence, earlier studies on the aspects of responsibility and needs, but especially investigations that consider all three allocation principles are of interest.

### 3.3.1 Studies on Responsibility-sensitive Egalitarianism

In the field of empirical economics, a growing literature regards the acceptance of some previously described theoretical concepts. The first study to be mentioned is the survey of Yaari and Bar-Hillel (1984). Although they do not relate any of their results to responsibility concerns, Fleurbaey and Maniquet (2005) reinterpret distributions proposed by respondents. If differences in utility functions were said to result from metabolic dissimilarities, chosen allocations were in line with the principle of compensation, whereas differences due to tastes provoked distributions that can be explained by the principle of natural reward.

In contrast, Clément and Serra (2001) explicitly focused on the influence of responsibility- and compensation-variables. In the context of dental health expenditures, effort (dental care) and talent (socio-demographic characteristics which are thought to have an effect on dental health) were both said to have an influence on costs and were systematically varied. Participants were familiarised with the principle of compensation and the equality principle, which means equal consideration of individual costs by the health authorities in the given contexts. The authors found that 26 out of their 39 participants regarded aspects of responsibility.

Furthermore, Boarini et al. (2006) investigated aspects of responsibility in several contexts including health expenditures. These were inspired by Dworkin's (1981b) insurance idea mentioned in the previous section. A majority of subjects opted for higher health insurance premiums if agents were said to be chain-smokers (75% of the respondents selected a higher amount) or regularly participate in dangerous sports (50%). The latter finding is of importance for our first context in the present study.

In a more sophisticated study, Schokkaert and Devooght (2003) presented hypothetical situations in a health expenditure context and also in an income distribution setting. They started by investigating the location of the responsibility cut and presented several two-person cases, where claimants differed with respect to one respective characteristic. The authors found that among their students from Belgium, Burkina Faso and Indonesia the delegation approach, but more often the control approach was followed. Nevertheless, neither among the different countries nor among participants from the same location was there general consensus. At the same time, with regard to the previously mentioned idea by Roemer (1993), they found minor cultural differences in locating the responsibility cut. Afterwards, respondents faced four-person situations that were intended to create conflicts between the principle of natural reward and the principle of compensation. In the health context, most students wanted to see an 'intermediate compensation', while in the income distribution case some support for 'countercompensation', where the punishment exceeded the negative consequences, became visible. Schokkaert and Devooght argued that they probably witnessed adjustments of both principles. Additionally, incentive considerations may have played a role at least in the income context.

In an experimental study, Cappelen, Sørensen and Tungodden (2006) combined a dictator game with a previous production phase to get further insights into the influence of effort and talent on income distributions. Interestingly, they found that respondents regularly held others responsible for differences with respect to productivity. The authors conclude that the responsibility cut is not between "choices and circumstances but between impersonal and personal factors" and, thus, question the "choice egalitarian view" (p. 18).

Moreover, Faravelli (2007) utilised contexts inspired by the study of Yaari and Bar-Hillel (1984) to investigate the responsibility cut. Here, differences in individual productivity were either due to different efforts or resulted from the fact that one hypothetical person was supposed to be handicapped. In the first case, respondents more often chose a utilitarian solution while in the second case the maximin principle gained most support. This setting is already very close to our study, but the principle of needs is replaced by the principle of equality in Faravelli's case.

To summarise this first review, some studies confirm the importance of individual control over relevant variables, while the investigation by Cappelen, Sørensen and Tungodden (2006) shows that this is not always the case. Moreover, the findings by Schokkaert and Devooght (2003) question the clear-cut distinction between the principle of natural reward and the principle of compensation suggested by Fleurbaey.

### 3.3.2 Merit in Macro-justice Contexts

Let us turn now to some studies on income redistribution that consider trade-offs between several allocation principles. Hence, at the moment we will focus only on the influence of merit concerns on the acceptance of the needs principle when this is contrasted with the efficiency principle, because this structure comes closest to the setting of the situations in our questionnaire. As already explained in the introduction of this chapter, merit is usually said to be determined by ability, effort and performance (see e.g. Miller, 1999). In all experiments being regarded participants had to evaluate different proposals for income distributions of a hypothetical society. The income vectors presented were systematically varied with respect to both average income, so that efficiency was modified, and the variance, which then operationalised the equality principle. Furthermore, poverty lines had been introduced to control for the needs principle. Finally, the classical merit definition was incorporated by changing the share of income, which was said to be determined by work effort and abilities of each individual in the hypothetical society.

The first study from the field of social psychology to be mentioned comes from Mitchell et al. (1993). They conclude that "subjects have a deep aversion to allowing people to fall below the poverty line [...] even if people at the bottom 'deserve' it because they are not working hard" (p. 636). Interestingly, the authors also speculate about possible reasons for their observation. Firstly, one motive could be that respondents may have feared falling into the lowest class in the future even if only hypothetical situations were regarded. Secondly, people may have wanted to minimise envy and hostility of the poor. This reason fits in some way to Harsanyi's (1977) argument of a rule utilitarianism, where future societal welfare plays a role. Thirdly, subjects may have found it emotionally rewarding to help the poor. Probably, they wanted to know that they live in a society where people in need receive help without regarding the causes for their needs. Finally, in the case of the highest degree of responsibility, 90% of each income level was said to be generated by effort and ability. But, nevertheless, this could have been interpreted in the way that still 10% are 'undeserving poor'.

With regard to the study of Mitchell et al., some shortcomings have been pointed out in the literature (see e.g. Scott et al., 2001). For example, equality and needs considerations have not been separated. The former principle was measured in absolute rather than in proportional terms so that at least below the poverty line both principles lead to similar recommendations. Furthermore, the minimum income level has not been varied systematically. At least this last point has been reconsidered by two of the authors (Ordóñez and Mellers, 1993). They conclude that there also exists a trade-off between the principles of needs and merit.

Two studies by four authors in the field of political science, viz. Scott et al. (2001) and Michelbach et al. (2003), took up the methodological approach of the two investigations just described. Besides a similar operationalisation of the principle of efficiency, they also varied the degree to which income is explained by effort and ability instead of luck. Moreover, equality was measured in proportional terms and the absolute poverty line was varied systematically and independently from equality concerns. The authors report that both the equality-efficiency trade-off and the sensitivity to needs were mediated by merit assumptions. Additionally, as already mentioned in the previous chapter, they observed gender differences. Interestingly, "men are still concerned with merit [...] even with poverty an explicit issue, whereas women are instead affected by [...] need" (Michelbach et al., p. 536). We will come back to this important gender aspect in the next section.

The macro-justice experiments presented in this subsection confirmed that support of lower income classes often declines if income is increasingly explained by effort and ability. Most importantly, this general observation even concerns people below the poverty line. They are then labeled 'deserving poor'.

### 3.3.3 Responsibility and Needs in Micro-justice Contexts

In the following subsection, we will report results from those micro-justice studies, which combine aspects of responsibility and needs. In this sense, they are very close to the setting of the situations in the present questionnaire and, therefore, will be described in some more detail.

To begin with, it should be pointed out that there exists a well-settled theory in the field of social psychology to explain reactions to aspects of responsibility. The so-called *attribution theory* has been initiated by Heider (1958) and tries to explain how people react to causal attributions of responsibility. According to this approach, individuals try to infer the causes of good or bad outcomes and hold agents responsible for them. Also, it is important for them to know to what extent this agent has influenced the outcome. Applying this more general concept to the present question of effects of responsibility, it follows that those contributions, for which responsibility is attributed to an individual, determine the reward. This concept seems to fit to the idea of responsibility by control, but one should keep in mind that the focus of attribution theory is on the behaviour of the person who evaluates the hypothetical context. Thus, it basically allows for the explanation of possible heterogeneities of individual preferences. The next two studies explicitly use this concept, and also Konow's (2001) principle of accountability originates from this theory.

In the first of the two papers to be considered from social psychology, Skitka and Tetlock (1992) propose a complex contingency model of distributive justice. They identify abstract distributive norms, attributes of both claimants and allocators, and resource constraints as important determinants for individual distribution decisions. In the first experiment reported in the article by Skitka and Tetlock all potential receivers of a scarce resource had unsatisfied basic needs, being it either for an organ, for a drug to treat the symptoms of 'Acquired Immune Deficiency Syndrome' (AIDS), or for housing for poor. In a first step, different allocation principles had to be ranked by participants. Then, causes for the needs described were varied and respondents had to state their feelings about the different situations. Afterwards, the limited resource had to be allocated among claimants who differed with respect to the cause and the urgency of their needs and with regard to the benefits of the possible help. Also, the number of available organs, drugs or houses was modified to analyse the effect of scarcity. Most importantly for the present study, the authors found that internal controllable causes of needs provoked most distaste and least sympathy. Moreover, needs and efficiency were the most prominent allocation values unless hypothetical individuals had internal control over the causes. This result is in accordance with the principle of natural reward and also holds for claimants with most severe needs. The authors speculate that under the assumption of scarcity the support for careless recipients may not be efficient since resources could be wasted by them in the future again.

Hence, from a social point of view, incentives for careful behaviour should be given. In a way, the idea that underlies Harsanyi's (1977) rule utilitarianism reappears.

However, it has to be noted that, in contrast to our study, all claimants were supposed to be in need for the scarce resource so that the impartial spectator was asked to decide on the applied allocation rule that selects the most deserving individuals.

Finally, in a modified questionnaire study reported by Skitka and Tetlock (1992) there were enough resources to fulfil all basic needs. Somewhat surprisingly, 23 out of 37 respondents denied giving the resource to some individuals in at least one out of three contexts. According to the authors this showed the strength of the responsibility principle.

The study by Farwell and Weiner (1996) considered a rather different question. The authors intended to investigate self-perceptions of own fairness in relation to other people in six distinct contexts. They identified three different allocation principles, viz. equality, proportional equity and needs, but argued that perceptions of aspects of responsibility are also regularly included in justice evaluations. Their Situation 6 especially regarded people in need. Respondents were asked to imagine a situation where they, but also other individuals, had to allocate monetary assistance to different subjects, all of them having acquired AIDS. Among other characteristics, possible hypothetical recipients differed with respect to the causes of their illness, being it promiscuous heterosexual sex (the responsibility case) or a blood transfusion (the no-responsibility case). Participants gave less money to those individuals who were supposed to be responsible for their fate, and expected this lower payment also from other respondents. Thus, Farwell and Weiner conclude that "studies are needed to determine the conditions under which responsibility is not used as input into equity evaluation" (p. 879). As before, all claimants were in need of the allocated resources. This was also the case in the next study, which is even closer to our questionnaire design.

Demuijnck and Le Clainche (2007) explicitly focused on the role of handicapped people in theoretical and empirical work on distributive justice. Although disabilities are regularly used as an example to explain undeserved inequalities, the authors also regarded a case which they classified as reflecting luck egalitarianism. Remember that here, the distinction between brute luck and option luck determines the location of the responsibility cut. In the third scenario presented in the study, Roemer's (1993) idea of a culture-dependent responsibility line was additionally taken up. Students from France and Cameroon faced a hypothetical situation, in which they had to allocate a limited amount of money between four individuals all of them suffering from the same handicap of having only one leg. But the causes for this disability differed and ranged from an injury in a car accident caused by someone else to a shot in the leg of a robber by the police during a hold-up. The results show that 50.6% of the French respondents and 22.1% of the students from Cameroon completely ignored risk-taking behaviour and opted for equal split. Only very few wanted to punish strictly. Instead, in France 25.9% and in Cameroon 36.0% of the subjects distinguished between different degrees of responsibility and also gave a basic amount of money to each person. The authors conclude that luck egalitarianism was not supported in this situation.

The last investigation to be presented comes closest to one of our situations in the present questionnaire but also to the survey introduced in chapter 4. In Konow's (2001) Question 6, a case was described where respondents should distribute money between two projects in a hypothetical country. The first project intended to prevent starvation of people in one part of the country, while the competing project in another area concerned an agricultural program that would permanently raise people from a subsistence level to a moderate standard of living. In a different version, Konow changed the amount that was needed to prevent starvation from 50% to 80% and 100% and, thus, created a needs-efficiency trade-off.[10] Moreover, in the initial 50%-case the malnutrition was either due to a drought or caused by the inhabitants who sold too much of their crops to buy radios or televisions. Although one may argue that access to radio and television also reflects basic needs, or that the worse-off people could not foresee the future need for crops, the case being considered seems to have established a trade-off between the principle of needs on the one hand and the principles of efficiency and responsibility on the other hand. Thus, aspects of responsibility are introduced by describing 'careless behaviour' instead of option luck.[11]

In telephone interviews, respondents faced only one out of the four different versions of this situation. Results reveal some significant differences and, therefore, confirm the trade-offs mentioned. In the initial case, 89% of the subjects were willing to completely regard basic needs (the average share of the total amount was 53.4%). However, this proportion dramatically decreased to 19% when the entire amount was necessary to prevent starvation. In the responsibility version, 75% of the participants wanted to fully consider basic needs (the average payment was 46.3% of the total amount). Although this change was statistically significant, the great majority of subjects still supported the people in need.

Since these results are very important for the present and the successive study, some difficulties of the underlying structure should be discussed. Firstly, basic needs are already fulfilled if the worse offs receive 50% of the available resource. However, this 'equal split' solution is a focal point in many distribution problems so that it could be too 'easy' for respondents to fully regard all basic needs. This may even be the case if aspects of responsibility are incorporated. Secondly, it remains unclear in the questionnaire what will happen

10 It should be noted that in our cases the benefits rather than the needs level are varied.

11 Note that Konow uses the expression 'accountability principle' instead of 'responsibility principle'.

if the worse-off group receives either more or less than 50% of the available amount of the resource. From the corresponding mean amounts it can be deduced that at least in the no-responsibility version some respondents paid more than half of the available money to the worse offs. Did they perhaps expect to equalise the living conditions in both parts of the country *beyond* basic needs? This possibility is a very important idea. In fact, the third questionnaire study in the present work also focuses on this solution. Thirdly, unfortunately, Konow did not use the responsibility version with respect to the needs modifications so that the influence on the needs-efficiency trade-off is not clear. However, as already explained in the introduction, this is exactly what we are going to do in the present study. Finally, in Konow's question it is not stated how many individuals live in each part of the country and, therefore, it remains unclear how many people are affected by each measure. However, Gyrd-Hansen (2004) argues that distributive decisions may be influenced by information about the relative proportion of a group that could be helped with a given amount of money.

To summarise this subsection, in income distribution problems aspects of merit seem to play a role even if as a consequence members of low income classes fall below the poverty line. This macro-justice result could be confirmed by most of the reviewed investigations on micro-justice contexts. In two studies from the field of social psychology, but also in the considered situation from Konow (2001), aspects of responsibility were found to have a significant influence even if unsatisfied basic needs are regarded. However, in the first two studies *all* claimants suffered badly. Moreover, Demuijnck and Le Clainche (2007) could not reveal strong effects of the fact that disabled people were supposed to be responsible for their fate.

Thus, overall the empirical evidence on influences from aspects of responsibility on the fulfilment of basic needs is not very clear. Therefore, the present study aims to contribute to these still completely open questions.

## 3.4 The Questionnaire

In this section, the questionnaire versions will be introduced in some more detail. With regard to several previously presented empirical investigations, but especially with respect to the more sophisticated theoretical concepts, this investigation is less ambitious. Instead, similarly to studies by Clément and Serra (2001), Konow (2001), Demuijnck and Le Clainche (2007) and Faravelli (2007), or to the first part of the survey by Schokkaert and Devooght (2003), we basically consider opinions on the location of the responsibility cut. Nevertheless, the following situations will allow us to get some insights into the trade-off between the principles of needs and responsibility. Moreover, this will be done by investigating the influence of aspects of responsibility on the needs-efficiency trade-off. This is especially important since earlier micro-justice studies either considered cases where all claimants had unsatisfied basic needs or did not systematically vary the benefits from supporting the better-off group.

In the first subsection, the characteristics and intentions of the questionnaire modifications are discussed. Afterwards, relevant theoretical ideas are related to our settings. Finally, expectations about possible gender differences will be formulated.

### 3.4.1 Two Questionnaire Versions

As already explained in the previous sections, the questionnaires included modifications of two situations of the first study presented in the second chapter. In contrast to several other examinations, and also to the investigation presented in the following chapter, either-or decisions are regarded. The earlier descriptions of the contexts are now supplemented by information about the causes for the disastrous situations of the worse-off (group of) individual(s). Here, in the no-responsibility version of the questionnaire it is suggested that these worse offs are clearly not responsible for their fate, whereas in the responsibility case the reasons for their miserable situations originate from their risk-taking behaviour. Similar to the first study, the better-off group is successively enlarged in order to vary the benefits of the corresponding alternative.

The previously indicated modifications of the original questionnaire concerned situations 1 and 2.[12] Remember that in situation 1 respondents could either help a handicapped person or finance the education of an increasing number of intelligent children. In situation 2, either starving people in Africa or environmental programs in the home country of the respondent should be supported. Now, additional information on the causes for the distressed situation of the worse offs is given. In the no-responsibility version of situation 1, it was said that the retarded person is severely handicapped from birth. Hence, we described a context that is, according to Demuijnck and Le Clainche (2007), one of the most often used examples to declare that a person is not responsible for his or her unfortunate situation. Correspondingly, in the second context, the starvation of the Africans was said to be caused by a drought. Therefore, this case is very similar to the no-responsibility version of Konow's (2001) Question 6.

The risk-taking behaviour in the responsibility version was introduced in the first context by stating that the handicap was due to an accident from participating in a dangerous sport. This example is regularly given by theorists to explain the idea of voluntary choices in the concept of equality of

---

12 While the third situation has not been revised at all, pre-tests revealed that in the more complex situation 4 various relevant factors and motives simultaneously effected the decisions so that the influence from responsibility considerations could not be isolated.

opportunity.[13] Hence, we also follow an argument that has been stated in chapter 1. Theorists often use specific examples from which they derive their conclusions. However, they may be biased. Moreover, Boarini et al. (2006) report that 50% of participants in their survey opted for a higher health insurance premium if a person regularly participated in some dangerous sport. In the second situation, we said that the African economies being considered were widely damaged by failing experiments with self-bred grain. Again, it can be assumed that the countries were well aware of the risk they faced due to their experiments.

Nevertheless, while the no-responsibility versions seem to be unproblematic, the reader may have already observed some important differences between the two risk-taking behaviours being described. For example, it could be the case that the Africans had no choice but to take the risk if they wanted to improve their, probably, poor living conditions. In contrast, it can be assumed that the sportsperson was free to renounce the risk. Of course, as explained in section 3.2, the notion of 'free will' may also enclose various difficulties. Closely related to this concern is the fact that the starting point with respect to the welfare level before the risk-taking behaviour differed between the two responsible parties. The same argument may also hold for the two versions of situation 1. In contrast to the sportsperson in the responsibility version, the disabled individual in the no-responsibility case has never experienced a different life. This difference could to some degree explain higher support for alternative $x$ in the responsibility version.

Moreover, in the first situation the aspect of responsibility was formulated in a personalised way, whereas in the second context a kind of large-scale responsibility was considered.

### 3.4.2 Predictions from the Literature

As previously explained, the present questionnaire study may give insights into the trade-off between the principles of needs and responsibility. This will be done by incorporating the latter principle into the needs-efficiency trade-off investigated in chapter 2. Indeed, different theoretical concepts predict diverse outcomes in the given allocation problems. Let us regard the principle of responsibility first. Since the questionnaire situations describe different types of risk-taking behaviour that lead to the disastrous situation of some individuals, the difference between option luck and brute luck is the focal point of the investigation. Hence, with respect to this distinction our study is similar to the investigation by Demuijnck and Le Clainche (2007) described above on luck egalitarianism. Option luck exists if negative consequences follow from a conscious acceptance of a risk that an agent could have declined.

13 See e.g. Williams and Cookson (2000) for using this particular case with regard to the work of Arneson (1989) and Cohen (1989).

In contrast, brute luck happens to a person who faces negative consequences of risk-taking behaviour that he or she could not reasonably avoid. The reader will remember that the concepts of equality of resources or equality of opportunity regularly attribute responsibility to the first but not to the second type of luck.

However, there are some important differences between the two contexts in our questionnaire. In the first situation, where the handicap is said to be due to an accident from participating in a dangerous sport, the introduced aspect of responsibility is likely to be interpreted as a clear case of option luck. In contrast, as explained in the previous subsection, the voluntariness of the risk-taking behaviour in the second context may be questioned. Recall the objection by Lippert-Rasmussen (2001) against the concept of optional luck. He states that society may have failed to create good conditions of choice which are necessary to hold a person responsible for his or her behaviour. Following this line of argument, one may state that in our situation 2 the degree of option luck on the side of the Africans is reduced by the fact that outside institutions, like Western countries, could have prevented the need for such experiments described. Hence, it is possible that respondents want to compensate the worse offs in both version of the second context.

Furthermore, the fact that responsibility is at large in situation 2 introduces an aspect that can be described as 'diffusion of responsibility'. For example, Forsé and Parodi (2006, p. 3) ask with respect to the concept of merit: "Is it judged on strictly individual basis, or does the fact of belonging to a community come into play in one way or another?". Thus, overall, option luck is more likely to exist in the first context. But if the risk-taking behaviour is acknowledged in a situation, theoretical concepts that are based on responsibility by control predict differences between answers in the responsibility and the no-responsibility questionnaire version.

Nevertheless, in the present study the principle of responsibility is opposed to the needs principle. This has already been an important aspect in one theoretical conception presented in section 3.2. While theories which are based either on equality of resources or on equality of opportunity do not consider needs as a special case, Fleurbaey's idea of equality of selected functionings can certainly be interpreted as considering basic needs. Fleurbaey wants to prevent possibly enormous welfare losses and argues that there must be a certain index of previously identified functionings, which should be equalised by society without regarding any aspect of responsibility. Thus, in our basic needs contexts the worse-off individuals should always receive support no matter whether they are responsible for their fate or not. Therefore, it is also possible that the aspects of responsibility introduced in our questionnaire situations do not display any significant influence on decisions.

But now, the needs principle is contrasted with the principles of efficiency and responsibility, which both suggest helping the better offs. The results of the preceding chapter have already shown that the efficiency principle may be of relevance. Clearly, aspects of efficiency may play a role in both the responsibility and the no-responsibility version. Unfortunately, the structure of our questionnaire situations does not allow for a clear distinction of responsibility and efficiency considerations. Nevertheless, we may be able to investigate the influence of aspects of responsibility on the trade-off between the principles of needs and efficiency. We have already reported above that in income distribution studies a compensation of 'deserving poor' is often denied. Furthermore, merit aspects are regularly found to mediate different trade-offs. Thus, it is interesting to investigate effects of responsibility considerations in a different setting.

Additionally, as already argued in the previous section, Harsanyi's (1977) idea of rule utilitarianism that proposes evaluating behaviour from a societal viewpoint may play a role. If risk-taking behaviour is judged to be 'antisocial' because it inflicts costs on society, then misbehaving individuals may be punished by our respondents.

However, Harsanyi's argument could also be used in favour of the needs principle. Here, all individuals may benefit from the assurance that they live in a society where people in need are always helped. In this case, participants of our study may support the worse offs despite aspects of responsibility.

Especially in our second context, a related line of argument could lead to a stronger support for the Africans if their miserable situation results from experiments with self-bred grain. Respondents may want to honour this risk-taking behaviour, because they judge it as socially valuable in the sense that it could serve as a 'shining example' for other poor countries to actively try to improve their situation even if this includes the possibility of failure. Clearly, in this case the Africans are held to be the more deserving group.

To conclude this section, we will have a very brief look at possible gender differences with respect to responsibility considerations, while the reader may reconsider the literature review in the second chapter for a more detailed description of possible differences between female and male justice evaluations.

As already mentioned in the previous section, Michelbach et al. (2003) report that in their experiments the influence of merit on the equality-efficiency trade-off differed between both sexes. While at some point women were more in favour of the needs principle, men were always willing to consider aspects of merit. This result corresponds to findings by Eckel and Grossman (1996). They showed that women punished more often, but only if costs for the punishment were low. Also, Dickinson and Tiefenthaler (2002) state that aspects of merit, measured by results in a short test, more often influenced men than women. These findings, but also the previously revealed stronger female support of needs arguments instead of efficiency considerations, would suggest that females more often choose alternative $x$ in the present study.

However, an opposite observation is also possible. The literature review by Croson and Gneezy (2008) shows that in many contexts women are more risk-averse than men. Also, Eckel and Grossman (2000) concluded that risk attitudes are often relevant for gender disparities. Moreover, Croson and Buchan (1999) examined gender differences in a 'trust game' and found that women displayed more reciprocity than men. Therefore, females may be willing to punish both risk-taking behaviour and the infliction of costs on society more frequently compared to men.

Certainly, our study does not enable us to derive deeper insights into reasons for gender differences. Nevertheless, we may contribute to the question whether there are some gender-specific allocation principles.

## 3.5 The Sample

In the following section, the design and administration of the questionnaire study is described. Afterwards, the development of the final samples is illustrated in some more detail.

### 3.5.1 Questionnaire Implementation

In section 3.4, it has been illustrated that there exists a no-responsibility and a responsibility version of each situation. However, each respondent received the same type of both contexts. Hence, there was matching of the two different versions in each single questionnaire sheet. Such a structure was chosen to avoid a too obvious emphasis on the responsibility matter. This could have resulted if participants tried to figure out similarities and dissimilarities between the two given contexts.

Basically, the same survey procedures as in the first questionnaire investigation have been followed in the present study. Nevertheless, some essential differences have to be explained since they are also important for the description and interpretation of results. Most of them are due to a modified data base.

Similar to our preceding survey, the questionnaire sheets were completed by undergraduate students at the Department of Economics at the Universität Osnabrück. While situation 1 was administered in the years 2002 and 2003, situation 2 was only used in 2003. However, inspired by some earlier findings from the first questionnaire, which are reported in Gaertner, Jungeilges and Neck (2001), Gaertner and Jungeilges (2002) and Gaertner and Schwettmann (2005), the number of respondents was clearly expanded by including students from other countries. More precisely, undergraduate students from economics departments at the Universitat Autónoma de Barcelona and at the Katholieke Universiteit Leuven also completed the questionnaires in the year 2005.

Indeed, some differences between the implementations of the study in the three countries were unavoidable. Firstly, it is important to notice that all participants faced situations written in their mother tongue. This was done to prevent misunderstandings of given contexts, which may bias results concerning local effects. An English version of the questionnaire was translated into Catalan and Dutch, respectively. Certainly, some information has been adjusted to the specific context of a country. For example, in Barcelona in situation 2 'North Sea' was replaced by 'Mediterranean Sea' and the 'Federal Reserve' by the 'Federal Government', since the Spanish Central Bank is not allowed to make any profits.

Secondly, as before, respondents were asked to give verbal explanations for their decisions. Moreover, participants should state whether they would ever be willing to switch to option $y$. However, only answers of German students are analysed in the present text.

Thirdly, although all students attended courses at economics or business administration departments, a clear distinction between these two fields of study was impossible in Barcelona and Leuven, where different programs of studies contained elements of both fields. Nevertheless, in the previous investigation we could not detect any significant influence from the courses the students were enrolled in. Thus, in the following analyses, the corresponding information is not considered. Furthermore, it is completely uncommon for students in Leuven to receive work experience before starting their university careers. Because such a question would have been odd to them, it has been omitted in the Belgian questionnaire and, therefore, is also not incorporated into the following investigations.

Fourthly, similar to the first study students in Osnabrück were asked to complete the questionnaires during tutorials. However, in Barcelona and Leuven subjects completed the sheets during lecture time and were advised by a lecturer, although each of these groups was also rather small.

Finally, in all countries the present study was accompanied by further questions of the same or another investigation. In Osnabrück, in 2002, a third questionnaire version contained the four situations presented in the previous chapter. Moreover, the current questionnaire also included a modification of situation 4 with respect to responsibility considerations. This additional context was also presented in Osnabrück in 2003 and in Barcelona. However, the modification of aspects of responsibility was not properly formulated, as could be detected from written comments. Hence, this third context is not described here. Most likely, it did not have any influence on the other two situations, because it was placed after the first two contexts. In Leuven, a second, completely different study on the 'claims problem' was simultaneously performed. Results can be found in Bosmans and Schokkaert (2009). Both questionnaire types were distributed in alternating order to control for ordering effects. However, such effects could not be detected in any of the statistical investigations.

All differences concerning the implementation of the study at the three universities should be kept in mind when place effects are observed. However, we do not expect that the illustrated disparities have major influences on possible local differences.

### 3.5.2 Individual Characteristics and Sample Reductions

In Osnabrück 198 students in the year 2002 and 282 subjects in the year 2003 participated in the study. While situation 1 was presented in both years, situation 2 was only used in the second year. The corresponding numbers of participants in Barcelona and Leuven are 78 and 242, respectively, for both situations. However, following the procedure used in the previous investigation, only those respondents are considered who completed all situations of the questionnaire sheets received since a refusal to answer some questions obviously reflects either problems or unease with the given task. Thus, in Osnabrück 16 participants in the year 2002 and 19 in 2003 have been excluded from the sample, while in Barcelona 5 and in Leuven 2 subjects failed to consider all contexts. There were no differences with respect to the aspect of responsibility.

Next, with the exception of 'work experience' and 'field of study', the additionally allocated demographic questions were similar to those described in the preceding chapter. This is also the case for the 2003 sample from Osnabrück, where the previously explained modified demographic questions have been used. Hence, the same variables as before have been modelled. In situation 1, 87 out of 758 students, and in situation 2, 71 out of 576 subjects left at least one demographic question unanswered.[14] Interestingly, no Spanish and only 7 Belgian students are among these subjects. From this group, 28 participants in situation 1 (and 17 in situation 2) refused to answer any demographic question, but 48 (44) students only skipped the question about their expected future income. The reader will remember this 'item non-response problem' from chapter 2. Hence, the question arises again whether to exclude such cases from the sample, which allows us to analyse all variables of interest but introduces the possibility of a sample selection bias, or to include all available answers of these individuals on other items, which would extend the sample size but eliminate the possibility to investigate the influence of the missing variables. It seems to be plausible to focus only on the 48 students identified for situation 1 in the discussion in the following paragraphs, because most of the remaining 39 subjects also left out several or even all other demographic questions.

As before, a closer look at the resulting sample shows that 36 out of these 48 students are female. Indeed, the estimation of a binary logit model with MISSING as the dependent dichotomous variable reveals that the variables AGE and MALE display a statistically significant influence on the probability of observing a missing value for the income variable. Hence, the missingness mechanism is not MCAR. McFadden's $R^2$ equals 0.142, indicating that the fit of the model is not very high. Nevertheless, preliminary $\chi^2$ tests on justice evaluations reveal that members of this group switched significantly less often

14 Notice that the questions on 'work experience' and on the 'field of study' are not considered here.

from alternative $x$ to $y$ in both contexts compared to the remaining sample.[15] Thus, there could be a sample selection bias with respect to the dependent variables.

Thus, what should be done? Certainly, as already described above, neither the gain of the previously explained sample reduction nor the benefit from including at least the additional 48 students comes without some costs. In the present chapter, the focus is on the influence of aspects of responsibility. Clearly, from a theoretical point of view, answers to the question on future income are not supposed to be influenced by responsibility considerations so that it seems to be more important to include the additional 48 respondents into the sample and, thereby, abandon the possibility to control for income expectations. Nevertheless, most results for the reduced sample will be reported in the text. It should be noticed that this procedure differs from the one followed in the previous chapter. There, gender differences were the central subject matter of the study. But as females and males noticeably differed with respect to future income expectations, the incorporation of the corresponding variable seemed to be more important than using the larger sample for situations 1 and 4.

In Table 3.1 the individual characteristics for the larger sample are given, whereas in Table 3.15 in Appendix 3.8 the reduced sample is described that allows the incorporation of future income variables. Moreover, respective correlation coefficients for the former sample are presented in Table 3.2. Besides the previously introduced variables, two additional sample attributes are included. Firstly, in order to control for the influence of aspects of responsibility in multivariate regression models the binary variable RES is constructed and reflects the questionnaire version. Further $\chi^2$ tests confirmed that the two versions were randomly distributed among the different groups of the samples. Secondly, respondents come from different countries. Thus, additional place dummy variables are incorporated to allow for local disparities. In Tables 3.1 and 3.15, comparisons of mean values with respect to context, place and gender are possible. To start with, the proportion of students from each university differs between the two situations due to the fact that in Osnabrück only situation 1 was used in both years. Next, consider local differences. Most strikingly, students in Osnabrück are remarkably older than their counterparts in Barcelona and Leuven. One possible reason is the fact that at least in the western *Bundesländer* in Germany young people have to attend school for 13 years before they enter the university. Furthermore, male Germans attend compulsorily military or civilian service so that they regularly start their university career even one year later. Finally, Belgian students have usually no work experience. Nevertheless, due to the large range of the age variable especially in Osnabrück and Barcelona there is no complete separation of the

15 However, none of the descriptive results significantly varied between the larger and the reduced sample.

Table 3.1: Variable descriptions

| | | Total | | Place | | | |
|---|---|---|---|---|---|---|---|
| | | | | Osnabrück | | Barcelona | Leuven |
| Code | Description | Sit. 1 n=719 | Sit. 2 n=549 | Sit. 1 n=413 | Sit. 2 n=243 | Sit.1+2 n=73 | Sit.1+2 n=233 |
| $AGE$ | Age of proband (in years) | 20.95 (2.47) | 20.42 (2.34) | 22.55 (1.92) | 22.49 (1.81) | 19.11 (1.60) | 18.69 (0.86) |
| $MALE$ | Proband is male: 0=No, 1=Yes | 0.53 (0.50) | 0.50 (0.50) | 0.54 (0.50) | 0.48 (0.50) | 0.40 (0.49) | 0.55 (0.50) |
| $RES$ | Version: 0=No responsibility, 1=Responsibility | 0.50 (0.50) | 0.49 (0.50) | 0.51 (0.50) | 0.50 (0.50) | 0.48 (0.50) | 0.49 (0.50) |
| $PAR_1$ | Worker, craftsman | 0.18 (0.38) | 0.18 (0.39) | 0.17 (0.37) | 0.17 (0.38) | 0.37 (0.49) | 0.14 (0.35) |
| $PAR_2$ | Employee / civil servant in the public sector | 0.27 (0.44) | 0.26 (0.44) | 0.26 (0.44) | 0.25 (0.43) | 0.16 (0.37) | 0.31 (0.46) |
| $PAR_3$ | Employee in the private sector | 0.26 (0.44) | 0.26 (0.44) | 0.26 (0.44) | 0.26 (0.44) | 0.33 (0.47) | 0.24 (0.43) |
| $PAR_4$ | Self-employed | 0.28 (0.45) | 0.28 (0.45) | 0.29 (0.46) | 0.29 (0.45) | 0.14 (0.35) | 0.31 (0.47) |
| $PLACE_O$ | Universität Osnabrück (Sit.1 in 2002 and 2003, Sit.2 in 2003) | 0.57 (0.50) | 0.44 (0.50) | 1.00 (—) | 1.00 (—) | 0.00 (—) | 0.00 (—) |
| $PLACE_B$ | Universitat Autònoma de Barcelona (in 2005) | 0.10 (0.30) | 0.13 (0.34) | 0.00 (—) | 0.00 (—) | 1.00 (—) | 0.00 (—) |
| $PLACE_L$ | Katholieke Universiteit Leuven (in 2005) | 0.32 (0.47) | 0.42 (0.50) | 0.00 (—) | 0.00 (—) | 0.00 (—) | 1.00 (—) |

Note: Given are mean values. Standard deviations are stated in parentheses.

Continuation: Variable descriptions

| Code | Description | Total | | Gender | | | |
|---|---|---|---|---|---|---|---|
| | | | | Women | | Men | |
| | | Sit. 1 n=719 | Sit. 2 n=549 | Sit. 1 n=341 | Sit. 2 n=275 | Sit. 1 n=378 | Sit. 2 n=274 |
| $AGE$ | Age of proband (in years) | 20.95 (2.47) | 20.42 (2.34) | 20.57 (2.18) | 20.19 (2.07) | 21.29 (2.66) | 20.66 (2.58) |
| $MALE$ | Proband is male: 0=No, 1=Yes | 0.53 (0.50) | 0.50 (0.50) | 0.00 (—) | 0.00 (—) | 1.00 (—) | 1.00 (—) |
| $RES$ | Version: 0=No responsibility, 1=Responsibility | 0.50 (0.50) | 0.49 (0.50) | 0.50 (0.50) | 0.49 (0.50) | 0.51 (0.50) | 0.50 (0.50) |
| $PAR_1$ | Worker, craftsman | 0.18 (0.38) | 0.18 (0.39) | 0.20 (0.40) | 0.20 (0.40) | 0.16 (0.37) | 0.17 (0.37) |
| $PAR_2$ | Employee / civil servant in the public sector | 0.27 (0.44) | 0.26 (0.44) | 0.29 (0.45) | 0.29 (0.45) | 0.25 (0.43) | 0.24 (0.43) |
| $PAR_3$ | Employee in the private sector | 0.26 (0.44) | 0.26 (0.44) | 0.23 (0.42) | 0.24 (0.43) | 0.28 (0.45) | 0.28 (0.45) |
| $PAR_4$ | Self-employed | 0.28 (0.45) | 0.28 (0.45) | 0.27 (0.44) | 0.25 (0.44) | 0.30 (0.46) | 0.30 (0.46) |
| $PLACE_O$ | Universität Osnabrück (Sit.1 in 2002 and 2003, Sit.2 in 2003) | 0.57 (0.50) | 0.44 (0.50) | 0.56 (0.50) | 0.46 (0.50) | 0.58 (0.49) | 0.43 (0.50) |
| $PLACE_B$ | Universitat Autònoma de Barcelona (in 2005) | 0.10 (0.30) | 0.13 (0.34) | 0.13 (0.34) | 0.16 (0.37) | 0.08 (0.27) | 0.11 (0.31) |
| $PLACE_L$ | Katholieke Universiteit Leuven (in 2005) | 0.32 (0.47) | 0.42 (0.50) | 0.31 (0.46) | 0.38 (0.49) | 0.34 (0.48) | 0.47 (0.50) |

Note: Given are mean values. Standard deviations are stated in parentheses.

Table 3.2: Correlation matrix for individual characteristics

| | Situation 1 (n=719) | | | | | | | | |
|---|---|---|---|---|---|---|---|---|---|
| | $AGE$ | $MALE$ | $PAR_1$ | $PAR_2$ | $PAR_3$ | $PAR_4$ | $PLACE_O$ | $PLACE_B$ | $PLACE_L$ |
| $AGE$ | 1.000 | 0.147 | 0.051 | −0.028 | −0.029 | 0.008 | 0.754 | −0.250 | −0.635 |
| $MALE$ | | 1.000 | −0.050 | −0.044 | 0.059 | 0.036 | 0.022 | −0.086 | 0.033 |
| $PAR_1$ | | | 1.000 | −0.282 | −0.276 | −0.294 | −0.037 | 0.167 | −0.068 |
| $PAR_2$ | | | | 1.000 | −0.357 | −0.380 | −0.015 | −0.078 | 0.066 |
| $PAR_3$ | | | | | 1.000 | −0.372 | 0.001 | 0.054 | −0.036 |
| $PAR_4$ | | | | | | 1.000 | 0.024 | −0.109 | 0.045 |
| $PLACE_O$ | | | | | | | 1.000 | −0.391 | −0.804 |
| $PLACE_B$ | | | | | | | | 1.000 | −0.233 |
| $PLACE_L$ | | | | | | | | | 1.000 |
| | Situation 2 (n=549) | | | | | | | | |
| | $AGE$ | $MALE$ | $PAR_1$ | $PAR_2$ | $PAR_3$ | $PAR_4$ | $PLACE_O$ | $PLACE_B$ | $PLACE_L$ |
| $AGE$ | 1.000 | 0.099 | 0.026 | −0.028 | 0.009 | −0.016 | 0.784 | −0.220 | −0.637 |
| $MALE$ | | 1.000 | −0.041 | −0.057 | 0.047 | 0.054 | −0.031 | −0.080 | 0.086 |
| $PAR_1$ | | | 1.000 | −0.283 | −0.282 | −0.295 | −0.035 | 0.188 | −0.094 |
| $PAR_2$ | | | | 1.000 | −0.354 | −0.371 | −0.031 | −0.087 | 0.091 |
| $PAR_3$ | | | | | 1.000 | −0.369 | 0.006 | 0.061 | −0.048 |
| $PAR_4$ | | | | | | 1.000 | 0.019 | −0.124 | 0.066 |
| $PLACE_O$ | | | | | | | 1.000 | −0.349 | −0.765 |
| $PLACE_B$ | | | | | | | | 1.000 | −0.336 |
| $PLACE_L$ | | | | | | | | | 1.000 |

Note: The given numbers are Pearson correlation coefficients (Pearson's $r$).

samples. However, from Table 3.2 it can be seen that there exists a high correlation only between the place of the investigation and the age of a respondent. These observations also hold for the reduced sample. If the age of a participant displays an influence on the dependent variable, this effect may influence the estimated place effects. Thus, it should be separated.[16] Moreover, and in contrast to the first study, the squared value of the age variable is also incorporated in the following models because of the strong local differences. Thus, a nonlinearity to the age effect is introduced in the way that the marginal effect of AGE on the examined dependent variable depends in turn on the initial age from which the considered increase started.[17] Another local discrepancy concerns the parental background of a student. In Barcelona, compared to the other two places, more respondents classify their parent's background as 'worker' or 'craftsman', while less of them state either 'employee/civil servant in the public sector' or 'self-employed'. Finally, from the data presented in Table 3.15 in the Appendix it can be observed that respondents from Barcelona are particularly pessimistic about their future income, while German students are mostly optimistic.

With respect to the gender samples the same differences as in the first questionnaire investigation can be observed. Men are somewhat older and also more optimistic about their future income. Furthermore, the proportion of female students is highest in Barcelona.

To summarise, despite some sample reductions, sufficiently large samples are available, which also allow considering several potential influences on the effect of responsibility considerations on the distributive decisions being regarded.

## 3.6 Results

In chapter 2, several statistical tools have been introduced and applied in order to detect gender differences with respect to both the initial fulfilment of the equity axiom and possible reconsiderations if the better-off group is successively enlarged. Now, the same methods will be applied to control for the additional aspect of responsibility. Moreover, differences between places and, again, between females and males are considered in detail. Descriptive results and corresponding $\chi^2$ tests are presented first. Afterwards, multivariate regression models are estimated to get further insights into decision structures and, also, to evaluate the statistical relevance of previous one-dimensional comparisons. Here, we distinguish between binary response models and or-

16 Indeed, in some regression models for situation 2 we could observe differences between the three places only if we excluded the variables AGE and $AGE^2$, but this effect could be traced to the different ages of respondents in the corresponding samples. See our argumentation in subsection 2.4.4.

17 See Borooah (2002, p. 19) for a similar explanation.

dered or multinomial response models. Finally, gender differences are investigated in the last subsection.

### 3.6.1 Descriptive Results

In Tables 3.3 and 3.4 relative frequencies for all possible decision patterns in both contexts are presented. The two questionnaire versions are separated and, moreover, results are distinguished with respect to the place of the investigation. Let us start by examining effects of responsibility considerations for the total samples. In situation 1, some minor disparities can be observed; the fulfilment of the equity axiom declined by 4.6 percentage points, whereas choices in accordance with sequence 1111 can be noticed slightly more frequently. None of these changes are statistically significant. In situation 2, results of both versions are almost identical. Hence, the aspects of responsibility introduced does not seem to have any relevant effect in the given contexts.

Next, we have a look at results from the three origins. In fact, two different comparisons are possible. On the one hand, the influence of responsibility considerations can be regarded for each place separately. On the other hand, results for each questionnaire version can be investigated with respect to local differences. In both cases, disparities in the evaluation of responsibility matters may become visible. Regarding each origin individually, it can be seen that for situation 1 in Osnabrück the fulfilment of the axiom declined and, consequently, the relative frequency of sequence 1111 increased if aspects of responsibility were introduced. More surprisingly, choices in accordance with sequence 0000 can also be observed more often. Consequently, due to this movement to the two 'unconditional' decision patterns the relative frequency of a switch from alternative $x$ to alternative $y$ occurred significantly less regularly ($\chi^2$ value=3.959, p=0.047). Unfortunately, sample sizes for Barcelona are rather small so that seemingly stronger changes are not statistically significant. Especially, the consideration of responsibility reduced the unconditional support for the handicapped person – it declined from 60.5% to 48.6% and increased the relative frequencies for all different switching behaviours after initially fulfilling the equity axiom. Also for the Belgian sample, some smaller changes can be detected. The acceptance of the equity axiom went down by about 7 percentage points and so did the relative frequency of sequence 0000 if aspects of responsibility were introduced.

Results did not change remarkably in situation 2. Aspects of responsibility displayed no effect in Osnabrück and only minor influences on decisions in Barcelona, where the unconditional support of the worse offs in the responsibility case declined again. In contrast, respondents in Leuven seem to 'honour' the risk-taking behaviour of the Africans. Here, the fulfilment of the equity axiom and the relative frequency of sequence 0000 increased. Nevertheless, all differences are not statistically significant. Therefore, it can be deduced

Table 3.3: Relative frequencies - All possible decisions: Situation 1

| | No responsibility | | | | Responsibility | | | |
|---|---|---|---|---|---|---|---|---|
| Sequence | Total (n=359) | Osnabrück (n=203) | Barcelona (n=38) | Leuven (n=118) | Total (n=360) | Osnabrück (n=210) | Barcelona (n=35) | Leuven (n=115) |
| 0 0 0 0 | 0.370 | 0.369 | 0.605 | 0.297 | 0.364 | 0.419 | 0.486 | 0.226 |
| 0 0 0 1 | 0.033 | 0.025 | 0.053 | 0.042 | 0.028 | 0.029 | 0.057 | 0.017 |
| 0 0 1 0 | 0.0 | 0.0 | 0.0 | 0.0 | 0.006 | 0.010 | 0.0 | 0.0 |
| 0 0 1 1 | 0.159 | 0.187 | 0.026 | 0.153 | 0.142 | 0.143 | 0.114 | 0.148 |
| 0 1 0 0 | 0.003 | 0.0 | 0.0 | 0.008 | 0.003 | 0.0 | 0.0 | 0.009 |
| 0 1 0 1 | 0.006 | 0.010 | 0.0 | 0.0 | 0.008 | 0.005 | 0.029 | 0.009 |
| 0 1 1 0 | 0.008 | 0.005 | 0.026 | 0.008 | 0.003 | 0.0 | 0.029 | 0.0 |
| 0 1 1 1 | 0.209 | 0.232 | 0.158 | 0.186 | 0.189 | 0.176 | 0.171 | 0.217 |
| 1 0 0 0 | 0.0 | 0.0 | 0.0 | 0.0 | 0.006 | 0.0 | 0.0 | 0.017 |
| 1 0 0 1 | 0.003 | 0.0 | 0.0 | 0.008 | 0.003 | 0.0 | 0.0 | 0.009 |
| 1 0 1 0 | 0.0 | 0.0 | 0.0 | 0.0 | 0.003 | 0.0 | 0.0 | 0.009 |
| 1 0 1 1 | 0.006 | 0.010 | 0.0 | 0.0 | 0.006 | 0.010 | 0.0 | 0.0 |
| 1 1 0 0 | 0.008 | 0.015 | 0.0 | 0.0 | 0.003 | 0.005 | 0.0 | 0.0 |
| 1 1 0 1 | 0.003 | 0.0 | 0.0 | 0.008 | 0.006 | 0.005 | 0.0 | 0.009 |
| 1 1 1 0 | 0.003 | 0.005 | 0.0 | 0.0 | 0.003 | 0.0 | 0.0 | 0.009 |
| 1 1 1 1 | 0.189 | 0.143 | 0.132 | 0.288 | 0.231 | 0.200 | 0.114 | 0.322 |
| % Switch | 40.1 | 44.3 | 23.7 | 38.1 | 35.8 | 34.8 | 34.3 | 38.3 |
| % Fulfilment of equity axiom | 78.8 | 82.8 | 86.8 | 69.5 | 74.2 | 78.1 | 88.6 | 62.6 |

Note: A choice of alternative x is coded as 0, a decision in favour of y is coded as 1.

Table 3.4: Relative frequencies - All possible decisions: Situation 2

| Sequence | No responsibility Total (n=178) | No responsibility Osnabrück (n=122) | No responsibility Barcelona (n=38) | No responsibility Leuven (n=118) | Responsibility Total (n=271) | Responsibility Osnabrück (n=121) | Responsibility Barcelona (n=35) | Responsibility Leuven (n=115) |
|---|---|---|---|---|---|---|---|---|
| 0 0 0 0 | 0.468 | 0.467 | 0.711 | 0.390 | 0.458 | 0.438 | 0.600 | 0.435 |
| 0 0 0 1 | 0.036 | 0.025 | 0.105 | 0.059 | 0.018 | 0.008 | 0.0 | 0.035 |
| 0 0 1 0 | 0.029 | 0.016 | 0.0 | 0.051 | 0.015 | 0.0 | 0.029 | 0.026 |
| 0 0 1 1 | 0.119 | 0.082 | 0.0 | 0.161 | 0.148 | 0.124 | 0.086 | 0.191 |
| 0 1 0 0 | 0.011 | 0.016 | 0.0 | 0.008 | 0.004 | 0.0 | 0.029 | 0.0 |
| 0 1 0 1 | 0.004 | 0.0 | 0.0 | 0.008 | 0.0 | 0.0 | 0.0 | 0.0 |
| 0 1 1 0 | 0.004 | 0.0 | 0.0 | 0.008 | 0.022 | 0.025 | 0.0 | 0.026 |
| 0 1 1 1 | 0.065 | 0.098 | 0.026 | 0.042 | 0.092 | 0.091 | 0.114 | 0.087 |
| 1 0 0 0 | 0.011 | 0.008 | 0.026 | 0.008 | 0.007 | 0.008 | 0.0 | 0.009 |
| 1 0 0 1 | 0.007 | 0.016 | 0.0 | 0.0 | 0.0 | 0.0 | 0.0 | 0.0 |
| 1 0 1 0 | 0.014 | 0.008 | 0.0 | 0.025 | 0.007 | 0.017 | 0.0 | 0.0 |
| 1 0 1 1 | 0.007 | 0.008 | 0.026 | 0.0 | 0.011 | 0.008 | 0.057 | 0.0 |
| 1 1 0 0 | 0.007 | 0.008 | 0.0 | 0.008 | 0.011 | 0.017 | 0.0 | 0.009 |
| 1 1 0 1 | 0.0 | 0.0 | 0.0 | 0.0 | 0.0 | 0.0 | 0.0 | 0.0 |
| 1 1 1 0 | 0.036 | 0.066 | 0.026 | 0.008 | 0.041 | 0.074 | 0.0 | 0.017 |
| 1 1 1 1 | 0.183 | 0.180 | 0.079 | 0.220 | 0.166 | 0.190 | 0.086 | 0.165 |
| % Switch | 21.9 | 20.5 | 13.2 | 26.3 | 25.8 | 22.3 | 20.0 | 31.3 |
| % Fulfilment of equity axiom | 73.4 | 70.5 | 84.2 | 72.9 | 75.6 | 68.6 | 85.7 | 80.0 |

Note: A choice of alternative x is coded as 0, a decision in favour of y is coded as 1.

that the aspects of responsibility which were introduced exhibited only minor effects on decisions in both situations even if we distinguish between the three different places. Surprisingly, in contrast to our expectations, some students seemed to 'reward' the risk-taking behaviour in the first context in Osnabrück and in the second situation in Leuven, while the Spanish sample is probably too small to detect significant influences.

In view of country differences detected in earlier studies on this questionnaire, a second kind of assessment may regard local disparities in each questionnaire version. Let us take a second look at the descriptive data in the two tables. We will only comment on those differences that are found to be significant at the 5% level.

In situation 1, for both questionnaire versions answers from Belgian respondents are remarkably different from those given by their counterparts in Osnabrück and Barcelona. Almost all $\chi^2$ tests on the overall distribution of answers on the possible decision patterns are highly significant. Furthermore, in both versions students from Leuven were significantly less likely to fulfil the equity axiom. In contrast, in the no-responsibility case an unconditional support for the handicapped person, viz. sequence 0000, can be found more regularly in Barcelona than in the other two places. Interestingly, this sequence was least often chosen in Leuven in the responsibility version. This is due to both the increased relative frequency in Osnabrück and the decreased value in Belgium.

In situation 2, there are only two important local differences. As before, participants from Barcelona more often decided in accordance with sequence 0000 in the no-responsibility version. However, the introduction of responsibility considerations reduced this discrepancy. Somewhat surprisingly, our German students were least likely to fulfil the equity axiom in the responsibility case. Especially the increased acceptance of the axiom by the Belgian respondents should be noticed here.

Clearly, it is worth mentioning that these comparisons are not adequate to identify 'cultural' effects. Firstly, more groups from the same countries should be regarded to make more reliable statements about justice attitudes. Secondly, especially the sample from Barcelona is rather small. Thirdly, a culturally based reason for possible local differences is not obvious since all students live in the Western European hemisphere, although nothing is known about their origins. Also, some differences with respect to the execution of the study in each country exist, but the effects of these disparities should be rather small. More likely, other factors, such as the age of a respondent or parental background, may have had an influence on the observed heterogeneity of some answers. This gives support for the idea of applying multivariate regression models to control at least for some known dissimilarities in the three samples. Even more importantly, local effects should also be separated from the influence of responsibility considerations. This argument is very much in line with the elaborations in chapter 1. Several individual characteristics may bias attitudes so that it is important to control for them.

To summarise, the one-dimensional comparisons firstly showed that in both contexts no significant effects of the incorporated aspect of responsibility can be observed. Hence, the principle of responsibility does not seem to have an influence on the needs-efficiency trade-off. However, secondly, certain honouring of risk-taking behaviour of the individual(s) in need could be detected for Osnabrück in situation 1 and for Leuven in situation 2. Thirdly, some stronger local differences have been identified.

Before we turn to the multivariate models, let us take a brief look at some verbal comments from Osnabrück. The focus is on those remarks that contain statements on the aspect of responsibility. In situation 1, 23 (or 11.0%) out of 210 participants who faced the responsibility questionnaire explicitly mentioned that the sportsperson is responsible for his or her fate. This proportion is unexpectedly low. One possibility is that students did not want to seem to be too harsh or unmerciful and, in order to justify themselves, pretended to be motivated by other reasons to deny support for worse offs. However, there are no remarkable differences between responses on the two versions with respect to several other arguments, like aspects of efficiency, described already in chapter 2. Additionally, 13.4% of the women but only 8.9% of the men mentioned aspects of responsibility. Nevertheless, this difference is not statistically significant.

In situation 2, only two subjects claimed that their decision was negatively influenced by the risk-taking behaviour of the Africans, while one respondent explicitly wanted to reward their behaviour. Furthermore, four students argued that the Germans are responsible for the pollution in their own country and one individual said that Western countries are responsible for African problems. Interestingly, this final argument follows the reasoning of Lippert-Rasmussen (2001) who criticises the notion of option luck.

A second question regarded those respondents who always opted for alternative $x$. They were asked to state whether they would ever be willing to switch to alternative $y$ if the better-off group is further extended. In situation 1, 83.6% of the subjects in the no-responsibility version and 80.2% in the responsibility case said that they would never switch from $x$ to $y$, no matter how many people were members of the better-off group. In situation 2, the corresponding numbers are 92.9% and 96.2%. Hence, there is again no effect of the consideration of aspects of responsibility. Furthermore, there are no gender differences with respect to this question. A great majority of both sexes in both groups wanted to support the worse offs unconditionally.

To summarise results of verbal comments, the aspects of responsibility did not play a role in most of the comments by the students. Also, the respective effect in situation 1 is lower than probably expected. However, as argued already in chapter 2, this observation does not necessarily mean that responsibility considerations had no influence on decisions at all. Respondents may not want to appear 'hard-hearted' in their verbal comments so that the influence of the effect being regarded could have been more indirect and subliminal.

### 3.6.2 Binary Response Models

The following multivariate regression models incorporate individual attributes and questionnaire characteristics that have been introduced in section 3.5. For that, the two samples, which were separated with respect to the questionnaire version in the previous subsection, are pooled. The dummy variable RES indicates the corresponding version, whereby RES=0 represents the no-responsibility and RES=1 the responsibility case. As explained above, the focus will be on the larger sample that also contains those students who only refused to answer the question on their expected future income. But results of the reduced sample are also mentioned and allow us to comment on both the possible sample selection effects and the influence of the included income expectations.

Let us start by considering binary logit models regarding the fulfilment of the equity axiom. In Table 3.5 estimated models for both situations are given. As can be seen from the LR statistics, the models are relevant. However, again, $R^2$ values are small, which means that the explanatory power is rather low. Again, only those effects are considered, which are found to be significant at least at the 5% level.

As can be deduced from all estimated coefficients for the responsibility dummy variable, there does not exist any relevant effect of this additional consideration on the probability of fulfilling the axiom. This observation does not only hold for both 'single effects' models but also for the two 'place effects' models. In the latter case, responsibility considerations are allowed to differ between the three places being regarded. However, additional likelihood-ratio tests reveal that the two product terms in the 'place effects' models do not significantly improve model fit.[18] Nevertheless, this time we report regression results of these extended models to familiarise the reader with the interpretation of verbal comments on other interactive models which are not explicitly presented in following subsections.

Surely, the absence of responsibility effects has already been identified in the preceding subsection, but now other influential factors are controlled for. Two of them are only important in situation 1. Firstly, respondents with a 'self-employed' parental background were significantly less likely to fulfil the equity axiom compared to those students who classified the main earner of their family as 'worker or craftsman'. Secondly, Belgian participants accepted the axiom remarkably less often than their counterparts in Osnabrück. The

18 Results of corresponding likelihood-ratio tests are $\chi^2_2 = 0.24$, p-value = 0.891, in situation 1 and $\chi^2_2 = 1.48$, p-value = 0.479, in situation 2.

Table 3.5: ML estimates of binary logit models
Dependent variable: Fulfilment of Equity Axiom

| Independent variables | Situation 1 (n=719) Single effects | Situation 1 (n=719) Place effects | Situation 2 (n=549) Single effects | Situation 2 (n=549) Place effects |
|---|---|---|---|---|
| *Constant* | 12.147 | 11.860 | 19.153* | 19.270* |
| | (6.767) | (6.789) | (9.052) | (9.117) |
| *AGE* | −0.736 | −0.710 | −1.573 | −1.571 |
| | (0.582) | (0.584) | (0.809) | (0.815) |
| $AGE^2$ | 0.013 | 0.013 | 0.034 | 0.034 |
| | (0.013) | (0.013) | (0.018) | (0.018) |
| *MALE* | −0.563** | −0.564** | −0.698** | −0.699** |
| | (0.191) | (0.191) | (0.210) | (0.210) |
| *RES* | −0.256 | −0.300 | 0.141 | −0.078 |
| | (0.183) | (0.254) | (0.201) | (0.284) |
| $PAR_2$ | −0.511 | −0.513 | −0.231 | −0.237 |
| | (0.300) | (0.301) | (0.313) | (0.314) |
| $PAR_3$ | −0.352 | −0.353 | −0.177 | −0.181 |
| | (0.307) | (0.307) | (0.312) | (0.312) |
| $PAR_4$ | −0.702* | −0.706* | −0.220 | −0.255 |
| | (0.294) | (0.295) | (0.309) | (0.311) |
| $PLACE_B$ | −0.267 | −0.437 | 0.400 | 0.326 |
| | (0.460) | (0.569) | (0.451) | (0.553) |
| $PLACE_L$ | −1.438** | −1.448** | −0.079 | −0.327 |
| | (0.364) | (0.414) | (0.387) | (0.439) |
| $PLACE_B *$ | — | 0.370 | — | 0.119 |
| *RES* | | (0.773) | | (0.729) |
| $PLACE_L *$ | — | 0.049 | — | 0.514 |
| *RES* | | (0.382) | | (0.428) |
| Log likelihood | −367.72 | −367.60 | −298.61 | −297.87 |
| LR statistic | 48.72** | 48.95** | 26.20** | 27.67** |
| McFadden $R^2$ | 0.062 | 0.062 | 0.042 | 0.044 |
| Mean dependent var. | 0.765 | 0.765 | 0.745 | 0.745 |

Note: Given are logistic coefficients (betas). Standard errors are reported in parentheses. Level of significance: $^*0.01 \leq p < 0.05$, $^{**}p < 0.01$.

corresponding odds ratio is $exp(-1.438) = 0.237$; the 95% confidence interval is 0.116 to 0.484. From the significance level of the estimated coefficient for the Leuven dummy variable in the 'place effects' model it can be seen that this difference is independent from aspects of responsibility.

However, the strongest influence results from the gender variable. In both situations for each model the exponent of the estimated coefficient is significantly lower than 1.0. Hence, men were astonishingly less likely to fulfil the equity axiom compared to females even if other possible factors are controlled for. This finding even strengthens the conclusions of the previous chapter especially with respect to situation 2.

Furthermore, it is important to notice that we also controlled for several interaction effects containing the responsibility variable. They were not found to significantly improve model fit so that all of them were excluded from the model by stepwise backward elimination.[19]

The basic findings also hold for the reduced sample where the future income dummies are incorporated.[20] However, in situation 1 the estimated coefficient for the responsibility variable equals −0.327 (S.E. 0.192) and is significant at least at the 10% level (p=0.089). Interestingly, this result also holds if the income variables are excluded from the model. Thus, a weak sample selection effect seems to exist. This is an important result.

Finally, from a negative and significant estimated coefficient for the dummy variable $FUT_3$ in situation 1 it becomes apparent that more optimistic respondents were remarkably less likely to fulfil the equity axiom compared to those with 'neutral' income beliefs. Again, product terms are not important.

### 3.6.3 Ordered and Multinomial Response Models

After examining the initial cases with only one better-off (group of) individual(s), we turn now to distributions in the case of successively increasing numbers of better offs. Again, either an ordered or a multinomial logit model seems to be the appropriate way to investigate the underlying decision problems. However, as before, the choice of the appropriate method is not unequivocal. Thus, a closer evaluation of results from both regression methods is necessary.

Primarily notice that 31 respondents in situation 1 and 68 students in situation 2 did not deliver a sensible answer pattern. Consequently, they are excluded from subsequent samples. In Table 3.6 relative frequencies for the five relevant sequences are presented for distinct groups. Here, the focus is again on the larger samples. Similar to the presentation of results in the preceding chapter, the index $z$ is used for representing each sequence of answers

19 The only exception is the product term MALE∗RES, which will be presented in subsection 3.6.4.

20 These tables are not presented here due to space restrictions.

Table 3.6: Relative frequencies - All sensible decision patterns

| | | Situation 1 | | | | | | | |
|---|---|---|---|---|---|---|---|---|---|
| | | Responsibility | | | | Gender | | | |
| | | RES=0 | RES=1 | | | MALE=0 | MALE=1 | | |
| Sequence | z | (n=345) | (n=343) | $s_o$ | $s_m$ | (n=330) | (n=358) | $s_o$ | $s_m$ |
| 0 0 0 0 | 5 | 0.386 | 0.382 | - | | 0.421 | 0.349 | - | |
| 0 0 0 1 | 4 | 0.035 | 0.029 | - | - | 0.036 | 0.028 | - | + |
| 0 0 1 1 | 3 | 0.165 | 0.149 | - | - | 0.173 | 0.142 | - | + |
| 0 1 1 1 | 2 | 0.217 | 0.198 | + | - | 0.212 | 0.204 | + | + |
| 1 1 1 1 | 1 | 0.197 | 0.242 | + | + | 0.158 | 0.277 | + | + |
| | | Situation 2 | | | | | | | |
| | | Responsibility | | | | Gender | | | |
| | | RES=0 | RES=1 | | | MALE=0 | MALE=1 | | |
| Sequence | z | (n=242) | (n=239) | $s_o$ | $s_m$ | (n=243) | (n=238) | $s_o$ | $s_m$ |
| 0 0 0 0 | 5 | 0.537 | 0.519 | - | | 0.584 | 0.471 | - | |
| 0 0 0 1 | 4 | 0.041 | 0.021 | + | - | 0.041 | 0.021 | + | - |
| 0 0 1 1 | 3 | 0.136 | 0.167 | + | + | 0.165 | 0.139 | + | - |
| 0 1 1 1 | 2 | 0.074 | 0.105 | + | + | 0.082 | 0.097 | + | + |
| 1 1 1 1 | 1 | 0.211 | 0.188 | + | - | 0.128 | 0.273 | + | + |

Note: A choice of alternative x is coded as 0, a decision in favour of y is coded as 1. $z$ represents the corresponding sequence in ordered logit models. $s_o$ and $s_m$ denote the signs of estimated marginal effects in the ordered or of coefficients in the multinomial logit models, respectively.

by a single value in the ordered logit model. For the two responsibility versions, the single crossing assumption is fulfilled only in situation 1, whereas in the gender case single crossing occurs in both contexts. This would support the application of an ordered logit model.

As explained in the description of statistical methods in subsection 2.3.3, there are additional assessing tools that require estimating the two models before evaluating their results. However, two previous technical notes are necessary. Firstly, as explained in chapter 2, all reported ordered logit models include a constant term when calculating the log likelihood values, but this has no consequences for other estimated results except for the threshold values.

Secondly, unlike the previous investigation, in some cases problems arose while estimating multinomial logit models. Because of empty cells, corresponding zero-values in denominators lead to undefined odds ratios. Besides some other groups, this difficulty appears in the responsibility version of situation 2, where sequence 0001 is absent from answers of the Spanish sample. For such cases Baltes-Götz (2006) recommends to combine some of the affected predictor categories. He admits that this method is "feasible but not

Table 3.7: Suggestive likelihood-ratio test for single crossing assumption

| Effects (model) | Ordered $L_O$ | Multinomial $L_M$ | $k$ | $\chi^2$ value: $2(L_M$-$L_O)$ |
|---|---|---|---|---|
| | Situation 1 (larger sample) | | | |
| Single | −553.37 | −535.46 | 9 | 35.81 |
| Gender (1) | −551.37 | −531.94 | 10 | 38.85 |
| Gender (2) | −551.43 | −531.43 | 11 | 40.01 |
| Gender (3) | −537.62 | −520.15 | 12 | 34.94 |
| | Situation 2 (larger sample) | | | |
| Single | −385.31 | −367.37 | 8 | $35.89^{\dagger}$ |
| Gender (1) | −385.23 | −366.05 | 9 | $38.37^{\dagger}$ |
| Gender (2) | −384.65 | −365.33 | 9 | $38.64^{\dagger}$ |
| Gender (3) | −383.90 | −361.44 | 12 | 44.93 |

Note: $L_O$ and $L_M$ are log likelihood values. $\chi^2$ values are compared with $\chi^2_{k(5-2)}$. Level of significance: $^{\dagger}0.05 \leq p < 0.10$, $^{*}p < 0.05$. $k$ = number of estimated coefficients in the ordered logit model.

always sympathetic" (p. 74, translation by the author). Indeed, for situation 2 the estimated multinomial logit models will not include the dummy variable PLACE$_B$. Consequently, answers of respondents from Leuven (PLACE$_L$=1) are compared with those of all remaining participants (PLACE$_L$=0). However, we have to generate comparable log likelihood values. Here, the dummy variable mentioned is dropped in the estimations of both multinomial and ordered logit models. All of these values are given in Table 3.7. Nevertheless, the ordered logit models reported later on include all variables in order to use all available information. It is for this reason that log likelihood values differ between the completely reported models and the corresponding values stated in Table 3.7.

Now, regard the results of $\chi^2$ tests for the single crossing assumption that are also given in Table 3.7. Here, different models that will be presented in due course are distinguished. As previously explained, high differences between respective log likelihood values should give reason for reservations about the application of the ordered logit model. A careful test on the appropriateness of the ordered logit models should use the 10% significance level. In this case, three models for the sample of situation 2 seem to be somewhat problematic. Nevertheless, notice again that this test only gives an overall measure for the suitability of the applied method.

Hence, based on the experiences in the previous chapter, a third 'test' is applied where the algebraic signs of estimated marginal effects of the ordered logit models and estimated coefficients from the multinomial logit models are considered. They are also given in columns s$_o$ and s$_m$, respectively, in Table 3.6. Again, an example may be helpful to clarify the statements of the signs. An estimated positive value for a marginal effect from the ordered logit model indicates that the probability of the considered decision pattern increases if the value of the dummy variable being regarded, i.e. RES or MALE, increases from 0 to 1. In contrast, an estimated positive coefficient in the multinomial logit model indicates that the probability of choosing the considered decision pattern compared to the base sequence, viz. sequence 0000, is higher for RES=1 or MALE=1 than for the opposite group indicated by a value of zero. From results in Table 3.6 it is visible that signs of marginal effects are more often 'incorrectly' specified in situation 2, while in the first context only the estimated 'crossing point' is somewhat misplaced in both the responsibility and the gender case. Conversely, similar discrepancies are not observed for estimated coefficients from multinomial logit models. Nevertheless, this assessment is not very reliable, since most of the estimates are not statistically significant. Particularly, the marginal effects in situation 2 are very close to zero, as will be shown next.

So, is the application of an ordered logit model in all cases feasible? In situation 1, there seem to be no major problems with respect to the larger sample. However, results are more unclear in situation 2. Consequently, as before, both approaches will be applied simultaneously, but findings should be carefully interpreted. Additionally, some results from the reduced samples are verbally presented.

Table 3.8 contains estimates of ordered logit models for both situations. Results appear to be very similar to the binary logit regressions presented in Table 3.5. This observation also holds for the reduced models. Firstly, and most importantly, responsibility considerations do not display any significant influence on the ordered dependent variable. Hence, the supposed responsibility of the individual(s) in need seems to be of no relevance for the distribution decisions of respondents. Moreover, we estimated 'place effects' models that included interaction terms of local dummy variables and the indicator RES and, therefore, allowed for local disparities with respect to the influence of responsibility considerations. Nevertheless, model fit did not significantly improve over the case of 'single effects' models so that these 'place effects' models are omitted in the present work.

However, two other effects are found to be important. On the one hand, in both 'single effects' models the estimated gender coefficients are negative and highly significant in both contexts. Corresponding p-values equal 0.003 in each of the models. Following the explanations in subsection 2.3.3, this has to be interpreted in the following way: For female respondents the probability of observing sequence 0000 is significantly higher and the probability of choosing sequence 1111 is significantly lower compared to their male counterparts. Moreover, in order to make further statements about gender effects on the probabilities for 'intermediate' sequences (i.e. $z_i$=2,3,4), marginal probabilities have to be computed. Corresponding values for the 'single effects'

Table 3.8: ML estimates of ordered logit models
Dependent variable: 5 Ordered Sequences

| Independent variables | Situation 1 (n=688) | Situation 2 (n=481) |
|---|---|---|
| $AGE$ | −0.663 | −1.416* |
| | (0.484) | (0.687) |
| $AGE^2$ | 0.015 | 0.031* |
| | (0.011) | (0.015) |
| $MALE$ | −0.423** | −0.545** |
| | (0.144) | (0.181) |
| $RES$ | −0.108 | −0.036 |
| | (0.139) | (0.175) |
| $PAR_2$ | −0.020 | 0.087 |
| | (0.212) | (0.264) |
| $PAR_3$ | −0.170 | 0.231 |
| | (0.213) | (0.262) |
| $PAR_4$ | −0.295 | −0.079 |
| | (0.210) | (0.264) |
| $PLACE_B$ | 0.360 | 0.469 |
| | (0.320) | (0.381) |
| $PLACE_L$ | −0.797** | −0.533 |
| | (0.280) | (0.341) |
| $\mu_1$ | −9.184 | −17.609* |
| | (5.573) | (7.674) |
| $\mu_2$ | −8.163 | −17.103* |
| | (5.571) | (7.672) |
| $\mu_3$ | −7.501 | −16.412* |
| | (5.570) | (7.669) |
| $\mu_4$ | −7.362 | −16.280* |
| | (5.570) | (7.668) |
| Log likelihood | -553.37 | -390.37 |
| LR statistic | 43.96** | 29.48** |
| (Pseudo-) $R^2$ | 0.022 | 0.024 |

Note: Given are logistic coefficients (betas). Standard errors are reported in parentheses. Level of significance: $^{*}0.01 \leq p < 0.05$, $^{**}p < 0.01$.

models are given in Table 3.9.[21] The underlying calculations follow the procedures described in subsection 2.3.3. Results for both situations show that gender disparities are strongest for the two extreme positions, which reflect an unconditional support for either group. This effect is even stronger for situation 2 compared to situation 1. Thus, gender differences with respect to the support of the worse-off individuals were not only relevant in the initial case but also with respect to enlargements of the better-off group(s). We will come back to this point in the next subsection.

On the other hand, there are some remarkable local differences especially in situation 1. Students from Leuven, compared to their counterparts in Osnabrück, were significantly less likely to act in accordance with sequence 0000 but more likely with regard to sequence 1111. The corresponding p-value equals 0.004. Results in Table 3.9 show that the probability of observing the decision pattern 0000 is 17.5% lower in Leuven and 8.4% higher in Barcelona compared to Osnabrück. The respective numbers for the sequence 1111 are only slightly lower. Moreover, from results of the 'place effects' models in both contexts, which are not explicitly presented, it can be concluded that the absence of influences from aspects of responsibility did not depend on the place of the investigation. Furthermore, it should be mentioned that several other interaction effects have been controlled for. However, the applied stepwise backward elimination removed all of these variable products from the final model.

Finally, in situation 2 there are some significant effects of the age of a respondent on the ordered dependent variable. The estimated negative coefficient for AGE combined with the positive value for $AGE^2$ means that if the age of a student is increased, his or her answer relates to a lower value $z$. However, the older the respondents are the lower this effect is.

A brief look at results from reduced samples, which are not explicitly presented due to space restrictions, reveals that the inclusion of future income variables combined with the underlying sample reduction has no influence on the identified results for the effects of the variables for responsibility, place and gender. This finding is important, because earlier we identified some differences with respect to future income expectations especially between the three places. Moreover, the income dummy variables are of no relevance. Nevertheless, in the second context the age of a respondent is no longer important. Again, it is not clear whether this observation is due to the inclusion of the additional future income variables or to the sample reduction. Hence, the regression is repeated on the smaller sample but without the two dummies. As before, the effect of AGE is not important so that, obviously, the sample reduction causes the changes.

21 The also considered 'place effects' models give very similar results. Therefore, they are omitted in this table. Moreover, each model includes all single variables presented.

Table 3.9: Ordered logit models - Selected marginal probabilities

| Model | Variable | $Pr'(z_i = 1)$ | $Pr'(z_i = 2)$ | $Pr'(z_i = 3)$ | $Pr'(z_i = 4)$ | $Pr'(z_i = 5)$ |
|---|---|---|---|---|---|---|
| | | | | Situation 1 | | |
| Single effects | $MALE$ | 0.070 | 0.029 | −0.001 | −0.003 | −0.096 |
| | $RES$ | 0.018 | 0.007 | −0.000 | −0.001 | −0.024 |
| | $PLACE_B$ | −0.055 | −0.027 | −0.003 | 0.001 | 0.084 |
| | $PLACE_L$ | 0.142 | 0.048 | −0.010 | −0.006 | −0.175 |
| Gender: Model 1 | $MALE$ | 0.115 | 0.047 | −0.001 | −0.004 | −0.157 |
| | $RES$ | 0.065 | 0.026 | −0.000 | −0.002 | −0.088 |
| Gender: Model 2 | $MALE$ | 0.037 | 0.016 | −0.000 | −0.001 | −0.051 |
| | $PLACE_B$ | −0.051 | −0.025 | −0.003 | 0.001 | 0.077 |
| | $PLACE_L$ | 0.094 | 0.035 | −0.005 | −0.004 | −0.120 |
| Gender: Model 3 | $MALE$ | 0.103 | 0.042 | −0.001 | −0.004 | −0.141 |
| | $RES$ | 0.064 | 0.025 | −0.000 | −0.002 | −0.087 |
| | $PLACE_B$ | −0.069 | −0.035 | −0.005 | 0.001 | 0.108 |
| | $PLACE_L$ | 0.100 | 0.036 | −0.005 | −0.004 | −0.127 |
| | | | | Situation 2 | | |
| Single effects | $MALE$ | 0.085 | 0.024 | 0.021 | 0.001 | −0.131 |
| | $RES$ | 0.006 | 0.002 | 0.001 | 0.000 | −0.008 |
| | $PLACE_B$ | −0.066 | −0.021 | −0.022 | −0.002 | 0.110 |
| | $PLACE_L$ | 0.084 | 0.022 | 0.018 | 0.001 | −0.125 |
| Gender: Model 1 | $MALE$ | 0.096 | 0.027 | 0.023 | 0.001 | −0.148 |
| | $RES$ | 0.017 | 0.005 | 0.004 | 0.000 | −0.026 |
| Gender: Model 2 | $MALE$ | 0.037 | 0.010 | 0.009 | 0.001 | −0.056 |
| | $PLACE_B$ | −0.095 | −0.032 | −0.036 | −0.004 | 0.167 |
| | $PLACE_L$ | 0.043 | 0.011 | 0.010 | 0.001 | −0.064 |
| Gender: Model 3 | $MALE$ | 0.046 | 0.013 | 0.011 | 0.001 | −0.070 |
| | $RES$ | 0.028 | 0.008 | 0.006 | 0.000 | −0.042 |
| | $PLACE_B$ | −0.138 | −0.049 | −0.060 | −0.008 | 0.255 |
| | $PLACE_L$ | 0.075 | 0.020 | 0.016 | 0.001 | −0.112 |

Note: Sums of marginal probabilities in each row do not always equal zero due to rounding. $Pr'(.)$ represents $\frac{\partial Pr(.)}{\partial x_{il}}$.

It has previously been argued that especially for situation 2 due to a violation of the single crossing assumption, the estimation of an ordered logit model may not be the appropriate approach. However, reconsider the arguments in favour of this method discussed in subsection 2.6.2. While the ordered logit model estimates only one equation from which single effects can be calculated, the multinomial logit model uses multiple regressions and identifies various effects for one variable from pairwise comparisons. Additionally, in contrast to the previous study, some empty cells prevent the usage of all available information in the multinomial logit model. Nevertheless, the statistical constraints mentioned could necessitate the consideration of the second approach.

Estimated results of multinomial logit models are summarised in Table 3.10. Again, only 'single effects' models are considered, since the omitted 'place effects' models yielded almost identical log likelihood values. Hence, as before, the place of the investigation has no influence on effects of the variable RES.

Basically, the presented results confirm earlier findings. In no case does the responsibility dummy variable show any significant influence on the compared probabilities. Thus, similar to all estimated regressions so far, we are not able to detect any relevance of responsibility considerations for the underlying decision problem.

However, the estimated coefficients give some more insights into possible differences, especially with respect to the gender of a respondent and also to the place of the investigation. Gender differences are particularly strong if the probability of observing sequence 1111 over sequence 0000 is regarded. In both contexts the positive and highly significant estimated coefficients for the variable MALE shows that this odds ratio is clearly higher for males than for females. Similar differences concerning the other sensible sequences are not apparent. These observations confirm both earlier descriptive results and estimated marginal effects of the ordered logit model. We will come back to this point in the following subsection.

Furthermore, students from Belgium were remarkably more likely to choose sequence 1111 over sequence 0000 compared to their German counterparts in situation 1 and to respondents in Osnabrück and Barcelona in situation 2.[22] In the first context, Spanish students decided less often in accordance with sequence 0011 than with sequence 0000 compared to German participants. In situation 2, respondents in Leuven were more likely to act in accordance with sequence 0011 than with the base sequence compared to students from the other two universities.

There are some additional effects visible. Comparing the probabilities of observing an unconditional support for the intelligent child(ren) with the like-

22 Remember that due to empty cells, students from the latter two cities are pooled in situation 2. Consequently, Belgian answers are compared with those of the resulting larger group.

Table 3.10: Multinomial logit models

| Independent variables | Situation 1 (n=688) | | | | Situation 2 (n=481) | | | |
|---|---|---|---|---|---|---|---|---|
| | 1111 | 0111 | 0011 | 0001 | 1111 | 0111 | 0011 | 0001 |
| *Constant* | 4.255 | 3.239 | 11.420 | −6.810 | 20.219* | 3.865 | 12.746 | 24.886 |
| | (6.236) | (7.468) | (11.978) | (17.509) | (9.184) | (11.388) | (9.613) | (37.010) |
| $AGE_c$ | 0.678 | 0.255 | 0.994 | −0.668 | 2.429* | 0.645 | 1.693 | 2.712 |
| | (0.663) | (0.778) | (1.205) | (1.790) | (0.963) | (1.188) | (1.010) | (3.624) |
| $AGE_c^2$ | −0.014 | −0.008 | −0.028 | 0.010 | −0.053* | −0.015 | −0.034 | −0.066 |
| | (0.014) | (0.017) | (0.027) | (0.040) | (0.022) | (0.027) | (0.023) | (0.088) |
| $MALE$ | 0.695** | 0.192 | 0.073 | 0.104 | 0.865** | 0.406 | −0.067 | −0.516 |
| | (0.222) | (0.216) | (0.239) | (0.461) | (0.260) | (0.344) | (0.279) | (0.578) |
| $RES$ | 0.238 | −0.062 | −0.084 | −0.157 | −0.093 | 0.341 | 0.204 | −0.707 |
| | (0.212) | (0.210) | (0.233) | (0.448) | (0.248) | (0.337) | (0.273) | (0.571) |
| $PAR_2$ | 0.296 | −0.438 | 0.183 | 0.335 | −0.159 | 0.441 | −0.267 | −0.278 |
| | (0.337) | (0.310) | (0.365) | (0.669) | (0.389) | (0.519) | (0.382) | (0.721) |
| $PAR_3$ | 0.387 | −0.075 | 0.177 | 0.206 | −0.053 | −0.276 | −0.751 | −1.197 |
| | (0.339) | (0.300) | (0.374) | (0.677) | (0.367) | (0.552) | (0.410) | (0.898) |
| $PAR_4$ | 0.674* | −0.148 | 0.504 | 0.161 | 0.153 | 0.653 | −0.286 | −0.304 |
| | (0.332) | (0.306) | (0.360) | (0.711) | (0.377) | (0.508) | (0.394) | (0.755) |
| $PLACE_B$ | −0.115 | −0.890 | −1.630** | −0.457 | — | — | — | — |
| | (0.500) | (0.482) | (0.628) | (0.949) | | | | |
| $PLACE_L$ | 1.381** | 0.078 | −0.265 | −0.487 | 1.041** | −0.179 | 1.572** | 1.569 |
| | (0.430) | (0.433) | (0.492) | (0.925) | (0.390) | (0.495) | (0.433) | (0.828) |
| Model fit | LL: −535.46, LR test: 79.8**, $R^2$: 0.041 | | | | LL: −367.37, LR test: 63.9**, $R^2$: 0.052 | | | |

Note: The base sequence is 0000. Values are logistic coefficients (betas). Standard errors are reported in parentheses. Level of significance: $^*0.01 \leq p < 0.05$, $^{**}p < 0.01$. The variable $PLACE_B$ is omitted in situation 2 due to insufficient numbers of responses for answer category 0001. The model fit is described by the Log likelihood value (LL), the Likelihood-ratio test (LR test) and McFadden's $R^2$.

lihood for the unconditional help for the handicapped person, the resulting odds ratio is significantly higher for students from a 'self-employed' parental background compared to those from a 'worker or craftsman' environment. This discovery is very much in line with some earlier results in this and the previous chapter. Moreover, the strong effect of the variable AGE in situation 2, already identified in the ordered logit regressions, is also confirmed, but it only concerns the contrast between the two unconditional decision patterns. Lastly, we incorporated several possible interaction effects but, again, they are all removed from the final model by stepwise backward elimination.

Finally, multinomial logit models are also estimated for both reduced samples and include dummy variables for future income expectations of respondents. Some minor differences between these models and those reported in Table 3.10 exist. However, all of them are due to the sample reduction but not to the additional variables. As before, future income expectations do not display any significant influence on the decisions being considered. Furthermore, the previously detected gender and place effects persist in these regressions.

To conclude these rather extensive two subsections, several advanced statistical methods have been applied in order to separate the effects of responsibility considerations from confounding influences of other individual and questionnaire attributes. Here, significant influences from the dummy variable RES are completely absent. This observation is independent from the choice of the statistical approach. In contrast, particularly effects of the place of the investigation and the gender of a respondent are found to be of greater importance in all regression models. The significant influence of the place of the investigation on justice evaluations is independent from aspects of responsibility. In both version students from Leuven either acted less often in accordance with the equity axiom or decided less frequently in the spirit of the axiom. The influence of gender on responsibility considerations will be investigated in the next section.

### 3.6.4 The Role of Gender

In subsection 3.4.2, it was already argued that gender differences with respect to responsibility considerations are possible. Furthermore, similar to the investigation presented in chapter 2, a sufficiently large sample is available so that thorough investigations of the influence of gender on justice evaluations are possible. In the previous two subsections, some of the differences between women and men that have been discovered in the first investigation could be confirmed or even strengthened. Male students were significantly less likely to fulfil the equity axiom being considered in both contexts. Moreover, in this sample a successive enlargement of the better-off groups did not diminish observed disparities between both sexes. In fact, men were more likely than women to unconditionally support alternative $y$ instead of always helping the worse offs. In this subsection, two further aspects are considered. Firstly, gender effects on the influence of responsibility considerations are analysed. Secondly, place differences with respect to all observed gender disparities may lead to more complex statements about justice attitudes of males and females.

*Descriptive Results*

We will begin by looking at relative frequencies of all possible decision patterns. In Tables 3.11 and 3.12 corresponding values for female and male samples are given for both situations, and in each context for both questionnaire versions. Here, the total sample but also separate answers from Osnabrück and Leuven are regarded. The number of respondents in Barcelona is simply too small to make sensible statements.

Reconsider the relevant findings in chapter 2, which were entirely based on a sample from Osnabrück. In situation 1, women tended to switch more frequently while men were more likely to choose in accordance with sequence 1111. Moreover, there were remarkable gender disparities in the fulfilment of the equity axiom. However, differences with respect to sequence 0000 could not be observed. In situation 2, no gender differences could be detected. Thus, in order to investigate the validity of these earlier findings for the present samples, we should start by comparing female and male answers in the no-responsibility case.

In both total samples of the present study, the equity axiom was clearly more frequently fulfilled by women in the no-responsibility version of both situations. According to the $\chi^2$ test for $2 \times 2$ contingency tables these differences are significant in the first (p=0.007) but not in the second context (p=0.133). They partly confirm earlier results of binary models reported in Table 3.5. There, gender differences for the total sample containing both questionnaire versions revealed that women were significantly more likely to fulfil the axiom in both contexts.

Furthermore, in both contexts sequence 1111 is significantly more often observed for males than for females (p=0.002 in situation 1 and p=0.015 in situation 2), while the decision pattern 0000 was more frequently chosen by females in both situations (p=0.004 and p=0.052, respectively).[23] Notably, these differences not only underpin the previous findings but even strengthen them. While the switching behaviour was almost equally likely for both sexes in the present case, the unconditional choices reflect a much stronger disagreement between sexes. What is more, gender disparities are also apparent in the second context. But here, they were clearly driven by respondents from Leuven. These observations correspond to previously described results of the ordered logit models, which have been summarised in Table 3.8. There, it has been revealed for both total samples that females were more likely to act in the spirit of the equity axiom.

23 It has already been explained above that we are also considering significant results at the 10% level if sample sizes are rather small.

Table 3.11: Relative frequencies: Situation 1 - Women and men

| Sequence | No responsibility | | | | | | Responsibility | | | | | |
|---|---|---|---|---|---|---|---|---|---|---|---|---|
| | Total | | Osnabrück | | Leuven | | Total | | Osnabrück | | Leuven | |
| | Women n=172 | Men n=187 | Women n=95 | Men n=108 | Women n=54 | Men n=64 | Women n=169 | Men n=191 | Women n=97 | Men n=113 | Women n=51 | Men n=64 |
| 0 0 0 0 | 0.448 | 0.299 | 0.432 | 0.315 | 0.370 | 0.234 | 0.367 | 0.361 | 0.371 | 0.460 | 0.314 | 0.156 |
| 0 0 0 1 | 0.041 | 0.027 | 0.042 | 0.009 | 0.037 | 0.047 | 0.030 | 0.026 | 0.031 | 0.027 | 0.020 | 0.016 |
| 0 0 1 0 | 0.0 | 0.0 | 0.0 | 0.0 | 0.0 | 0.0 | 0.006 | 0.005 | 0.010 | 0.009 | 0.0 | 0.0 |
| 0 0 1 1 | 0.163 | 0.155 | 0.200 | 0.176 | 0.167 | 0.141 | 0.172 | 0.115 | 0.175 | 0.115 | 0.157 | 0.141 |
| 0 1 0 0 | 0.0 | 0.005 | 0.0 | 0.0 | 0.0 | 0.016 | 0.0 | 0.005 | 0.0 | 0.0 | 0.0 | 0.016 |
| 0 1 0 1 | 0.006 | 0.005 | 0.011 | 0.009 | 0.0 | 0.0 | 0.006 | 0.010 | 0.010 | 0.0 | 0.0 | 0.016 |
| 0 1 1 0 | 0.006 | 0.011 | 0.0 | 0.009 | 0.019 | 0.0 | 0.0 | 0.005 | 0.0 | 0.0 | 0.0 | 0.0 |
| 0 1 1 1 | 0.186 | 0.230 | 0.200 | 0.259 | 0.204 | 0.172 | 0.225 | 0.157 | 0.196 | 0.159 | 0.294 | 0.156 |
| 1 0 0 0 | 0.0 | 0.0 | 0.0 | 0.0 | 0.0 | 0.0 | 0.0 | 0.010 | 0.0 | 0.0 | 0.0 | 0.031 |
| 1 0 0 1 | 0.006 | 0.0 | 0.0 | 0.0 | 0.019 | 0.0 | 0.0 | 0.005 | 0.0 | 0.0 | 0.0 | 0.016 |
| 1 0 1 0 | 0.0 | 0.0 | 0.0 | 0.0 | 0.0 | 0.0 | 0.0 | 0.005 | 0.0 | 0.0 | 0.0 | 0.016 |
| 1 0 1 1 | 0.006 | 0.005 | 0.011 | 0.009 | 0.0 | 0.0 | 0.006 | 0.005 | 0.010 | 0.009 | 0.0 | 0.0 |
| 1 1 0 0 | 0.012 | 0.005 | 0.021 | 0.009 | 0.0 | 0.0 | 0.0 | 0.005 | 0.0 | 0.009 | 0.0 | 0.0 |
| 1 1 0 1 | 0.006 | 0.0 | 0.0 | 0.0 | 0.019 | 0.0 | 0.006 | 0.005 | 0.010 | 0.0 | 0.0 | 0.016 |
| 1 1 1 0 | 0.0 | 0.005 | 0.0 | 0.009 | 0.0 | 0.0 | 0.0 | 0.005 | 0.0 | 0.0 | 0.0 | 0.016 |
| 1 1 1 1 | 0.122 | 0.251 | 0.084 | 0.194 | 0.167 | 0.391 | 0.183 | 0.272 | 0.186 | 0.212 | 0.216 | 0.406 |
| % Switch | 39.0 | 41.2 | 44.2 | 44.4 | 40.7 | 35.9 | 42.6 | 29.8 | 40.2 | 30.1 | 47.1 | 31.3 |
| % Fulfilment equity axiom | 84.9 | 73.3 | 88.4 | 77.8 | 79.6 | 60.9 | 80.5 | 68.6 | 79.4 | 77.0 | 78.4 | 50.0 |

Note: A choice of alternative x is coded as 0, a decision in favour of y is coded as 1. The 'total' samples include respondents from all three places, viz. Barcelona, Leuven and Osnabrück.

Table 3.12: Relative frequencies: Situation 2 - Women and men

| | No responsibility | | | | | | Responsibility | | | | | |
|---|---|---|---|---|---|---|---|---|---|---|---|---|
| | Total | | Osnabrück | | Leuven | | Total | | Osnabrück | | Leuven | |
| | Women | Men | Women | Men | Women | Men | Women | Men | Women | Men | Women | Men |
| Sequence | n=141 | n=137 | n=64 | n=58 | n=54 | n=64 | n=134 | n=137 | n=62 | n=59 | n=51 | n=64 |
| 0 0 0 0 | 0.525 | 0.409 | 0.484 | 0.448 | 0.444 | 0.344 | 0.507 | 0.409 | 0.419 | 0.458 | 0.549 | 0.344 |
| 0 0 0 1 | 0.043 | 0.029 | 0.016 | 0.034 | 0.093 | 0.031 | 0.030 | 0.007 | 0.016 | 0.0 | 0.059 | 0.016 |
| 0 0 1 0 | 0.035 | 0.022 | 0.031 | 0.0 | 0.056 | 0.047 | 0.007 | 0.022 | 0.0 | 0.0 | 0.0 | 0.047 |
| 0 0 1 1 | 0.113 | 0.124 | 0.078 | 0.086 | 0.167 | 0.156 | 0.179 | 0.117 | 0.161 | 0.085 | 0.216 | 0.172 |
| 0 1 0 0 | 0.007 | 0.015 | 0.0 | 0.034 | 0.019 | 0.0 | 0.0 | 0.007 | 0.0 | 0.0 | 0.0 | 0.0 |
| 0 1 0 1 | 0.0 | 0.007 | 0.0 | 0.0 | 0.0 | 0.016 | 0.0 | 0.0 | 0.0 | 0.0 | 0.0 | 0.0 |
| 0 1 1 0 | 0.0 | 0.007 | 0.0 | 0.0 | 0.0 | 0.016 | 0.030 | 0.015 | 0.048 | 0.0 | 0.020 | 0.031 |
| 0 1 1 1 | 0.050 | 0.080 | 0.094 | 0.103 | 0.019 | 0.063 | 0.097 | 0.088 | 0.113 | 0.068 | 0.078 | 0.094 |
| 1 0 0 0 | 0.021 | 0.0 | 0.016 | 0.0 | 0.019 | 0.0 | 0.007 | 0.007 | 0.016 | 0.0 | 0.0 | 0.016 |
| 1 0 0 1 | 0.007 | 0.007 | 0.016 | 0.017 | 0.0 | 0.0 | 0.0 | 0.0 | 0.0 | 0.0 | 0.0 | 0.0 |
| 1 0 1 0 | 0.021 | 0.007 | 0.016 | 0.0 | 0.037 | 0.016 | 0.015 | 0.0 | 0.032 | 0.0 | 0.0 | 0.0 |
| 1 0 1 1 | 0.007 | 0.007 | 0.016 | 0.0 | 0.0 | 0.0 | 0.007 | 0.015 | 0.016 | 0.0 | 0.0 | 0.0 |
| 1 1 0 0 | 0.0 | 0.015 | 0.0 | 0.017 | 0.0 | 0.016 | 0.0 | 0.022 | 0.0 | 0.034 | 0.0 | 0.016 |
| 1 1 0 1 | 0.0 | 0.0 | 0.0 | 0.0 | 0.0 | 0.0 | 0.0 | 0.0 | 0.0 | 0.0 | 0.0 | 0.0 |
| 1 1 1 0 | 0.043 | 0.029 | 0.078 | 0.052 | 0.019 | 0.0 | 0.022 | 0.058 | 0.048 | 0.102 | 0.0 | 0.031 |
| 1 1 1 1 | 0.128 | 0.241 | 0.156 | 0.207 | 0.130 | 0.297 | 0.097 | 0.234 | 0.129 | 0.254 | 0.078 | 0.234 |
| % Switch | 20.6 | 23.4 | 18.8 | 22.4 | 27.8 | 25.0 | 30.6 | 21.2 | 29.0 | 15.3 | 35.3 | 28.1 |
| % Fulfilment equity axiom | 77.3 | 69.3 | 70.3 | 70.7 | 79.6 | 67.2 | 85.1 | 66.4 | 75.8 | 61.0 | 92.2 | 70.3 |

Note: A choice of alternative x is coded as 0, a decision in favour of y is coded as 1. The 'total' samples include respondents from all three places, viz. Barcelona, Leuven and Osnabrück.

Next, compare answers to both the no-responsibility and the responsibility questionnaire versions in the two situations. Let us start by looking at the total samples. In situation 1, the fulfilment of the equity axiom went down somewhat for both sexes so that gender differences remained significant (p=0.010). Correspondingly, again facing the responsibility version men were much more likely to act in accordance with sequence 1111 (p=0.012). Fairly surprisingly, while women less often tended to support the handicapped person unconditionally, the corresponding relative frequency for men went up. Hence, there are no longer any gender differences with respect to sequence 0000 in the responsibility case. Consequently, men were less likely to switch from alternative $x$ to $y$ compared to both women in the responsibility version (p=0.012) and men in the no-responsibility case (p=0.021). Thus, it seems as if women reacted as probably expected, while men were more likely to display an unconditional support for either alternative.

This result cannot be confirmed in situation 2. There were virtually no effects of responsibility considerations on answers of male students. In contrast, if responsibility considerations were introduced, females fulfilled the axiom more often. As a result, women are now significantly more likely than men to support the Africans initially (p=0.000). Other gender differences remained the same. Hence, in some way females seem to have honoured the risk-taking behaviour of the Africans, whereas males completely ignored this fact.

Findings for both situations are a bit disturbing, but they become clearer if results from two places are investigated separately. In Osnabrück, opposite developments for women and men are visible in situation 1 if relative frequencies for the two questionnaire versions are compared. Women in the responsibility case, compared to women facing the opposite version, less often fulfilled the axiom (p=0.089) and, hence, were more likely to choose in accordance with sequence 1111 (p=0.040). In contrast, men switched less frequently (p=0.027) and acted more regularly in accordance with sequence 0000 (p=0.027) if the handicap is due to participating in some dangerous sports. This discrepancy cannot be observed for the Belgian samples, where both sexes reacted in the way 'expected' with regard to the aspect of responsibility, although the effect is not statistically significant for the total Belgian sample. Here, men responded even slightly more strongly with regard to the decrease of relative frequencies of both the fulfilment of the axiom and the choice represented by sequence 0000. Consequently, here gender differences are even more apparent if the handicapped person is supposed to be responsible for his or her own fate. Thus, the 'troubling' results for situation 1 can be explained by the risk-honouring behaviour of German males.

In contrast, in the second context observed changes of answers in the responsibility case are mainly due to reactions of Belgian women to the aspect of risk-taking behaviour. There, astonishingly 92.2% of the females fulfilled the equity axiom in the responsibility case. This value is higher than in the no-responsibility case (p=0.067), and also significantly larger than the corresponding value for males in the responsibility version (p=0.004). Also, in the responsibility version women were more likely than men to choose in accordance with sequence 0000 (p=0.025), while the difference in the relative frequency for sequence 1111 remains significant (p=0.025). In Osnabrück, the acceptance of the axiom declined for men and increased for women in the responsibility version; the resulting difference between both sexes is statistically significant at the 10% level (p=0.080).

To summarise, in situation 1 some male students from Osnabrück honoured the risk-taking behaviour of the sportsperson and females punished it to some extent, while in situation 2 women in Leuven and – to some degree – in Osnabrück, rewarded the experiments of the Africans. Now, it is interesting to see whether multivariate regression models confirm these one-dimensional comparisons.

*Binary Response Models*

Various regression models have already been estimated in the preceding subsections. For each situation, these models are supplemented by three different sets of interaction effects in order to investigate different influences from the gender dummy.

Firstly, the product term MALE∗RES is added to see whether the effect of responsibility considerations on the dependent variable is influenced by the gender of respondents. Remember, that in such cases the single dummy variable for gender and the indicator of the questionnaire version, RES, are conditional on the other product term being zero.

Secondly, local differences with respect to gender disparities are allowed for, which are now analysed without considering different effects of the aspect of responsibility. This is due to the fact that interaction terms including the dummy variable RES are not incorporated in the second 2-way interaction model of each situation.

Thirdly, three-way interaction terms are used. Following the suggestions of Jaccard (2001, p. 25), RES is interpreted as the focal independent variable, whereas MALE is the first-order moderator variable, because it is supposed to directly influence the effect of responsibility considerations on the distributive decision. Consequently, the place dummies are second-order moderator variables, since they are supposed to moderate the influence of the first-order variable, viz. gender. As explained in subsection 2.3.4, this model must also include all lower order interaction terms in order to be hierarchically well-formulated.

Now, consider the binary logit models reported in Table 3.13. If we run likelihood-ratio tests to determine whether each regarded set of product terms improves model fit over the cases presented in Table 3.5, we find that in none of the cases a statistically significant improvement at the 5% level can be

Table 3.13: ML estimates of binary logit models - Gender effects
Dependent variable: Fulfilment of Equity Axiom

| Independent variables | Situation 1 (n=719) 2-way | | 3-way | Situation 2 (n=549) 2-way | | 3-way |
|---|---|---|---|---|---|---|
| *Constant* | 12.199<br>(6.766) | 12.032<br>(6.808) | 12.658<br>(6.857) | 19.156*<br>(9.086) | 17.275<br>(9.041) | 17.375<br>(9.205) |
| *AGE* | −0.737<br>(0.582) | −0.729<br>(0.585) | −0.765<br>(0.589) | −1.588<br>(0.813) | −1.401<br>(0.807) | −1.411<br>(0.822) |
| $AGE^2$ | 0.013<br>(0.013) | 0.013<br>(0.013) | 0.014<br>(0.013) | 0.035<br>(0.018) | 0.030<br>(0.018) | 0.030<br>(0.018) |
| *MALE* | −0.621*<br>(0.279) | −0.282<br>(0.263) | −0.634<br>(0.404) | −0.394<br>(0.281) | −0.334<br>(0.291) | 0.029<br>(0.407) |
| *RES* | −0.323<br>(0.294) | −0.257<br>(0.184) | −0.669<br>(0.410) | 0.527<br>(0.318) | 0.139<br>(0.201) | 0.280<br>(0.405) |
| $PAR_2$ | −0.514<br>(0.301) | −0.505<br>(0.302) | −0.492<br>(0.303) | −0.215<br>(0.314) | −0.264<br>(0.315) | −0.255<br>(0.317) |
| $PAR_3$ | −0.353<br>(0.307) | −0.339<br>(0.309) | −0.334<br>(0.310) | −0.162<br>(0.312) | −0.206<br>(0.314) | −0.196<br>(0.315) |
| $PAR_4$ | −0.705*<br>(0.294) | −0.673*<br>(0.296) | −0.660*<br>(0.297) | −0.197<br>(0.311) | −0.257<br>(0.312) | −0.274<br>(0.316) |
| $PLACE_B$ | −0.267<br>(0.460) | −0.493<br>(0.549) | −1.146<br>(0.692) | 0.395<br>(0.452) | 1.111<br>(0.687) | 0.960<br>(0.835) |
| $PLACE_L$ | −1.438**<br>(0.364) | −1.006*<br>(0.432) | −1.349*<br>(0.553) | −0.086<br>(0.388) | 0.274<br>(0.465) | −0.036<br>(0.539) |
| $MALE*$<br>$RES$ | 0.108<br>(0.376) | — | 0.616<br>(0.523) | −0.656<br>(0.413) | — | −0.708<br>(0.565) |
| $MALE*$<br>$PLACE_B$ | — | 0.595<br>(0.805) | 1.816<br>(1.257) | — | −1.271<br>(0.792) | −1.238<br>(1.040) |
| $MALE*$<br>$PLACE_L$ | — | −0.771<br>(0.399) | −0.272<br>(0.588) | — | −0.631<br>(0.446) | −0.653<br>(0.594) |
| $PLACE_B*$<br>$RES$ | — | — | 1.334<br>(1.020) | — | — | 0.369<br>(1.331) |
| $PLACE_L*$<br>$RES$ | — | — | 0.595<br>(0.634) | — | — | 0.812<br>(0.743) |
| $MALE * RES*$<br>$PLACE_B$ | — | — | −2.339<br>(1.686) | — | — | −0.214<br>(1.627) |
| $MALE * RES*$<br>$PLACE_L$ | — | — | −0.904<br>(0.799) | — | — | −0.204<br>(0.926) |
| Log likelihood | -367.67 | -365.09 | -363.55 | -297.33 | -296.68 | -294.09 |
| LR statistic | 48.80** | 53.97** | 57.05** | 28.75** | 30.05** | 35.23** |
| McFadden $R^2$ | 0.062 | 0.069 | 0.073 | 0.046 | 0.048 | 0.057 |

Note: Given are logistic coefficients (betas). Standard errors are reported in parentheses. Level of significance: $^*0.01 \leq p < 0.05$, $^{**}p < 0.01$.

observed. This finding also holds for the reduced samples including variables on income expectations. Additionally, we experimented with models that included only one place dummy – and corresponding product terms – at the same time to compare answers from one country with the combination of the two other places. However, no significant effects could be observed. It is possible that our samples from different places are still too small to detect significant gender differences with respect to the consideration of aspects of responsibility.

Nevertheless, let us briefly comment on some results in order to get at least an impression of possible gender disparities. The first two-way interaction model in situation 1 contains a negative and statistically significant estimated coefficient for the gender dummy variable. Hence, in the no-responsibility case (the condition is RES=0) men were less likely to fulfil the equity axiom, which corresponds to the descriptive results for the total sample.

In the second two-way interaction model, the estimated coefficient of the product MALE$*$PLACE$_L$ is negative and significant at least at the 10% level (the corresponding p-value equals 0.054 so that this result cannot be seen from the table).[24] Thus, in general the effect of gender on the initial support for the handicapped person may have been different in Leuven compared to Osnabrück. Indeed, the overall difference between relative frequencies for women and men is rather low in Osnabrück compared to Leuven.

The three-way interaction terms do not reveal any local disparities in the influence of gender on responsibility considerations. Also, only some minor effects are visible in situation 2.

Finally, let us briefly mention some results of the reduced samples where future income variables are additionally included in the regressions. Here, surprisingly changes occurred. German females were less likely to fulfil the axiom if the handicapped person was supposed to be responsible compared to the case where the retarded person was said to be handicapped from birth. Moreover, the influence of aspects of responsibility on the fulfilment of the equity axiom is remarkably different for male respondents in Osnabrück. These findings confirm some of our earlier observations from the descriptive results. However, some scepticism about these clearer differences might be reasonable. The inclusion of future income dummy variables could have had an influence, but further regressions on the reduced sample data without these predictors yield similar results. Thus, the strengthened gender effects seem to be entirely due to the exclusion of 48 respondents from Osnabrück. Evidently, a sample selection bias exists which is especially due to the varied income question in the year 2003. Hence, one should again be careful in interpreting the results of the reduced sample.

24 The $\chi^2$ value for the corresponding likelihood-ratio test with regard to the two product terms is statistically significant at the 10% level (p-value=0.072).

*Ordered and Multinomial Response Models*

Again, extensions of the better-off groups in both situations are considered. Here, we will only focus on the larger samples. It has already been argued in subsection 3.6.3 that in situation 1 the application of ordered logit models seems to be unproblematic for the different gender models. In contrast, results of the 'suggestive' likelihood-ratio test summarised in Table 3.7 revealed significant differences at the 10% level in the second situation. Nevertheless, in the following paragraphs we will present only results of ordered logit models, while multinomial logit models are omitted in order to save space. This is for three reasons. Firstly, the estimation of some multinomial logit models caused problems due to empty cells. Secondly, likelihood-ratio tests on the relevance of (sets of) product terms could not reveal any significant improvement of model fit compared to models where no product terms are included. Thirdly, results of both types of regression models are astonishingly similar so that one may skip presentations of more extensive models.

Results of ordered logit models are presented in Table 3.14.[25] Likelihood-ratio tests show that only for model 1 of situation 1 the inclusion of a product term significantly improves model fit ($\chi_1^2 = 4.00$, the critical value for $\alpha$=0.05 equals 3.84). In this model, which includes the product term MALE∗RES, the negative and significant estimated coefficient for the gender variable confirms that women were more likely to choose in accordance with sequences that are closer to the spirit of the equity axiom. Furthermore, the negative estimated coefficient for RES is statistically significant at the 10% level (p=0.052). This means that for females (MALE=0) in the total sample the probability of perceiving sequence 1111 increases and the likelihood of observing sequence 0000 decreases if we move from RES=0 to RES=1. In contrast, as the positive and significant estimated coefficient for the interaction term implies, this reaction is different for males. This observation is confirmed by model 3 in situation 1, which includes three-way interaction terms. The significant effect of the product term MALE∗RES reveals that the main influence comes from the German sample, since the estimated coefficient is conditioned on $PLACE_B$=$PLACE_L$=0.

The observed differences can also be deduced from marginal probabilities summarised in Table 3.9 in the previous subsection. For models 1 and 3 they show that differences between females and males were astonishingly high for those sequences, which denote an unconditional support for either alternative $x$ or $y$.

Lastly, estimated results for model 2 in situation 1 presented in Table 3.14 reveal that the overall effect of gender on observed decision patterns differed between Leuven and Osnabrück. The corresponding coefficient for the product term MALE∗$PLACE_L$ is negative and significant at the 10% level

25 In order to keep the presentation manageable, parental background dummies and the variables AGE and $AGE^2$ are omitted although they are included in the regressions.

Table 3.14: ML estimates of ordered logit models - Gender effects
Dependent variable: 5 Ordered Sequences

| Independent | Situation 1 (n=688) | | | Situation 2 (n=481) | | |
|---|---|---|---|---|---|---|
| variables | Model 1 | Model 2 | Model 3 | Model 1 | Model 2 | Model 3 |
| $MALE$ | −0.700** | −0.227 | −0.632* | −0.617* | −0.236 | −0.296 |
| | (0.203) | (0.189) | (0.269) | (0.253) | (0.270) | (0.381) |
| $RES$ | −0.397 | −0.110 | −0.394 | −0.109 | −0.037 | −0.181 |
| | (0.204) | (0.139) | (0.271) | (0.255) | (0.175) | (0.372) |
| $PLACE_B$ | 0.385 | −0.332 | 0.467 | 0.471 | 0.722 | 1.161 |
| | (0.321) | (0.382) | (0.511) | (0.381) | (0.480) | (0.716) |
| $PLACE_L$ | −0.782** | −0.540 | −0.579 | −0.530 | −0.272 | −0.476 |
| | (0.281) | (0.319) | (0.390) | (0.341) | (0.390) | (0.483) |
| $MALE*$ $RES$ | 0.559* | — | 0.819* | 0.144 | — | 0.123 |
| | (0.280) | | (0.368) | (0.351) | | (0.524) |
| $MALE*$ $PLACE_B$ | — | 0.040 | 0.071 | — | −0.569 | −0.966 |
| | | (0.511) | (0.716) | | (0.621) | (0.924) |
| $MALE*$ $PLACE_L$ | — | −0.586 | −0.197 | — | −0.526 | −0.443 |
| | | (0.309) | (0.433) | | (0.377) | (0.533) |
| $PLACE_B*$ $RES$ | — | — | −0.219 | — | — | −0.798 |
| | | | (0.650) | | | (0.874) |
| $PLACE_L*$ $RES$ | — | — | 0.069 | — | — | 0.363 |
| | | | (0.449) | | | (0.546) |
| $MALE * RES*$ $PLACE_B$ | — | — | −0.088 | — | — | 0.663 |
| | | | (1.022) | | | (1.248) |
| $MALE * RES*$ $PLACE_L$ | — | — | −0.809 | — | — | −0.154 |
| | | | (0.613) | | | (0.745) |
| $\mu_1$ | −9.301 | −9.422 | −10.072 | −17.617* | −16.068* | −16.250* |
| | (5.563) | (5.599) | (5.617) | (7.666) | (7.684) | (7.723) |
| $\mu_2$ | −8.278 | −8.395 | −9.040 | −17.110* | −15.560* | −15.742* |
| | (5.561) | (5.597) | (5.615) | (7.664) | (7.682) | (7.721) |
| $\mu_3$ | −7.612 | −7.732 | −8.369 | −16.419* | −14.865 | −15.046 |
| | (5.559) | (5.595) | (5.613) | (7.661) | (7.679) | (7.718) |
| $\mu_4$ | −7.471 | −7.592 | −8.227 | −16.286* | −14.732 | −14.912 |
| | (5.559) | (5.595) | (5.613) | (7.660) | (7.679) | (7.718) |
| Log likelihood | -551.37 | -551.43 | -547.84 | -390.29 | -389.29 | -388.13 |
| LR statistic | 47.96** | 47.84** | 55.01** | 29.65** | 31.66** | 33.97** |
| (Pseudo-) $R^2$ | 0.024 | 0.024 | 0.028 | 0.024 | 0.026 | 0.028 |

Note: Given are logistic coefficients (betas). Standard errors are reported in parentheses. Level of significance: *$0.01 \leq p < 0.05$, **$p < 0.01$. All models also include the variables $AGE$, $AGE^2$, $PAR_2$, $PAR_3$ and $PAR_4$.

(p=0.057). But this outcome only confirms earlier findings on local disparities.

In situation 2, stronger gender effects on the influence of responsibility considerations are not visible.

So, what can be concluded with respect to the influence of gender on the effect of responsibility considerations? From the descriptive data it was observed that there were some clear but unexpected overall gender differences concerning the evaluation of the risk-taking behaviour of worse-off individuals. While especially males from Germany 'honoured' the risk-taking behaviour of the sportsperson, women in Leuven rewarded the experiments of the Africans. To some degree these findings could be confirmed by different multivariate regression models, although most of the observed effects were not 'strong' enough to show statistical significance, which might be due to the still relatively low sample sizes in some cases. In the concluding section, our observations will be interpreted.

## 3.7 Conclusions

The underlying intention of the present investigation was to shed some more light on the trade-off between the principle of needs and a version of the principle of responsibility. This was done by incorporating certain aspects of responsibility into the previously considered needs-efficiency trade-off. Thus, the responsibility principle may moderate this conflict. As we said at the outset of this chapter, aspects of responsibility have only recently been introduced by economic theorists into welfare economic reasoning and, in particular, into egalitarian concepts. Moreover, it has been explained that two central questions have to be answered by a theory of distributive justice that aims at incorporating responsibility ideas. Firstly, the location of the responsibility cut that regards the basis on which responsibility is attributed, must be defined. Secondly, the operationalisation of responsibility-sensitive distribution concepts has to be described. Here, especially Bossert and Fleurbaey in a series of papers have identified two basic principles that are logically independent. While the principle of compensation introduces egalitarian concerns, the principle of natural reward establishes the idea of responsibility. Consequently, each theoretical approach fulfils both principles to a certain degree, whereas a complete satisfaction of both notions is impossible.

In subsection 3.4.2 it has been explained that the hypothetical situations in the present questionnaire introduced a kind of risk-taking behaviour on the side of the individuals in need. Thus, the focus is on Dworkin's concept of option luck that is used by several theories to identify the location of the responsibility cut, while others have their reservations about this. Nevertheless, we also argued that the case for option luck seems to be much more obvious in the first situation of the questionnaire, which is an often mentioned example in the theoretical literature, whereas the second context also contained some countervailing aspects.

However, the aim of the present work is to investigate conflicts between justice principles. Therefore, the aspect of responsibility has been incorporated into the well-established trade-off between the needs or equality principle and the principle of efficiency. This results in a rather complex situation, where the needs principle is challenged by efficiency and responsibility considerations. While many theoretical concepts, which formulate principles of responsibility, are not able to differentiate between diverse contexts, in particular Fleurbaey (1995b, 1998, 2008) has focused on the context of needs, and claimed that society should identify certain functionings, which form an index that should be equalised over individuals without regarding any information on aspects of responsibility.

Various statistical instruments have been applied in order to thoroughly analyse answers on both contexts of the present questionnaire. The most general result of this investigation is that we could not detect any negative significant influence of responsibility considerations on the acceptance of the needs principle by our students. Several explanations for this observation are possible.

Firstly, it might be doubted that the location of the responsibility cut is uncontroversial in both situations. It has already been argued in subsection 3.4.1 that especially the behaviour of the sportsperson in situation 1 is one of the most prominent examples in the literature for a case of option luck. In that sense, we regarded an argument by Schokkaert (1999) that has been mentioned in the first chapter. Theorists may be biased by some prominent examples in their research community. For this, it is of special interest to see whether opinions of theorists on certain cases, such as being handicapped after participating in a dangerous sport, are shared by laymen. In contrast, even more scepticism about the free choice of the Africans and the diffusion of responsibility being described obviously weakened the case for responsibility-sensitivity in the second situation.

Secondly, in both contexts the relevant information for possible aspects of responsibility may be covered by several other details, which are important for the principles of needs and efficiency. Subjects may have simply missed this point. This could also be seen from the small number of comments on this aspect in the verbal answers. Indeed, a good deal of information is necessary in both contexts to create the intended trade-off. But this objection points towards a deeper problem of all empirical investigations. The question is, how obvious specific decision alternatives should be pronounced by the phrasing and the framing of a situation. In fact, some studies intensely direct the attention of respondents to those aspects in which the researcher is interested. However, reconsider again possible biases of theoretical conception that have been discussed in chapter 1. Is it not possible that an empirical researcher who is mostly interested in the uncovering of effects of responsibility considerations could be tempted to push participants of a questionnaire study towards that direction? Clearly, the question arises of how obvious some offered alternatives could be stated without being called 'manipulative'?

Furthermore, in real life situations it is probably more often the case that a decision-maker has available a variety of information on different aspects of the underlying situation so that it is up to him or her which particular information to use.

With regard to the two contexts in the present questionnaire, the responsibility of the sportsperson in situation 1 seems to be especially clear. Also, it was explicitly intended to formulate the aspect of responsibility in the second context in a rather mild and cautious way. In fact, each respondent received similar versions of the two situations. By this procedure, biases from a different version of the respective other context should be avoided.

A third argument for the absence of negative influences from aspects of responsibility can be identified. For some students, it might have been tough to make an either-or decision and, possibly, completely reject the help for people in need. Indeed, several empirical studies that revealed effects of information about the responsibility of individuals for their own fate offered the possibility of a continuous split of a given resource.[26] It is possible that the complete denial of help could be seen as too harsh a punishment for previous misbehaviour. In fact, in the following questionnaire study the restriction of either-or decisions will be relaxed. However, results of the first investigation already revealed that a majority of subjects rejected at some point the support for worse offs and chose instead in accordance to the principle of efficiency. Moreover, many theoretical approaches on influences from responsibility considerations do not distinguish between different contexts.

Nevertheless, the findings of both studies presented may suggest a different reading. It seems to be possible that a certain group of respondents would react to both the principle of responsibility and the efficiency principle. Thus, additionally introduced information on aspects of responsibility may only have minor effects due to the already existing efficiency arguments. In contrast, another group of subjects probably objects to all kinds of violation of the principle of needs. Certainly, this interpretation cannot be 'proved' by the present data, but it is consistent with many empirical findings that reveal a strong heterogeneity of opinions on fair allocations. And clearly, this observation also holds for theorists who propose different justice concepts.

However, despite the just discussed – and often weakened – reservations about the location of the responsibility cut in both questionnaire situations, several theoretical ideas, like those who demand equality of resources or equality of opportunities, predict a stronger effect of aspects of responsibility. Nevertheless, in general this influence is not observable. Obviously, it is impossible

26 Examples are the investigations by Skitka and Tetlock (1992), Farwell and Weiner (1996) and Konow (2001).

to show that something does not exist. But it is also important to recognise that the principle of responsibility, which has been operationalised by the concept of option luck, has strongly been criticised for being inappropriate in situations, where basic needs are regarded. This line of argument follows from Fleurbaey's (1998) concept of equality of selected functionings. In that sense, especially findings from our first context, which is most uncontroversial with regard to the aspect of responsibility being described, explicitly support this theoretical hypothesis.

Furthermore, the previously mentioned idea of societal utility reappears in two ways. Firstly, all people may gain from the knowledge that they live in a society where individuals in need are always helped. Secondly, in the context of the African starvation the risk-taking behaviour could be interpreted as being socially valuable. Consequently, the Africans 'deserve' to be supported.

Some additional points are particularly worth mentioning. In chapter 1, various possible biases of justice evaluations have been discussed. In the present study, two factors proved to be important. On the one hand, certain local differences have been revealed. As argued already above, these variations are far removed from showing cultural effects. It is quite difficult to explain why respondents in Belgium should possess different justice attitudes compared to participants from Germany or Spain. If more comprehensive comments on such disparities are desired, one should use several additional samples from different places in the three countries being regarded. Moreover, other groups of society have to be incorporated to obtain reliable insights into the cultural dimension of equity evaluations. Nevertheless, clear local effects have been identified. As explained in the first chapter, it is important to control for these influences in order to receive unbiased justice attitudes.

On the other hand, we focused again on gender differences. As before, the reviewed empirical work was not conclusive with respect to the expected influence of aspects of responsibility on answers of men and women. While females are usually found to be more risk-averse, males more often regarded aspects of merit in income distribution experiments. Again, the relatively large sample size allowed us to analyse gender effects. Furthermore, the inclusion of respondents from different places offered the opportunity to investigate local differences with respect to gender effects. The results were a little bit of a surprise. Firstly, the strong gender differences, which have been revealed by the first questionnaire study, have not only been confirmed but even strengthened. This was basically due to respondents from Belgium. Now, in both situations male respondents less often accepted the equity axiom and were less likely to unconditionally support the worse offs. Secondly, results on the influence of aspects of responsibility on answers from men and women are rather complex. While male students in Osnabrück honoured the risk-taking behaviour of the sportsperson, females in Leuven rewarded the risky experiments of the Africans.

Obviously, there are different perceptions of the hypothetical behaviours in the contexts being described. It could be possible that male students, compared to their female counterparts, were better able to identify with the sportsperson in situation 1. In contrast, maybe women in Belgium interpreted the second situation differently and evaluated the risk-taking behaviour in a more positive way. As explained above, the different starting points may have played a certain role. While the sportsperson already knew a better life and was probably equally well off compared to the intelligent children, the Africans may have been supposed to be clearly worse off than inhabitants of the country of respondents. Possibly, these differences have dissimilar effects on women and men.

Still, we are not able to give conclusive reasons for observed gender differences. Nevertheless, it is important to recognise such observations as potential biases. Moreover, gender-specific justice concepts are possible. Faravelli (2007) argues that if information gaps in hypothetical situations exist, individual characteristics may guide the filling of these gaps. This idea seems to be very reasonable in all of our investigations.

Finally, three technical remarks are necessary. Firstly, again we did not apply advanced statistical methods proposed in the specialised literature on the treatment of item non-responses. However, we found it important to mention the possible selection bias. This intention is partly based on the elaborations about biases in the first chapter. Moreover, it is very interesting to see that the question on future income expectations of respondents mainly excluded females from the sample. In the present investigation, we relied on the larger sample, since the observed selection bias seems to have more important consequences. However, in the previous study, the future income variable was of major interest. Nevertheless, in both chapters, tests on the corresponding smaller or larger samples have been reported.

Secondly, we experimented with ordered and multinomial logit models. In the literature, a reliable tool to evaluate the appropriateness of both approaches is not available. Each model has advantages and disadvantages so that both methods are simultaneously presented and discussed.

Thirdly, there is no consensus in the literature about the most appropriate way to interpret interaction terms. We decided to follow the suggestions by Jaccard (2001), which may be seen as less advanced. Nevertheless, if significant effects were observed, they always confirmed findings from descriptive data and one-dimensional statistical tests.

Clearly, the two studies introduced so far are closely related. The theoretical background is rather similar, and the applied statistical methods are identical. The investigation that has been presented in this chapter has introduced responsibility as an important additional principle of justice into the previous needs-efficiency trade-off. Now, we are prepared to turn to the third empirical investigation. Here, many similarities to its predecessors will be recognised. However, several modifications will be described, which intend to examine additional trade-offs between the four principles of distributive justice. Thus, a completely different allocation conception is proposed that is based on more than one notion of justice.

## 3.8 Appendix

Table 3.15: Variable descriptions (incl. income expectations)

| | Total | | Osnabrück | | Women | | Men | |
|---|---|---|---|---|---|---|---|---|
| | Sit. 1 | Sit. 2 | Sit. 1 | Sit. 2 | Sit. 1 | Sit. 2 | Sit. 1 | Sit. 2 |
| Code | n=671 | n=505 | n=365 | n=199 | n=305 | n=242 | n=366 | n=263 |
| $AGE$ | 20.83 | 20.23 | 22.54 | 22.44 | 20.38 | 19.92 | 21.21 | 20.51 |
| | (2.47) | (2.28) | (1.94) | (1.81) | (2.17) | (1.98) | (2.63) | (2.49) |
| $MALE$ | 0.55 | 0.52 | 0.57 | 0.53 | 0.00 | 0.00 | 1.00 | 1.00 |
| | (0.50) | (0.50) | (0.50) | (0.50) | (—) | (—) | (—) | (—) |
| $RES$ | 0.50 | 0.50 | 0.51 | 0.50 | 0.50 | 0.49 | 0.51 | 0.50 |
| | (0.50) | (0.50) | (0.50) | (0.50) | (0.50) | (0.50) | (0.50) | (0.50) |
| $PAR_1$ | 0.17 | 0.18 | 0.16 | 0.15 | 0.19 | 0.19 | 0.16 | 0.17 |
| | (0.38) | (0.38) | (0.36) | (0.36) | (0.39) | (0.39) | (0.37) | (0.37) |
| $PAR_2$ | 0.27 | 0.27 | 0.27 | 0.26 | 0.30 | 0.31 | 0.25 | 0.24 |
| | (0.45) | (0.44) | (0.45) | (0.44) | (0.46) | (0.46) | (0.43) | (0.43) |
| $PAR_3$ | 0.26 | 0.26 | 0.26 | 0.26 | 0.23 | 0.24 | 0.28 | 0.28 |
| | (0.44) | (0.44) | (0.44) | (0.44) | (0.42) | (0.43) | (0.45) | (0.45) |
| $PAR_4$ | 0.28 | 0.28 | 0.29 | 0.29 | 0.26 | 0.24 | 0.30 | 0.31 |
| | (0.45) | (0.45) | (0.45) | (0.45) | (0.44) | (0.43) | (0.46) | (0.46) |
| $PLACE_O$ | 0.54 | 0.39 | 1.00 | 1.00 | 0.51 | 0.38 | 0.57 | 0.40 |
| | (0.50) | (0.49) | (—) | (—) | (0.50) | (0.49) | (0.50) | (0.49) |
| $PLACE_B$ | 0.11 | 0.14 | 0.00 | 0.00 | 0.14 | 0.18 | 0.08 | 0.11 |
| | (0.31) | (0.35) | (—) | (—) | (0.35) | (0.39) | (0.27) | (0.31) |
| $PLACE_L$ | 0.35 | 0.46 | 0.00 | 0.00 | 0.34 | 0.43 | 0.35 | 0.49 |
| | (0.48) | (0.50) | (—) | (—) | (0.48) | (0.50) | (0.48) | (0.50) |
| $FUT_1$ | 0.16 | 0.18 | 0.18 | 0.24 | 0.20 | 0.22 | 0.13 | 0.15 |
| | (0.37) | (0.39) | (0.38) | (0.43) | (0.40) | (0.41) | (0.34) | (0.36) |
| $FUT_2$ | 0.37 | 0.36 | 0.27 | 0.17 | 0.45 | 0.44 | 0.30 | 0.29 |
| | (0.48) | (0.48) | (0.45) | (0.38) | (0.50) | (0.50) | (0.46) | (0.45) |
| $FUT_3$ | 0.47 | 0.46 | 0.55 | 0.59 | 0.35 | 0.34 | 0.57 | 0.56 |
| | (0.50) | (0.50) | (0.50) | (0.49) | (0.48) | (0.48) | (0.50) | (0.50) |

Note: Variable descriptions are analogous to those given in Table 3.1. The following codes are added: $FUT_1$: Future income below average ($< 50\%$), $FUT_2$: Average future income ($= 50\%$), $FUT_3$: Future income above average ($> 50\%$). Given are mean values. Corresponding numbers for Barcelona and Leuven are similar to the values stated in Table 3.1. Hence, they are omitted.

# 4 The Acceptance of Truncated Efficiency

## 4.1 Introduction

Let us start this chapter by reconsidering once again the four allocation principles that are said to be behind several distinct theories of distributive justice. Firstly, the most fundamental notion is the principle of equality, but here each theory has to state what the corresponding equalisandum is. Secondly, the principle of efficiency demands the maximisation of the sum of benefits from a given quantity of a certain resource. Therefore, it has to be distinguished from Pareto efficiency. However, the underlying notion is regularly represented by a combination of the Pareto criterion and a version of the compensation principle. In this case, an allocation is said to be efficient if it is not Pareto dominated by another allocation, even if one allows for hypothetical lump-sum redistributions. Thirdly, the principle of responsibility demands the acceptance of outcomes which follow from individual differences with respect to responsibility-variables that have to be defined by the theoretical conception. Fourthly, according to the principle of needs, unsatisfied basic needs of each individual should be fully regarded.

Certainly, the four notions could recommend conflicting allocations in distribution situations so that trade-offs between these principles are of special interest. One remarkable result of the two preceding empirical studies was the notable proportion of subjects who reconsidered their initial support for worse-off individuals, when opposite better-off groups were successively enlarged. The respondents objected to the spirit of the equity axiom that underlies the difference principle. Such decisions can be interpreted in two ways. On the one hand, aspects of efficiency are increasingly appealing in the given contexts and, thereby, explain the relevance of this principle even if the fulfilment of basic needs is offered as an alternative. On the other hand, a well-known pitfall of the unconditional support for worse offs can be witnessed, which has already been described in the discussion on the difference principle in the first chapter with respect to the criticism by Harsanyi (1975). It is sometimes called the 'bottomless pit problem' and relates to those concepts which solely focus on improvements for worse offs, no matter how small they are, and, as a result, accept any sacrifice of alternative benefits for better offs, even if they are massive.[1] With regard to the structure of the situations described in our questionnaires, the possible 'wastefulness' of the difference principle becomes increasingly apparent. Nevertheless, Elster (1995, p. 94) describes the dilemma of both the difference principle and utilitarian concerns by saying that "the former theory has too much potential for waste and the latter too little capacity for compassion to be fully acceptable as a theory of justice". More generally, we observe a trade-off between the principles of needs or equality and the principle of efficiency.

However, Elster goes on to argue that the combination of different distribution concepts could allow for attenuating possible concerns being immanent in single principles. Particularly, he mentions *truncated utilitarianism* as an important alternative. This allocation concept demands maximising total welfare subject to a certain *floor level* of individual welfare of all people. Consequently, this level which introduces a constraint to inequality is lexicographically preferred to utilitarian reasoning in the way that the latter freely unfolds only after fully regarding the floor level. However, reconsider the discussion on theories of distributive justice in subsection 1.2.1. There, it was argued that the underlying informational requirements of utilitarianism are probably too strong in many contexts. Therefore, as already said above, it is more convenient to apply the Pareto criterion and a formulation of the compensation principle as weaker assumptions for the efficiency principle. In the present chapter, the focus is on this less demanding definition. Consequently, the more appropriate name for the allocation conception being regarded might be *truncated efficiency*.

Hence, in view of our previous empirical results it is obvious to ask whether the idea of truncated efficiency can serve as a well accepted compromise solution if we confront laymen with correspondingly modified situations of our earlier questionnaires.

But if this conception seems to be a candidate for an acceptable compromise between different justice theories, what can be said about the attention that truncated efficiency has received in the theoretical literature on distributive justice? Maybe, the reader will remember that we described the considered idea already in chapter 1. It was explained that Rawls (1971) explicitly rejects this mixed conception, where the floor level is given by a certain social minimum. Firstly, he argues that "the difficulty here is the same as that with intuitionist doctrines generally" and asks "how [...] the social minimum [is] to be selected and adjusted to changing circumstances" (p. 316). Secondly, the application of utilitarian reasoning beyond the acceptance of the social minimum suffers from the same shortcomings as utilitarianism in general so that "there are still reasons for choosing the difference principle [...] over that of utility even in the restricted context of a mixed conception" (pp. 324-325).

---

1 See e.g. Brighouse (2001) for this expression. According to Demuijnck and Le Clainche (2007), other just as catchy terms are 'slavery of the talented' or 'social hijacking'.

Indeed, both the interpretation of the floor level and the definition of the applied principle beyond this level are crucial for the evaluation of truncated efficiency. One possibility to state this idea in line with our four allocation principles is to regard a combination of the principles of needs and efficiency, whereby the former receives absolute priority. But then, it has to be explained what is meant by the term 'needs'. In fact, some writers try to define the floor level as an absolute poverty line. As illustrated by Moore (1978), the idea of helping people in need with the aim of allowing them a life at the poverty line can already be observed from historical examples. Moreover, truncated efficiency is reflected in the structure of modern welfare states. Most prominently, Boulding (1962, p. 83) formulates that "[...] society lays a modest table at which all can sup and a high table at which the deserving can feast". Indeed, beyond the consideration of needs, the notion of just deserts plays a crucial role in many conceptions. The intention is to preserve incentives in society in order to maximise overall production and, correspondingly, average income (see e.g. Frohlich and Oppenheimer, 1992). Similarly, in the realm of political theory, Raphael (1970) describes the welfare state as a combination of the principles of needs and merit, whereby the latter is based on effort and ability. Accordingly, after the fulfilment of everyone's basic needs, competition for additional resources should be implemented.

However, as already explained in the introduction of chapter 3, some theorists do not accept merit or effort as distinct notions. For example, Rawls (1971, p. 15) claims that we need a conception of justice "that nullifies the accidents of natural endowment and the contingencies of social circumstances" that consider, for example, talents and effort. Similar ideas are stated by Nozick (1974) and Hayek (1976), while Miller (1999) cites several authors who maintain that merit is a distinct allocation principle. Furthermore, the incorporation of incentive considerations is usually seen as being problematic since this may lead to a 'second best ethics' (see e.g. Schokkaert and Devooght, 2003). But even if one does not acknowledge the relevance of merit, truncated efficiency may be just as plausibly derived from efficiency considerations directly. Clearly, in view of the discussion of principles in the first chapter and with regard to our empirical results in chapters 2 and 3, at least to some degree the relevance of efficiency seems to be convincing. In view of this argument, Scott et al. (2001, p. 752) criticise the studies of Frohlich and Oppenheimer (1992) by pointing out that "since they did not distinguish between efficiency and merit in their design they cannot determine why groups allowed inequality when maximizing income". Indeed, we are also going to independently vary information which is relevant for the application of the principles of efficiency and responsibility in order to control for the influence of both notions. However, it is important to note that we decided to apply a micro-justice setting while almost all theoretical, but also a larger proportion of empirical work on truncated efficiency, regards macro-justice examples. Nevertheless, in the first chapter we have argued that the distinction between small- and large-scale situations is basically a contextual effect that should not demand completely different justice theories.

Especially due to the work by Frohlich and Oppenheimer (1992) truncated efficiency has received attention in empirical investigations on equality-efficiency trade-offs. It is important to recognise that in order to determine the floor constraint two different concepts are applied in empirical studies, which are reviewed in the next section. The two approaches reflect different understandings of truncated efficiency which appear to be surprisingly essential. Firstly, in some studies participants who opted for the application of truncated efficiency were additionally asked to state their preferred value for the floor level (see e.g. Frohlich and Oppenheimer, 1992, or Herne and Suojanen, 2004).[2] This procedure allows for an unrestricted but maybe less obvious choice of a parameter for the floor. Secondly, in other studies additional information on an explicit poverty line is given (examples are studies by Mitchell et al., 1993, Michelbach et al., 2003, or Faravelli, 2007). In this case, one possibility for the location of the floor is directly 'proposed' in the description of the hypothetical situation.

In the first approach, the identification of the floor level by respondents usually follows unobservable motives. Indeed, Frohlich and Oppenheimer (1992) report that in their study on the acceptance of different hypothetical income distributions participants from North America located the floor level very close to the 'real' poverty line in their society while subjects from Poland chose a level that was well above the corresponding value in their home country. Certainly, the choices of these values are very illuminating. However, it is not clear whether respondents were aware of these lines so that they may have followed either the principle of needs or the principle of equality. But especially in the latter case, we would then witness aspects of intuitionism since a complete equalisation is still rejected. Clearly, Rawls (1971) criticises the weak normative foundations of intuitionism while the empirical relevance is often acknowledged. In the next chapter, it will be explained that corresponding preferences can be represented by isoelastic social welfare functions, which allow displaying different degrees of inequality aversion.

In contrast, following the second approach observed in empirical studies, a distinction is introduced between the principle of needs, which can be fulfilled by accepting the given poverty line, and the principle of equality, which demands to further increase welfare of worse offs beyond this level. Consequently, the value of the social minimum, as used in mixed conceptions described by Rawls, can be deduced from the needs principle. Hence, this special case of truncated efficiency is, at least to some degree, normatively motivated. Therefore, this idea could directly mitigate Rawls's criticism of mixed distribution principles with regard to the arbitrariness of the floor level.

2 Alternatively, Traub et al. (2005) infer *implicit* levels from preferences of subjects over different income distributions.

Furthermore, the interpretation of the poverty line as the floor level allows for a separation of the maximin principle and truncated efficiency, as empirically demonstrated, for example, by Michelbach et al. (2003). The difference between both ideas can be stated in the following way: While the maximin equity criterion represents the case where utilitarianism is constrained by a floor that is maximised, truncated efficiency asks for a minimisation of the floor level until a given poverty line is reached.[3] However, it should be noted again that the situations in the questionnaire are constructed in the way that allocations in accordance with the maximin principle also fulfil the principle of equality.

Similar to our studies presented in chapters 2 and 3, the current questionnaire investigation regards again equality-efficiency trade-offs in settings with two hypothetical groups. However, now a continuous split of the additionally given resource is possible so that a larger set of allocations is available. Furthermore, the idea of a poverty line is introduced in the way that the absolute amount of the resource, which is necessary to satisfy all basic needs of the worse-off group, is explicitly stated. In contrast to our previous investigations, a complete recognition of needs is possible, whereas a total equalisation of both groups regarded is still unfeasible. Thus, applications of different distribution principles beyond the fulfilment of the needs principle are available. Also, more detailed information on the benefits of offered alternatives is given so that we can distinguish between the principle of efficiency and maximin or egalitarian behaviour.[4] Moreover, due to the possibility of a continuous division of the resource, new solutions with respect to the principle of equality, but also compromises between efficiency and equality concerns, are available beyond the fulfilment of needs. Above, we have noted that merit or responsibility considerations and efficiency arguments may enhance the acceptance of truncated efficiency. Thus, as before, we will independently vary information on aspects of responsibility and efficiency so that the relevance of these two principles can be analysed.

In the next section, various empirical studies that explicitly allow for choices in accordance with the idea of truncated efficiency are reviewed and discussed. Afterwards, an axiomatic formulation of this rule from social choice literature is summarised. In the fourth section, the setup of hypothetical situations in the questionnaire is presented and compared with the two previous studies, while in section five the sample is described. Various results are presented in the sixth section. Section seven offers some conclusions.

---

3 See Faravelli (2005, pp. 19-20) for a similar explanation.

4 Notice once again that maximin behaviour also leads to efficient solutions in the Paretian sense. However, the principle of efficiency departs from this definition.

## 4.2 Empirical Studies on Truncated Efficiency

In the following review of empirical studies on the acceptance of truncated efficiency, it will become apparent that results are mixed. Frohlich and Oppenheimer (1992) find very strong support for this concept. Because of the importance of their study for other investigations – including the present work – their experiment will be presented in some detail, first. Then, various subsequent studies will be reviewed in the second subsection. They followed the general idea of Frohlich and Oppenheimer, but also articulated some concerns.

### 4.2.1 The Experiments by Frohlich and Oppenheimer

First of all, the experiments by Frohlich and Oppenheimer (1992) were not the first investigations that examined the acceptance of truncated efficiency. For example, Alves and Rossi (1978) found that income levels are judged to be fair if they result from work effort, but they have to exceed a given minimum level. Also, Mellers (1982) showed that respondents obeyed different merit rules to determine fair salaries in diverse contexts, but these earnings should be above a poverty line that was explicitly given in the questionnaire.

Furthermore, the book by Frohlich and Oppenheimer (1992) summarises several of their own precedent experiments and also studies of their collaborators. Previous articles include Frohlich, Oppenheimer and Eavey (1987a, 1987b), Frohlich and Oppenheimer (1989, 1990), and Lissowski, Tyska and Okrasa (1991). However, to simplify matters in this section we will refer to the book from 1992, when we mention their names without a year specification.

In total at least 488 university students from the United States, Canada and Poland participated in the experiments reported by Frohlich and Oppenheimer.[5] They initially received verbal sketches of four principles for income distributions in a hypothetical society: maximising the minimum income level, i.e. the Rawlsian approach, maximising the average income, which is attributed to Harsanyi's utilitarian concept, and maximising the average income subject to either a certain floor or a range constraint. The latter constraint is defined by the absolute difference between the richest and the poorest individual in society. Respondents were carefully trained to understand the meaning and the consequences of each principle. Additionally, they had to pass a test about various aspects of the principles. Then, at the end of the first part of the experiment, the students had to rank the four rules. With respect to the third and fourth principle presented, they were also asked to state the required parameter. Afterwards, the highest ranked principle of each respondent was used for selecting the 'best' income vector out of an unknown set of

5 It is impossible to quote an unequivocal number from the elaborations of the authors. Besides several other statements, 488 is the highest value we could determine from the tables in the book (p. 210). However, Frohlich and Oppenheimer (p. 56) also remark that ninety-eight experiments with groups of five were run.

different income distributions for society. The subject was randomly placed in an income class of his or her selected distribution and received a monetary payoff based on the hypothetical income in their class.

Certainly, participants were made aware of this procedure before they decided on the ranking of allocation rules. Furthermore, it is important to clarify that rather high values for the floor or the range constraint resulted either in 'pure' Rawlsianism or in 'pure' utilitarianism if none or only one of the previously unknown income vectors fulfilled the constraint.

Out of 414 subjects, who completed all relevant questions (Frohlich and Oppenheimer, p. 99), 57.5% ranked the principle of maximising average income subject to a floor level highest, while 25.6% decided in favour of the utilitarian solution. The maximin criterion was most prominent for only 7.6% of the students.

Frohlich and Oppenheimer explicitly claim that they offer an empirical rejection of the Rawlsian difference principle. Hence, they carefully point out the similarities between Rawls's assumptions about the original position and the structure of the experiment (Frohlich and Oppenheimer, pp. 26-31). Firstly, respondents had only restricted information regarding their personal situation and the structure of society. Thus, complete uncertainty about the position in the future income distribution is achieved, which points to the impartial spectator approach discussed in the first chapter. Therefore, the decision on the allocation rule had to be made behind a veil of ignorance. Secondly, the agenda of available principles was known to the students, but they were also allowed to develop their own rules. Thirdly, however, Frohlich and Oppenheimer admit that it is impossible for an experimental setting to reflect the high stakes in the original position, where subjects are thought to decide on life chances in future societies.[6]

The more often cited findings of the studies by Frohlich and Oppenheimer come from the second part of their experiment. After deciding on an individual ranking of principles, participants were placed in groups of five and asked to reach agreement on one principle by discussing possible consequences. Thus, the fourth Rawlsian dictum for the original position should be realised, which demands an extensive open discussion that results in an unanimous agreement. The previous uncertainty about the position in the future income distribution was preserved, but now different income vectors were used, which also contained higher income values. Only if an agreement was reached, a subset of income distributions was selected on the basis of the chosen principle. Otherwise, a vector was randomly picked from the total set of all unknown and possibly undesired vectors.

6 This point has already been made in chapter 1 and led us to the application of hypothetical questionnaire situations without any monetary payments in all of our investigations.

Again, results are striking. Frohlich and Oppenheimer (p. 60) report choices of 81 groups.[7] Among them, 77.8% supported the principle of maximising average income subject to a floor level, while only 1.2% followed the difference principle. Frohlich, Oppenheimer and Eavey (1987a, p. 630) report that in the discussions "most individuals wanted to balance the security of a high floor with the possibility of increasing the average income in the hope that they might fall into one of the higher income classes". From this acceptance of the mixed concept, the authors conclude that there are pluralistic justice beliefs.

Another important finding from the discussions among participants concerns the choice of a floor level, which has extensively been debated by the students. In North America, but not in Poland, the selected values among the groups followed a normal distribution. Moreover, although real poverty lines in the corresponding countries were not mentioned in the experiment, the mean values of the chosen floor levels were at the respective poverty line in North America, but well above this threshold in Poland. Besides these local differences, other individual characteristics had no influence. Frohlich and Oppenheimer argue that local habits might have influenced bargaining processes. They conclude that further experiments are needed to anticipate the outcome of such bargaining situations for constraint parameters.

Finally, besides cultural effects the authors also investigated other possible influences on the choice of allocation rules. They varied the size of the stake and the variance of payoffs, regarded losses instead of gains, controlled post-choice stability and considered choices without any reference to justice terms. However, the support for the principle being regarded remained impressively strong.

### 4.2.2 Some Concerns and further Investigations

The experiments just described and their results provoked quite a lot of discussions. They also inspired several studies that modified the empirical setting and often observed less support for maximising average income subject to a floor constraint.

A first problem, which has already been formulated by Frohlich and Oppenheimer, but also picked up by Miller (1992) and Herne and Suojanen (2004), is linked to the previously mentioned inappropriateness of experiments to reflect the significance of decisions in the original position. In almost all empirical studies risk only concerns the payoffs that participants may receive on the basis of their choices, which should lead to less risk-aversion. However, as Miller (1992) correctly objects, arguments used in the reported group dis-

7 Again, it is not easy to determine how many groups reached agreement. This is especially due to different experimental structures at various places. See the elaborations of Frohlich and Oppenheimer on pages 55 to 60.

cussions and low support for maximising average income show that students assumed more often income distributions in a society than simply a game to play. Nevertheless, as already discussed in chapter 1, hypothetical situations without monetary incentives are possibly equally suitable to trigger earnestness of respondents.

The second point is more a remark than a criticism. Frohlich and Oppenheimer convincingly reason that discussions about principles by their students reflect the decision procedure in Rawls's original position. However, results of such a bargaining process between subjects holding opposing justice concepts may depend on different bargaining abilities or, as already observed in the experiments by Frohlich and Oppenheimer, cultural influences on bargaining behaviour. Although these findings are extremely valuable, several successive studies asked instead for individual decisions. It might also be possible that the observed compromise solution is to some degree due to this kind of discussion process. Traub et al. (2005, p. 285) explicitly argue in this direction and also comment that group discussions "would have shifted the focus of [their own] experiment to the analysis of deliberative democracy". Although we should keep this argument in mind, the strong support for truncated efficiency in the experiments by Frohlich and Oppenheimer, even before the discussion part has started, should be noted.

A third point relates to the Rawlsian assumption that agreement in the original position must be socially stable. Thus, as Rawls (1971) explains, only the difference principle or the utilitarian conception are possible candidates for such a settlement, since they can be defended by normative arguments. Nevertheless, as Miller (1992, p. 579) notes, especially Frohlich and Oppenheimer (1990) have shown that truncated efficiency is even accepted if subjects experienced the effects of their choices and had to pay a 'tax' to support worse-off individuals. Moreover, Miller argues that in several empirical investigations the principle of desert was found to be well accepted by laymen. Hence, if this notion is explicitly excluded by the difference principle, social stability may even decrease.

Fourthly, Scott et al. (2001) criticise the fact that Frohlich and Oppenheimer did not distinguish between the principles of efficiency and merit. Consequently, several studies on income distributions (e.g. Mitchell et al., 1993, Ordóñez and Mellers, 1993, Scott et al., 2001, and Michelbach et al., 2003) independently varied efficiency and merit information and confirmed both concepts as legitimate moral principles. Similar to our second questionnaire study in the present work, merit will be replaced by responsibility considerations in the following investigation. Nevertheless, we will also be able to distinguish aspects of efficiency and responsibility and analyse their respective influence on the acceptance of truncated efficiency.

A further concern, which has been mentioned above, regards the impossibility to discriminate between the equality and the needs principle in results by Frohlich and Oppenheimer. Indeed, their respondents from Poland chose floor levels that were well above the poverty line, whereas several values proposed by North American groups were very close to the corresponding level in their country. In this case, the floor level or poverty line should be varied independently of equality measures. This has been done, for example, by Ordóñez and Mellers (1993) and Scott et al. (2001). However, in the present questionnaire the floor level is not systematically changed, but relevant information for all other allocation principles is independently varied.

Finally, Scott et al. (2001) criticise that Mitchell et al. (1993) measure equality in absolute rather than proportional terms. Clearly, this argument also applies to the experiments by Frohlich and Oppenheimer. As we will see in the following sections, in the present questionnaire respondents were offered various different possibilities to consider aspects of equality.

So, what are the findings of other investigations on the concept of truncated efficiency? We will start by regarding macro-justice studies. Firstly, the needs principle, i.e. the consideration of the poverty line in the present context, is found to be important in various situations. Some of them have already been mentioned at the beginning of this section. Moreover, Mitchell et al. (1993, p. 636) conclude that "subjects have a deep aversion to allowing people to fall below the poverty line [...] even if people at the bottom 'deserve' it because they are not working hard". Additionally, Ordóñez and Mellers (1993) point out that especially democrats, liberals and women were in favour of a minimum salary.

Secondly, compared to findings by Frohlich and Oppenheimer, equality considerations were usually much stronger in subsequent studies if they were separated from the needs principle (see e.g. Scott et al., 2001, or Michelbach et al., 2003). Also, in the questionnaire study by Michelbach et al. 18% of respondents were in favour of the Rawlsian difference principle. This proportion is higher than before, but of course still represents a clear minority.

Thirdly, above the social minimum, both the principles of efficiency and merit seem to be well accepted in the studies by Scott et al. (2001) and Michelbach et al. (2003), while Mitchell et al. (1993) discovered that merit moderated the investigated equality-efficiency trade-off. Herne and Suojanen (2004) almost replicated the experimental structure used by Frohlich and Oppenheimer and found that in a veil of ignorance setting 62% of their participating groups decided in favour of maximising average income subject to a floor constraint. In contrast, if subjects knew their position in the future income distribution, 60% of them wanted to implement the Rawlsian maximin principle. The authors speculate that in a 'no veil of ignorance' setting respondents are better able to separate their personal interests from considerations of fairness.

In a somewhat different experimental setting, where no poverty line was given, Traub et al. (2005) found that a formula reflecting Boulding's hybrid model best described behaviour of respondents in an 'ignorance' or uncertainty scenario, which is, as they argued, closest to the Rawlsian original position. However, the reported floor level was zero. Thus, although the formula also reflected some inequality aversion, observed behaviour was closer to the maximisation of expected utility. Again, the lottery character of the experiment may have had an influence.

Most of these studies regarded macro-justice settings and, therefore, suffered from some shortcomings discussed already in the first chapter. For example, current welfare practices may have an influence if help for people in need is considered.

In contrast, there are especially two empirical studies that investigated the acceptance of truncated efficiency in micro-justice settings. Firstly, in Konow's (2001) Question 6, which has already been discussed in subsection 3.3.3, a situation was described where basic needs of one hypothetical group could be fulfilled before allocating the remaining resource to a "more attractive" (p. 149) alternative in favour of a second group. The corresponding results revealed that the acceptance of this poverty line declined if a higher amount of the given resource was necessary to fully regard basic needs.

Secondly, the investigation by Faravelli (2007) is rather similar to our questionnaire study. The contexts presented are inspired by the questionnaires used by Yaari and Bar-Hillel (1984). Here, two hypothetical people differ with respect to their utility functions. The 1333 students in the study were outside observers who had to individually distribute a certain amount of a given resource between both subjects. In the initial situation, they could choose between solutions which are – according to Faravelli – inspired by utilitarianism (this has been selected by 22.5% of the respondents), egalitarianism (37.9%), or Rawls's difference principle (39.6%). After considering this initial case, subjects received one out of three possible modifications. In the first two versions, differences of utility functions have been explained either by different abilities and a handicap or by varying effort levels. However, in the third context, instead of specifying causes for individual disparities, a floor was introduced with respect to individual utility levels. Obviously, this value represented a kind of poverty line. Besides the initially proposed solutions (only the utilitarian concept did not obey the floor constraint) 'utilitarianism with a floor' was added as a fourth possible distribution. The respective proportions for utilitarianism, egalitarianism and Rawlsianism were now 1.9%, 32.1% and 40.0%, while the new solution of truncated efficiency was selected by 26.1% of the participants. Faravelli concludes that "the introduction of a floor did not enable a solution accepted by all of the parties" (p. 1415). Additionally, he found senior students to be more likely to prefer 'utilitarianism with a floor'. Unfortunately, as Faravelli also notes, this fourth solution was neither included in the initial nor in the other two modified cases so that especially the effect of responsibility (or effort) was not analysable in more detail.

In this section we mentioned several starting points for the present study on the acceptance of truncated efficiency. In section 4.4 many of these aspects will reappear. However, before the setup of the questionnaire is presented, a further theoretical approach to the allocation concept being considered will be summarised in the next section.

## 4.3 An Example from Social Choice Theory

Repeatedly, the difference between the principles of equality and needs has been mentioned in this work, although it does not play a role in our first two studies. To state it once again, equality considerations naturally concern the comparison between two or more individuals. The Rawlsian difference principle also depends on such comparisons in order to identify the worse-off individuals. However, as Scott et al. (2001) explain, basic needs should be determined in absolute terms. For example, a certain poverty line could be regarded or previously defined basic needs must be fulfilled. As explained above, in the contexts of our third questionnaire the needs principle will establish the floor level for the concept of truncated efficiency.

In social choice theory, similar considerations have been formulated by Tungodden (2000). Although he does not explicitly look at truncated efficiency, his argument should be briefly sketched in this subsection.

In the largest part of his paper, Tungodden proves that a version of the leximin principle has to be endorsed for all plausible conceptions of equality if the promotion of equality is assigned absolute priority in concepts of justice. However, in his Section 6, he argues that if one focusses on equality advancement in distribution conflicts, the absolute circumstances of affected individuals are left unconsidered. Hence, as Tungodden reasons, a concern of an absolute value does not have its source in egalitarian considerations, but in a *humanitarian desire* to alleviate as much suffering as possible. Nevertheless, this alleviation can be distributed quite unequally.

In order to characterise the following situations, let us firstly introduce those parts of the formal framework used by Tungodden that are helpful to get an idea of the underlying argumentation. There exists a fixed population denoted by $N = 1, \ldots, n$. Each social alternative is characterised by an $n$-dimensional vector $u$, wherein each element represents the utility level of the corresponding person in the given state. However, instead of utility levels the values may also reflect vectors of income or of functionings or primary good indices.[8] Rankings of social alternatives solely depend on the numbers given

8 Due to the introduction of Suppes Principle (SU), Tungodden (p. 231) considers positions rather than individuals as the basic element when making individual comparisons. Suppes Principle reads as follows: For all $u$,$v$: if the utility level of every position (from the worse off to the best off) is at least as high in $u$ as in $v$, then $u$ is at least as just as $v$. Moreover, if there exists one position where the utility level is strictly higher in $u$ than in $v$, then $u$ is more just than $v$.

in these vectors and fulfil the usual assumptions of reflexive and transitive binary relations.

To introduce the idea of absolute poverty Tungodden defines an affluence line $z^H$ and an absolute poverty line $z^L$. Hence, if person $j$ is thought to live in absolute poverty in social state 1, this is expressed by the notion $z^L \geq u_j^1$.

Now, two cases of two-person distribution conflicts are of relevance. The first problem regards situations where both individuals live in destitution. Clearly, the equality perspective requires the application of the leximin principle. In contrast, the humanitarian concern, as interpreted above, probably demands different solutions below the absolute poverty line that may even be in accordance with the efficiency principle. Hence, in this specific case egalitarian and humanitarian concerns go into different directions. Consequently, justice does not always require equality promotion.[9] Although this observation is of some additional interest, it is neither followed up by Tungodden in his axiomatic illustration nor in our questionnaire situations so that corresponding empirical investigations have to be left for future examination.

Instead, we concentrate on Tungodden's second situation, in which only one person lives below the poverty line, while the other individual lives in affluence. In this situation, both humanitarian concern and equality promotion demand giving absolute priority to the worse-off person. To include this case in his model Tungodden (p. 241) proposes the following condition:

**Weak Absolute Priority of those Below the Absolute Poverty Line (WAPBAP)**: Given some $z^H \geq z^L > 0$ and for all $u, v$ if there exist $j, k$ such that:

(1) $j$ attains a strictly lower level of utility in $u$ than $v$, and $u_j \geq z^H$;

(2) $k$ attains a strictly higher level of utility in $u$ than $v$, and $z^L \geq u_k$;

(3) the utility of everyone else is the same in $u$ as in $v$,

then $u$ is at least as just as $v$.

Then, Tungodden proves that a justice relation that satisfies WAPBAP and SU also satisfies the condition Weak Povertymin (WPM). According to WPM the utility loss of one individual living in destitution outweighs each utility gain of any number of individuals living above the affluence line. Thus, if WAPBAP is extended in the way that it covers *all* two-person situations, the justice relation demands to give absolute priority to ease the suffering of those below the absolute poverty line. The reader may have noticed that this is the statement of our needs principle.

To summarise the relevance of the argumentation for the present study, the condition WAPBAP introduces a floor level that is similar to the idea of truncated efficiency. Furthermore, this condition leads to a clear implication for

9 With respect to this issue, Tungodden (p. 239) bases his argument on the work of Nagel (1991) and Temkin (1993).

justice relations with respect to individuals below that level. From Tungodden's point of view this condition is likely to be accepted even if the concrete specification of a level may cause some disagreement.

However, we are also interested in rules that may be applied above $z^L$. Again, Tungodden (p. 242) offers one alternative:

> "if [...] we assign absolute priority to equality promotion according to AP in all distributive conflicts where everyone is above the absolute poverty line, then we have to solve these conflicts in accordance with a version of the leximin principle".

Here, the condition Absolute Priority (AP) is taken from Vallentyne (2000). It says that equality is increased if a social alternative that considers only two individuals increases utility of a person below the mean who stays below the mean and decreases utility of a person above the mean who stays above the mean. But certainly, such an egalitarian perspective is not the only alternative if all people are above the poverty line. Instead, it is also possible that AP may be rejected, for example, in favour of a utilitarian solution. In this case, we would end up with the concept of truncated efficiency.

In this subsection, the possibility of truncated efficiency in the realm of social choice theory has been sketched. Indeed, the axiomatic framework introduced by Tungodden already allows for behaviour in accordance with truncated efficiency – even if this is not the main focus of the author. Nevertheless, his aim is to introduce a poverty line and to describe possible behaviours below and above this line. We are now ready to look at the structure of hypothetical situations in the present questionnaire study. Clearly, the setup is inspired by the theoretical and empirical work that has been presented in the previous sections, but also by our two preceding studies.

## 4.4 The Questionnaire

Based on the theoretical considerations introduced in sections 4.1 and 4.3, the setup of the questionnaire will be presented in the following section. After describing the general structure of the hypothetical situations, the contexts are introduced in some more detail.

### 4.4.1 General Structure of Hypothetical Situations

As shown in the previous section, truncated efficiency has been empirically investigated more frequently in the context of income distributions. Our idea is now to create micro-justice situations that also allow for allocations in accordance with this mixed conception. Moreover, the structure of this setting should be based on the two earlier studies in this work in order to make them comparable and to obtain a more complete impression of distributive behaviour for this type of empirical procedure. Hence, we will explain similarities between the studies in due course, but also point out important differences at the end of this subsection.

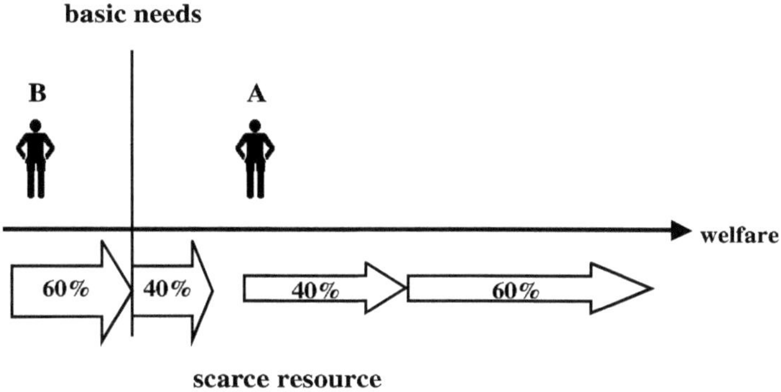


Figure 4.1: General structure of hypothetical situations

The basic structure of the following hypothetical situations is visualised in Figure 4.1. Similar to our earlier investigations, there are two groups of people, A and B, whereby it is agreed that the first group is better off than the second in terms of individual welfare or another equalisandum. Both groups are supposed to be of equal size initially. Furthermore, individuals in group B have unsatisfied basic needs. This fact is depicted by the dashed line. In contrast, individuals in A are well above this absolute threshold value. Similar to the minimum income level, one can imagine a certain index of basic needs that should be satisfied in order to live at the poverty line. Now, each participant in the study is supposed to act as an impartial decision-maker. He or she has available a unique amount of a scarce resource that can be distributed in a continuous fashion between A and B in order to further individual welfare of both groups. Note that in previous macro-justice studies on the acceptance of truncated efficiency welfare was measured in terms of earnings; hence improvements are obtained by reallocating these incomes. However, in our case the given resource is once again interpreted as 'manna from heaven'.

Here, group B is said to need about 60% of this additional resource to have all basic needs fulfilled. Certainly, this number is somewhat arbitrarily chosen. Nevertheless, in the discussion on Konow's (2001) Question 6 in subsection 3.3.3, it was noted that a corresponding value of no more than 50% of the given resource could 'too easily' result in a full regard of needs: Firstly, as noticed also by Konow, an equal split is always attractive in cases where an additional resource has to be distributed. Secondly, if less than 50% of the resource would be necessary to lift people in need on the poverty line, relatively low opportunity costs of such a decision may induce respondents to accept this distribution – even despite possibly existing reservations based on aspects of responsibility. Hence, in order to get a somewhat clearer impression of the 'strength' of the needs principle, a value of about 60% may seem appropriate. Indeed, Konow discovered in his study that increasing the necessary proportion from 50% to 80% and 100% significantly reduced the full consideration of basic needs from 89% to 45% and 19% of the respondents, respectively. Therefore, the first question of the present study relates to the acceptance of the needs principle if there are enough resources but another alternative is offered.

If group B receives more than 60% of the additional resource, its situation in terms of individual welfare can be further improved. Nevertheless, even with 100% of the given amount a complete equalisation is impossible so that maximin behaviour is reasonable. This assumption takes up the suggestion by Gyrd-Hansen (2004, p. 1113) in her questionnaire study on distributional aspects of health gains that the "preference for treating the patient group with the worse health status [...] would not have appeared as strong, had the study not been designed such that equality in final health status is on offer". Hence, this characteristic of our hypothetical situations creates another possible challenge to the maximin principle.

So far, the structure allows for regarding basic needs and, additionally, promoting more equality beyond this level. Now, this is contrasted with efficiency considerations if at least part of the available resource is given to group A. In Figure 4.1 the higher benefits from such an allocation are expressed by the arrows. While their volume corresponds to the amount of the distributed resource, the length describes the achieved individual welfare gain as measured on the horizontal axis. Consequently, for example the two 40%-arrows show that giving 40% of the available amount of the scarce resource to group A causes a welfare gain that is twice as high as the corresponding gain for group B. An identical efficiency interpretation would be that group A needs only half of the respective amount required for group B to receive the same welfare profit.

Hence, each share allocated to group A corresponds to a rejection of the maximin equity criterion and, moreover, to a refusal of the needs principle if the proportion is higher than 40%. Consequently, the principle of truncated efficiency demands giving exactly 60% of the resource to group B in order to fully consider basic needs and to allocate the remaining amount to the more beneficial group A.

Furthermore, as we have already discussed more extensively in chapter 1, the fact that the decision-maker is asked to distribute 'manna from heaven' may enhance the wish to split up the resource evenly between both parties if potential receivers are supposed to have equal claims based on other principles. This is an important contrast to earlier macro-justice studies on truncated efficiency, in which income redistributions are usually considered. Also, note that a division of the resource was not available in the two preceding questionnaire studies but has already been considered in the questionnaire modification by Gaertner (1994).

In our case, there are different ways to choose an egalitarian solution. Firstly, respondents could distribute the given resource evenly and give 50% to each group. However, then they would ignore the full consideration of the basic needs of group B. Secondly, decision-makers may completely fulfil the needs of group B and, afterwards, split up the remaining amount equally. Thus, they would give 80% to group B. Thirdly, instead of focusing on equal amounts one may consider equal gains in terms of benefits that have to be defined later on.

Certainly, besides the allocations mentioned, which may be motivated by 'pure' distribution mechanisms, the structure of the hypothetical situations also allows for several 'intermediate' allocations. They may represent compromises between certain allocation rules and are based on the idea that Rawls (1971) has called intuitionism. Especially, different degrees of inequality aversion, which can be represented by an isoelastic social welfare function, lead to various distinct solutions of the equality-efficiency trade-off. They have been mentioned in the first chapter and will be discussed in more depth in the following chapter 5.

Let us summarise two of the major aims of the present study so far. Firstly, we contrast the principles of needs and efficiency, when the allocation of the first 60% of the given resource is regarded. Certainly, helping people in need can be seen as an almost infinite utility gain. However, as our previous studies and several other empirical investigations on the acceptance of the needs principle have revealed, it is possible that respondents regard benefits of available alternatives as being even more valuable. Secondly, the question arises as to what happens beyond the fulfilment of basic needs. Here, the idea of truncated efficiency is only one possible motive among several others.

Based on the initial situation, we also consider important extensions that are inspired again by the two previous questionnaire investigations. Firstly, in a within-subject design, the benefits of supporting group A are increased two times. Thus, the preliminary trade-off between the principle of efficiency and either the needs principle or the maximin equity criterion is tightened; it may become more and more appealing to increase the initial share for group A. Consequently, it is possible that these modifications also encourage support of truncated efficiency.

Secondly, and similar to the second questionnaire study, aspects of responsibility are introduced by using two different questionnaire versions, in which group B is supposed to be either not responsible or responsible for the existence of unsatisfied basic needs. Although the way in which responsibility is incorporated is very much in line with the relevant literature cited in chapter 3 and, thus, makes it possible to check for the influence of aspects of responsibility on the consideration of basic needs, it is important to note that individuals in group B are not supposed to be responsible for the lower ability of their projects to generate benefits. Furthermore, it could be argued that the possibility to split the given resource in a continuous manner leads to reactions that are easier to detect compared to the strict either-or decisions.

In the present case, the setting diverges from income redistribution cases, where an individual may be held accountable for the income due to work effort. Clearly, the issue of incentives does not have any disturbing influence in the present study. Furthermore, in contrast to the structure of our previous investigation, it is possible to 'heal' the consequences of self-induced basic needs by spending at least 60% for group B. However, as a result there are less resources left for improving individual welfare of both groups beyond the basic needs level. Thus, similar to the first two studies, opportunity costs could play a role. Therefore, we may observe an additional but more complex behavioural effect that could be called *delayed responsibility*. Respondents may wish to regard aspects of responsibility only after completely regarding basic needs, although group B is supposed to be responsible for its unsatisfied needs, but not for the lower benefits beyond needs. Overall, allocations in favour of group B may become less attractive if aspects of responsibility are incorporated. Hence, the observation of truncated efficiency could be furthered in the responsibility version of the questionnaire.

To summarise, there are three very important differences between the present study and the two preceding investigations. Firstly, continuous splits instead of either-or decisions are considered. Therefore, on the one hand, a larger set of possible allocations is available, which also includes distributions based on intuitionism. On the other hand, it should be easier to detect behavioural changes resulting from variations with respect to the principles of efficiency and responsibility. Secondly, a complete regard of basic needs is possible, which could lead to a higher acceptance of the principle of needs. Thirdly, more detailed information about the benefits of alternatives above the poverty line is given so that the compensation principle can be applied.

### 4.4.2 Two Questionnaire Situations

In the following subsection, the two hypothetical contexts in the questionnaire will be discussed in some more detail, while complete texts are given in Appendix 4.8.1. The situations follow the structure just described. In both contexts respondents are asked to distribute a certain resource – development aid in the first (situation 'Aid') and fuel in the second case (situation 'Fuel') – between either two islands or two settlements. It is explicitly stated that these resources are available only once and, moreover, nothing is said about the source of the development aid or fuel; hence it should be interpreted as 'manna from heaven'. Also, in both contexts groups A and B are said to be of equal size in the initial case.

After this preliminary information, the questionnaire described what each group intended to do with its received share of the scarce resource. In situation 'Aid', both islands are planning to connect households to the power supply system (projects 'Power A' and 'Power B'). However, in order to incorporate aspects of efficiency, costs per household on B are said to be twice as high as the corresponding costs on A, so that the same benefit, measured in number of households, is obtained at higher costs. Similarly, in situation 'Fuel', saw mills are the only source of income to lift the two settlements above subsistence level, on which the inhabitants would otherwise live. The operation of the mill for one additional hour per day costs twice as much in B as in A. Hence, the reader will have noticed that this structure allows for applying the previously described compensation principle. Here, the better-off island or settlement could make hypothetical transfers of connected households or working hours of the mill towards the worse-off group. Thus, efficiency beyond basic needs can be regarded.

It should be noted that in both contexts, the two groups to be considered are never responsible for these differences. Furthermore, to allow following the maximin principle, group A is unambiguously always better off than group B even if the latter group receives all available resources. While this structure is explicitly stated for situation 'Aid', respondents in situation 'Fuel' have to deduce this fact from the given numbers. Contrary to maximin behaviour, giving the total amount to group A is also a feasible alternative in both contexts. In this case, either each household on island A receives electricity or, correspondingly, the saw mill in settlement A can work in total nine hours per day.

Finally, the aspect of needs is introduced in absolute terms. In situation 'Aid', 60% of the development aid is necessary to prevent a famine on island B (project 'Food B'). Certainly, this context is inspired by situation 2 of the two preliminary questionnaire studies and also by Konow's (2001) Question 6. However, in the discussion of Konow's example in subsection 3.3.3 it has been objected that a clear statement on consequences of payments above or below the amount which is necessary to fully regard basic needs is missing. Therefore, we describe the effects of allocating a smaller amount to island B in the way that a smaller number of households would receive enough food. In situation 'Fuel', 40,000 out of 70,000 litres are needed to heat all houses during the whole winter period. This setting has been inspired, for example, by Mack and Lansley (1985) who find that a great majority of respondents in Britain count things such as a bath, a bedroom or a heated house as basic needs. However, in contrast to the first situation, *all* households are unheated for a certain period of time if settlement B receives less than the stated quantity of fuel.

Next, consider variations with respect to benefits and aspects of responsibility. In situation 'Aid', benefits of the project on island A are increased by lowering the costs for connecting one household to the power supply system, while the corresponding costs on island B remain unchanged. Simultaneously, the number of inhabitants of island A is successively increased in parts b) and c) so that the proportion of households to be helped on A, given a constant amount of money, always remains the same. Hence, we distinguish this share of households from the number of concerned households.[10] Consequently, if the number of households to be helped should be kept constant, the amount for A has to be reduced in parts b) and c). However, the principle of efficiency as defined before would demand focusing on the sum of households to be helped. Hence, we may also observe an increasing amount for island A. This rather complicated structure follows on from two assumptions. Firstly, it should always be clear how many inhabitants are on both islands, but also what proportion of all inhabitants are affected. This follows from the criticism on Konow's (2001) Question 6. Secondly, the possibility should remain to give the whole amount to the better-off group so that the number of inhabitants has to be increased if costs per households decline.

In situation 'Fuel' benefits of group A are varied by increasing the number of households in settlement A. Since all households gain from each working hour of the mill, a consecutively increasing number has the effect that, for example, an additional man-hour in part b) increases the number of beneficiaries compared to settlement B and also compared to settlement A in part a). This idea is very carefully formulated in parts b) and c) in the questionnaire by pointing out that not only the number of households, but also the capacity of the mill and the number of workers is doubled or tripled.[11] Therefore, it is still reasonable to give the entire quantity to group A, which then results again in a total of nine working hours per day.

As before, aspects of responsibility are incorporated by designing two different versions of the questionnaire. In the no-responsibility versions the needs of group B are caused either by an unexpected drought (situation 'Aid') or by the bankruptcy of the shipping company (situation 'Fuel'). In contrast, in the responsibility versions it was stated in the first context that island B has fatally misused pesticides despite warnings from the United Nations, while in the second context the inhabitants of settlement B wasted energy needed for the winter period. It is important to notice that in the present study aspects of responsibility differ from the cases of option luck being considered in the previous investigation. Now, the miserable situation of worse-off individuals has been caused by their *careless behaviour*.

10 Alternatively, the corresponding percentage number could be interpreted as the probability of a single household to get an electricity connection if these are randomly distributed. This probability is constant in all parts of the situation.

11 The formulation of the efficiency variation was somewhat ambiguous in the first year, 2005, of the investigation so that this situation was reformulated in 2006. Hence, the 2005 sample of this situation is completely discounted.

It seems to be reasonable to assume that negative consequences of the reported misbehaviour are known to the worse-off groups. Moreover, individuals in both groups were free to choose an alternative behaviour and, therefore, have not been forced by outside parties or conditions. Furthermore, we tried to describe misbehaviour which seems to be plausible. Finally, it has to be noted that we considered hypothetical groups rather than individuals. This fact may have weakened the individual responsibility of described people.

Some differences between the two questionnaire situations have previously been mentioned. To recapitulate, firstly different contexts are considered, which may already yield differences in answer patterns. Secondly, in situation 'Aid' only some households suffer badly if needs are only partly regarded, whereas in the case of a respective decision in situation 'Fuel' all households have to forgo heating for a certain period of time. Thirdly, a similar observation can be made with respect to efficiency considerations. In the first situation, some households receive an electricity connection while others remain disconnected, whereas in the second situation all households in a settlement gain from the additional working time of the saw mill.

However, the two situations differ with respect to one further important aspect, which has not been noted yet. In situation 'Fuel', the income enhancing investment into the mill in settlement B is only possible after using up another 40,000 litres of fuel to heat the houses. Clearly, this setting is closer to comparable macro-justice surveys, where worse-off individuals are also supposed to firstly use additional income for their basic allotments. In contrast, in situation 'Aid' two different projects on island B, viz. projects 'Power B' and 'Food B', are proposed. Thus, here it is possible to separate the fulfilment of basic needs from efficiency considerations with respect to island B. This setting is inspired again by the previous discussion on Konow's (2001) Question 6 in subsection 3.3.3. There, it was argued that some respondents may have allocated some money to the agricultural project of the better-off part of the country to improve the prospects of both areas simultaneously. A similar consideration of 'cross-effects' has also been observed from verbal answers in our first questionnaire study presented in chapter 2. One possible interpretation is that these respondents traded off today's basic needs and the possibility of a better life in the future. Nonetheless, such reasoning is also driven by aspects of efficiency. By offering the possibility to split the given amount between both projects on island B it can be controlled for this argument. Moreover, as will be explained in the results section, the influence of aspects of responsibility, which only consider the existence of unsatisfied basic needs, can also be observed from this separation.

### 4.4.3 Test Questions

Frankly speaking, the hypothetical allocation problems presented may be more difficult to penetrate compared to the situations in the two preliminary questionnaire studies. Therefore, participants were asked to answer some test questions after reading part a) of each situation. This serves two advantages: Firstly, respondents have to review important aspects of the situations described. Secondly, those subjects who fail to answer every test question correctly reveal that they have some severe problems in understanding at least one principle being considered. Thus, they are not included in the sample.

Especially in social psychology or political science this tool is very common. For example, Scott et al. (2001, p. 753) applied a short test to confirm that participants have been successfully manipulated by all variables that were relevant for understanding the underlying distribution principles. If respondents failed to correctly answer these questions, they were excluded from the final data set. Frohlich and Oppenheimer (1992, p. 37) also used test questions about several aspects of the allocation mechanisms to be considered. According to the authors, respondents frequently initially failed the test, but then they had the possibility to resit for as long as it took them to pass this test. The second procedure has the advantage of having more participants in the final sample. However, respondents may get the misleading impression that there are also right and wrong answers when they have to make their distribution decisions in the main part of the questionnaire – even if they are informed that this is not the case.

In the present study, respondents received four test questions in each context which are also presented in Appendix 4.8.1. For didactic reasons they follow the order of information given in the questionnaire texts, but in different succession in the two settings. In situation 'Aid' the first two questions intend to clarify that a certain amount of money invested in either electricity project helps twice as many households on island A as on island B. This aspect of efficiency is also emphasised in questions 2 and 3 of situation 'Fuel'. Here, the third question also points out that the mills do not have to work full hours. Furthermore, the third question of situation 'Aid', and the first question of situation 'Fuel', stress again the consequences of spending less than the necessary quantity of the corresponding resource with regard to all unsatisfied basic needs. Thus, here the needs principle is involved. Moreover, depending on the questionnaire version, the causes for the existence of these needs are repeated in order to point towards the aspect of responsibility. Finally, question 4 in each context is intended to illuminate that group A is unambiguously always better off than group B so that the maximin criterion appears to be another option. Particularly, in situation 'Fuel' this information has to be noted since it is not explicitly stated in the text.

### 4.4.4 Interpretation of Answers

Some introductory remarks concerning the way respondents are asked to specify their preferred distributions seem to be necessary. After reading through the description of a hypothetical situation and answering four test questions, participants received tables with distribution options. Although such predetermined allocations may influence the way respondents think about possible solutions, the admittedly somewhat demanding calculations should be simplified by presenting these proposals. Another problem may arise if virtually plausible allocations have been overlooked when preparing the tables. For example, Schokkaert and Devooght (2003, p. 221, footnote 8) report with respect to their questionnaire investigation on responsibility-fair compensation that they did not think about a certain 'countercompensation' possibility and only became aware of this, because they allowed respondents the possibility of adding their own proposals in a pre-test. Therefore, firstly, an earlier version of our current questionnaire has been presented to a sample of about 20 Ph.D. and graduate students in order to perceive possible problems with the wording of the situations and, additionally, to receive further distribution proposals. Secondly, in the final questionnaire version it was also possible for respondents to state their own allocations.

Table 4.1: Distribution principles and offered sequences

| | Situation 'Aid' (*a*) | | | Situation 'Fuel' (*b*) |
|---|---|---|---|---|
| Possible motive | Part a) | Part b) | Part c) | All parts |
| 'Strict efficiency' | 100-0-0 | 100-0-0 | 100-0-0 | 70-0 |
| Equality (additional resource) | 50-0-50 | 50-0-50 | 50-0-50 | 35-35 |
| Efficiency before needs (island B) | 20-40-40 | 20-40-40 | 20-40-40 | — |
| Truncated efficiency | 40-0-60 | 40-0-60 | 40-0-60 | 30-40 |
| Compromise I: Needs & Efficiency & Constraint | 30-10-60 | 30-10-60 | 30-10-60 | 20-50 |
| Needs & Equality (remaining resource) | 20-20-60 | 20-20-60 | 20-20-60 | 15-55 |
| Needs & Equality (proportional gain) | 13-27-60 | 13-27-60 | 12-28-60 | 10-60 |
| Needs & Equality (absolute gain) | 13-27-60 | 8-32-60 | 5-35-60 | — |
| Compromise II: Needs & Maximin & Constraint | 10-30-60 | 10-30-60 | 10-30-60 | 5-65 |
| Maximin | 0-40-60 | 0-40-60 | 0-40-60 | 0-70 |

(*a*) Sequences in situation 'Aid' denote the allocated amount (in thousands) to project 'Power A' - project 'Power B' - project 'Food B'.
(*b*) Sequences in situation 'Fuel' denote the allocated amount (in thousands) to settlement A - settlement B.

The presumable interpretations of the proposed distributions in the questionnaire are summarised in Table 4.1. Here, decisions are represented by sequences. In situation 'Aid', the first number of each sequence states the amount (in thousands) that should be given to the project on island A, the second figure corresponds to the electricity project on island B while the third digit represents the money for food on island B. In situation 'Fuel', there are only two projects so that the first number corresponds to fuel for settlement A and the second value to fuel for settlement B. Most of the underlying principles have previously been discussed. Giving all resources to group A may be interpreted as following an idea of 'strict efficiency', although nothing is known about utility gains of group B below the poverty line. Moreover, there are two additional possibilities, which partly ignore unsatisfied basic needs of island B in situation 'Aid': Respondents can split the given amount either strictly equally (sequence 50-0-50) or they could consider aspects of efficiency of supporting island B before needs are completely fulfilled (20-40-40).[12] As explained above, only the first alternative is also available in situation 'Fuel' (35-35). After fully considering needs, subjects may follow different conceptions to allocate the remaining quantity of the resource. Truncated efficiency, different kinds of equality and the maximin criterion have previously been mentioned. Furthermore, two additional compromises between different principles are offered, one with a stronger concern for the more beneficial project ('Compromise I') and one that more pronounces the aspect of equality more strongly ('Compromise II'). The second distribution also results in an equalisation of resources that are available to each saw mill during the winter period. Nevertheless, these are only proposals, and other allocations based on the equality-efficiency trade-off may be observed.

Clearly, since respondents are also allowed to state their own distributions, a great variety either of chosen or of additionally proposed allocations is expected.[13]

Based on the two questions stated already in subsection 4.4.1, several questions are of greater importance in this study. Firstly, and most generally, we want to know which allocations are actually chosen – and how often. Secondly, based on the two previous chapters, we are interested in the fulfilment of basic needs. Here, aspects of efficiency and responsibility may have an influence. Thirdly, beyond considering basic needs various distribution concepts are conceivable. Here, the prominence of truncated efficiency is of greater interest. Fourthly, the aspect of responsibility is directly linked to the existence of unsatisfied needs, but we have already speculated that there could also be a delayed effect in the sense that respondents do not take responsibility arguments into account until basic needs are fully considered. Fifthly,

12 Certainly, from this argument other allocations may result. They will be included in this category later on. Moreover, in chapter 5 we will argue that we may even observe a motive that we will call 'equality of additional resources'.

13 For example, Dickinson and Tiefenthaler (2002) asked 157 participants in their dictator game to split up a given amount of 60 tokens and received 28 different answers.

as mentioned before, there are some contextual differences between the two situations. These may result in certain disparities of answering behaviours. Finally, individual characteristics of respondents have also been gathered so that we are able to control for such influences on all examined decisions. Especially the influence of the sex of a respondent will be investigated more carefully, again.

In order to receive some further insights into decision motives participants were asked for verbal comments on their choices. However, because there are so many different aspects in this study, on which respondents did not always comment, verbal answers are only examined with respect to some specific questions.

## 4.5 The Sample

In the following section, the implementation of the questionnaire study and some relevant sample characteristics are illustrated. Also, similar to the two previous studies, individual characteristics have been collected so that a more detailed sample description is possible. Moreover, based on the answers to the introduced test questions the development of the final data set is explained.

### 4.5.1 Questionnaire Implementation

Participants in the study were students at the Universität Osnabrück. All of them attended an undergraduate lecture in microeconomic theory at the Department of Economics in the years 2005 or 2006. As in the previous investigations, students were asked to complete the questionnaires during tutorials. In the year 2005, the current investigation comprised three different contexts, but due to time restrictions each student only received two of them. They were given in alternating order. However, the third hypothetical situation is not considered in this work. In contrast, in 2006 all participants faced the situations 'Aid' and 'Fuel'.

Furthermore, in both years the allotted booklets also contained a respective second questionnaire study. These were in no way related to the investigation to be presented here. Summaries of the corresponding questionnaires can be found in Bosmans and Schokkaert (2009) for 2005 and in Amiel, Cowell and Gaertner (2009) for 2006. Due to different extents of these appended studies it took respondents about 30 minutes in the latter but 45 minutes in the earlier year to complete all items. Introductorily, similar to the first two studies, students received instructions.[14] The order of questions was alternated with respect to the two different studies and the various contexts. Moreover, responsibility and no-responsibility versions were handed out in turn. Firstly, this was done to receive an almost equal number of answers on

14 See the instructions for tutors in Appendix 2.7.3.

all different versions of questions. Secondly, it should be more difficult for the students to simply copy their answers from each other.

In Table 4.2 descriptions and sample means for all variables used in the following statistical analyses are summarised. Due to the alternations mentioned, some questionnaire characteristics have been incorporated. Here, by using dummy variables we are able to control for ordering effects of different studies (ORDER 1) and of different situations in the present investigation (ORDER 2). As before, each respondent only received either the responsibility or the no-responsibility version of the questionnaire. Hence, a respective dummy variable (RES) is introduced again to analyse the effect of responsibility considerations. With the help of $\chi^2$ tests we confirmed that the two questionnaire versions were randomly distributed among different groups of the samples. Unfortunately, in the year 2005 the hypothetical situation 'Fuel' contained a misleading wording in parts b) and c). Consequently, for this context only answers from the year 2006 are analysed. In contrast, the 'Aid' sample includes replies from both years of the investigation. Thus, a time dummy variable (YEAR 05) is incorporated to detect differences between the answers of the two years.

### 4.5.2 Explanation of Demographic Questions

Similar to the preceding studies, respondents were asked about some socio-demo-graphic characteristics. The corresponding sheet is also given in Appendix 4.8.1, and descriptions of resulting variables can be found again in Table 4.2. Obviously, this part differs from earlier versions with respect to some questions. As before, participants were requested to state their age and their gender. The dummy variable MALE equals 1 if the student is male.

As discussed earlier, the question on work experience of respondents was somewhat imprecisely formulated in the two previous questionnaires, which resulted in slightly unspecific interpretations. Therefore, now students were asked whether they attended a training before starting their studies (dummy variable JOB). The underlying idea is that experiences during a longer working period have an impact on certain attitudes and justice evaluations. Thus, the reformulated question exhibits the advantage of excluding those who only had worked part-time or as a side-line, or had completed their military or civilian service.

In contrast to the two earlier studies, students had to answer all remaining questions on a 7-point scale. This setup is supposed to offer several advantages. Firstly, a kind of graphical presentation of alternatives may alleviate the answering of a question where a numerical statement is expected (see Amiel, Cowell and Ramos, 2007, for a similar presumption). Secondly, an odd number of answer categories either allows for choosing the medium position or makes it possible to indicate the distance from this average rank. Thirdly, participants in experiments rarely like to choose extreme positions

Table 4.2: Variable descriptions: Overall and reduced samples

| | | Situation 'Aid' | | | | Situation 'Fuel' | | | |
|---|---|---|---|---|---|---|---|---|---|
| | | Overall | Reduced sample | | | Overall | Reduced sample | | |
| Variable code | Description | sample n=485 | Total n=419 | Females n=167 | Males n=252 | sample n=289 | Total n=205 | Females n=85 | Males n=120 |
| *AGE* | Age of proband (in years) | 22.38 | 22.36 | 21.86 | 22.69 | 22.26 | 22.27 | 21.64 | 22.73 |
| | | (1.78) | (1.70) | (1.55) | (1.72) | (1.72) | (1.76) | (1.60) | (1.73) |
| *FAMILY* | Income of parents: 1=Very low, 7=Very high | 4.39 | 4.42 | 4.40 | 4.44 | 4.43 | 4.42 | 4.36 | 4.46 |
| | | (1.16) | (1.14) | (1.12) | (1.16) | (1.13) | (1.15) | (1.18) | (1.12) |
| *FUTURE* | Expected income: 1=Very low, 7=Very high | 4.79 | 4.79 | 4.69 | 4.85 | 4.79 | 4.76 | 4.60 | 4.87 |
| | | (0.96) | (0.94) | (0.89) | (0.97) | (0.91) | (0.91) | (0.90) | (0.90) |
| *JOB* | Professional training: 0=No, 1=Yes | 0.19 | 0.20 | 0.20 | 0.20 | 0.16 | 0.18 | 0.12 | 0.23 |
| | | (0.40) | (0.40) | (0.40) | (0.40) | (0.37) | (0.39) | (0.32) | (0.42) |
| *MALE* | Proband is male: 0=No, 1=Yes | 0.59 | 0.60 | 0.00 | 1.00 | 0.58 | 0.59 | 0.00 | 1.00 |
| | | (0.49) | (0.49) | | | (0.50) | (0.49) | | |
| *POLITICS* | Political attitude: 1=Far to the left, 7=Far to the right | 3.87 | 3.87 | 3.61 | 4.05 | 3.85 | 3.84 | 3.71 | 3.93 |
| | | (1.00) | (1.00) | (0.93) | (1.01) | (0.93) | (0.95) | (0.87) | (1.00) |
| *REPEATER* | Participation in both years: 0=No, 1=Yes | 0.18 | 0.18 | 0.16 | 0.19 | 0.30 | 0.26 | 0.25 | 0.28 |
| | | (0.38) | (0.38) | (0.36) | (0.40) | (0.46) | (0.44) | (0.43) | (0.45) |
| *ORDER 1* | Order of studies: 0=This study second, 1=This study first | 0.50 | 0.51 | 0.55 | 0.48 | 0.50 | 0.50 | 0.51 | 0.49 |
| | | (0.50) | (0.50) | (0.50) | (0.50) | (0.50) | (0.50) | (0.50) | (0.50) |
| *ORDER 2* | Order of questions: 0=Sit.'Aid' second, 1=Sit.'Aid' first | 0.50 | 0.52 | 0.52 | 0.52 | 0.49 | 0.55 | 0.58 | 0.53 |
| | | (0.50) | (0.50) | (0.50) | (0.50) | (0.50) | (0.50) | (0.50) | (0.50) |
| *RES* | Version: 0=No responsibility, 1=Responsibility | 0.50 | 0.50 | 0.47 | 0.52 | 0.51 | 0.50 | 0.45 | 0.54 |
| | | (0.50) | (0.50) | (0.50) | (0.50) | (0.50) | (0.50) | (0.50) | (0.50) |
| *YEAR 05* | 0=Year 2006, 1=Year 2005 | 0.40 | 0.39 | 0.37 | 0.40 | 0.00 | 0.00 | 0.00 | 0.00 |
| | | (0.49) | (0.49) | (0.49) | (0.49) | | | | |

Note: The reported numbers are mean values. Standard deviations are given in parentheses.

so that, in order to still get meaningful results, offering at least seven alternatives seems to be an appropriate number. Finally, a qualitatively ordered variable derived from such a point scale can more easily be interpreted than, for instance, the unequal categories for expected income or the different occupational categories in our first two questionnaire investigations.

Earlier we have argued that the profession of the main earner of a family may have a formative influence on attitudes of adolescents. Now, this question is replaced by an income scale (FAMILY), on which respondents should rate the parental income situation during their childhood which ranges from 'very poor' (FAMILY=1) to 'very rich' (FAMILY=7). One may argue that this is an unsuitable or at least very vague measure for possible parental influences. However, firstly Skitka and Tetlock (1992) reason that family income is an appropriate proxy for social background that in turn is supposed to have an influence on moral arguments. And Miller (1992) also reports that 'class' is supposed to be one of the major influences on distributive attitudes, besides 'gender' and 'culture'. Secondly, surely one does not receive a precise income measurement from this question. But what is more interesting is the perception of the income situation in the parents' house by a respondent. Additionally, the employment categories occasionally used in the previous studies caused confusions, because respondents had problems either to sort out which parent is the 'head of the household' or to assign this parent to one of the occupational groups.

As before, subjects had to indicate their expected position on the income distribution scale in ten years' time. Although they are supposed to decide as an impartial spectator with respect to the hypothetical situations, it was already argued in preceding chapters that participants may feel more empathy towards 'their' group of society. Thus, again their choice could range from 'very poor' (FUTURE=1) to 'very rich' (FUTURE=7).

In addition, participants were asked to state their political orientation on a scale which ranges from 'far to the left' (POLITICS=1) to 'far to the right' (POLITICS=7). Several sociological studies reveal that political attitudes have an influence on moral arguments. An informative overview can be found, for example, in Mitchell et al. (1993). However, the reviewed papers often apply more extensive sets of questions to distinguish between conservative and liberal attitudes. In several investigations, political viewpoints are found to have clear impacts in particular on the evaluation of aspects of responsibility. For example, Skitka and Tetlock (1992) found that even with a sufficient quantity of resources conservative students were significantly less likely to support people in need if these were responsible for their own fate. Additionally, Cappelen et al. (2007) summarise that in political theory it is known that right-wingers hold individuals responsible for much more characteristics and choices than left-wingers do. Nevertheless, instead of implementing a more extensive set of questions on this point we adopted the single question on political orientation as utilised, for example, by Amiel and Cowell (2002).

Since the questionnaire, which all students were expected to complete without any monetary compensation, was already rather lengthy, an even more extensive version could probably deter participants from taking part in the study. Hence, further possible questions not only on political attitudes but also on religious background, working ethics, citizenship or 'migrational background' are abandoned, even if in other studies they are sometimes found to display a certain influence. Additionally, although students were informed that the questionnaire was anonymous, some of them may have hesitated to answer such deeper personal questions.

A final but important individual characteristic of some respondents is the fact that they probably participated in the investigation in both years being considered. If students fail the final exam of the microeconomic theory course they can either resit the exam in the following semester or wait a full year and attend the lecture and also the tutorials once again.[15] Clearly, this problem also existed in the two earlier studies, especially in the years 1990 and 2003. However, in these cases there was no information on repeaters available. In order to identify those students, a further question has been added. From this information a dummy variable (REPEATER) is modelled. Due to different sample structures of the two situations this variable has different implications in both contexts. Participating in the questionnaire in two successive years could have had various, possibly countervailing consequences. Students could get annoyed, because they faced the same questionnaire twice, but in this case they were also able to refuse to complete it. What is more, students who failed the exam were selected by their skills in microeconomic theory. However, the corresponding effect is not supposed to be significant with respect to moral judgements. Therefore, probably the most interesting question is, whether the answering of the questionnaire itself had an influence on the moral arguments of respondents. For example, after the first completion of the questionnaire they may have reflected the hypothetical situations or discussed them with their classmates. Thus, students could change their attitudes. Hence, in situation 'Fuel', where only the sample of the year 2006 is considered, we incorporate the variable REPEATER in the following regressions, although it seems to be rather unlikely that there is a stronger effect. Indeed, no impact of this variable on any decision has been discovered.

The case is more complicated in situation 'Aid'. Here, respondents from two years are included. However, those students who attended the tutorials in both years are likely to be counted twice. Thus, we may run into greater problems if it were detected that justice evaluations of these 'repeaters' significantly differed from those who attended the questionnaire study for the first time. Therefore, we ran various statistical tests with the 2006 sample for situation 'Aid' in order to check for the influence of this variable. The corre-

15 Of course, some students even resit the exam in the following semester, fail again and, therefore, probably attend the tutorials in the next year.

sponding results will be presented in subsection 4.6.4, where we will discuss this point more extensively. However, in neither case are attitudes of repeaters found to differ significantly from evaluations of non-repeaters. Thus, findings with respect to situation 'Fuel' are confirmed. Moreover, estimated coefficients for the corresponding dummy variable YEAR 05 do not indicate any significant influences. Therefore, it has been decided to leave these students in the 'Aid' sample. The main reason is that we aim at investigating all attendees of this course to receive a more representative picture of justice attitudes of this group of students. Consequently, the variable REPEATER is not included in the regressions of the overall sample of situation 'Aid'.

### 4.5.3 Answers on Test and Demographic Questions

The tutorials are usually held by graduate students. However, in order to motivate subjects to participate in the study the author of this work visited all tutorials and informed students about the importance of their answers for the project. Moreover, by this, an equal treatment of respondents with respect to introductory information should be reached. In situation 'Aid', a total of 508 questionnaires were handed out. 15 students did not complete the questions on the hypothetical contexts. Another 8 subjects only rejected the demographic questions so that there remain 485 respondents in the overall sample. In situation 'Fuel', we distributed 303 booklets and received 296 completed answer sheets with respect to the contextual questions. Out of this group, 7 subjects failed to state all demographic characteristics. Thus, there remain 289 students in the total sample.

These numbers are further reduced when answers on test questions are considered. In situation 'Aid' the four questions were correctly answered by 97.3%, 94.0%, 95.7% and 92.8% of the subjects, respectively. In total, 419 students (86.4%) gave correct statements on all four test questions. Correspondingly, in situation 'Fuel' we observe 97.9%, 90.7%, 88.6% and 86.2% right answers to the four test questions. Although these numbers are again rather high, 'only' 205 subjects (70.9%) made no mistake at all in this part. Thus, there are some differences between the test results in both situations. It is possible that either the structure of situation 'Fuel' is more complex or that the corresponding test questions are more difficult to answer. The latter point may have had some relevance for the fourth question in each situation. While in situation 'Aid' it is explicitly stated in the text that island A is unambiguously always better off than island B, in situation 'Fuel' respondents had to figure out this fact on their own from the given numbers. Indeed, 26 students only failed to answer this question correctly in the 'Fuel' case. Nevertheless, the value of such tests seems to be unquestionable, because students who misunderstood at least one central aspect of the given hypothetical situation can be identified and left out from the final sample.

It is interesting to see which individual or questionnaire characteristics have had a significant influence on the quality of answers on the test questions. Therefore, a binary dependent variable has been modelled that takes on the value 1 if the respective person correctly answered all four questions of the situation being considered. In anticipation of the following statistical analyses, the characteristics described above are used as independent variables in a binary logit model. The results for both contexts are summarised in Table 4.3. In situation 'Aid' older students and respondents without work experience were less likely to give correct answers. But there was only one effect relevant in both contexts. If situation 'Aid' was presented first (ORDER 2=1), the probability of understanding all relevant information as intended significantly increased. Thus, either reading through situation 'Aid' improves the understanding of the underlying structure of otherwise similar contexts or situation 'Fuel' tends to confuse some respondents. Nonetheless, the test questions enable us to identify those participants who completely assimilated the relevant information.[16] Nevertheless, results in the following section will uncover more effects of the order of questions. Therefore, it is important to control for these influences by adequate statistical methods.

Besides explanations of all incorporated variables, Table 4.2 also reports mean values and standard deviations for the overall and the reduced samples. We also distinguish between women and men, but this discrimination will be considered later on in more detail. The reduced 'total' samples contain those respondents who correctly answered all corresponding test questions. Only these groups will be used in the following statistical investigations. For both situations, two-sample $t$-tests have been run to compare mean values of individual variables, but no significant differences between the reduced sample and the sample of excluded cases could be detected.

The graphs in Figure 4.2 show the distributions of those four individual variables for the reduced sample of situation 'Aid' that are not coded as dummy variables. Obviously, the majority of participants were between 21 and 23 years old. The perceived income of the parents, the expected income in 10 years' time and, especially, political attitudes of students are normally distributed over the possible categories, with very few respondents at the extreme positions. Nevertheless, the mean values for the two income variables are above 4.0 so that, on average, participants supposed their families' and their own future income to be above average.

Furthermore, in Table 4.4 correlation coefficients according to Pearson are presented for the reduced samples. Although several of our variables are ordinal, Pearson's $r$ offers a reasonable approximation for usually applied correlations, such as Spearman's rho. Moreover, Pearson's $r$ is also appropriate to determine correlations between continuous and dichotomous variables, like

16 Note that repeaters are not more likely to correctly answer these test questions. Hence, a 'learning effect' is absent even in this part.

Table 4.3: ML estimates of binary logit models: Test questions
Dependent variable: Correct Test Questions

| Independent variables | Situation 'Aid' (n=485) | Situation 'Fuel' (n=289) |
|---|---|---|
| *Constant* | 5.561* | 1.666 |
| | (2.178) | (2.618) |
| *AGE* | −0.205* | −0.015 |
| | (0.092) | (0.113) |
| *FAMILY* | 0.126 | −0.059 |
| | (0.117) | (0.121) |
| *FUTURE* | −0.021 | −0.105 |
| | (0.143) | (0.155) |
| *JOB* | 1.134* | 0.519 |
| | (0.488) | (0.517) |
| *MALE* | 0.523 | 0.195 |
| | (0.287) | (0.290) |
| *POLITICS* | −0.063 | 0.005 |
| | (0.143) | (0.149) |
| *REPEATER* | — | −0.562 |
| | | (0.315) |
| *ORDER 1* | 0.320 | −0.028 |
| | (0.273) | (0.270) |
| *ORDER 2* | 0.570* | 0.754** |
| | (0.277) | (0.272) |
| *RES* | −0.159 | −0.069 |
| | (0.271) | (0.268) |
| *YEAR 05* | −0.321 | — |
| | (0.274) | |
| Log likelihood | -184.56 | -166.92 |
| LR statistic | 16.73 | 14.55 |
| McFadden $R^2$ | 0.043 | 0.042 |
| Mean dependent var. | 0.864 | 0.709 |

Note: Asymptotic standard errors are reported in parentheses. Level of significance: *$0.01 \leq p < 0.05$, **$p < 0.01$.

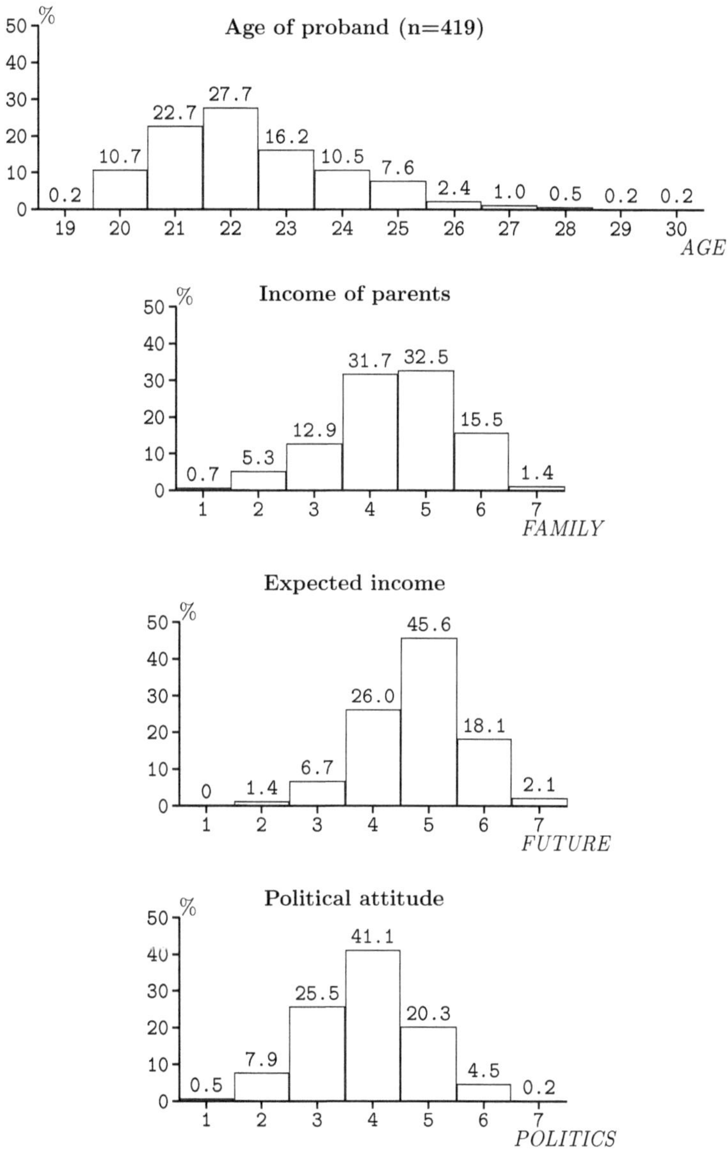


Figure 4.2: Demographics: Situation 'Aid'

Table 4.4: Correlation matrix for individual characteristics

| | Situation 'Aid' (n=419) | | | | | |
|---|---|---|---|---|---|---|
| | *AGE* | *FAMILY* | *FUTURE* | *JOB* | *MALE* | *POLITICS* |
| *AGE* | 1.000 | −0.011 | −0.027 | 0.641 | 0.239 | 0.143 |
| *FAMILY* | | 1.000 | 0.162 | 0.084 | 0.015 | 0.124 |
| *FUTURE* | | | 1.000 | 0.026 | 0.081 | 0.165 |
| *JOB* | | | | 1.000 | −0.001 | 0.093 |
| *MALE* | | | | | 1.000 | 0.214 |
| *POLITICS* | | | | | | 1.000 |
| | Situation 'Fuel' (n=205) | | | | | |
| | *AGE* | *FAMILY* | *FUTURE* | *JOB* | *MALE* | *POLITICS* |
| *REPEATER* | 0.273 | 0.032 | 0.051 | −0.021 | 0.031 | 0.124 |
| *AGE* | 1.000 | −0.023 | −0.001 | 0.657 | 0.306 | 0.082 |
| *FAMILY* | | 1.000 | 0.104 | 0.050 | 0.040 | 0.031 |
| *FUTURE* | | | 1.000 | 0.014 | 0.145 | 0.153 |
| *JOB* | | | | 1.000 | 0.138 | 0.066 |
| *MALE* | | | | | 1.000 | 0.118 |
| *POLITICS* | | | | | | 1.000 |

Note: Given numbers are Pearson correlation coefficients (Pearson's $r$).

AGE and MALE. Hence, this coefficient seems to be adequate to describe relations between our variables. As before, we observe higher correlations between AGE on the one hand and JOB and MALE on the other hand. Moreover, failing to pass the final exam results in older respondents. In section 2.4.4 we have already summarised reasons for including the variable AGE. Nevertheless, the results reported in the following section also hold if we run regression without controlling for the age of a respondent. Furthermore, due to the low variance of the variable AGE we do not control for non-linear effects ($AGE^2$) in the following regressions.

## 4.6 Results

In this section, the stated conjectures at the end of section 4.4.4 are considered. Starting with the initial case in each situation, an overview is given about chosen allocations in general, but also relative frequencies of the fulfilment of the needs principle and, beyond it, distributions in accordance with truncated efficiency and the maximin principle. Afterwards, modifications with regard to aspects of efficiency and responsibility are considered.

Furthermore, based on the findings in the two preceding investigations in chapters 2 and 3, the influences of individual attributes and sample characteristics on various decisions are investigated in a further subsection. Throughout all investigations, differences between the two hypothetical settings become apparent and have to be carefully explained.

### 4.6.1 Basic Results from the Initial Case

Several distribution alternatives, summarised in Table 4.1, have been offered to respondents. In Figures 4.3 and 4.4 relative frequencies for these response categories are given for the no-responsibility version of both contexts. We will start by investigating answers to part a) of each situation.

A first impression of the graphical presentations is that in neither case does one single category exist that has been selected by almost all students. However, as explained in subsection 4.4.4, due to the great variety of possible answers this is no surprise. Nevertheless, some of the presented distributions were more prominent among respondents.

To begin with, there are several possibilities to follow the idea of equalising the additional resources. In situation 'Aid' 27.1% of the students wanted to balance the remaining amount of money after fully considering basic needs, and another 21.4% equalised benefits measured either in number or in proportion of households on both islands. In situation 'Fuel', only 2.9% wanted to split the remaining 30,000 litres of fuel evenly, but 46.1% enabled both saw mills to work one additional hour. The differences between the two contexts are difficult to explain. Maybe students found it easier to calculate allocations that equalise benefits in situation 'Fuel'. But more importantly, overall almost 50% of the participants opted for equality arguments in both cases. This is a very strong result.

In contrast to these results, pure equality of the given amount, i.e. sequences 50-0-50 and 35-35, did not play a role. Hence, the needs principle seems to prevent such choices.

In each figure, to the right of the equality allocations explained above, those choices are found which reflect a stronger support for the worse-off group B. An almost equal share of respondents in both situations acted either in accordance with the maximin criterion or with a compromise solution displaying greater weight to group B.[17] However, in the 'Aid' context 18.6% preferred 'Compromise II' and only 4.8% the solution following from the maximin principle, while in situation 'Fuel' a small group chose a trade-off solution but 30.4% preferred maximin behaviour. Thus, especially the maximin criterion

17 Note that in each context only one compromise solution in favour of each group has been proposed. Certainly, there are several other possible compromise solutions, and indeed, as explained in the footnotes for both figures, some respondents stated their own compromises. However, they are included in the given relative frequencies. Moreover, the corresponding numbers for sequence 20-40-40 in situation 'Aid' also contain some other 'efficiency before needs' allocations with respect to island B.

Figure 4.3: Response categories: Situation 'Aid' - No responsibility

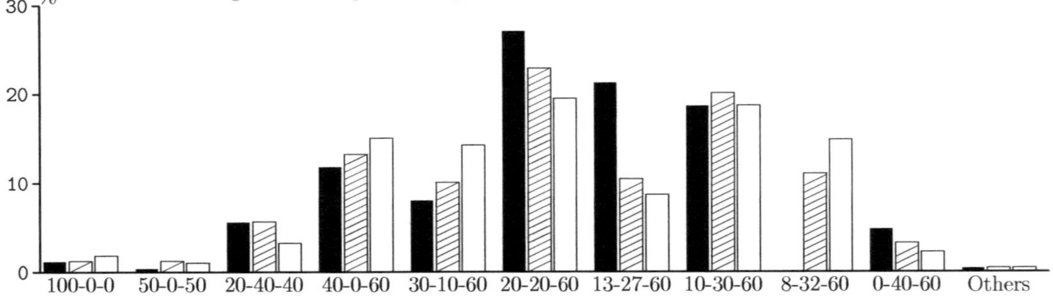


Percentage frequencies (n=205)

| Part | 100-0-0 | 50-0-50 | 20-40-40 (*a*) | 40-0-60 | 30-10-60 (*b*) | 20-20-60 | 13-27-60/ 12-28-60 | 10-30-60 (*c*) | 8-32-60/ 5-35-60 | 0-40-60 (*d*) | Others |
|---|---|---|---|---|---|---|---|---|---|---|---|
| a) | 1.4 | 0.5 | 5.7 | 11.9 | 8.1 | 27.1 | 21.4 | 18.6 | — | 4.8 | 0.5 |
| b) | 1.4 | 1.4 | 5.7 | 13.3 | 10.0 | 22.9 | 10.5 | 20.0 | 11.0 | 3.3 | 0.5 |
| c) | 1.9 | 1.0 | 3.3 | 15.2 | 14.3 | 19.5 | 8.6 | 18.6 | 14.8 | 2.4 | 0.5 |

(*a*) Included are the sequences 50-25-25 (2 subjects in a), 1 person in b) and c)), 40-20-40 (1 subject in b)), 35-35-50 (1 subject in a), b) and c)), 30-20-50 (1 subject in a), b) and c)).

(*b*) Included are the sequences 35-5-60 (1 subject in b) and c)), 25-15-60 (2 subjects in b)), 27-13-60 (1 subject in c)).

(*c*) Included are the sequences 18-22-60 (1 subject in c)), 17-23-60 (1 subject in b)), 15-25-60 (5 subjects in a) and b), 4 people in c)), 6-34-60 (1 subject in c)).

(*d*) Included is the sequence 0-0-100 (1 subject in a)).

Figure 4.4: Response categories: Situation 'Fuel' - No responsibility

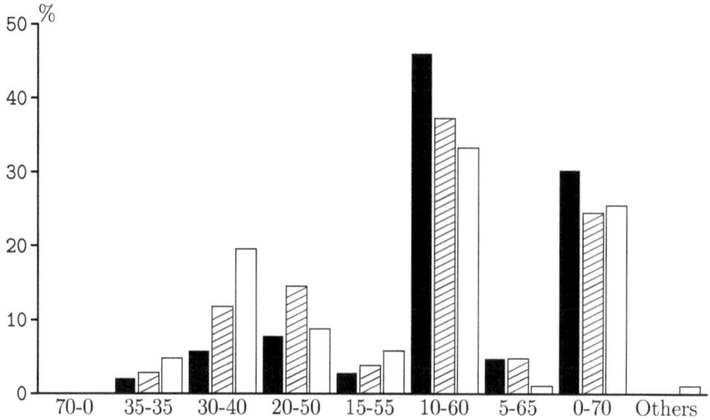


Percentage frequencies (n=102)

| Part | 70-0 | 35-35 | 30-40 | 20-50(*a*) | 15-55 | 10-60 | 5-65(*b*) | 0-70 | Others |
|---|---|---|---|---|---|---|---|---|---|
| a) | 0.0 | 2.0 | 5.9 | 7.8 | 2.9 | 46.1 | 4.9 | 30.4 | 0.0 |
| b) | 0.0 | 2.9 | 11.8 | 14.7 | 3.9 | 37.3 | 4.9 | 24.5 | 0.0 |
| c) | 0.0 | 4.9 | 19.6 | 8.8 | 5.9 | 33.3 | 1.0 | 25.5 | 1.0 |

(*a*) Included is the sequence 25-45 (1 subject in a)).
(*b*) Included are the sequences 2.5-67.5 (1 subject in a)), 7.5-62.5 (1 subject in b)).

was much more prominent in the 'Fuel' context. We will come back to this point at the end of this subsection.

On the left hand side of each figure, decisions in favour of those frequencies can be found that express a stronger support for the better-off group. Here, 'Compromise I' was equally prominent in both situations but, more interestingly, the allocation following from the principle of truncated efficiency was supported by only 11.9% of the students in the 'Aid' and 5.9% in the 'Fuel' case. Hence, at least in part a) of the no-responsibility version of each context this concept was clearly less often followed than in several earlier studies especially in the realm of income redistributions.

Additionally, in situation 'Aid', respondents were offered the possibility to split up the money for island B between projects 'Power B' and 'Food B'. Thus, they were able to separate needs considerations from a concern for future development of that island. In the given no-responsibility version, 5.7% of the probands decided to pay less than 60% of the money to project 'Food B'. The frequency is rather low but this point will be reconsidered if aspects of responsibility are incorporated.

Next, some more general decisions are of interest. They are summarised in Table 4.5 for the currently regarded part a) of the two no-responsibility versions (RES=0), but also for the two modifications, i.e. with respect to responsibility (RES=1) and efficiency (parts b) and c)), which will be regarded later on. From the given values it can be observed that basic needs were completely fulfilled by a great majority in both samples. Furthermore, relative frequencies of choices in accordance with the countervailing principles of maximin and truncated efficiency have previously been discussed. Additionally, it is also reasonable to contemplate two continuous variables since respondents were allowed to state a split of the given resources. On the one hand, certainly the amount given to the better-off group A in each context is of interest. On the other hand, one may also focus on those participants who followed the needs principle and look at the amount they were willing to spend for group B *beyond* the needed amount. Thus, we hope to get further insights into possible decision patterns beyond the fulfilment of needs. Both variables will become more important in the following subsections. At the moment, apparently the difference between mean values of both amounts being considered is very small in situation 'Aid', where students focused more on equal split of the remaining resource beyond needs. In contrast, due to more frequent equalisations of benefits, the corresponding difference is larger in the second context.

To summarise, although responses of the students spread over all possible answer categories, we are able to identify some more general observations. The needs principle has been fulfilled by the great majority of respondents in the two contexts. However, since only about 60% of the available resource was necessary to fully regard basic needs, this higher proportion of students compared to our two previous studies could have been expected. Furthermore,

Table 4.5: Summary of decisions

| Decision | Part | Situation 'Aid' RES=0 (n=210) | Situation 'Aid' RES=1 (*a*) (n=209) | Situation 'Fuel' RES=0 (n=102) | Situation 'Fuel' RES=1 (*a*) (n=103) |
|---|---|---|---|---|---|
| 'Fulfilment of needs' (%) | a) | 92.4 | 86.6 | 98.0 | 87.4** |
| | b) | 91.4 | 86.1 | 97.1 | 83.5** |
| | c) | 93.8 | 87.1* | 94.1 | 79.6** |
| 'Maximin' (%) | a) | 4.8 | 5.3 | 30.4 | 6.8** |
| | b) | 3.3 | 3.3 | 24.5 | 4.9** |
| | c) | 2.4 | 2.9 | 25.5 | 8.7** |
| 'Truncated efficiency' (%) | a) | 11.9 | 21.1* | 5.9 | 21.4** |
| | b) | 13.3 | 21.1* | 11.8 | 26.2** |
| | c) | 15.2 | 22.5 | 19.6 | 29.1 |
| Mean amount for A (in Thsd.) | a) | 20.64 | 24.41** | 9.34 | 19.13** |
| | b) | 21.06 | 25.34** | 12.08 | 21.72** |
| | c) | 21.38 | 25.70* | 14.07 | 23.04** |
| Mean amount for B beyond needs (*b*) (in Thsd.) | a) | 20.99 | 17.00** | 21.18 | 13.44** |
| | b) | 21.01 | 16.78** | 18.61 | 11.98** |
| | c) | 20.66 | 17.35* | 17.34 | 12.01** |

(*a*) Results of statistical comparisons between the samples RES=0 and RES=1 are also given in this column. $\chi^2$ tests for $2 \times 2$ contingency tables are used with respect to the binary decisions 'fulfilment of needs', 'maximin' and 'truncated efficiency'; two-sample $t$-tests for means are applied for 'mean amount for A' and 'mean amount for B beyond needs'. Level of significance: $^*0.01 \le p < 0.05$, $^{**}p < 0.01$.

(*b*) Considered are only those respondents who fulfilled basic needs.

the principle of equality was most often followed beyond the full consideration of needs. Here, several different allocations can be interpreted in this way. The fact that the resource was interpreted as 'manna from heaven' and the possibility of a continuous split have probably increased the prominence of these solutions.

Furthermore, the allocation based on the maximin criterion was often chosen in situation 'Fuel', but not in situation 'Aid'. Here, one can only speculate that this might have been due to different evaluations of hypothetical situations by our respondents. It is possible that in the 'Aid' context students evaluated a connection to the power supply system as an essential tool for the development of both islands, even though island A was said to be better off in either case. Accordingly, the maximin solution may have seemed to be too harsh in this context. Furthermore, in situation 'Fuel' a single focusing on settlement B could have been even more appealing because it enables the saw mill to work 1.5 hours per day, almost – albeit not exactly – the same time as the mill in settlement A. This line of reasoning takes up the argument of Gyrd-Hansen (2004) in the sense that we may observe differences with respect to support of worse-off individuals if a complete equalisation of groups being considered is either possible or impossible.

Finally, truncated efficiency did not receive as much attention as possibly expected. However, the following modifications of the initial decision problem may alter this observation.

### 4.6.2 Aspects of Responsibility

The first variation of both initial hypothetical situations to be regarded concerns aspects of responsibility. In order to investigate this effect we compare now the previously described findings with corresponding results from the responsibility versions. Later on, multivariate regression models are applied to receive further insights into the statistical significance of any possibly detected influences on the equality-efficiency trade-off. We start by focusing on the fulfilment of basic needs. For this, Table 4.5 states relative frequencies for the two separated samples in part a) of each situation. Obviously, both the usage of pesticides in situation 'Aid' and the waste of energy in situation 'Fuel' reduced the willingness of respondents to support the worse-off groups. The reported significance levels in columns RES=1 relate to $\chi^2$ tests for $2 \times 2$ contingency tables between both samples. Differences are statistically significant at the 10% level (p=0.054) in the first and at the 1% level in the second context. Thus, although the acceptance of the needs principle was rather high in each case, especially in situation 'Fuel' a significant decline can be observed if groups in need are supposed to be responsible for their own fate. To state it even more explicitly, due to these aspects of responsibility 13.4% of the respondents in situation 'Aid' and, correspondingly, 12.6% in situation 'Fuel' accepted the idea of letting group B either starve or live in unheated houses during the winter period, even though it would have taken only about 60% of the given resources to avoid such suffering. However, these results are in line with some findings on responsibility considerations in micro-justice contexts reported in subsection 3.3.3. Nevertheless, in the present study the acceptance of the needs principle was very high in both versions of each situation. However, in chapter 3 we could not detect any significant influence from aspects of responsibility on the consideration of unsatisfied basic needs of worse-off individuals. It is possible that the observed effect of responsibility considerations is due to the possibility of splitting up the given resources in a continuous manner, which allows for more individual allocations.

In each situation, the departure from the needs principle lead to stronger support especially for one alternative below the needs level. This can be seen from Figures 4.5[18] and 4.6.[19] In the 'Aid' context we allowed for separating the development aid for island B between the consideration of needs and building up the power supply system. Consequently, sequence 20-40-40 has been offered as one alternative, in which needs are not fully considered before some money is also spent on the second project on B. It has already been argued above that such allocations may be observed if respondents either misunderstood the underlying situation or wanted to emphasise the investment into the future of island B. Responsibility considerations offer a further explanation: Since inhabitants of island B are thought to be responsible for the famine, but not for the lower benefits from financial aid for the power supply project compared to island A, one could possibly be willing to deny a full consideration of basic needs and spend some more money on the alternative project for B instead. Indeed, aspects of responsibility increased the relative frequency from 5.7% to 9.6% in part a), but these differences were not statistically significant.

Because several reasons for supporting such sequences are conceivable, a closer look at the verbal comments of these respondents may be helpful. In total there were 46 students choosing 20-40-40 or a related sequence in either part a), b) or c). 15 respondents declined to state a reason for their decision, 11 wanted to equalise the distribution of development aid even among all projects, and another 7 students argued that the power supply project is also important. Only 3 participants mentioned responsibility considerations, whereas 4 respondents showed some misunderstanding of the underlying context. Hence, in general it seems to be possible that for this group of students aspects of needs and responsibility were less important than efficiency considerations.

In situation 'Fuel', a similar allocation decision was not available. Here, in contrast to the first situation, an equal split of the given resource (35-35) was significantly more often supported when the shortage of fuel in settlement B was due to wasting energy. Clearly, the significant increase reflects the willingness of the students to take aspects of responsibility into consideration.

Next, consider the effects of responsibility concerns on relative frequencies of other proposed allocations in Figures 4.5 and 4.6. At the moment, let us focus again on part a) in each case. As before, $\chi^2$ tests are applied to

18 Similar to the footnotes of Figure 4.3 the following sequences are included in the categories: In category 20-40-40: 40-60-0 (1 subject in a)), 40-20-40 (1 subject in c)), 35-15-50 (1 subject in a)), 30-30-40 (2 subjects in a) and b), 1 person in c)), 30-20-50 (1 subject in a) and c), 2 people in b)), 25-20-55 (1 subject in c)).
In category 20-10-60: 28-12-60 (1 subject in a), b) and c)), 27-13-60 (1 subject in b)), 25-15-60 (1 subject in a) and b)).
In category 10-30-60: 15-25-60 (2 subjects in a) and b), 1 person in c)).
In category 0-40-60: 0-0-100 (2 subjects in a)).

19 Similar to the footnotes of Figure 4.4 the following sequence is included in category 20-50: 25-45 (1 subject in a)).

Figure 4.5: Response categories: Situation 'Aid' - Responsibility

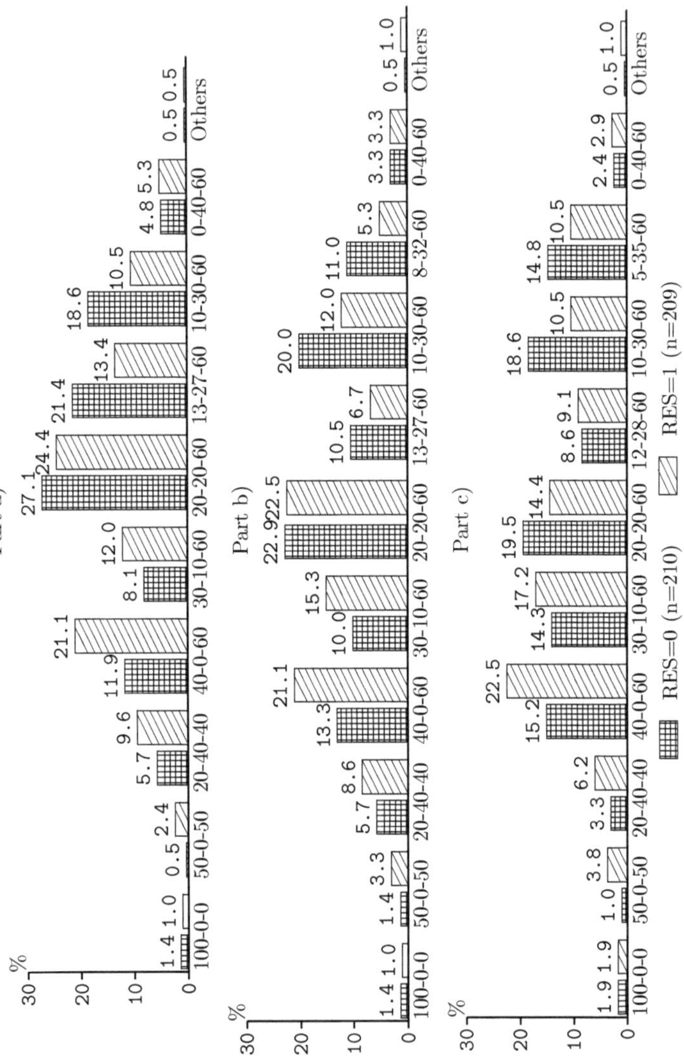

Figure 4.6: Response categories: Situation 'Fuel' - Responsibility

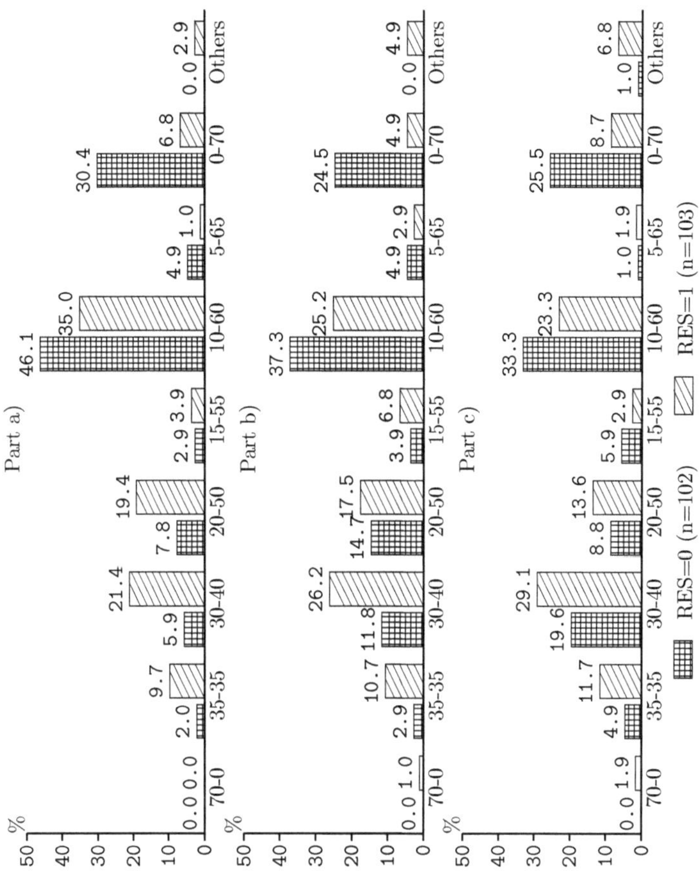

find evidence against the hypothesis $H_0$ that the distribution of responses on stated allocations was similar between the versions RES=0 and RES=1. This procedure results in a $10 \times 2$ table in the 'Aid' context and a $8 \times 2$ table in the 'Fuel' case. The hypothesis $H_0$ is rejected in both situations ($\chi^2_9$=20.698, p=0.014 and $\chi^2_7$=42.040, p=0.000). Hence, there were significant differences with respect to answering behaviours due to aspects of responsibility.

Obviously, equality beyond basic needs was more often supported in both situations if members of worse-off groups were not supposed to be responsible for their own fate. While about half of all participants in both no-responsibility samples chose these balancing allocations, the relative frequencies slightly decreased if aspects of responsibility were incorporated. Similar observations are apparent for both the 'Compromise II' solution in favour of island B in situation 'Aid' and, most astonishingly, the allocation corresponding to the maximin principle in situation 'Fuel'. From Table 4.5 it can be seen that the latter difference is statistically significant at the 1% level. Hence, aspects of responsibility also had a strong influence on the emphasis of the worse-off position of group B.

Nevertheless, some contextual effects can also be detected. As argued above, in situation 'Aid' the connection of households to the power supply system on the better-off island A can be interpreted as a sort of development program that should get at least a small amount of the resource, while in situation 'Fuel' the saw mill in the better-off settlement A already works for two hours per day.

Concerning allocations that express a stronger support for group A, the supposed responsibility of the worse offs remarkably increased the probability of choosing allocations in accordance with both truncated efficiency and compromise solutions in favour of better-off individuals. While in each situation the acceptance of the first principle was rather low in the no-responsibility case, it increased to more than 21% in both contexts if the worse-off individuals were supposed to be responsible for their own fate. The $\chi^2$ tests in Table 4.5 show the statistical significance of these differences; the corresponding p-values are 0.012 in situation 'Aid' and 0.001 in situation 'Fuel'.

Indeed, these are important findings. Certainly, given our hypothetical situations one could argue that truncated efficiency is quite attractive since the corresponding allocations are close to an equal distribution of the additionally given resource. Furthermore, beyond the fulfilment of the needs principle, supporting the better-off groups with a certain amount gives back a higher benefit, measured in number of households or in working hours, than paying the same amount to their opponents. So, there should already be plausible reasons to spend at least 40% of the resource for the project of group A in each context. But surprisingly, it seems to need the additional inclusion of aspects of responsibility to make truncated efficiency a prominent allocation concept.

This is astonishing since responsibility considerations are only connected with the existence of unsatisfied basic needs, but they are not the reason for differences beyond needs. Thus, besides direct consequences on the fulfilment of the needs principle, a delayed responsibility effect is also observed. This finding is underpinned by the mean values reported in Table 4.5. The values of the 'mean amount for A' concern all respondents. The additionally stated results of two-sample $t$-tests reveal some overall differences: Respondents were willing to make significantly higher payments to the better-off groups if the worse offs were supposed to be responsible for their situation. Furthermore, when the focus is only on those participants who gave at least enough resources to group B to respect basic needs, we find again highly significant differences in both contexts. This is probably the clearest evidence for the supposed delayed responsibility effect.

In total, aspects of responsibility had a strong effect on answers in part a) of each hypothetical situation. This finding will be reconsidered and clearly confirmed in the following subsections. At first, variations of benefits are taken into account. Afterwards, multivariate regression models will allow for additional insights into decision patterns.

### 4.6.3 Aspects of Efficiency

Similar to the two previous questionnaire studies, the size of the better-off group is successively enlarged in each context. Thus, the equality-efficiency trade-off should become more and more apparent. As already explained in subsection 4.4.2, the cost reduction for the connection of one household on island A described in situation 'Aid' caused some more difficulties compared to the rather obvious extension of settlement A in situation 'Fuel'. In this subsection we will study the effects of these variations in particular by means of several previously introduced figures.

To begin with, consider once again the relative frequencies of the no-responsibility version for both contexts in Figures 4.3 and 4.4 on pages 206 and 207. When we move from part a) to part c) in situation 'Aid', a decline of the relative frequency of the 'equal split' sequence 20-20-60 can be observed. But this is not the case for the idea of 'equal gain', which is measured either in equal proportions (13-27-60 in a) and b), 12-28-60 in c)) or in number of households (13-27-60, 8-32-60, 5-35-60 in the respective parts).[20] Moreover, the allocation in accordance with the maximin principle did not play any role, while support for the distribution explained by 'Compromise II' (10-30-60) in favour of island B remained almost equally high in all parts. In contrast, an increasing number of respondents can be identified who attached

20 Note again that this gain should be separated from a direct utility interpretation. It is unclear how much utility each island receives from one additionally connected household. Thus, either numbers or proportions of households are regarded.

more importance to the project on island A if this alternative becomes less expensive. To some degree this is visible from the frequencies of the allocations corresponding either to 'Compromise I' (30-10-60) or to truncated efficiency.

Results are even more obvious in situation 'Fuel'. Although solution 10-60, which corresponds to an equal gain of working hours, was most often chosen in all three parts, the relative frequency of this sequence declined. Respectively, an increasing number of students opted for a stronger support for settlement A. Here, the answers seemed to successively proceed – almost wavelike – towards the left hand side of the horizontal axis. Consequently, in part c) significantly more participants than in part a) chose the allocation in accordance with truncated efficiency ($\chi^2_2$=7.663, p=0.006). Nevertheless, on the other side of the scale a remarkable number of probands followed the allocation suggested by the maximin principle unconditionally, i.e. also in both extensions. This is again similar to findings for 'Compromise II' in situation 'Aid'.

Observations with respect to truncated efficiency and the maximin criterion can also be confirmed for both contexts if the more general results in Table 4.5 on page 209 are examined. Furthermore, apparently the full regard of basic needs can be detected for an equally high share of respondents in all parts of situation 'Aid', while the corresponding values for situation 'Fuel' declined somewhat if the size of settlement A was increased. It may be possible that in cases, where aspects of efficiency gain more and more attention, living without heating in settlement B is considered to be less severe than the famine on island B. In the 'Aid' context, changes of the mean amounts also given are not very meaningful. As previously explained, participants who are willing to retain equality in terms of numbers of recipients should give a decreasing amount of money to island A in parts b) and c). This may cancel out other effects on the mean amount. Additionally, giving the same amount to the better-off group in each case could be interpreted as a kind of efficiency consideration with some concern for equality aspects. We will reconsider this point in chapter 5.

In contrast, in situation 'Fuel' stronger efficiency considerations result in a higher amount for settlement A. In fact, the mean amount for A significantly increases if we proceed from part a) to part c) while the mean amount for B beyond needs remarkably decreases. By this, a greater concern for efficiency arguments is clearly visible.

So far, the consequences of efficiency variations were less obvious in situation 'Aid' compared to situation 'Fuel'. This might be due to the structure of both contexts being described. Nevertheless, it seems that in each case it is particularly those respondents who had previously chosen an equal split beyond basic needs in part a) who tended to switch to solutions with a higher benefit in parts b) and c). We will reconsider this observation in the following paragraphs. However, it is rather plausible that the modifications being regarded turned the attention of these participants towards a convincing reason to distinguish between both hypothetical groups.

Next, it should be examined whether variations of benefits displayed different effects if the previously described aspects of responsibility were simultaneously introduced. Note that this situation is the clearest case of plurality of justice principles in this work. However, it is important to notice that already in part a) the help for the better-off group was more beneficial in terms of numbers of households or working hours so that we do not check for effects of responsibility alone.

Relative frequencies for different response categories can be found in Figures 4.5 and 4.6 on pages 212 and 213. In situation 'Aid', $\chi^2$ tests show that the distribution of answers on the proposed response categories were significantly different at the 5% level between the samples RES=0 and RES=1 in part b) ($\chi^2_{10}$=19.507, p=0.034), but not in part c) ($\chi^2_{10}$=17.213, p=0.070). In contrast, in situation 'Fuel' the corresponding differences between both questionnaire versions were statistically significant at the 1% level in all parts. Hence, if aspects of efficiency were increasingly emphasised, the influence of responsibility consideration on allocation decisions diminished only in the first context. The reason for this observation is not obvious. From the indicated statistical results in the RES=1 columns in Table 4.5 it can be seen that in both situations the difference between the two versions with respect to the acceptance of truncated efficiency declined. This was mainly due to the stronger reaction to aspects of efficiency by those participants who faced the no-responsibility version.

In chapter 3, we have already speculated that only a certain proportion of respondents in all samples may be sensitive to both efficiency and responsibility considerations. This explanation could also be of relevance in the present study. Firstly, the results just presented show that if we move from the no-responsibility to the responsibility version, a certain proportion of subjects decided in favour of a solution that prefers the better offs. However, if we only regard the no-responsibility case and move from part a) to part c) a more similar proportion of students opted for the solutions with a higher benefit. Secondly, we witnessed a greater heterogeneity of justice attitudes, which did not disappear if the modifications mentioned were introduced. Despite the first observations, the solutions in accordance with truncated efficiency were most prominent when aspects of efficiency and responsibility were simultaneously included. But even in this case, a great majority of respondents obviously followed alternative conceptions.

To conclude, responsibility as well as efficiency considerations promoted the acceptance of truncated efficiency. Nevertheless, if both effects were varied at the same time, the strongest support for the allocation that corresponds to this mixed concept could be observed. Other differences – but also similarities – between the responsibility and the no-responsibility sample remained more or less the same in parts b) and c). Therefore, with respect to truncated efficiency the effect of responsibility was only to some degree influenced in turn by efficiency considerations.

Finally, since the benefits of supporting group A were varied in a within-subject design, we are able to investigate how individual respondents reacted to these changes. However, the interpretation of individual behaviours is not straightforward so that we will deal with possible decision motives in much more detail in chapter 5.[21] Obviously, several 'pure' allocation principles are independent from efficiency modifications. For example, respondents who wanted to follow the ideas of 'strict efficiency', truncated efficiency, different equality conceptions or the maximin criterion should have chosen the same allocation in all three parts of the situation.[22] Furthermore, participants who opted for one of the two classes of compromise solutions, and, thereby, traded off the principles of equality and efficiency, should have chosen corresponding compromises in all parts of a situation. All of the choices mentioned reflect a consistent compliance with one single conception.

In contrast, other respondents seemed to 'switch' from one principle to another. For example, one may seem to follow the idea of 'equal split beyond needs' in part a), choose a compromise in part b) and finally decide in accordance with truncated efficiency in part c). In particular these 'switches' caused the observed effects of efficiency variations. In chapter 5, we will argue that many of these possible reconsiderations of initial allocations do not necessarily reflect a change of principles, but can be explained by a certain degree of inequality aversion that represents again a compromise between equality and efficiency considerations. Nevertheless, in the present section, we will distinguish between the previously described compliance with a single concept and a possible change from one principle to another, although we know now that the latter behaviour could also be explained by the trade-off mentioned. However, it is interesting to see which allocations have been chosen in each respective group and, in the next subsection, which factors influenced these decisions. Furthermore, this is the only possibility to investigate the evolution of behaviour in all three parts of a questionnaire situation.

In total 51.8% of the respondents in situation 'Aid' and 56.6% in situation 'Fuel' seemed to choose in accordance with the same allocation concept in all parts. The slightly lower value for the first context could be due to the more complex variations in this situation. Figures 4.7 to 4.10 in Appendix 4.8.2 present corresponding results.

To begin with, take a look at those respondents who seem to have followed the same concept in all three parts of a respective situation. In situation

21 Notice once again that we do not 'know' the reasons behind each choice but have to try to figure out possible motives.

22 One important exception is the aim to equalise numbers of benefitting households on both islands in situation 'Aid', but we are certainly also able to identify respondents who followed this concept.

'Fuel' (Figure 4.7), it can be seen that equal benefits and the maximin principle were undoubtedly the most important ideas. If responsibility considerations have been incorporated, truncated efficiency replaced the maximin equity criterion. Additionally, the aspect of responsibility displayed a central influence, which can also be observed from the relative frequency of the maximin solution. In situation 'Aid' (Figure 4.8), different modifications of the equality principle have most often been chosen, but in the responsibility version the allocation 40-0-60 was the most prominent single response. Obviously, the acceptance of truncated efficiency was remarkably influenced by additional aspects of responsibility. Overall, responsibility considerations displayed a significant influence on the distribution of responses on all categories ($\chi^2_{10}$=28.354, p=0.002).

But which allocations have been chosen by those participants who reconsidered their initial allocation at least once if support for group A yielded more and more benefits? The answer can be found in Figures 4.9 and 4.10 in the Appendix. Here, due to smaller sample sizes we do not distinguish between the responsibility and the no-responsibility versions. In both situations, the initially favoured idea of equality beyond needs, which is either displayed by the allocation 10-60 in situation 'Fuel' or by sequence 20-20-60 in situation 'Aid', was less attractive in parts b) and c), whereas particularly allocations in accordance with truncated efficiency in the first and with 'Compromise I' in the second case received more attention.

Somewhat surprisingly, in situation 'Aid' an equal gain, measured either in number or percentage of households, for both islands became more popular even for this group of 'switching respondents'. Moreover, in situation 'Fuel' the maximin solution was also chosen by some of these subjects. Certainly, part of these results can be explained by inconsistent behaviour of respondents.[23] Nevertheless, in chapter 5 we will show that a stronger support for the worse offs is also reasonable if we introduce a higher degree of inequality aversion.

To summarise, efficiency variations had some effect in situation 'Aid' and a rather strong influence in situation 'Fuel'. Especially if aspects of responsibility were involved, further efficiency considerations increased support for truncated efficiency.

### 4.6.4 The Influence of Individual or Sample Characteristics

In section 4.5, we have already presented several individual characteristics of respondents but also some additional attributes of the questionnaire. Results of the two previous questionnaire studies have shown that some characteristics may be important for analysing justice evaluations. Gender plays the most

---

23 For example, in situation 'Fuel' one person has chosen allocation 0-70 in parts a) and c), but 5-65 in part b).

prominent role, here. Furthermore, in line with the discussion of explanatory studies in subsection 1.4.2, we not only want to identify the acceptance of single allocation principles but also intend to investigate why certain behaviours are displayed. Hence, in the following subsection, multivariate regression models will be applied in order to answer especially two questions: Firstly, it will be examined whether some of the earlier results, for example the influence of aspects of responsibility, also hold if we control for individual and questionnaire attributes. Secondly, additional insights into the influence of some individual and questionnaire characteristics, e.g. gender or ordering effects, could be gained. In chapter 2, we elaborated already on various logit models. In the present chapter, only binary logit models are applied to analyse influences on the three dichotomous variables given in Table 4.5, i.e. observing allocations in accordance with the fulfilment of the needs principle, truncated efficiency and maximin behaviour. Afterwards, ordinary least square (OLS) models will be applied with respect to the remaining two variables in Table 4.5, representing the corresponding amounts given either to group A or to group B beyond basic needs. Similar to the procedure in chapter 3, the no-responsibility and the responsibility samples are pooled so that the dummy variable RES indicates the questionnaire version faced by the respondent.

In Table 4.6, maximum likelihood estimates of corresponding binary logit models for part a) of each situation are summarised.[24] As previously detected from the descriptive data, the probability of observing a fulfilment of basic needs was significantly lower in both contexts if the worse-off group was supposed to be responsible for the existence of unsatisfied needs. In situation 'Aid', the odds for witnessing a fulfilment over a rejection if facing the responsibility version of the questionnaire are $exp(-0.689) = 0.502$ times the corresponding odds in the no-responsibility case. The respective value in the 'Fuel' context, $exp(-2.097) = 0.123$, is even lower. This discrepancy between the two situations might be due to the possibility that a famine is supposed to be even more severe than unheated houses. Only for situation 'Aid' one more attribute is found to display a significant influence. If students evaluated their political position as being more to the right, they were less likely to act in accordance with the needs principle. This finding also holds for parts b) and c). At least the direction of this effect could have been expected.[25]

Beyond the fulfilment of the needs principle, influences on the acceptance of truncated efficiency are of major interest in Table 4.6. Again, the effect of aspects of responsibility is remarkable in both contexts. Furthermore, it

24 In Tables 4.6 and 4.8 only results for part a) are stated, while corresponding numbers for parts b) and c) are verbally described.

25 Note that we also experimented with dummy variables that are similarly coded as those in the two previous questionnaire studies. Here, parental background, future income expectations and political attitudes were each represented by three dummy variables. However, results are very similar to those presented in the given tables.

Table 4.6: ML estimates of binary logit models for part a)

Dependent binary variables: Needs, TE, Maximin

| Independent variables | Situation 'Aid' (n=419) | | | Situation 'Fuel' (n=205) | | |
|---|---|---|---|---|---|---|
| | Needs | TE | Maximin | Needs | TE | Maximin |
| *Constant* | 1.895 | −6.082* | 7.320 | 4.414 | 0.015 | 1.313 |
| | (3.231) | (2.561) | (4.946) | (5.752) | (4.524) | (3.926) |
| *AGE* | 0.104 | 0.125 | −0.530* | −0.063 | −0.121 | 0.088 |
| | (0.139) | (0.105) | (0.229) | (0.240) | (0.196) | (0.169) |
| *FAMILY* | −0.035 | −0.109 | −0.325 | −0.048 | −0.261 | 0.176 |
| | (0.143) | (0.120) | (0.189) | (0.264) | (0.203) | (0.177) |
| *FUTURE* | −0.022 | 0.389* | 0.331 | 0.104 | 0.158 | −0.242 |
| | (0.182) | (0.159) | (0.247) | (0.355) | (0.261) | (0.216) |
| *JOB* | 0.556 | −0.059 | 2.122** | 1.445 | 0.135 | −0.419 |
| | (0.620) | (0.439) | (0.766) | (1.236) | (0.786) | (0.747) |
| *MALE* | 0.014 | 0.131 | 0.586 | 0.401 | 0.896 | 0.471 |
| | (0.361) | (0.310) | (0.529) | (0.635) | (0.514) | (0.436) |
| *POLITICS* | −0.361* | 0.009 | −0.104 | 0.133 | 0.007 | −0.236 |
| | (0.175) | (0.143) | (0.244) | (0.308) | (0.236) | (0.206) |
| *REPEATER* | — | — | — | −0.130 | −0.095 | −0.336 |
| | | | | (0.690) | (0.559) | (0.522) |
| *ORDER 1* | −0.526 | 0.143 | 0.283 | −0.760 | −0.632 | 0.460 |
| | (0.334) | (0.275) | (0.466) | (0.594) | (0.443) | (0.402) |
| *ORDER 2* | 0.289 | −0.932** | 0.446 | 0.575 | −0.145 | −1.010* |
| | (0.328) | (0.285) | (0.474) | (0.591) | (0.438) | (0.414) |
| *RES* | −0.689* | 0.711* | 0.075 | −2.097** | 1.488** | −2.007** |
| | (0.337) | (0.282) | (0.464) | (0.796) | (0.504) | (0.474) |
| *YEAR 05* | 0.227 | 0.175 | 0.691 | — | — | — |
| | (0.343) | (0.279) | (0.467) | | | |
| Log likelihood | -133.04 | -173.51 | -74.95 | -45.84 | -71.95 | -82.04 |
| LR statistic | 15.45 | 27.85** | 16.76 | 15.64 | 19.58* | 32.49** |
| McFadden $R^2$ | 0.055 | 0.074 | 0.101 | 0.146 | 0.120 | 0.165 |
| Mean dependent variable | 0.895 | 0.165 | 0.050 | 0.927 | 0.137 | 0.185 |

Note: Asymptotic standard errors are reported in parentheses. Level of significance: *$0.01 \leq p < 0.05$, **$p < 0.01$. The binary dependent variables are '(Needs) Fulfilment of needs', '(TE) Choosing in accordance with truncated efficiency', '(Maximin) Choosing in accordance with maximin'.

can be observed that in situation 'Aid' students who were more optimistic about their future income were also more likely to act in accordance with this principle. This result is in line with some of our findings in the two earlier questionnaire investigations. There, more sanguine future income expectations made respondents act more in line with efficiency considerations.

The allocation in accordance with the maximin criterion can only be observed for 5.0% of our students in situation 'Aid'. Here, older respondents or those without work experience were less likely to choose the corresponding distribution. These results are difficult to explain but the number of corresponding participants is low.

In situation 'Fuel' none of the individual characteristics display a stronger influence on the choice of allocations corresponding to either truncated efficiency or maximin. Presumably, this fact is due to the rather small sample size.

Concerning additional questionnaire characteristics, the ordering of the two situations turns out to have an influence on observing behaviour in accordance with truncated efficiency in the 'Aid' case. If this context was presented to the respondent first, then the corresponding allocation was less likely to be perceived. This observation holds in parts a), b) and c). Hence, it seems as if situation 'Fuel' has biased respondents towards such decisions. Moreover, if situation 'Fuel' was first, then, at least in part a), the allocation following from the maximin principle was more often chosen in that context. All these observations are rather difficult to explain. Therefore, multivariate regression models become even more important, because they allow for separating influences from questionnaire features. Additionally, due to the alternated order of questions the relevance of this ordering effect should have been considerably weakened.

In the previous subsection, we distinguished between respondents who complied with one allocation concept in all parts of a situation, and students who seemed to switch from one rule to another if efficiency information was varied. Hence, it is interesting to see which factors display an influence on the fact that a participant always seemed to apply the same principle. This behaviour has been modelled as a further binary variable, which takes on the value 1 if the chosen allocations are supposed to follow from the same distribution conception. Corresponding ML estimates of binary logit models are presented in Table 4.7. Apparently, in situation 'Aid' male students were significantly more likely than their female counterparts to act in accordance with the same conception. This point was also made in chapter 2. As argued there, women seem to switch more frequently if the given context is modified, while men try to detect an overall structure behind a situation and be guided more by abstract rules. This line of reasoning closely follows the arguments of Gilligan (1982).

Furthermore, the ordering of situations played again a role in the 'Aid' context. From the negative and highly significant estimated coefficient for the

Table 4.7: Binary logit models: Compliance

Dependent binary variable: Compliance with one Conception

| Independent variables | Situation 'Aid' (n=419) | Situation 'Fuel' (n=205) |
|---|---|---|
| *Constant* | 1.452 | 1.543 |
| | (1.933) | (2.939) |
| *AGE* | −0.070 | −0.076 |
| | (0.082) | (0.126) |
| *FAMILY* | −0.108 | −0.025 |
| | (0.092) | (0.130) |
| *FUTURE* | 0.041 | −0.096 |
| | (0.111) | (0.165) |
| *JOB* | 0.172 | 0.961 |
| | (0.338) | (0.547) |
| *MALE* | 0.627** | 0.089 |
| | (0.222) | (0.317) |
| *POLITICS* | 0.092 | 0.080 |
| | (0.106) | (0.155) |
| *REPEATER* | — | 0.664 |
| | | (0.371) |
| *ORDER 1* | −0.249 | 0.112 |
| | (0.202) | (0.292) |
| *ORDER 2* | −0.615** | 0.401 |
| | (0.203) | (0.296) |
| *RES* | 0.090 | 0.015 |
| | (0.202) | (0.295) |
| *YEAR 05* | 0.287 | — |
| | (0.208) | |
| Log likelihood | -277.54 | -135.54 |
| LR statistic | 25.24** | 9.54 |
| McFadden $R^2$ | 0.043 | 0.034 |
| Mean dependent variable | 0.518 | 0.566 |

Note: Asymptotic standard errors are reported in parentheses. Level of significance: $^{*}0.01 \leq p < 0.05$, $^{**}p < 0.01$.

variable ORDER 2 we can conclude that respondents who faced situation 'Aid' first were significantly less likely to follow their initially identified principle also in parts b) and c). Maybe, students who had to answer situation 'Fuel' before they turned to the 'Aid' case, were more experienced in evaluating the structure of these situations. Hence, we would expect to observe a positive and significant estimated coefficient for the second equation in Table 4.7. Indeed, the estimated value is positive, but the corresponding p-value equals 0.175 and, therefore, does not reflect any statistically significant influence.

As already described above, for both situations Table 4.5 also states mean values for variables that either reflect the given amount for the better-off group A or the quantity given to group B beyond the necessary value for completely fulfilling basic needs. Since respondents were allowed to state any reasonable number, we can model continuous variables from these statements and apply OLS models. The common representation is given in equation (4.1). Let

$$y_i^* = \beta_0 + \beta_1 x_{i1} + \cdots + \beta_k x_{ik} + \varepsilon_i \tag{4.1}$$

be the latent regression, where $y_i^*$ is an unobserved continuous variable that represents the optimal payment, evaluated from individual i's perspective, either for group A or for group B. It is assumed that the $l = 1, \ldots, k$ independent variables, which represent individual or questionnaire characteristics, determine the size of $y_i^*$. The model also includes a constant term. Moreover, the terms $\varepsilon_i$ denote the individual-specific effects. They are assumed to be independently and normally distributed. The available set of data for $i = 1, \ldots, n$ individuals has been utilised to estimate equation (4.2):

$$\widehat{y_i} = \widehat{\beta_0} + \widehat{\beta_1} x_{i1} + \cdots + \widehat{\beta_k} x_{ik}. \tag{4.2}$$

Here, $\widehat{y_i}$ is the observed amount distributed by individual $i$ to group A or B, respectively. Hence, we estimate $k + 1$ parameters $\widehat{\beta_l}$ for $l = 0, 1, \ldots, k$ by applying the method of OLS.

The correspondingly estimated equations are presented in Table 4.8. The results confirm the earlier observations concerning the influence from aspects of responsibility on allocation decisions. While the estimated amount for island A in situation 'Aid' increases by 3.648 units if island B has used pesticides, the estimated amount for settlement A in situation 'Fuel' is 10.078 units higher if settlement B has wasted energy. Both increases are statistically significant at the 1% level. Even more interestingly, there seems to have occurred a similar effect for the amount for group B beyond the consideration of basic needs in both context. Thus, obviously, besides the direct effect on the acceptance of the needs principle there exists a delayed responsibility effect in the sense that suffering groups are hold responsible for causing their misfortune beyond the direct effects of their careless behaviour. As expected,

Table 4.8: OLS estimates for part a)

| | Situation 'Aid' | | Situation 'Fuel' | |
|---|---|---|---|---|
| Independent variables | Amount for A (n=419) | Amount for B beyond needs (n=371) | Amount for A (n=205) | Amount for B beyond needs (n=190) |
| *Constant* | −7.129 | 45.133** | 9.763 | 21.205 |
| | (13.311) | (11.114) | (14.496) | (13.036) |
| *AGE* | 0.690 | −0.987* | −0.051 | 0.111 |
| | (0.566) | (0.478) | (0.622) | (0.565) |
| *FAMILY* | −0.480 | 0.197 | −0.487 | 0.497 |
| | (0.624) | (0.524) | (0.644) | (0.580) |
| *FUTURE* | 1.554* | −0.621 | 0.415 | −0.476 |
| | (0.762) | (0.645) | (0.816) | (0.716) |
| *JOB* | −4.347 | 2.248 | −2.841 | 1.336 |
| | (2.326) | (1.949) | (2.618) | (2.340) |
| *MALE* | 2.738 | −0.694 | 0.301 | −0.596 |
| | (1.528) | (1.279) | (1.570) | (1.432) |
| *POLITICS* | 1.954** | −0.570 | 0.205 | −0.599 |
| | (0.725) | (0.620) | (0.771) | (0.737) |
| *REPEATER* | — | — | 0.561 | −0.132 |
| | | | (1.787) | (1.645) |
| *ORDER 1* | 0.555 | 0.643 | −0.491 | 1.780 |
| | (1.392) | (1.158) | (1.444) | (1.300) |
| *ORDER 2* | −2.992* | 2.993* | 0.728 | −1.449 |
| | (1.390) | (1.156) | (1.462) | (1.315) |
| *RES* | 3.648** | −3.856** | 10.078** | −7.808** |
| | (1.388) | (1.155) | (1.462) | (1.315) |
| *YEAR 05* | 0.687 | 0.612 | — | — |
| | (1.427) | (1.186) | | |
| Adjusted $R^2$ | 0.064 | 0.051 | 0.167 | 0.145 |
| F-statistic | 3.844** | 2.978** | 5.080** | 4.213** |

Note: Given are non-standardised coefficients. Standard errors are reported in parentheses. Level of significance: $^{*}0.01 \leq p < 0.05$, $^{**}p < 0.01$. The dependent variable 'Amount for B beyond needs' concerns only those respondents who fully considered needs.

the possibility of dividing the resource in a continuous fashion leads to more sensible reactions to the introduction of aspects of responsibility.

The estimated coefficients in Table 4.8 reveal some additional influential factors in situation 'Aid'. Similar to some earlier results from the binary logit model, students who were more optimistic about their future income, but also respondents who judged their political view as being more to the right, were willing to give a higher amount to the project on island A which yields a higher benefit. The directions of these effects are probably as expected. Additionally, older students payed less to project 'Power B'. This is in line with previous observations, especially in chapter 2, on the acceptance of the maximin principle. Finally, ordering effects are identified again in the 'Aid' context. Facing this situation first made participants give less to island A and more to island B beyond basic needs. We have already commented on this aspect above. Again, the absence of any further influences in situation 'Fuel' might be due to the smaller sample size.

*Gender Differences*

The influence of the sex of the allocator plays a prominent role in this work. Hence, special attention is given, again, to disparities in allocation decisions of women and men. Preliminary $\chi^2$ tests reveal that only in situation 'Aid', the distribution of answers on all possible response categories was significantly different between female and male respondents. Here, remarkable differences can be observed for the (not reported) total sample in parts a) (corresponding p-value=0.001) and b) (p=0.039), but not in part c) (p=0.111). Furthermore, a distinction between the no-responsibility and the responsibility sample reveals that gender differences can be detected for the first sample – the p-values are 0.007, 0.061, and 0.025 in parts a), b) and c) – but do not exist for the latter sample – corresponding p-values are 0.075, 0.688, and 0.435. Hence, gender differences seemed to occur only if aspects of responsibility were absent. However, judgements of both sexes conformed to each other especially if the worse-off group was supposed to be responsible for the existence of unsatisfied basic needs.

But in what way did female answers differ from male responses? In order to get some more insights into female and male behaviour, the values stated in Table 4.5 have been reproduced in Table 4.9, but now, distinct samples of both sexes for different questionnaire versions are considered. Furthermore, results on respective statistical tests are reported in the 'male' columns. Here, the hypotheses $H_0$ states that either relative frequencies or mean values for men are similar to corresponding values for women. Note that sample sizes in situation 'Fuel' are rather small. In the 'Aid' context there are no gender differences with respect to the fulfilment of the needs principle; for both sexes the proportion of participants who completely regarded basic needs went down if the hypothetical worse-off group was supposed to be responsible. The 'Fuel' case provoked some more gender disparities. Again, the acceptance of

Table 4.9: Summary of decisions - Females and males

| | | Situation 'Aid' | | | | Situation 'Fuel' | | | |
|---|---|---|---|---|---|---|---|---|---|
| | | No responsibility | | Responsibility | | No responsibility | | Responsibility | |
| Decision | Part | Females (n=88) | Males (*a*) (n=122) | Females (n=79) | Males (*a*) (n=130) | Females (n=47) | Males (*a*) (n=55) | Females (n=38) | Males (*a*) (n=65) |
| 'Fulfilment of needs' (%) | a) | 93.2 | 91.8 | 86.1 | 86.9 | 100.0 | 96.4 | 81.6 | 90.8 |
| | b) | 88.6 | 93.4 | 86.1 | 86.2 | 97.9 | 96.4 | 76.3 | 87.7 |
| | c) | 94.3 | 93.4 | 88.6 | 86.2 | 93.6 | 94.5 | 73.7 | 83.1 |
| 'Maximin' (%) | a) | 5.7 | 4.1 | 3.8 | 6.2 | 25.5 | 34.5 | 5.3 | 7.7 |
| | b) | 3.4 | 3.3 | 2.5 | 3.8 | 21.3 | 27.3 | 2.6 | 6.2 |
| | c) | 1.1 | 3.3 | 2.5 | 3.1 | 23.4 | 27.3 | 5.3 | 10.8 |
| 'Truncated efficiency' (%) | a) | 11.4 | 12.3 | 16.5 | 23.8 | 2.1 | 9.1 | 15.8 | 24.6 |
| | b) | 8.0 | 17.2 | 17.7 | 23.1 | 8.5 | 14.5 | 23.7 | 27.7 |
| | c) | 9.1 | 19.7* | 19.0 | 24.6 | 12.8 | 25.5 | 23.7 | 32.3 |
| Mean amount for A (in Thsd.) | a) | 18.57 | 22.14 | 21.10 | 26.42* | 8.67 | 9.91 | 19.87 | 18.69 |
| | b) | 18.16 | 23.15* | 23.09 | 26.71 | 11.86 | 12.27 | 22.24 | 21.42 |
| | c) | 18.91 | 23.16 | 23.32 | 27.15 | 13.72 | 14.36 | 23.16 | 22.97 |
| Mean amount for B beyond needs (*b*) (in Thsd.) | a) | 21.31 | 20.76 | 19.30 | 15.63* | 21.33 | 21.04 | 13.87 | 13.22 |
| | b) | 23.10 | 19.57* | 17.97 | 16.05 | 18.64 | 18.58 | 12.41 | 11.75 |
| | c) | 22.48 | 19.33 | 19.76 | 15.85 | 17.95 | 16.83 | 12.68 | 11.67 |

(*a*) Results of statistical comparisons between the samples 'Females' and 'Males' are also given in this column. $\chi^2$ tests for $2 \times 2$ contingency tables are used with respect to the binary decisions 'fulfilment of needs', 'maximin' and 'truncated efficiency'; two sample $t$-tests for means are applied for 'mean amount for A' and 'mean amount for B beyond needs'. Level of significance: $^{*}0.01 \leq p < 0.05$, $^{**}p < 0.01$.

(*b*) Considered are only those respondents who fulfilled basic needs.

the needs principle declined for both groups in the responsibility version. However, this decline is statistically significant only for the female sample. Corresponding $\chi^2$ tests that are not given in Table 4.9 produce p-values of 0.002, 0.002, and 0.011 in parts a), b) and c), respectively. Hence, in this context women seem to have reacted more strongly to aspects of responsibility than men. The reader will remember that in subsection 3.4.2 we reviewed already some studies which revealed that women are more willing than men to punish antisocial behaviour.

Men also allocated more often than women in accordance with the maximin principle in situation 'Fuel', although the difference was not statistically significant and declined remarkably for both sexes if aspects of responsibility were included. The other extreme position beyond the consideration of basic needs is represented by truncated efficiency. The corresponding allocation has also been more often chosen by male respondents in both contexts. Surprisingly, this observation was not influenced by responsibility considerations. Furthermore, efficiency variations in parts b) and c) left gender differences unchanged in situation 'Fuel' and even increased them in the 'Aid' context. The highest support for truncated efficiency can be observed among male participants who faced the responsibility version of the 'Fuel' case.

Obviously, men tended to follow efficiency arguments more often. This finding is also underpinned by results for the two continuous variables – at least in situation 'Aid'. On average, male participants wanted to give a higher amount to island A and a lower sum beyond needs to group B. Thus, similar to results in the previous two chapters, it may be deduced from the descriptive data that male respondents preferred the more extreme positions on the given scale of alternatives, whereas females appeared to be more in favour of compromise solutions. Here, especially truncated efficiency seems to be a masculine principle. Moreover, these findings confirm again earlier results of chapters 2 and 3 in the way that men – in contrast to women – were more likely to follow efficiency considerations. Additionally, with respect to aspects of needs in the 'Fuel' case, women reacted more strongly to responsibility information.

Now, let us regard some regression models. The sample descriptions in Table 4.2 on page 197 show that on average female respondents are younger. In both situations the corresponding p-value of a two-tailed, two-sample $t$-test for means equals almost zero. This observation is probably due to the compulsory military or civilian service of men in Germany. Also, women were somewhat less optimistic about their future income (p=0.099 for situation 'Aid', p=0.038 for situation 'Fuel'). As in section 2.4.4, this could be interpreted either as a lack of self confidence or simply as a realistic evaluation of the current income differences between women and men in today's Germany. Furthermore, on average political attitudes of women were described as being more to the left compared to their male counterparts (p=0.000 for situation 'Aid', p=0.093 for situation 'Fuel'). Finally, in the 'Fuel' context less women than men reported having work experience. Thus, overall there existed certain gender differences with respect to demographic characteristics. Moreover, these attributes have changed between the two years of the investigation. This conclusion can be derived from some differences between the two situations. Hence, controlling for these factors seems to be advisable.

The first regression results are summarised in Table 4.7 on page 223. It has previously been reported that male students were significantly more likely to follow the same distributive principle in all parts of situation 'Aid'. All further regression models in Tables 4.6 and 4.8 do not reveal any additional gender differences. However, if one would be more generous and also mark statistically significant coefficients at the 10% level, in the latter table we would witness gender disparities in the previously expected direction with respect to the given amount to island A in parts a) and b) and with regard to the amount for island B beyond the full regard of needs in part c) of situation 'Aid'. Similarly, in the binary logit model for truncated efficiency in situation 'Fuel', the corresponding p-value for the estimated positive coefficient in Table 4.6 equals 0.081. Moreover, it was argued above that in situation 'Fuel' women reacted more strongly with respect to the acceptance of the needs principle if aspects of responsibility were introduced. Indeed, these differences can be found if the total sample is split up into a male and a female part. There are no remarkable influences from the responsibility dummy variable for the first group but significant effects at the 5% level for the female sample in all parts of situation 'Fuel'.

Finally, in the case of the binary logit models we experimented with interaction effects of the gender dummy variable and other individual and questionnaire attributes. Corresponding regression results will be reported only verbally to save space. Similar to the study presented in chapter 2, the effect of gender on the decisions being considered strongly depended on the age of the respondent. With respect to the acceptance of the needs principle in situation 'Aid', estimated coefficients for the interaction term are positive and significant in parts a) ($\beta_{MALE*AGE_c}$=0.451, p=0.052) and b) ($\beta_{MALE*AGE_c}$=0.577, p=0.013). From the positive signs of the estimated coefficients for the gender dummy variable and the negative estimated coefficients for the age variable it can be concluded that the negative effect of AGE on the acceptance of the needs principle is significantly stronger for females than for males. Exactly the same observation can be made with respect to the allocation in accordance with truncated efficiency in parts b) ($\beta_{MALE*AGE_c}$=0.378, p=0.056) and c) ($\beta_{MALE*AGE_c}$=0.552, p=0.009) of situation 'Aid'. While on average males have already been more likely to act in accordance with truncated efficiency, the disparity mentioned even increased if respondents were older. Surprisingly, in parts b) and c) of situation 'Fuel' the age of a participant had the opposite effect in the case of the maximin principle compared either to the study presented in chapter 2 or to the observations for the needs principle in the first context. Now, older women were more likely to accept the needs principle while the opposite was the case for men. Overall, it is interesting to notice that both sexes seem to pass through different stages of moral development. According to Gilligan (1982), these stages, but also the pace of the passing, may differ between females and males.

To summarise these paragraphs, in the current investigation gender differences are not as strong as in previous studies. However, at least from the descriptive data and also from some regression results, certain disparities are detected. They confirm findings from others studies in the literature, but also some earlier results in previous chapters. Certainly, it may well be the case that controlling for other factors could already explain a great part of gender differences. Nevertheless, it is also possible that sample sizes are still too small to generate enough statistical power to confirm the observed disparities.

*Repeaters*
A final point, which has to be investigated separately, concerns the possible influence of repeaters in the current sample. Apparently, in situation 'Fuel' the fact that a subject had already participated in the study one year before had no influence at all on any decision. This can be seen from the estimated coefficients in the models represented in Tables 4.6, 4.7 and 4.8. However, as already explained in subsection 4.5.2, it is not feasible to incorporate the respective dummy variable REPEATER in regression models in situation 'Aid'. The main problem would result from the fact that an individual who completed the questionnaire in both years would be identified as a repeater in the year 2006 but as a non-repeater in the previous year. Thus, it is fundamentally important to investigate whether the completion of the questionnaire in both years caused significant biases of answer patterns. In such a case repeating participants should have been omitted from the 2006 sample. Again, relevant results will be summarised and presented only verbally because of the already great number of tables and figures in this chapter. Basically, the statistical tools presented above were employed again to obtain the following results. Certainly, only the 'Aid' sample of the year 2006 was utilised.

Firstly, we distinguished between non-repeaters (n=344) and repeaters (n=75) in order to examine whether there were significant differences in response behaviour. A $\chi^2$ test was conducted to find evidence against the hypothesis $H_0$ that the distribution of answers on the proposed allocations were identical in both groups. This hypothesis could not be rejected at the 5% level in all parts of situation 'Aid'. Next, $\chi^2$ tests for $2 \times 2$ contingency tables were run in order to identify significant differences with respect to the relative frequency of the binary choices 'fulfilment of needs', 'truncated efficiency', and 'maximin'. Again, no remarkable disparities at the 5% level could be detected. Afterwards, $t$-tests for mean values for the continuous variables 'amount for A' and 'amount for B beyond needs' were applied. No differences in any part of the situation were apparent.

Secondly, repeaters and non-repeaters may have differed with respect to some individual characteristics. Indeed, it is not surprising that repeaters were older than their non-repeating classmates. Moreover, a smaller proportion of them had work experience. Then, regression models were estimated. Here, similar to the models in the 'Fuel' context, the additional dummy variable REPEATER was incorporated. However, neither in any binary logit model nor in the two OLS regression models did the estimated coefficients display a significant influence on the corresponding dependent variables.

Thirdly, we reduced the samples used in the present chapter by excluding all repeaters from the group of 2006. Some descriptive results for this reduced sample are presented in Figure 4.11 on page 246 in Appendix 4.8.2. A comparison of these frequencies with the results presented in Figures 4.3 on page 206 and 4.5 on page 212 could not reveal any remarkable differences. Then, all regressions presented in this chapter have been rerun with the reduced sample. Results were in most cases identical with respect to significant estimated coefficients. If differences occurred, they mainly showed lower significance levels, which was most likely due to the previous sample reduction by 75 students.

Hence, there is no evidence that the completion of the questionnaires in the previous year had any influence on evaluations of respondents. Thus, it seems to be reasonable to also include the repeaters in the sample. This inclusion allows us to analyse answers from all students of that year.

## 4.7 Conclusions

At the beginning of the present work, it has been explained that the following three empirical investigations will regard trade-off relations between distinct justice principles. Also, it was explained that these studies should be based on prior theoretical reasoning. Thus, the common basis for our questionnaire surveys was the current theoretical debate on the possible pluralism of justice ideals, as it can be found for example in the work of Rawls (1971), Walzer (1983), Miller (1999) or Konow (2001, 2003). Despite the multitude of different theories of justice, four different allocation principles have been deduced from theoretical concepts. However, since the dispute on the combination of different allocation principles that are said to be behind justice theories is not resolved yet, it has also been argued in chapter 1 that empirical investigations may play a constructive role in the ongoing debate.

The present study included the four allocation principles into one single questionnaire structure and created several trade-offs between them. Clearly, the study has been based on the two preceding investigations. Nevertheless, some important modifications were necessary to consider all research questions stated in subsection 4.4.4. But before we conclude by summarising the corresponding answers found in this study, the trade-offs being regarded between the allocation principles and their corresponding operationalisations in the questionnaire should be briefly mentioned again, because they are of relevance for the following chapter and, more generally, for the statement of the present work.

Firstly, the principle of needs plays the most prominent role in all three studies presented. It has been introduced in the current questionnaire in a very specific way by modifying the idea of a poverty line to be found in several preceding macro-justice studies. The interpretation of needs should be in absolute terms, where each subject requires a certain quantity of a well-defined bundle of the equalisandum to be considered. In the present case, only one group was said to live below this level, but the additional resource sufficed to cover all respective needs. This last characteristic is the first departure from the structure of the initial two studies.

Secondly, and also similar to some previous macro-justice investigations, the principle of equality could be separated from needs considerations if the latter had already been fulfilled. Equality could be regarded in several different ways in our contexts. One may aim at equalising the individual shares of the distributed resource or regard the general well-being. However, similar to the two previous studies, a complete equalisation of individual welfare was not possible since the worse-off individuals continued to be worse off in all cases. Furthermore, beyond the full consideration of needs, the remaining resource could be allocated either evenly or by focusing on equal benefits. These alternatives were available due to the second modification of the initial structure, i.e. the possibility of a continuous split of the given resource.

The third principle regards efficiency, which is most often in conflict with aspects of needs or equality. The discussion by Rawls (1971, 1974a) and Harsanyi (1975) about the relationship between the difference principle and utilitarianism is the most prominent example. Similar to the first and second investigation, the benefits of the alternative in favour of the better offs were successively increased in order to examine the corresponding trade-off. If worse-off individuals live below the poverty line, statements on differences with respect to the benefits of alternatives are actually impossible since respondents have to make assumptions about utility gains of these worse offs. But from observed reconsiderations of initial choices in favour of worse-off subjects, the relevance of the efficiency principle can be inferred. Nevertheless, beyond the fulfilment of basic needs, information on the success of different projects was given for both groups so that the application of the compensation principle was feasible. This is a third important modification of the structure of previous studies.

Finally, as before responsibility was connected to the existence of unsatisfied needs. Again, two different versions were presented, which introduced an additional trade-off between the principles of needs and responsibility.

Besides the consideration of trade-offs, a further allocation criterion received special attention. The concept of truncated efficiency is usually motivated either by merit or by efficiency concerns. However, the structure of our hypothetical situations allowed considering the effects of variations with respect to the principles of efficiency and responsibility on the idea of truncated efficiency.

Now, let us reconsider some of the questions stated in subsection 4.4.4. Firstly, with regard to the previously analysed fulfilment of basic needs, we also observed a very high acceptance of the needs principle even if aspects of efficiency and responsibility were varied. This is in contrast to our earlier investigations. The most likely reason for this convincing agreement is the fact that only 60% of the available resource sufficed to fully regard all basic needs. Nevertheless, if aspects of responsibility were introduced, a significant decline of the full regard of basic needs could partly be observed. This is again in contrast to results of the second investigation presented in chapter 3, but confirms several earlier studies on truncated efficiency reviewed in subsections 3.3.2 and 3.3.3. However, it is important to note that the character of the responsibility consideration has changed. While in the second investigation this aspect was introduced as risk-taking behaviour, the present study described careless behaviours. But it must be mentioned that even if these aspects reduced the acceptance of the needs principle, the great majority of students still supported this idea.

Furthermore, the principles of efficiency and responsibility were found to be of greater importance beyond the full consideration of basic needs. The influence from efficiency concerns was most clearly visible in situation 'Fuel', where in parts b) and c) relative frequencies of given allocations increased for solutions yielding a higher benefit. In this context, efficiency modifications have been presented in a more obvious way, which may have influenced the results.

The importance of responsibility considerations is surprising since they were only connected to the existence of unsatisfied needs. One plausible reason for this delayed responsibility effect relates to the possibility of a continuous split of the resource so that influences of responsibility matters have been better visible than before. Furthermore, again the description of careless behaviour mentioned could have highlighted the responsibility of the worse offs. Therefore, many respondents seemed to be well aware of these aspects but, nevertheless, the needs principle served as a constraint. Thus, the important role played by both principles beyond aspects of needs confirmed earlier results from several macro-justice studies.

Among allocations which displayed the acceptance of the needs principle, equality arguments seemed to be most prominent. It is very likely that the consideration of an additional resource ('manna from heaven') has promoted this result, which is also in line with findings by Faravelli (2007). Moreover, several different possibilities of regarding the equality principle found their supporters.

However, this observation changed to some degree when efficiency or responsibility concerns were introduced. Maybe initially respondents did not detect any clear arguments, which supported moral claims of either group on the additional resource and, therefore, decided in favour of the equality principle. This result is to some extent in accordance with Konow's (2003) argument that equality is not a distinct justice principle, but follows if other principles do not justify a departure from an egalitarian solution.

In contrast to findings reported by Frohlich and Oppenheimer, the allocation in accordance with truncated efficiency has been chosen less often in both contexts regarded. This result occurred despite the fact that several arguments can be found in defence of truncated efficiency against other rules that are more in favour of the worse offs: the corresponding distribution was close to an equal split of the given resource, help for the better-off group yielded more and more benefit and in one version the worse-off individuals were even said to be responsible for their fate. Indeed, it has been observed that the relative frequency of the corresponding allocation was clearly influenced by aspects of responsibility and, at least in situation 'Fuel', efficiency. Nevertheless, the relative frequencies observed are very close to the rather low numbers reported by Faravelli (2007) for a similar solution concept. Surely, it is a mere guess, but perhaps Miller's (1992) scepticism about studies using a macro-context is justified. He argues that these investigations carry the risk that respondents infer solutions for income distribution problems from current practises of the welfare state in their home country. Consequently, if we regard micro-justice contexts, support of formerly popular conceptions may decline.

The alternative allocation, which follows from the maximin principle, was almost completely ignored in situation 'Aid', but received tremendous support in the no-responsibility version of situation 'Fuel'. We have previously argued that in the former context a connection to the power supply system may be of importance for both islands, whereas the maximin solution in the latter case led to almost equal levels of well-being.

Furthermore, we distinguished between a consistent compliance with one single conception and a possible switch from one principle to another due to efficiency variations. The idea of truncated efficiency proved to be very important for those respondents who reconsidered their initially chosen allocation. But we also argued that this switching behaviour could be explained to some degree by trade-offs between the principles of equality and efficiency. We will come back to this point in the next chapter.

Nevertheless, as predicted in the elaborations in chapter 1 and described in subsection 4.4.2, there were some more contextual differences. Also, ordering effects have been detected, but the alternated order of situations and the applied statistical methods controlled for these influences. Another helpful technical tool was the usage of test questions that allowed the identification of those respondents who misunderstood central points of the given contexts.

Finally, individual characteristics revealed some additional aspects. For example, the inclusion of students who had to repeat the course may be problematic. But we could not reveal any bias. Political orientation and future income expectations of respondents showed the effects previously expected. Moreover, gender played a role again. In line with results reported in the literature, men were more frequently found to follow only one principle but reacted less often to aspects of responsibility than women. Additionally, truncated efficiency seemed to be a masculine concept, while women were more in favour of compromise solutions. However, due to smaller sample sizes, gender differences have been less apparent compared to our previous two studies. As before, the age of a subject moderated the influence of gender on the acceptance of the needs principle and truncated efficiency.

To conclude, the structure of the presented study enabled us to investigate several different aspects of justice attitudes and the acceptance of allocation principles. Especially, the consideration of needs and the recognition of truncated efficiency have been analysed. The structure and theoretical interpretation of all studies will be finally reviewed and summarised in the following chapter.

## 4.8 Appendices

### 4.8.1 Appendix A: The Questionnaires

The following pages contain two different questionnaires. Both are part of a larger international research project concerning the problem of distributive justice. The questions do not aim at your knowledge, there are no "right" or "wrong" answers. In fact, we would be interested in your view. The analysis only serves scientific purposes and is anonymous.

**Situation Development Aid**

a) Imagine you have to decide on the distribution of a unique development aid amounting to **100,000 monetary units (MU)**. Different projects on two islands, A and B, each with **10,000 households** are considered as recipients. Although both islands are poor, the standard of living is higher on island A than on island B.

The government of island A would use the allotted amount to enlarge the power supply system (project "Power A"). The electricity connection of one household costs **10 MU**, so that for example **10,000 MU** are needed for 10% of the households.

The poorer island B also offers an investment into the power supply system (project "Power B"). Due to the unfavourable geographic conditions of the island, **20 MU** per household are necessary here, hence for example **20,000 MU** for 10% of the households respectively. However, independently of the realisation of project "Power B" the living conditions on B would be lower than on island A.

Moreover, due to an unexpected drought the inhabitants of island B are threatened by a famine. In order to grant all households the subsistence level of food, **60,000 MU** would be needed (project "Food B"). With a lower amount a respective smaller number of households would receive a sufficient quantity.

*In order to further clarify the described situation, we would like to ask you to answer the following questions:*

- How many households on island A would receive an electricity connection by an investment of 30,000 MU into project "Power A"?
  ...... households.

- And how many households on island B would receive an electricity connection by a payment of 30,000 MU into project "Power B"?
  ...... households.

- Suppose island B receives an amount of 30,000 MU for project "Food B". How many households would then have enough food despite the danger of a famine due to the drought? ...... households.

- Please make clear to yourself again: Is there any possibility within the limits of the development aid project to fully equalise the living conditions on both islands?
  Yes. □ No. □

Please state now, how you allocate the amount of 100,000 MU between the 3 projects of both islands. You may either pick one of the given allocations by a $\surd$ or state your own alternative in the last column.

| **Power A** (Thsd.) | 100 | 50 | 40 | 30 | 20 | 20 | 13 | 10 | 0 | ..... |
|---|---|---|---|---|---|---|---|---|---|---|
| **Power B** (Thsd.) | 0 | 0 | 0 | 10 | 20 | 40 | 27 | 30 | 40 | ..... |
| **Food B** (Thsd.) | 0 | 50 | 60 | 60 | 60 | 40 | 60 | 60 | 60 | ..... |
| **Your choice:** | □ | □ | □ | □ | □ | □ | □ | □ | □ | □ |

b) Imagine that the initial situation would have been the following: There exist **20,000 households** on island A, while the number of households on island B remains **10,000**. Again, the connection of respectively 10% of the households on island A with the power supply system costs 10,000 MU, but now this means **5 MU** per household. The conditions of both projects on island B remain unchanged, so that the electricity connection still costs **20 MU** per household. How should the amount of 100,000 MU be allocated?

| **Power A** (Thsd.) | 100 | 50 | 40 | 30 | 20 | 20 | 13 | 10 | 8 | 0 | ..... |
|---|---|---|---|---|---|---|---|---|---|---|---|
| **Power B** (Thsd.) | 0 | 0 | 0 | 10 | 20 | 40 | 27 | 30 | 32 | 40 | ..... |
| **Food B** (Thsd.) | 0 | 50 | 60 | 60 | 60 | 40 | 60 | 60 | 60 | 60 | ..... |
| **Your choice:** | □ | □ | □ | □ | □ | □ | □ | □ | □ | □ | □ |

c) Please imagine again a modified initial situation: There exist **30,000 households** on island A, while the number of households on island B remains **10,000**. Again, the connection of respectively 10% of the households with the power supply system costs **10,000 MU** which now means **3 MU** per household. The conditions of both projects on island B remain unchanged. Which allocation of the amount of 100,000 MU should be chosen?

| **Power A** (Thsd.) | 100 | 50 | 40 | 30 | 20 | 20 | 12 | 10 | 5 | 0 | ..... |
|---|---|---|---|---|---|---|---|---|---|---|---|
| **Power B** (Thsd.) | 0 | 0 | 0 | 10 | 20 | 40 | 28 | 30 | 35 | 40 | ..... |
| **Food B** (Thsd.) | 0 | 50 | 60 | 60 | 60 | 40 | 60 | 60 | 60 | 60 | ..... |
| **Your choice:** | □ | □ | □ | □ | □ | □ | □ | □ | □ | □ | □ |

Please give a brief explanation for your allocations!

### Situation Aid: Responsibility Version

"...Moreover, the inhabitants of island B are threatened by a famine, because they ignored warnings of the Food and Agricultural Organization of the UN and used pesticides which made the crop unusable. In order to grant all households..."

- Suppose island B receives an amount of 30,000 MU for project "Food B". How many households would then have enough food despite the danger of a famine due to the usage of pesticides? ...... households.

### Situation Fuel

a) Imagine two almost equal settlements, A and B, far in the North. For the last time before the annual closure of their ports in winter, both villages can be reached by a tankship. The cargo capacity of the only available ship is restricted to **70,000 litres**.

Both settlements need diesel fuel for both the operation of their respective saw mill and the heating of residential houses. The mills are the only income source of the inhabitants of both villages, who otherwise live at subsistence level.

Settlement A has already enough fuel available for the heating. Moreover, the stock suffices for a daily **two hour** operation of the saw mill. Each **additional 10,000 litres** of fuel would allow for operating the mill for one more hour per day.

Settlement B has not available any reserve of diesel fuel, because the shipping company, who was commissioned to deliver **40,000 litres** of fuel in autumn, declared bankruptcy. This quantity would be necessary to heat the residential houses in settlement B during the whole winter period. A smaller quantity would leave all houses unheated for some time.

If settlement B received an additional quantity of fuel, an operation of the saw mill would also be possible. The operation of the mill for one hour per day requires **20,000 litres** of fuel respectively.

*In order to further clarify the situation described, we would like to ask you to answer the following questions:*

- Suppose that settlement B receives a total of 20,000 litres of diesel fuel. Is this quantity sufficient to heat the houses during the entire winter despite the absent delivery in autumn?
  Yes. ☐ No. ☐
- How many **additional** hours per day could the saw mill in settlement A be operated if the settlement receives 50,000 litres of diesel fuel?
  ...... additional hours per day.

- How many hours per day could the saw mill in settlement B be operated if the settlement receives a total of 50,000 litres of fuel, of which 40,000 litres are needed for the heating? (Please note that it does not need to be clock hours).
  ...... hours per day.

- Please make clear to yourself again: Is there a possibility in the given situation that the living conditions in both settlements are fully equalised with the help of the fuel delivery?
  Yes. □ No. □

Please state now, how much of the 70,000 litres of fuel the tankship should deliver to each settlement. You may either pick one of the given allocations by a √ or state your own alternative in the last column.

| **Settlement A** (Thsd.) | 70 | 35 | 30 | 20 | 15 | 10 | 5 | 0 | ..... |
|---|---|---|---|---|---|---|---|---|---|
| **Settlement B** (Thsd.) | 0 | 35 | 40 | 50 | 55 | 60 | 65 | 70 | ..... |
| **Your choice:** | □ | □ | □ | □ | □ | □ | □ | □ | □ |

b) Imagine that the initial situation would have been the following: Settlement A has **twice** as many inhabitants as settlement B. At the same time, the mill in A has **twice** the capacity and employs at the same wage level **twice** as many people as the mill in B. All other details remain unchanged. Therefore, the stock of fuel in settlement A suffices for both the heating of the residential houses and a two hour operation of the saw mill per day. Each additional hour still requires a further 10,000 litres. The situation of settlement B remains unchanged. How much of the 70,000 litres should the tankship deliver to each settlement?

| **Settlement A** (Thsd.) | 70 | 35 | 30 | 20 | 15 | 10 | 5 | 0 | ..... |
|---|---|---|---|---|---|---|---|---|---|
| **Settlement B** (Thsd.) | 0 | 35 | 40 | 50 | 55 | 60 | 65 | 70 | ..... |
| **Your choice:** | □ | □ | □ | □ | □ | □ | □ | □ | □ |

c) Please imagine again a modified initial situation: Settlement A has **three times** as many inhabitants as settlement B. At the same time, the mill in A has **three times** the capacity and employs at the same wage level **three times** as many people as the mill in B. All other details on both settlements remain unchanged again. How much of the 70,000 litres should the tankship deliver to each settlement?

| **Settlement A** (Thsd.) | 70 | 35 | 30 | 20 | 15 | 10 | 5 | 0 | ..... |
|---|---|---|---|---|---|---|---|---|---|
| **Settlement B** (Thsd.) | 0 | 35 | 40 | 50 | 55 | 60 | 65 | 70 | ..... |
| **Your choice:** | □ | □ | □ | □ | □ | □ | □ | □ | □ |

Please give a brief explanation for your allocations!

### Situation Fuel: Responsibility Version

"...Settlement B does not have available any reserve of diesel fuel, because the inhabitants used up the required 40,000 litres of fuel as a result of already wasting energy in autumn. This quantity would be necessary..."

- Suppose that settlement B receives a total of 20,000 litres of diesel fuel. Is this quantity sufficient to heat the houses during the entire winter despite the waste of energy in autumn?
  Yes. □ No. □

## Additional Information

*Finally, we would be grateful for some information about yourself. Please note that the questionnaire is anonymous and that your answers serve only scientific purposes.*

*If necessary, mark the appropriate answers clearly by a $\surd$.*

- Are you female □ or male □ ?
- What is your age? ...... years
- Have you already completed a professional training? Yes. □ No. □
- Please state with the help of this scale how you would rate your own income prospects in the year 2015.

  very low — very high

  □——□——□——□——□——□——□
- Please consider the income situation of the family in which you grew up. How would you rate this income during your childhood?

  very low — very high

  □——□——□——□——□——□——□
- How would you rate your political views on a scale from "far to the left" to "far to the right"?

  far to the left — far to the right

  □——□——□——□——□——□——□
- Have you already participated before in a similar survey of our department? Yes. □ No. □

### 4.8.2 Appendix B: Additional Results

Figure 4.7: Compliance with one conception: Situation 'Fuel'

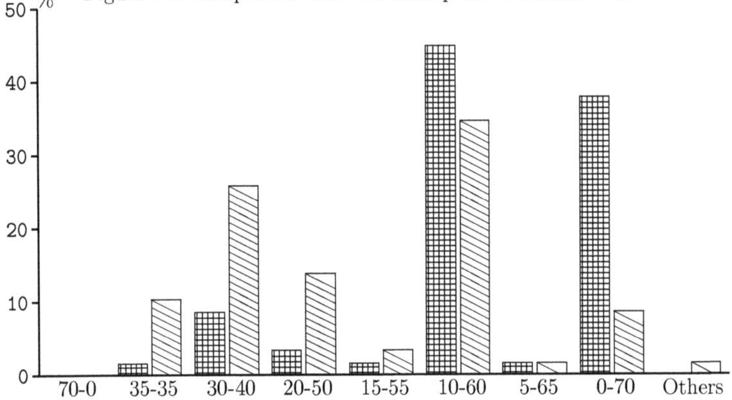


Percentage frequencies

| Sample | 70-0 | 35-35 | 30-40 | 20-50 | 15-55 | 10-60 | 5-65 | 0-70 | Others |
|---|---|---|---|---|---|---|---|---|---|
| *RES*=0 (n=58) | 0.0 | 1.7 | 8.6 | 3.4 | 1.7 | 44.8 | 1.7 | 37.9 | 0.0 |
| *RES*=1 (n=58) | 0.0 | 10.3 | 25.9 | 13.8 | 3.4 | 34.5 | 1.7 | 8.6 | 1.7 |

Figure 4.8: Compliance with one conception: Situation 'Aid'

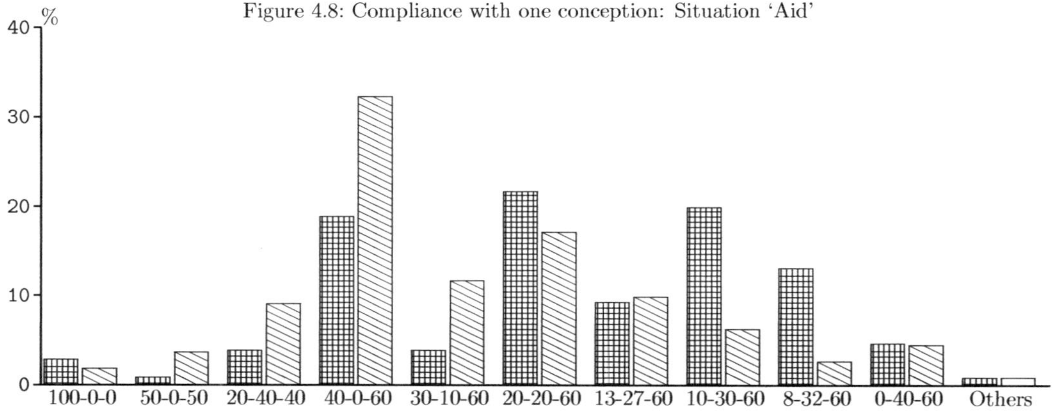


Percentage frequencies

| Sample | 100-0-0 | 50-0-50 | 20-40-40 | 40-0-60 | 30-10-60 | 20-20-60 | 13-27-60/ 12-28-60 | 10-30-60 | 8-32-60/ 5-35-60 | 0-40-60 | Others |
|---|---|---|---|---|---|---|---|---|---|---|---|
| *RES*=0 (n=106) | 2.8 | 0.9 | 3.8 | 18.9 | 3.8 | 21.7 | 9.4 | 19.8 | 13.2 | 4.7 | 0.9 |
| *RES*=1 (n=111) | 1.8 | 3.6 | 9.0 | 32.4 | 11.7 | 17.1 | 9.9 | 6.3 | 2.7 | 4.5 | 0.9 |

Figure 4.9: Reconsideration of initial choice: Situation 'Fuel'

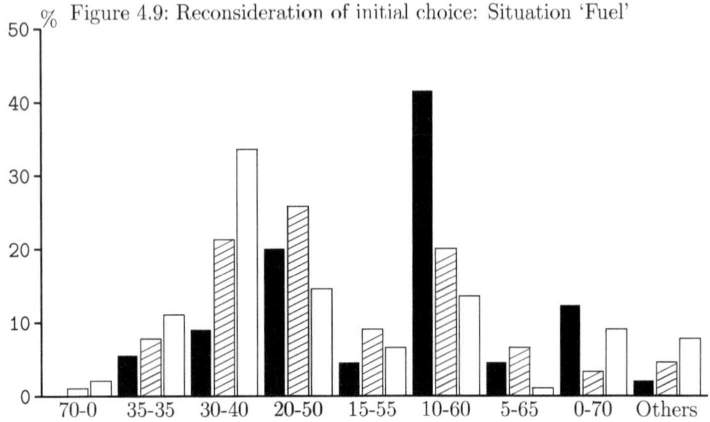


Percentage frequencies (n=89)

| Part | | 70-0 | 35-35 | 30-40 | 20-50 | 15-55 | 10-60 | 5-65 | 0-70 | Others |
|---|---|---|---|---|---|---|---|---|---|---|
| ■ | a) | 0.0 | 5.6 | 9.0 | 20.2 | 4.5 | 41.6 | 4.5 | 12.4 | 2.2 |
| ▨ | b) | 1.1 | 7.9 | 21.3 | 25.8 | 9.0 | 20.2 | 6.7 | 3.4 | 4.5 |
| □ | c) | 2.2 | 11.2 | 33.7 | 14.6 | 6.7 | 13.5 | 1.1 | 9.0 | 7.9 |

Figure 4.10: Reconsideration of initial choice: Situation 'Aid'

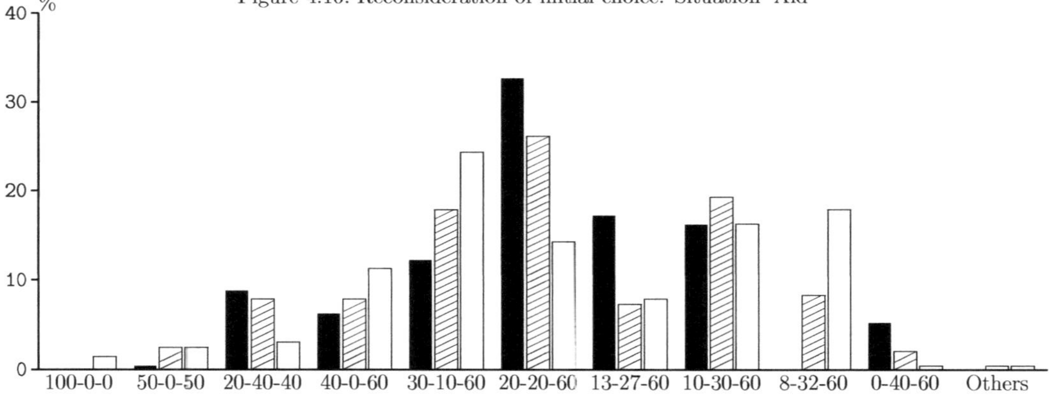


Percentage frequencies (n=202)

| Part | 100-0-0 | 50-0-50 | 20-40-40 | 40-0-60 | 30-10-60 | 20-20-60 | 13-27-60/ 12-28-60 | 10-30-60 | 8-32-60/ 5-35-60 | 0-40-60 | Others |
|---|---|---|---|---|---|---|---|---|---|---|---|
| a) | 0.0 | 0.5 | 8.9 | 6.4 | 12.4 | 32.7 | 17.3 | 16.3 | — | 5.4 | 0.0 |
| b) | 0.0 | 2.5 | 7.9 | 7.9 | 17.8 | 26.2 | 7.4 | 19.3 | 8.4 | 2.0 | 0.5 |
| c) | 1.5 | 2.5 | 3.0 | 11.4 | 24.3 | 14.4 | 7.9 | 16.3 | 17.8 | 0.5 | 0.5 |

Figure 4.11: Response categories: Situation 'Aid' (without repeaters)

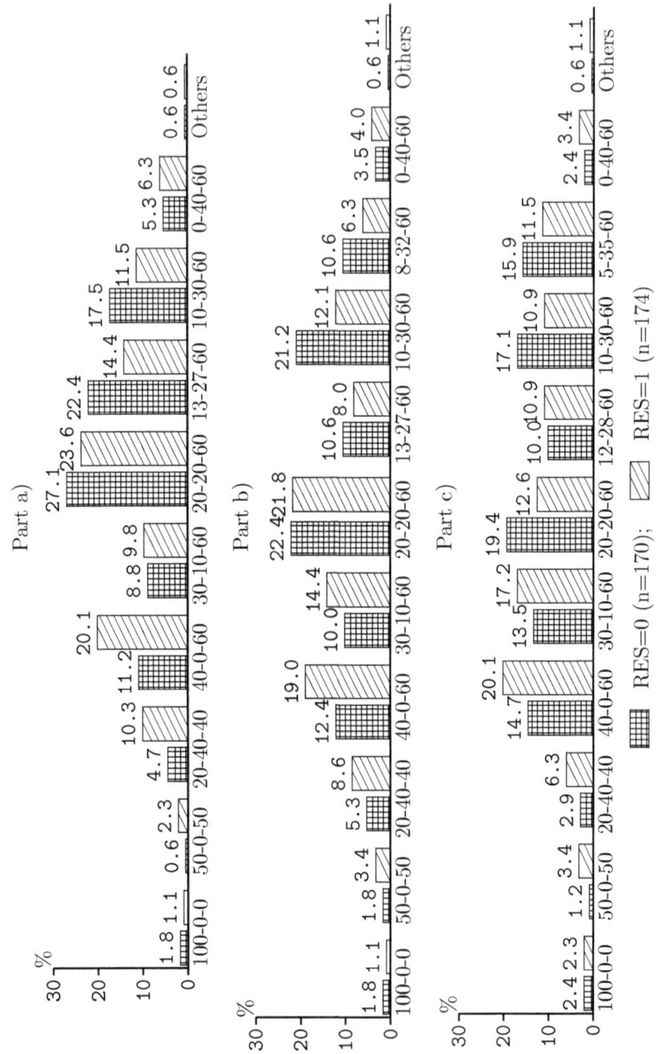

# 5 A Graphical Approach to Pluralism

## 5.1 Introduction

In chapter 1, it has been argued that empirical investigations within the realms of distributive justice should be based on theoretical arguments in order to profoundly claim relevance in the process of either discussing existing or developing new justice approaches. Consequently, the three preceding chapters on our empirical investigations contained careful introductions and explanations of theoretical ideas, which inspired the corresponding questionnaire study.

Also in chapter 1, it has been described that by now there are several axiomatically formulated and extensively discussed justice theories. However, by recalling Sen's (1984) famous flute example, it was explained that these morally sound theoretical concepts may lead to conflicting allocation proposals. As a consequence, modern theories of justice start to regard pluralities of distribution principles. Here, it is generally accepted to distinguish four basic allocation principles, viz. equality, efficiency, responsibility and needs. They are said to underlie different theories of justice and to explain potential conflicts.

Plurality of allocation principles is a rather new approach in the theoretical literature. One proposal suggested by Rawls (1971) requires absolute priority of his difference principle, which focusses on primary goods, over the maximisation of the total sum of individual happiness. Clearly, in our setting this solution solves the trade-off between the needs and the efficiency principle. Even more recently, as explained in chapter 3, the principle of responsibility has been introduced into welfare economics. While some concepts solely focus on this idea, others acknowledge the superiority of the needs principle, when it conflicts with aspects of responsibility.

Numerous empirical investigations reveal the existence of a pluralistic conception of allocation principles, but it is not clear whether they have had a strong impact on theoretical conceptions. Nevertheless, Schokkaert (1999) argues that empirical observations already played an important role in recent developments of welfare economics. Moreover, in particular the different arguments stated in subsection 1.3 in favour of theoretically based empirical investigations in the field of distributive justice describe the possibility of a constructive role of such studies in the process of discussing pluralistic justice conceptions among theorists.

Indeed, the first study in the present work aimed at investigating the acceptance of an equity axiom from social choice theory that underlies Rawls's difference principle in cases where it conflicts with the principle of efficiency. Moreover, in the second study aspects of responsibility were introduced into the existing structure of trade-offs between the principles of equality or needs and efficiency. The third investigation differed in some important ways from the first two studies. Although again a trade-off between the principles of needs and efficiency was described, a full regard of basic needs was possible. Thus, besides examining the priority of the needs principle, behaviour beyond the fulfilment of basic needs could be analysed. Here, we explicitly focused on the conception of truncated efficiency that demands the maximisation of the sum of total welfare subject to a floor level of individual welfare. Moreover, aspects of responsibility have been introduced again and, thereby, allowed for a full analysis of four allocation principles. Additionally, the possibility to split up the available amount of resources in a continuous fashion offered several new allocation possibilities. Clearly, the theoretical grounds are the least solid with respect to truncated efficiency. For example, Rawls (1971) doubts the social stability of mixed concepts and the moral foundation for the combination of different allocation principles that he calls intuitionism. Nevertheless, a corresponding allocation behaviour can be observed in our investigation, but also in various other empirical studies.

Hence, in this chapter, we are going to lead the reader back to theoretical grounds and offer a consistent presentation of all three surveys. Particularly, we are interested in interpretations of *all* possible allocation decisions. Consequently, results of the investigations will not be reconsidered in detail since they have already been extensively discussed in each of the three preceding chapters. Moreover, the results presented differed with respect to the context, to various samples and to the studies regarded so that it is impossible to review them here.

In order to use an accessible and convincing way to present possible similarities and differences between the studies, a graphical approach has been chosen. This procedure is inspired by work from public economics as well as health economics. In the former research field, Atkinson and Stiglitz (1987) already showed implications of different normative theories of the state by presenting their results with the help of several figures. In turn, this approach is based on earlier work, for example by Buchanan (1976) or Mishan (1977). Graphical presentations of the consequences of the difference principle and other distribution concepts were also introduced by Rawls (1971, pp. 76-78). In the realms of health economics especially Wagstaff (1991) discusses ethical questions related to the equity-efficiency trade-off by applying this graphical framework. In particular, concerns about inequality with respect to resource allocations based on quality-adjusted life years (QALYs) are expressed with the help of an isoelastic formulation of a social welfare function. This approach is inspired, for example, by Atkinson (1970) or Alexander (1974) and will also be explained in this chapter. Moreover, and most importantly for the following presentation, Williams and Cookson (2000) graphically represent implications of various philosophical theories of distributive justice and apply them to the allocation of QALYs.

The graphical approach implies advantages that will become visible in due course. For example, several inherent assumptions and constraints of each questionnaire structure can easily be visualised. Nevertheless, some necessary simplifications of complex theoretical concepts behind reviewed allocation principles have to be noted. Several of them will be discussed in subsection 5.2.1. Probably the strongest simplification is connected to the introduction of the welfarism theorem. However, the main purpose is to develop a graphical representation of distributive consequences of all four allocation principles. Furthermore, especially in the third questionnaire investigation, several trade-offs between these principles have been considered and should also be regarded in the following diagrams. Therefore, in some way the first two studies pave the way by successively introducing graphical representations of the most prominent justice concepts and the underlying allocation principles, before the more complex structure of the third study is visualised.

The chapter is organised in the following way. Besides identifying important assumptions and restrictions of the chosen approach, the second section also contains a description of the basic graphical structure. In the third section, the equality-efficiency trade-off of the first study is presented, including variations of information being relevant for the principle of efficiency. Also, motives for all possible allocation decisions are described. Afterwards, different effects observed that follow from additionally introduced information on aspects of responsibility in the second survey are explained. All these elaborations are then needed in section five to discuss the structure and allocations observed in the third questionnaire study. Section six briefly summarises the findings.

## 5.2 Setting the Scene

To start with, we will introduce the general idea and set the scene for the following graphical presentations of the different structures that underlie the hypothetical situations used in the three previous questionnaire studies. Clearly, this graphical approach contains several implicit assumptions, while others are explicitly required to reflect some of the theoretical concepts. All assumptions consequently lead to a restriction of the situation in question. Moreover, it is not intended to reproduce each situation of the questionnaire in every detail, since the general structure is often supplemented by several additional aspects. Instead, the focus will be on the broader structure of decision problems. Moreover, possible motivations for behaviours should be identified. In the next subsection, we will describe some restrictions and assumptions that are relevant for the following figures. Afterwards, in the second subsection the fundamental structure of all graphs will be introduced.

### 5.2.1 Some General Assumptions and Restrictions

As Williams and Cookson (2000) emphasise, it is impossible to fully describe philosophical ideas or theoretical conceptions by presenting them in a simple graph. Instead, consequences of each concept will be portrayed in a 'welfaristic' setting. In their seminal paper, Blackorby, Donaldson and Weymark (1984), based on earlier work by Sen (1977, 1984), elaborate that the *welfarism theorem* allows for the application of a diagrammatic approach. Just to refresh our minds, the theorem states that three conditions, viz. *unrestricted domain*, *Pareto indifference*, and *binary independence of irrelevant alternatives*, imply that a single ordering on the space of utility tuples, which contain individual utilities, can represent all social orderings of available alternatives.[1] Due to its consequentialistic nature, welfarism excludes non-utility features of the alternatives, for example procedural aspects. Hence, only individual utility derived from different social alternatives is used for forming social evaluations. It should be clear that the welfarism theorem introduces some very strong restrictions on the presentation of philosophical ideas. Williams and Cookson (2000, p. 1866) openly formulate the general statement of fact by saying: "What we are attempting here is the brutal task of forcing high minded philosophical theories about distributive justice into the procrustean bed of welfare economics!".

Now, let us remind the reader of some relevant properties of the concept of a Paretian social welfare function (SWF), which is applied to arrive at a complete ordering of social alternatives.[2] It considers utility of each individual under these alternatives and is Paretian in the sense that individual judgments are regarded which result from individual utility maximisation. Furthermore, it is also assumed that losses an gains can be determined and interpersonally compared. A SWF enables us to draw social indifference contours in utility space which represent allocations that are judged equally just. Clearly, the ultimate aim is the determination of a single SWF on which all members of society agree. However, not only the three questionnaire investigations presented, but also various other studies cited in this work, have revealed that the justice evaluations people hold are heterogeneous. Therefore, the resulting *social indifference curves* that will be described are more likely to represent individual allocation preferences rather than societal preferences.

Nevertheless, as already argued with respect to the equity axiom introduced in chapter 2, the situations presented in the questionnaire are structured in the way that all observers are supposed to agree on the fact that one (group of) individual(s) being considered is clearly worse off than the other. Hence, there is agreement on ordinal utility levels.

---

1 We refer those readers who are interested in the details of these axioms to the inspiring elaborations of Blackorby, Donaldson and Weymark (1984).

2 See e.g. Atkinson and Stiglitz (1987) for the following elaborations.

Besides the crucial assumption of a welfaristic approach other suppositions are also relevant for the hypothetical situations that will be graphically presented. All contexts reflect distribution problems between two (groups of) individuals so that we are able to remain in the two-dimensional utility space. Therefore, it is implicitly assumed that other groups in society are either not affected or equally influenced by the alternatives being regarded. Hence, they are supposed to be indifferent towards the available options. In social choice theory, this postulation is usually introduced with the help of a *separability axiom.*[3]

Closely related to this presumption is the fact that in all contexts an additional resource has to be allocated. This important assumption has already been discussed in the first chapter. Also, the available money is assumed to be set aside in an equitable way. However, from this assumption it follows that allocation decisions only concern the additional resource. Thus, redistribution of existing incomes or other previously allocated resources, which is most often regarded in macro-justice studies, is impossible. Clearly, this supposition is due to the Pareto efficiency postulate that prevents the groups considered from falling below their initial endowment level. Consequently, a fixed starting point is given in each of the following graphs. Hence, the location of respective levels in utility space also contains information about the relative position of the two (groups of) individuals being regarded. However, this does not exclude hypothetical compensations that are considered with respect to the compensation principle.

Starting from this endowment point, all allocations which are available due to the additional resource define the utility possibility set in the following figures. Here, Pareto efficient allocations are denoted by the *utility possibility frontier*. In the social welfare maximisation process corresponding points on this frontier are not Pareto-dominated by other feasible allocations. Moreover, it is assumed that utility which is derived from the distributed good, is monotonically increasing for both parties. Nevertheless, additional – and for some allocation principles necessary – information about possible utility gains is not always given in the questionnaire texts. Thus, they may depend on assumptions made by participants. The reader will remember that Faravelli (2007) argues that these assumptions are influenced by socio-demographic attributes of the decision-maker. Consequences will become apparent in due course.

Furthermore, Williams and Cookson (2000) discuss several philosophical concepts that restrict the utility possibility set. Particularly, ethical constraints may reduce the set of originally feasible allocations. For example, libertarians would reject allocations that originate from governmental mea-

3 See e.g. Hammond (1976) or Tungodden (2000) with respect to the different situations in our questionnaires. However, note that Tungodden's axiom presented in chapter 4 has been explicitly stated by him without requiring the separability axiom.

sures, e.g. taxation, to change outcomes that result from a process of free decision-making of adults. Another example is Rawls's theory. According to his first principle, all individuals should enjoy the same level of basic liberties. Thus, allocations that do not fulfil this precondition are excluded from the opportunity set. However, in the following drawings especially the Rawlsian approach is applied in a different way. Here, other ethical constraints, like his first principle of justice, are assumed to be already fulfilled before the situations described in the questionnaire appear so that the focus is on the difference principle.

Now, let us turn to assumptions about allocation principles that are supposed to motivate certain distributive behaviour. As already explained above, social indifference contours are utilised to reflect different allocation concepts followed by respondents. These concepts originate from different theories of justice, which are based on (combinations of) our four allocation principles. It is assumed that subjects do not switch between these (combinations of) principles if certain modifications, for example with respect to the principles of responsibility or efficiency, occur. Indeed, several concepts will recommend similar decisions even if these variations are considered. However, if the preferred allocation is changed this change should be based on the shape of the social indifference curve and, thereby, be explained by a certain distribution concept. For instance, switches from one allocation to another as a reaction to variations of benefits of available options are to be explained by preferences of participants that reflect trade-offs between aspects of efficiency and equality.

Such compromise solutions have already been discussed in the present work. We have explained that from Rawls's (1971) viewpoint the theoretical basis for these trade-offs being described is fragile since it is difficult to explain how individuals derive concrete weighting structures for the different principles. Nevertheless, empirical investigations have shown that participants often wish to consider several allocation principles simultaneously and, consequently, prefer compromises over the application of a single principle. But this does not necessarily mean that their behaviour is completely arbitrary. Instead, a certain degree of inequality aversion should result in a specific trade-off relation. Thus, if the benefit of one alternative is increased, the individual's trade-off conception should determine the resulting change in the distribution of the resource. Hence, even such hybrid principles demand certain reactions to modifications of the original situation. Therefore, we are also going to consider possible behaviour that is based on intuitionism.

### 5.2.2 The Basic Graphical Structure

It should be stated again that we do not intend to review the results of the questionnaire investigations but to present interpretations of all possible behaviours. We are now ready to have a first look at the graphical presentation of the structure of hypothetical situations in the first and second questionnaire study. This is given in Figure 5.1 where we also introduce some more general characteristics of all following graphs.

The axes state utility levels of the two groups being regarded. Additional utility is derived from the resource that has to be allocated by the external observer. Furthermore, all questionnaires describe situations in which one (group of) individual(s) is better off than the other. In all figures, this fact is represented by the location of the initial endowment point $z$ which is placed above the dashed 45°-line arising from the origin.[4] This line represents situations where both parties achieve equal individual utility levels. Moreover, as explained in the previous subsection, due to the Paretian restriction point $z$ limits the opportunity set to those allocations which yield at least the same utility levels for both groups as in this endowment point. Therefore, utility gains from all available alternatives of the allocation of the additional resource can be found to the north, east or northeast from $z$, whereby the horizontal axis states utility gains for the worse-off individuals.

Moreover, it is important to note underlying assumptions about the measurability and comparability of utilities in each situation. In the first two questionnaire studies, ordinally measurable and interpersonally comparable utility levels are suggested. Hence, all that is known is the fact that one group is better off under all alternatives. However, this assumption is changed in the third investigation, where the decision-maker gets to know the benefits above the poverty line. The consequences will be explained in due course.

Next, points $x$ and $y$ in Figure 5.1 represent utility levels for both groups if the entire resource is given to one of the two parties in the either-or decision being regarded. In this case, starting from utility levels given by point $z$, the upper indices $H$ and $L$ denote higher or lower utility gains for the better-off individual(s) from alternative $y$ compared to their worse-off counterpart(s) under alternative $x$. Nevertheless, as already explained in the previous subsection, the specific positions of $x$ and $y$ depend on the assumption about marginal utilities of both groups made by the external observer. But even if the available resource is completely distributed to the worse-off party, this (group of) subject(s) remains worse off. Consequently, point $x$ is also placed above the 45°-line. This characteristic reflects the fact that in neither questionnaire study is an equalisation of overall utility levels of both parties possible.

It should also be mentioned that further assumptions about individual utility functions are not necessary at the moment, since the axes already state utility levels that result from different alternatives.

A final aspect concerns the assumed shape of the utility possibility frontier that is described by the curves between points $x$ and $y^H$ or $y^L$ in Figure 5.1. In the first two questionnaires, no information about the shape of this frontier

4 The variable names in this chapter do not usually correspond to similarly named variables in the statistical section in chapter 2.

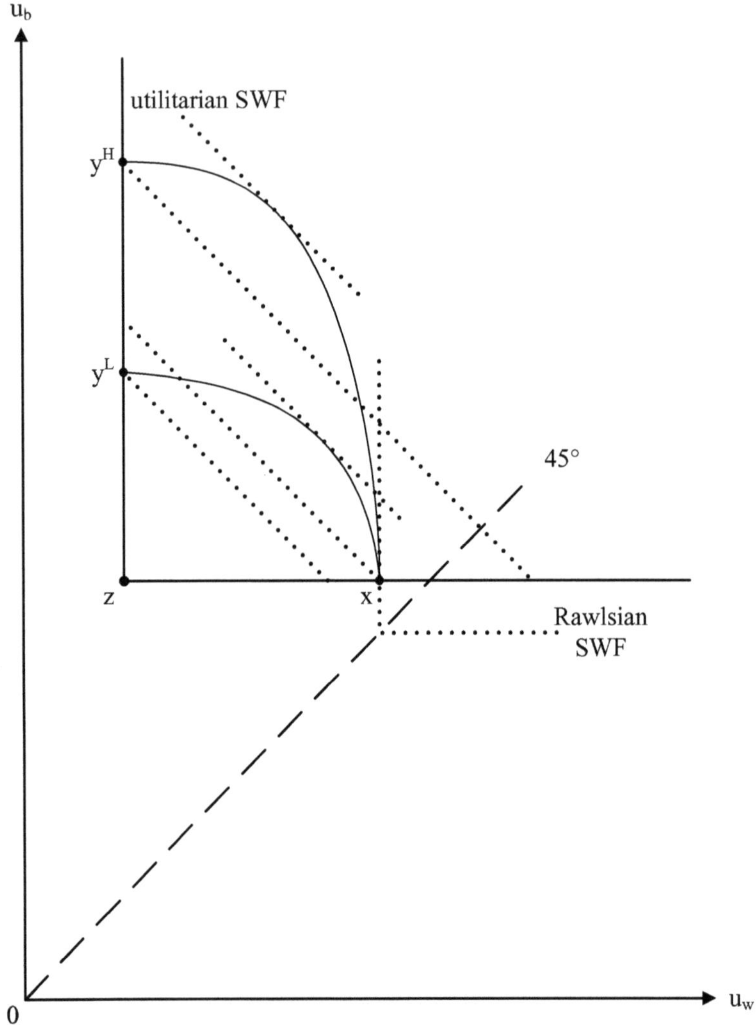


Figure 5.1: The basic graphical structure

is given, but in the next section, it will be illustrated that this lack of information has no consequences for the results. Nevertheless, in all of the following graphs the frontier is assumed to be continuous, concave to the origin, and monotonically decreasing from left to right. The first assumption allows for a continuous set of allocations between both groups, although in the first two studies only the intersections of the curve with the axes are available alternatives. The second supposition permits either strictly concave frontiers, as in Figure 5.1, or a linear relationship, as in the third questionnaire presented in Figures 5.6 and 5.7. The final assumption indicates that on the utility possibility frontier an increasing utility level for one party automatically corresponds to a decreasing level for the other party. This assumption excludes positive external effects that may occur if support of some (group of) individual(s) also increases the utility level of the counterpart. Certainly, this would be perfectly reasonable. For example, reconsider the first situation in the initial questionnaire where respondents had to decide between helping a handicapped person or furthering the education of an intelligent child. Here, some of our students argued that financing the education of an intelligent child may result in a better life for handicapped people in the future if the child decided to enter a research career, for instance, in medicine. Also, it could be claimed that utility of better offs increases if these individuals become aware that they live in a society in which people in need are supported. Clearly, these arguments are plausible, but we want to exclude them from the model. Consequences of a partly increasing utility frontier are discussed in Buchanan (1976), Mishan (1977), Atkinson and Stiglitz (1987) and Williams and Cookson (2000). The main effect would be that the Rawlsian and the egalitarian solution do not necessarily coincide.

In this section, the scene was set for the following graphical presentations where possible motives for chosen allocations in the three questionnaire studies should be described. Next, the underlying structures of hypothetical situations and possible distributions resulting from different allocation principles will be portrayed in more detail.

## 5.3 Efficiency and Equality in Either-or Decisions

We will start by considering possible decision motives in situations in the first questionnaire and in the no-responsibility version of the second questionnaire. Remember that the underlying structure could either be interpreted as a trade-off between the principles of needs and efficiency or as an equality-efficiency trade-off in a needs context. However, in the present analysis both relations lead to the same structure. Due to its clear and simple construction, the first context of the first questionnaire serves as the main example. In the initial case, a decision between support for a handicapped person who would be able to learn some very basic things and financing the education of an intelligent child is required. The child is supposed to be better off under each alternative. Furthermore, later on the group of better-off individuals is successively enlarged by introducing more and more intelligent children.

The first and probably most remarkable characteristic of this situation is the fact that only either-or decisions are possible. Consequently, the utility possibility frontiers in Figure 5.1 are of no relevance and, moreover, they are hypothetical with respect to their shape. Nevertheless, certainly such continuous frontiers also implicitly exist in this situation. Moreover, respondents possibly prefer to split up the given resource. This supposition can be deduced from results attained by Gaertner (1994) who used the present situation 1 of the first questionnaire but asked respondents to divide the given resource in a continuous fashion. Gaertner found that only 21 respondents out of 87 subjects, who made sensible statements, invested all the money into one of the two alternatives (unsurprisingly, 20 of these individuals opted for alternative $x$). In subsections 5.3.1 and 5.3.2, possible motives for compromise solutions will be described.

The first two of our questionnaires regard the acceptance of an equity axiom that underlies Rawls's difference principle. This axiom supposes ordinally measurable and interpersonally comparable utility levels. Thus, all that is known to the participants is the fact that the worse offs remain being worse off under both alternatives. In contrast, information on utility gains of the groups considered are not given. Consequently, decisions resulting from distribution concepts, which assume cardinal utilities and their interpersonal comparability, are influenced by assumptions of our students about utility differences under the two alternatives available. For example, some respondents may assume that the benefit for the handicapped person is higher than the gain for the intelligent child, while other subjects suppose the opposite relation.

In the questionnaire presently regarded, the principles of equality or needs and efficiency are of relevance. In this section it will be shown that three classes of allocation concepts, namely the maximin equity criterion, utilitarianism and mixed conceptions, may reflect different weights to these principles. Each of these three concepts is reflected by the structure of a respective SWF. As explained above, this function should indicate preferences of an external observer over different social states. In the present context, respondents have to evaluate and compare social welfare levels that result from alternatives $x$, for example the help for the handicapped person, and $y$, e.g. the support of the intelligent child.

### 5.3.1 Rawlsian and Utilitarian Reasoning

In Figure 5.1 on page 254, welfare contours resulting from social welfare functions that reflect either maximin or utilitarian reasoning are depicted by dotted lines. Since distribution concepts should be considered from a welfarist perspective, where social welfare serves as the maximand, Rawls's theory of justice is usually given as the utility-based maximin principle and, therefore, recommends the maximisation of (ordinally measurable) utility of the worse-off individual(s).[5] Hence, corresponding social welfare $W_R$ is given by

$$W_R = min(u_w, u_b), \tag{5.1}$$

where $u$ denotes the utility of the worse-off ($w$) or better-off ($b$) individuals, respectively. The social indifference contours resulting from the maximin SWF are L-shaped and centred on the 45°-line in our figures. In all three questionnaires, the worse-off people remain worse off, independently of the chosen alternative. Hence, according to the maximin principle social welfare is maximised if the entire additional amount is allocated to the worse-off people. In our contexts, these preferences are in accordance with both the equality and the needs principle. Consequently, in Figure 5.1 the indifference curve that corresponds to alternative $x$ denotes a higher social welfare compared to the corresponding contour for both alternatives $y^L$ and $y^H$.[6]

In contrast, a priori it is not clear which alternative will be preferred from a utilitarian perspective that is inspired by the efficiency principle. Utilitarianism is concerned about the sum of (cardinally measurable) individual utilities. Therefore, social welfare $W_U$ is given as

$$W_U = \alpha u_w + \beta u_b. \tag{5.2}$$

Here, $\alpha$ and $\beta$ are individual weights. In the case of classical utilitarianism individuals and their utility levels are equally weighted so that the constant slope of the resulting social indifference curves in utility space equals $-1$. Again, it is interesting to note that from this viewpoint the principle of equality is also behind utilitarianism. The respective contours corresponding to alternatives $x$ and $y$ are also given in Figure 5.1. However, since no information on utility gains for both groups is available, it is not clear whether the support of the better-off (group of) individual(s) leads to a higher ($y^H$) or lower ($y^L$) gain of social welfare compared to alternative $x$ in Figure 5.1. Thus, point $x$ lies either below or above the indifference curves corresponding to these alternatives. Hence, it solely depends on the marginal utilities assumed by the respondent in the concrete situation whether alternative $x$ or $y$ is preferred from a utilitarian perspective. Situation 3 in the first study is a good example. Here, participants had to decide whether to purchase dialysis machines or vitamins. The examination of verbal answers revealed that there was disagreement with respect to the benefits of the two alternatives.

5 See e.g. Rawls (1971, pp. 76-78) or Atkinson and Stiglitz (1987) for a more complete elaboration.

6 Once again, notice that alternative $x$ is Pareto efficient since it lies on the utility possibility frontier, but it does not necessarily fulfil our principle of efficiency.

Note again that this solution does not depend on the shape of the utility possibility frontier. This would only matter if a continuous split of the given resource is feasible. In that case, compromise solutions between both alternatives are possible. If the shape of the frontier is strictly concave as in Figure 5.1, the point where the respective slope equals -1 identifies the allocation that maximises social welfare according to equation (5.2).

### 5.3.2 Trading off Equality and Efficiency

Besides classical utilitarianism and the maximin principle, a third class of allocation rules will be considered. Here, these two concepts are interpreted as special cases of a more general kind of SWF, where efficiency and equality concerns are combined. Throughout the present work, we followed Rawls's (1971) designation and called this idea 'intuitionism'. Certainly, a necessary assumption in the present setting is that solutions with higher benefits are always accompanied by less equality.[7] However, in the first two questionnaires this supposition is only fulfilled if the utility gain is assumed to be higher for the better off(s) than for the worse off(s). Otherwise, alternative $x$ should be preferred according to both principles.

As already explained in the introduction of chapter 4, at least in empirical studies any possible arbitrary degree of inequality aversion can be observed. The most prominent function that incorporates such a degree is the isoelastic SWF. It offers the opportunity to reflect the equality-efficiency trade-off. We adopt the following formulation of Wagstaff (1991, 1993):

$$W_T = [(\alpha u_w)^{1-\tau} + (\beta u_b)^{1-\tau}]^{\frac{1}{1-\tau}}, \quad \tau \neq 1, \quad 0 \leq \tau < \infty. \tag{5.3}$$

Again, $\alpha$ and $\beta$ are individual weights. In this section it is assumed that $\alpha = \beta$, but this assumption will be relaxed later on. Furthermore, the value of $\tau$ reflects the degree of inequality aversion. For $\tau = 0$ the SWF in equation (5.3) is similar to the utilitarian case in equation (5.2). On the other side of the scale, the Rawlsian objective is attained if $\tau \to \infty$ and $\alpha = \beta$. In our case, due to the strict monotonic decrease of the utility possibility frontier the Rawlsian maximin criterion and egalitarian solutions focusing on equalising total utility of recipients are identical.

The attributes being described may explain the popularity of this variant of a SWF in the literature to reflect the trade-off mentioned. It was utilised, for instance, by Atkinson (1970) to define an inequality index, by Alexander (1974) as a direct philosophical objection to Rawls's maximin equity criterion, or by Atkinson and Stiglitz (1987) to distinguish different governmental objectives. Moreover, as will be shown in the next paragraphs, this function leads to indifference lines that are curves convex to the origin. According

7 In the next section, it is shown that also unequal weights to utility levels may yield a preference for alternatives that yield less benefit and, moreover, lead to more inequality.

to Rawls (1971, p. 77) these curves represent "a view less egalitarian than the difference principle, and perhaps more plausible at first sight". However, Rawls (1974b, p. 644) objects to a representation in which "we can shift smoothly from one moral conception to another simply by varying the parameter [$\tau$]". In particular, the missing theoretical foundation for the choice of $\tau$ is criticised.

Certainly, alternative formulations are possible. For example, in the context of health economics Bleichrodt, Diecidue and Quiggin (2004) propose using a rank-dependent QALY model instead, where equity weights in the decision process are applied. This approach seems to be similar to Gaertner's (1992) idea of weighting positions of individuals. Moreover, Bleichrodt, Doctor and Stolk (2005) argue that assumptions underlying the isoelastic SWF are usually not explicitly discussed. Therefore, and due to the difficulties in comparing different social welfare functions, Østerdal (2005) presents underlying axioms that lead to diverse allocation rules.

The literature just referred to constitutes important and necessary supplements to any application of the isoelastic SWF. However, it is probably one of the most often applied formulations to express trade-offs between the principles of equality and efficiency. Thus, it seems to be a natural candidate for a discussion and graphical representation of different allocation principles. Our aim is to investigate several choices observed and explain possible underlying preference structures. Moreover, Atkinson and Stiglitz (1987, p. 340) claim that equation (5.3) is "a useful device to explore the sensitivity of the findings to changing views about the social welfare function". Indeed, the empirical studies reviewed in the present work uncovered trade-off relations between different allocation principles, whereby the equality-efficiency trade-off is the most prominent one. Thus, the isoelastic SWF is a simple but, nevertheless, helpful tool to reflect at least justice preferences of participants in empirical investigations.

The band of indifference contours resulting from equation (5.3) is curved as, for example, given in Figure 5.2. The degree of the curvature depends on the value of $\tau$. The higher the degree of inequality aversion is, the stronger the respective curvature will be. The curves have to be symmetric with respect to the 45°-line. In Figure 5.2, a choice between alternative $x$ and a more beneficial choice, measured in assumed utility gain and represented by the distance $\overline{zy^c}$, is considered as an example. If we suppose $\tau_1 < \tau_2$, the curves corresponding to $\tau_1$ are less curved than those based on $\tau_2$ and reflect less inequality aversion. In the given situation, the social planner who is less inequality averse ($\tau_1$) prefers the more beneficial solution $y^c$, whereas the external observer with the higher degree of inequality aversion ($\tau_2$) chooses alternative $x$. As before, the shape of the utility possibility frontier has no effect in the present case, but it is easy to see from the given drawing that the usual optimisation conditions with respect to social welfare demands a

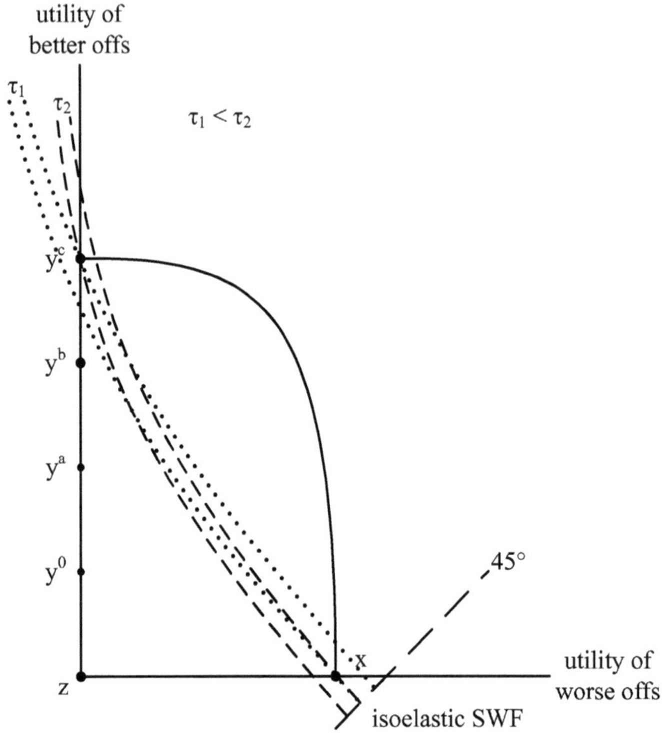


Figure 5.2: Equality-efficiency trade-offs and efficiency variations

compromise solution between the extreme alternatives $x$ and $y^c$ in the present case if a continuous split of the resource would be feasible.

Finally, besides the more fundamental objection to inequality, Williams and Cookson (2000) mention a second motivation for the occurrence of curving social indifference contours. Two special assumptions lead to convex welfare contours, which are symmetrical about the 45°-line. First, marginal social welfare from increasing individual utilities diminishes and, second, this schedule is identical for both groups.

To conclude this subsection, in the first and in the second questionnaire study we observed a strong heterogeneity of distribution behaviour. This can be explained by two facets. Firstly, different assumptions by our students about utility gains, which have been expressed in the diagrams by the location of point $y$, could lead either to an acceptance or to a rejection of alternative $y$. Secondly, different degrees of inequality aversion of respondents may result in distinct choices even if assumptions about utility gains are identical.

### 5.3.3 Effects of Efficiency Variations

In Figure 5.2, starting from the origin, points on the vertical axis represent different utility gains derived by the (group of) better off(s) from alternative $y$. As explained before, differences with respect to the assumptions by respondents about these gains are likely to exist. However, in the present case the stated points are interpreted as variations of utility levels under alternative $y$ in terms of utility, which result from a successive increase of the number of better offs. In the first context of the first questionnaire the number of intelligent children is successively increased to four in part c). Hence, the upper index of the respective labels denotes the corresponding part of the situation. In this subsection, we are mainly interested in possible motives for a reconsideration of an initial choice in favour of alternative $x$ which has regularly been observed in several contexts and for various samples in the first and second questionnaire study. Let us firstly regard social indifference curves that are based on the isoelastic SWF in equation (5.3) and which are given in Figure 5.2. To simplify matters marginal utility for the better-off group is assumed to be constant so that each additional person increases the utility gain from choosing alternative $y$ by the same amount. For $\tau_1$ a switch from alternative $x$ towards alternative $y$ increases social welfare if we move from three to four intelligent children, whereas for $\tau_2$ social welfare from supporting the worse-off individual is assumed to be higher in all parts being regarded.

Secondly, reconsider the case of the utilitarian SWF given in equation (5.2). Resulting indifference curves are presented in Figure 5.1 on page 254. Suppose, for example, that the points $y^L$ and $y^H$ reflect the cases of one child or two children, respectively. Again, a switch from alternative $x$ towards alternative $y^H$ increases corresponding social welfare.

It should be obvious that in the given setting each switch from helping the handicapped person towards supporting the intelligent children reflects some concern for the principle of efficiency. However, if alternative $x$ is preferred in all extensions being regarded, it cannot be deduced that efficiency concerns are absent. Here, only those students who reported that they would *never* switch towards alternative $y$ clearly followed the equality or needs principle.

In the present section, we intended to describe some very basic but, nevertheless, important characteristics of the graphical presentations of the preceding questionnaire studies. In order to analyse possible motives for allocation decisions, three different conceptions have been introduced, i.e. ideas based on the utilitarian, the maximin and classes of equality-efficiency trade-off concepts. Especially the last conception introduces some arbitrariness into the model. Nevertheless, even if the theoretical basis for this notion is weak, empirical investigations regularly observe such compromise solutions. Hence, isoelastic social welfare functions are able to reflect such decisions and, moreover, integrate them into our system of four distinct allocation principles. This idea will be further developed in the following sections.

A concluding note concerns the relationship between the needs and the equality principle with respect to our first and second questionnaire study. In this section, equality has been interpreted as overall equality of individual utility levels. Due to the specific structure of the hypothetical situations, where a complete equalisation of both parties with respect to their utility levels is not feasible, the needs principle and the equality principle suggest the same solution if a monotonically decreasing utility possibility frontier is assumed. However, in section 5.5 several other interpretations of the equality principle will be considered.

The application of the maximin criterion does not require focusing only on situations, where basic needs are regarded. The same holds true for equality concerns in general. Nevertheless, in the given contexts it is obvious to interpret support for the worse-off individual(s) also as a consideration of the needs principle. But this has no graphical consequences. Certainly, such an interpretation may have provoked stronger backing for alternative $x$. Thus, one should always keep in mind that support of the worse offs may solely be motivated by a concern for basic needs in our contexts. Moreover, it can be argued that basic needs should count as 'primary goods' in the Rawlsian sense (see e.g. Green, 1976, for a similar argumentation in the health context). However, as explained in chapter 1, the link between maximin preferences and Rawlsian reasoning is well established in the literature. Hence, the motivation to support worse-off individuals may result either from equality or, more likely, from maximin arguments. But in the first two questionnaire studies worse-off people continued to be worse off with respect to their basic needs so that a complete equalisation is never attainable.

## 5.4 Incorporating Aspects of Responsibility

Aspects of responsibility are the focal point of interest in the second questionnaire. We introduced corresponding information in our initial contexts. In the first situation, the disabled person is said to be handicapped either from birth or from participating in a dangerous sport. Moreover, in the second context, the starvation of the Africans is either due to a drought or caused by experiments with self-bred grain. In the following section, these considerations will be incorporated in the figures previously introduced. Here, some of the proposals presented in the paper by Williams and Cookson (2000) will be followed in the way that weighting schemes are applied to reflect possible considerations of differences in personal characteristics ascribed to the hypothetical groups. The authors motivate their approach explicitly by two theoretical concepts, which have already been explained in more detail in chapter 3. Firstly, Williams and Cookson refer to theories of equality of opportunity. Corresponding principles call for a compensation of suffering people only if their burdens do not result from their own free choices. Consequently, misery through no fault of one's own should yield a stronger concern for the utility of this disadvantaged group. In contrast, consequences of voluntary choices should not be compensated. The authors give the example of "becoming disabled due to a sports injury" (p. 1893), which is also one of the contexts described in our questionnaire. Secondly, the principle of desert, which has been noted in the margin, is mentioned by Williams and Cookson. In this case, differences in personal characteristics of groups being regarded may justify a different social evaluation of additional utilities for these individuals. A typical example are war veterans who are usually said to deserve a privileged treatment in health care contexts. However, note that weights only depend on individual characteristics and previous behaviour of hypothetical groups but not on their present utility level. Differences with respect to the latter should be taken into account by the degree of inequality aversion of the social planner.

Before we proceed with graphical presentations of possible reactions to aspects of responsibility, the underlying idea of a social welfare function should be reconsidered. At the beginning of this chapter, it was explained that these functions reflect the evaluations of social welfare assigned to different social states by an external observer. The motivation for 'punishing' certain behaviour, that was described in chapter 3, fits quite well into this interpretation. Accordingly, future social welfare may increase if 'socially costly' actions can be abandoned by punishing such misbehaviour through a denial of compensation for possibly resulting disadvantages.

From the answers to our second questionnaire, we can deduce three different reactions of respondents to this additionally given information about the causes of the miserable situation of the worse offs. Firstly, utility gains of individuals who are thought to be responsible for their own fate should receive less weight. Consequently, alternative $y$ should be more often selected in the initial case and/or if the better-off group is enlarged. However, we could not detect a significantly higher support for corresponding allocations in either of the two contexts. Secondly, aspects of responsibility may not provoke any remarkable differences between answers to both versions of the question being regarded. In fact, this case occurred most frequently in our second investigation. In chapter 3, it was argued that either responsibility facets may be too weak to show a noticeable reaction in either-or decision problems or needs aspects may simply be too dominant. Thirdly, some respondents could even give more weight to the utility of worse-off individuals if their misfortune was supposed to be a result of their own behaviour. Especially, the behaviour of the sportsperson in situation 1 was rewarded by male students in Osnabrück, while the experiments of the Africans in situation 2 were honoured by female respondents in Leuven. As previously explained, the latter case could be interpreted in the way that these hypothetical individuals deserve more support due to their willingness to change their disastrous situation. Again, future social welfare may increase if more starving people can be motivated to try changing their fate, even if this means some risk-taking behaviour.

In order to incorporate the weighting schemes just described, and to reflect the observed reactions to the additional information on aspects of responsibility given in the questionnaires, different graphical possibilities will be presented in the following paragraphs. As before, the plotted utility possibility frontiers are arbitrary and may, therefore, describe any initial or extended part of a certain situation.

Moreover, it should be remarked that we are not able to predict certain behaviours. Instead our aim is to interpret choices observed in the investigations presented before. To state it even more clearly, the following presentations are not able to explain – or even to predict – the effects of various different aspects of responsibility in the questionnaires but to rationalise observations.

In Figures 5.3 to 5.5, the endowment point $z$ is chosen as the origin. Consequently, the labels of the axes, viz. 'utility of better offs' and 'utility of worse offs', should indicate the position of $z$ in the actual utility space. Also, in all three figures the dotted curves reflect social preferences of those respondents who faced the no-responsibility version of the questionnaire, while the dashed contours are related to participants who received the responsibility version. It should be noted that *both* questionnaire versions are likely to evoke different weighting schemes compared to the 'equal-weights cases' described so far in this chapter. For example, in situation 2 of the no-responsibility version of the second questionnaire study, the better-off groups are said to live in the home country of the respondent. Hence, it is possible that he or she gives higher weight to the utility of these hypothetical groups. Nevertheless, we will focus only on situations where additional aspects of responsibility are introduced. Other modifications are straightforward and left to the imagination of the reader.

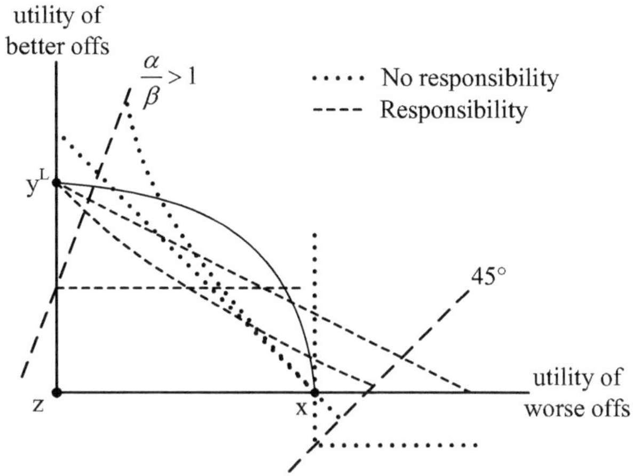


Figure 5.3: Aspects of responsibility: Negative effect

In Figure 5.3, the no-responsibility situation considers a case, where alternative $x$ yields a higher utility gain for the worse offs compared to the utility gain of the better-off individuals under alternative $y^L$. This can be seen from the comparison of the lines $\overline{zy^L}$ and $\overline{zx}$. Thus, efficiency and equality considerations, and of course all compromises between both principles, favour alternative $x$. This is also denoted in the graph where all three classes of (dotted) social indifference curves represent a higher social welfare in point $x$ than in point $y^L$. In contrast, in the responsibility version classical utilitarianism and the given trade-off preferences favour alternative $y^L$ despite its smaller utility gain for the better offs compared to the benefit from alternative $x$ for the worse offs. From equation (5.2) it can be seen that in the case of utilitarianism the weight given to the utility of the worse offs should decline so that we have $\alpha < \beta$. This leads to a flatter (dashed) line in Figure 5.3. In the present case, the change is strong enough to assign a higher social welfare to alternative $y^L$ than to option $x$.

Similarly, in equation (5.3) the weight to utility level $u_w$ decreases compared to the weight to $u_b$. So, $\alpha < \beta$ holds again. As a result, the slope of the (dashed) curve is also flatter, while the curvature remains unchanged, because it only depends on the degree of inequality aversion $\tau$. In the situation presented in the graph, a participant whose behaviour can be reflected by a respective isoelastic social welfare function would switch from alternative $x$ to choice $y^L$ if aspects of responsibility are added. Thus, the social planner chooses the allocation that favours the less beneficial solution with regard to individual utility which also increases inequality.

Also, one may take into consideration incorporating individual weights in the maximin SWF and, thereby, allow for a trade-off between the principles of equality and responsibility without regarding the efficiency principle. I am in two minds concerning the appropriateness of this idea. Let us assume that social welfare $W_M$ is given as

$$W_M = min(\alpha u_w, \beta u_b). \tag{5.4}$$

Now, the slope of the corresponding line through the origin equals $\frac{\alpha}{\beta}$ and, thus, depends on the weighting of individual utility levels in equation (5.4). In Figure 5.3, this line, which is denoted by $\frac{\alpha}{\beta} > 1$, is steeper than the 45°-line so that points on it always denote combinations of utility levels that systematically place the 'misbehaving' worse-off group at a disadvantage. In the case presented in the diagram, social welfare in point $y^L$ is again higher than the corresponding value in point $x$, as can be seen from the dashed L-shaped indifference curve (only the horizontal part is visible).

At first sight, this possibility is appealing. It seems to be plausible that a decision-maker supports worse-off people without regarding aspects of efficiency, but switches towards helping the better offs as soon as aspects of responsibility are introduced on the side of the worse-off party. However, in the contexts described in our second and third questionnaire aspects of responsibility are always combined with the efficiency principle so that a separate evaluation of the equality-responsibility trade-off is not possible. Moreover, for example Wagstaff (1991) argues that equation (5.4) follows from the isoelastic SWF in equation (5.3) if $\tau \to \infty$. But this statement is inconsistent since the interpretation of the parameters $\alpha$ and $\beta$ changes. While they indicate positive weights on utility levels in the isoelastic SWF, a higher value for a parameter in the function given in equation (5.4) means less utility for the corresponding group. Consequently, in order to draw the respective line in Figure 5.3 we assumed that $\alpha > \beta$.

Furthermore, consider points on this steeper line. Firstly, they no longer reflect any concern for equality but represent a fixed 'degree of inequality' between individual utility levels. Secondly, this degree is determined by effects of responsibility concerns on the slope $\frac{\alpha}{\beta}$. However, with respect to the isoelastic SWF it has been argued that the value of $\tau$ already represents the corresponding inequality aversion. Thus, the SWF in equation (5.4) seems to be incoherent. Therefore, in the following presentations we will express effects of responsibility considerations by equations (5.2) and (5.3) that also include a concern for the efficiency principle. This is in line with comments by Williams and Cookson (2000, p. 1879) who report with respect to theories of responsibility-sensitive egalitarianism that "equal opportunity theorists generally accept the need for balancing equality goals with efficiency goals".

Moreover, in subsection 5.5.3 a further possibility to incorporate aspects of responsibility will be discussed. In that case, the 'path' of L-shaped indifference contours starting in the endowment point $z$ is turned with respect to the

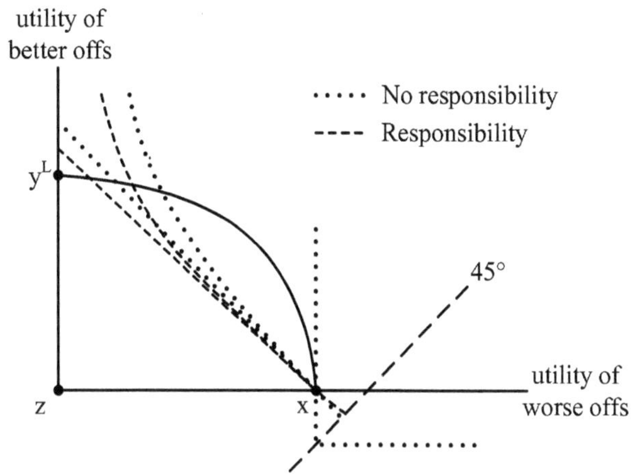


Figure 5.4: Aspects of responsibility: No effect

weights given to utility levels of both groups. However, due to the either-or decision regarded in our second questionnaire the two available single alternatives in the graphs, corresponding to the first two questionnaires, would lay on the same L-shaped curve in such a case, no matter what the slope of the 'path' looks like. Thus, a decision in favour of either option cannot be explained so that this possibility is ignored in the present section.

In the straightforward case in Figure 5.4, an almost similar situation as in Figure 5.3 is considered. Again, in the questionnaires the worse-off (group of) individual(s) is supposed to be responsible for the current misfortune. So, the external observers may give less weight to the utility gain received by this (group of) individual(s). As before, $\alpha < \beta$ should hold in equations (5.2) and (5.3), but now the effect is not strong enough to cause a switch from alternative $x$ to alternative $y$. In the graph, this effect is basically due to the fact that participants face an either-or decision. Hence, differences between the evaluations of alternatives $x$ and $y$ may not be strong enough to reveal an influence from aspects of responsibility. Clearly, as already explained in chapter 4, if alternatives along the utility possibility frontier were available, effects of responsibility considerations should be detected more easily.

After these explanations, the situation presented in Figure 5.5 should also be straightforward. Here, alternative $y^H$ leads to a higher utility gain for the better offs compared to the benefit received by the worse offs from alternative $x$. But due to the higher weight, which the external observer assigns to the latter (group of) individual(s) while maximising social welfare in the responsibility case, option $x$ is favoured in accordance with both the principle of efficiency and trade-off preferences between efficiency and equality. For

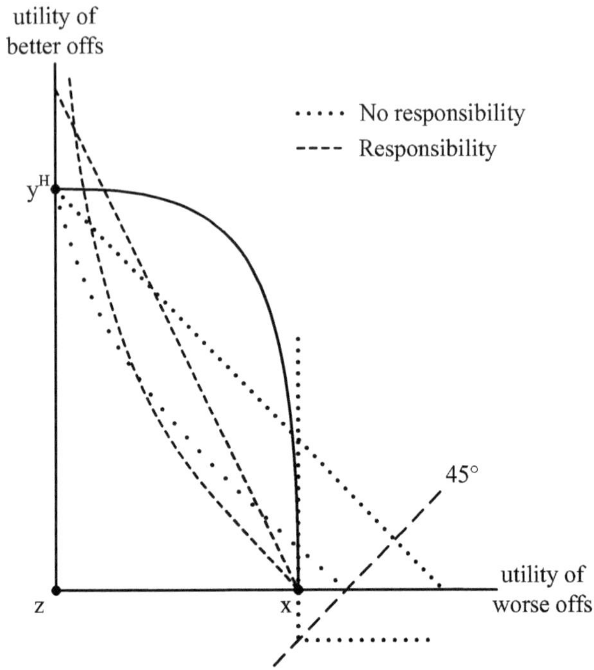


Figure 5.5: Aspects of responsibility: Positive effect

example, in the second situation of our questionnaire this case would occur either if the disastrous behaviour of the Africans does not originate from their own free will or if they deserve compensation for their risk-taking behaviour, although it led to a dreadful outcome.

In this section, it has been demonstrated that individual differences of hypothetical groups, for example previous (mis)behaviour, can be integrated in the graphical presentations of the situations. This has been done by assigning different weights to individual utility levels. While we followed arguments by Williams and Cookson (2000) and stated that influences on maximin preferences seem to be less plausible, the principle of efficiency and compromises between equality and efficiency are sensitive to individual attributes. Basically, these personal disparities regarded aspects of responsibility, but it should be clear that other characteristics may also differ. For example, in the second situation of the first and second questionnaire the better-off groups were supposed to live in the same country as the student who had to allocate the given resource. Certainly, introduced weights could also allow for this kind of personal differences. However, especially because of the consideration of basic needs and of the either-or characteristic of decisions, some disparities have no significant effect on distributions proposed by our students. Hence, the determination of values for $\alpha$ and $\beta$ is an empirical question that cannot be answered by our graphical presentations. Furthermore, the shape of the utility possibility frontier does not play a role in the situations presented up to now. But some previously introduced assumptions will be changed in the following section on the third questionnaire study. From this point of view, the preceding two sections paved the way for the graphical presentation of this final and most complex investigation.

## 5.5 The Analysis of Truncated Efficiency

The hypothetical situations in the third questionnaire study deviate with respect to some important characteristics from the construction of the two investigations previously described. Particularly, three of these departures, which have already been outlined in chapter 4, are necessary to create the intended new structure. Certainly, the graphical presentation should also incorporate the relevant modifications.

Firstly, a divisible resource is regarded. It has been argued in the preceding sections that the consideration of indivisible goods constrains the sensibility of the questionnaire instrument to detect reactions to aspects of either responsibility or efficiency. Also, obviously compromise solutions are only directly visible if respondents are allowed to state continuous splits of the resource. In this case, the comparison of social welfare levels originating from only two alternatives is replaced by a more advanced optimisation process on the side of the external evaluator who has to compare more than two alternatives now.

Secondly, it should be clear from elaborations in the previous sections that, as soon as one allows for a continuous division, the shape of the utility possibility frontier becomes important. However, additional information about this frontier at least with regard to its section above the poverty line is given in the third questionnaire. It is intended to create a constant rate of substitution between gains of both groups being considered in the corresponding situations.

Thirdly, the available resource suffices to fully regard basic needs of the worse-off group. Thus, in contrast to our previous questionnaires the needs principle and the maximin criterion can be separated from other egalitarian concerns. However, the explicit inclusion of the aspect of needs requires a more refined graphical presentation.

In the next subsection, consequences of the three modifications are explained in some more detail in our graphs. Afterwards, the allocations which have been proposed to the respondents in the questionnaire are presented and possible motivations for their selection are identified. Finally, responsibility and efficiency considerations are added to complete the graphical presentation of four allocation principles.

### 5.5.1 Graphical Consequences of Three Modifications

Throughout this section, situation 'Aid' in the third questionnaire will serve as a benchmark. However, sometimes we will depart from this context since priority should be given to the more general structure of the situations. Let us briefly review the basic characteristics of this first context. Respondents are asked to imagine two islands, A and B. No matter which allocation of the given resource is chosen, the former island is unambiguously always better off than the latter. Both governments offer investment projects for the development aid. This money can be distributed by the external observer in a continuous fashion. On both islands, the power supply system should be extended. However, due to unfavourable geographic conditions, the costs for connecting one additional household on island B are twice as high as the respective costs on island A. Furthermore, on the worse-off island a severe famine threatens the inhabitants. About 60% of the available resource is needed to save all households from starvation, but of course it is also possible to give less money to island B.

Additionally, in the 'Aid' context it is possible to invest in the power supply system of island B without fully regarding basic needs. Nevertheless, this is a specific facet of situation 'Aid' that will not be presented in the more general graphical presentation of the basic structure underlying the third questionnaire.

With the help of this context, the graphical consequences of the three main changes in the third questionnaire study described in the introduction of this chapter will be explained. The structure is presented in Figure 5.6. In this graph utility of the better offs is given again on the vertical axis, whereas the respective value for the worse-off group is stated on the horizontal axis. As before, point $z$ denotes the endowment point in terms of utility. None of the two islands can fall below this initial level. Giving the entire additional resource to one of the two parties would shift utility levels either to point $A$ or to point $H$. Similar to the two previous settings, it is not possible to equalise overall individual utility levels of the two groups. Consequently, both point $z$ and point $H$ are located above the 45°-line that starts from the origin of the utility space being regarded.

Now, a continuous split of the resource is possible so that we can draw a line between points $A$ and $H$. It should be noted that in contrast to the earlier figures this line reflects actually available solutions and is, therefore, not hypothetical. Certainly, all points below the boundary $\overline{AH}$ are also feasible, but since Pareto efficiency is assumed only points on this utility possibility frontier are considered.

Moreover, the allocated development aid in the situation regarded can be interpreted as additional income. It will be transformed by the proposed projects on both islands into utility that is measured either in the number of households connected to the power supply system or, as a special case on island B, in the number of households living at the poverty line. This understanding of the additional resource is similar to the interpretation of income in macro-justice studies, where income is interpreted as utility. In such investigations, a certain part of the allocated amount is also firstly used in order to satisfy basic needs.

But the question may arise, why the utility possibility frontier should be linear. The underlying assumption is that at least above the poverty line marginal utility from development aid is constant rather than decreasing for both parties. Thus, each additional monetary unit allows for connecting a constant number of households to the power supply system. However, this number differs between the two islands. This supposition is also implicitly made in macro-justice studies in the way that an additional unit of income results in the same utility gain no matter whether a rich or poor recipient is regarded. Furthermore, for example, Yaari and Bar-Hillel (1984, p. 9) note that "if [our resource] is subject to a 'law of diminishing marginal efficacy' then we may suppose that the variations allowed for in the question are small enough to make this effect negligible". Therefore, a linear frontier seems to be reasonable in our contexts.

Another important theoretical aspect can be deduced from the gradient of this line. As long as the slope is lower than $-1$ the previously introduced compensation principle holds at least above the poverty line. In the case being considered, the number of households that can be connected to the power supply system on island A by a fixed amount of aid is twice as high as the corresponding number on island B. Hence, giving a certain amount to island A would allow for a full hypothetical compensation (measured in

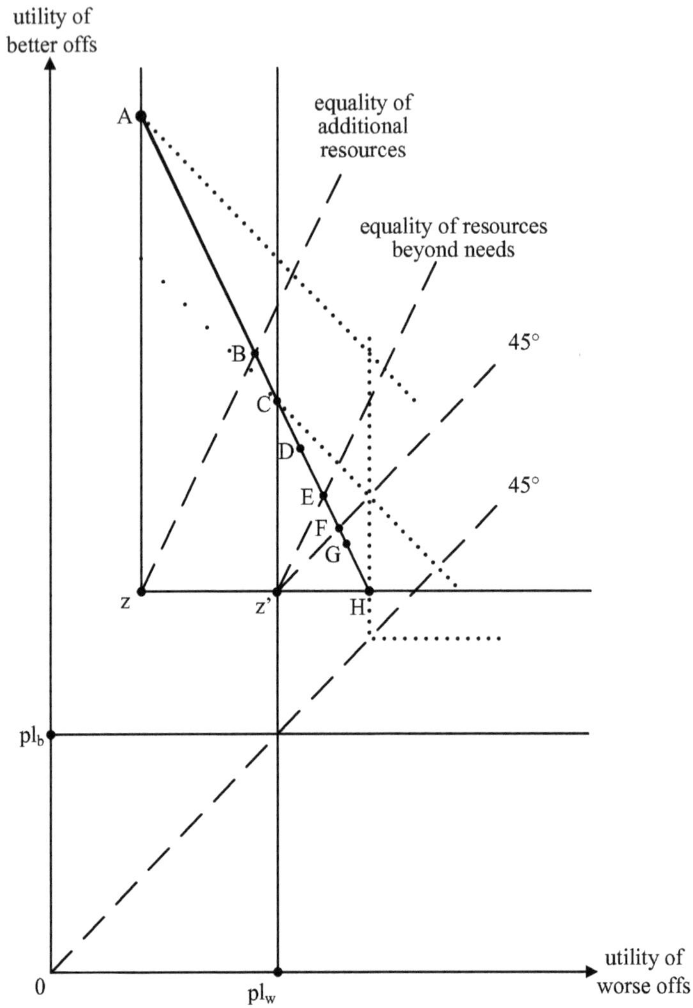


Figure 5.6: Truncated efficiency – Part a)

number of households) of island B by island A, but still leaves some benefit for island A.

So far, allocations above the poverty line have been considered. However, if the alleviation of hunger on the worse-off island is compared with connections to the power supply system on either island, the previously explained utility considerations are no longer suitable. Williams and Cookson (2000, especially pp. 1887-1889) discuss different options to introduce the idea of a poverty line into a graph in utility space. In our case we adopt the idea to incorporate a side constraint. Accordingly, equality with respect to this social minimum is required without permitting a trade-off with other distribution principles. Only beyond this level, other allocation aspects may be considered.

In Figure 5.6, poverty lines for both groups have been introduced by indicating certain minimum levels, $pl_b$ and $pl_w$. Allocations below these levels in the shaded areas do not satisfy all basic needs. The endowment point $z$ is also placed in the region below $pl_w$, because the worse-off island requires part of the development aid to prevent the famine. If respondents are willing to fully regard these basic needs – and consider other distributive principles only thereafter – point $z'$ results as a new (hypothetical) endowment point. In this case, the relevant utility possibility frontier shrinks to the section $\overline{CH}$. However, it is also possible that respondents do not accept this constraint. These subjects may choose an allocation reflected by a point on the frontier between $A$ and $C$. In fact, the third questionnaire study explicitly intended to investigate the relevance of this poverty line and, by this, the acceptance of the needs principle under various modifications.

### 5.5.2 Offered Allocations and Possible Motives

In this subsection, several allocations being proposed to the students in the questionnaire are identified in Figure 5.6. Moreover, some possible motivations for these distributions are presented and graphically explained.

Let us start by considering solutions below the poverty line $pl_w$ of the worse offs. The minimum level is expected to be ignored if respondents judge the principle of efficiency to be more important than the needs principle. On the one hand, this evaluation can be expressed in terms of classical utilitarianism, so that all resources are given to the more beneficial group (point $A$). Here, the highest respective social indifference curve, denoted by the dotted line, is reached. In chapter 4, we have called this behaviour 'strict efficiency'. However, the assumption of higher utility gains on island A compared to island B has to be fulfilled even if the welfare of the worse-off island B is below the poverty line.

On the other hand, points to the left of point $C$ may result from compromises between the standards of equality and efficiency. Here, corresponding social indifference curves, which are not given in Figure 5.6, are tangents to the utility possibility frontier.[8]

With respect to point $B$, another motive is also plausible, since equality of additional resources is reached. In the figure, this allocation leads to a higher utility gain for the more beneficial island A. But this is only reasonable if one solely focuses on utility measured in number of households connected to the power supply system, and ignores possibly higher utility gains of those below the poverty line. Note that in situation 'Aid' this was possible, because respondents could distinguish between two projects on island B. If this had not been the case, the utility gain of the poorer island should be measured in the number of households that can be prevented from starvation. However, in the latter case, comparisons of different utility dimensions are critical, as it has already been explained above. Overall, it seems to be more likely that the resulting allocation in point $B$ reflects a concern for equality of additional resources instead of utility concerns.

The most interesting position on the utility possibility frontier is point $C$. Here, basic needs of the worse-off group are fully regarded, whereas the remaining development aid is completely given to the electricity project on island A. The graphical presentation of the situation enables us to visualise three possible motives for the allocation corresponding to point $C$. Firstly, the basic structure of the hypothetical situation intends to create a setting in which truncated efficiency offers a plausible solution. While a 'hard nosed' utilitarian may prefer point $A$, a utilitarian, who nevertheless acknowledges the lexicographical priority of the needs principle, will maximise social welfare according to equation (5.2) along the line $\overline{CH}$.[9] Clearly, this argument is in line with the original idea of 'truncated utilitarianism'. Certainly, the benefits of those below the poverty line could be higher than any gain for individuals above this line.

Secondly, respondents who trade-off the principles of equality and efficiency and actually prefer a point to the left of $C$ – but to the right of $A$ – could be constrained by the poverty line. Although they are concerned about the more beneficial project on island A, the needs principle is too determined. Again, utility gains below the poverty line may be assumed to be higher in any case. It was for this reason that we called this allocation rule 'truncated efficiency' rather than 'truncated utilitarianism'. The former expression accentuates the fact that not only the classical utilitarianism but also a trade-off relation

8 It should already be mentioned that equality and needs considerations necessarily require the same allocation only to the left of the poverty line $pl_w$.

9 The former case is not at all hypothetical: Remember that in the case described by Konow (2001) the proportion of subjects who preferred the principle of efficiency over needs even if there were enough resources to fully regard all basic needs was surprisingly large.

with a stronger emphasis on efficiency considerations is truncated by the needs principle.[10]

A third motive to choose in accordance with point $C$ goes in the opposite direction. It has already been explained above that point $B$ may be favoured by those respondents who want to split the additional resource evenly between the two parties, and, therefore, ignore different utility gains of both parties from the resource. Nevertheless, this consideration may be constrained again by the poverty line. Indeed, a small extra amount of money would suffice to fully regard basic needs despite the more unequal distribution of the additional resource. This allocation concept could be called *truncated equality of additional resources*. However, it is not clear from the results presented in chapter 4 how many respondents really argued in that way.

Some points to the right of $C$ on the utility possibility frontier may be chosen for rather obvious reasons. An allocation reflected by point $E$ is probably motivated by a concern for equality of additional resources beyond the full regard of basic needs. The corresponding subsidiary line starts in $z'$, i.e. the new hypothetical endowment point. It shows a slope of 2 and, thereby, reflects the differences in marginal utility associated with the two electricity projects. Furthermore, a choice indicated by point $F$ is probably provoked by the desire to equalise benefits of both groups beyond basic needs. Consequently, the 45°-line originates in $z'$ and, thus, ignores the overall inequality with regard to individual utility levels. In chapter 4, we argued that the assumption of 'manna from heaven' could have provoked these considerations. Note that the allocation represented by point $F$ reflects a higher amount of development aid for the worse offs even beyond basic needs compared to the better offs. Hence, the former group is compensated for differences with respect to benefits, which are caused by unfavourable outside conditions but do not result from some possible 'misbehaviour' of the inhabitants of island B.

Respondents opting for a distribution that is represented by point $H$ especially consider the general worse-off situation of island B. In the graph, they would try to come as close as possible to the 45°-line starting from the origin of utility space. The maximin principle is one option to reflect this preference.[11] By horizontally moving to the 45°-line in Figure 5.6, higher L-shaped indifference curves with the locus about this line are reached. Nevertheless, subjects who trade-off the principles of equality and efficiency may also favour a single focus on worse-off individuals. In fact, correspondingly curved social indifference contours, which are symmetrical about the 45°-line, may be a tangent to each point on the line $\overline{AH}$. Moreover, any point between $C$ and $H$

10 It should be pointed out that truncated efficiency presupposes 'complete' interpersonal comparability. Hence, it demands comparability of both utility levels and utility differences.

11 Remark again that, in fact, the Rawlsian difference principle only demands interpersonally comparable and ordinally measurable utilities.

– including points $E$ and $F$ – can also be explained by such preferences for a compromise between equality and efficiency. Points $D$ and $G$ explicitly suggest two of these allocations. In the given model they can only be rationalised by a certain degree of inequality aversion.

Thus, what can be visualised by the graphical presentation of the initial situations in the third questionnaire? Most importantly, allocations corresponding to point $C$ primarily reflect the acceptance of the needs principle. Additionally, in many cases the poverty line seems to constrain efficiency considerations, but the idea of truncated equality of additional resources is also possible. Above the poverty line, various distributions can be motivated by different specifications of equality concerns. Furthermore, preferences for compromises between efficiency and equality may have inspired several choices of participants in the study. In the following subsections, possible effects of responsibility and efficiency variations on decisions are discussed by describing revised choices in the graphs. Thus, these two principles are also incorporated in the diagrammatic presentation and lead to a more complete picture of the underlying structure.

### 5.5.3 Aspects of Responsibility Reconsidered

Some possibilities to include aspects of responsibility into a graphical presentation have already been shown in section 5.4. Therefore, the relevant effects for the present case will be discussed rather briefly. To start with, in the two previous questionnaire studies at least some respondents seemed to honour the risk-taking behaviour either of the sportsperson or of the Africans. In contrast, in the present contexts of the third questionnaire study such 'positive' effects for the worse offs seem to be implausible. Neither the usage of pesticides despite several warnings from the UN in the first nor the waste of energy in the second context seems to give good reason for rewarding this behaviour. Thus, the only personal difference between worse offs and better offs in each situation concerns the 'negative' aspect of responsibility; other dissimilarities are displayed by different utility levels and should, therefore, solely be regarded by the shape of the social indifference contour.

In the situation presented in Figure 5.6 only classical utilitarian and trade-off preferences with regard to the principles of equality and efficiency are supposed to be influenced by responsibility variations. It has already been explained in section 5.4 why we suppose that 'pure' equality conceptions and maximin arguments remain unaffected. As before, different weights are attached to utility levels of both groups being regarded so that the fraction $\frac{\alpha}{\beta}$ from equations (5.2) and (5.3) may decrease if worse offs are supposed to be responsible for their fate. This change leads again to flatter indifference contours compared to the no-responsibility case. The decrease has two effects in Figure 5.6. Firstly, tangential points of the utility possibility frontier and those indifference curves, which result from certain trade-off preferences between efficiency and equality, should lie more to the left than before. Thus, the corresponding amount distributed to the worse-off group should decrease. Note that a change of the chosen allocation can be observed as soon as the aspect of responsibility is strong enough to vary the fraction $\frac{\alpha}{\beta}$. However, due to the either-or decision demanded this was not the case in the first two studies. In contrast, in the third investigation the mean amounts given to 'misbehaving' individuals significantly decreased in the responsibility version of situations 'Aid' and 'Fuel'.

Secondly, the 'pressure' on the poverty line may increase. The just described movement to the left along the line $\overline{CH}$ increases the number of subjects who are constrained by this minimum level. Hence, allocations in accordance with point $C$ should be observed more often. However, although indifference lines of those respondents who follow classical utilitarian arguments are also flatter, their choice should be unchanged, no matter whether it is either in accordance with point $A$ or with point $C$. In chapter 4, it has been shown that especially in situation 'Fuel' more respondents refused to accept the constraint in the responsibility version.

Finally, Williams and Cookson (2000, pp. 1881-1883) discuss a further alternative to incorporate personal differences of recipients. Let us reconsider Figure 5.6 on page 272. Here, we identified a point $z'$ from which a 45°-line starts that corresponds to L-shaped social welfare contours. Imagine now, that these contours are not symmetrical about this 45°-line through point $z'$, but about some flatter line that leads to a "target level of equality" on the 45°-line through the origin 0. In our context this would mean that benefits from development aid are shared between both parties with greater weight to improvements of the worse-off island. Thus, a certain "inequality-reducing path" is preferred to other also available paths towards the 45°-line arising from the origin 0. In fact, in the present investigation the no-responsibility cases may reflect this situation so that a larger benefit beyond basic needs should be permitted to the worse-off group. In Figure 5.6 this would lead to allocations represented by a point on the frontier between points $F$ and $H$. Moreover, in the responsibility case the slope of the path mentioned that starts in the endowment point should increase.

Although it can well be imagined that participants of our questionnaire study also followed such a path towards a target level for both groups and favoured the worse offs, especially two difficulties of this idea can be identified. Firstly, it may be asked why the better-off group should at all receive part of the resource in the given situation if the focus is on equalising utility levels. Williams and Cookson (p. 1881) argue that in their context "need for health" is regarded. Hence, the existing needs of the better offs have to be considered, too. However, in the present study the inhabitants of island A are supposed to live already above the poverty line. Secondly, it is difficult to see why the target point on the 45°-line arising from the origin should change in the responsibility case and indicate a new target, where *both* groups reach a higher utility level. Certainly, for technical reasons this assumption is necessary to reflect unequal weights to utility levels of both groups in the graph.

Nevertheless, an assumed trade-off between equality and efficiency is possibly better able to explain the allocation behaviours being regarded. On the one hand, the higher benefits of supporting the group of better offs can explain why a respondent is willing to allocate at least part of the resource to these individuals despite the facts that they do not live below the poverty line and that the other group is worse off. On the other hand, different evaluations of characteristics of recipients can be incorporated by changing the weights to the corresponding utility levels of both groups. Therefore, the isoelastic SWF seems to be a more convincing instrument to rationalise the graphical consequences of several allocation decisions.

To summarise, responsibility considerations can be incorporated into the graphical presentation of the underlying structure of the third questionnaire study. In particular, preferences that reflect trade-offs between the principles of equality and efficiency should be sensitive to these aspects and result in a reduction of resources allocated to the worse-off group. In the study conducted this change in evaluations of available alternatives could immediately be detected due to the possibility of splitting up the given amount in a continuous fashion.

### 5.5.4 Efficiency Variations Reconsidered

In the final subsection, one possibility to incorporate efficiency variations into the graphical presentation of situations in the third questionnaire study will be presented and discussed. The benefits of the project proposed by the better-off group in the 'Aid' context is increased by lowering the costs for connecting one household to the power supply system. While in part a) twice as many households on island A as on island B can be connected, in part b) the corresponding relation is 4 to 1. The implications of this alteration are considered in Figure 5.7.

Here, the linear utility possibility frontier is turned in point $H$, where the utility gain of the better-off group remains zero. Since the slope of this line indicates the rate of substitution between numbers of connected households on both islands, this value decreases from $-2$ to $-4$. In order to compare the effects of this modification, the frontiers corresponding to both part a) ($\overline{A^a H^a}$) and part b) ($\overline{A^b H^b}$) are given in the graph. The upper index, which is used for the labels of the points, denotes the corresponding part. Furthermore, points that have been named by the same capital letter regularly indicate distributions that are supposed to be inspired by the same allocation concept.

Now, the aim is to identify and compare the distributions following from the application of (combinations of) allocation principles in both parts. The corresponding points in the graph will be compared with respect to their position on the horizontal axis. Clearly, paying the same amount of money

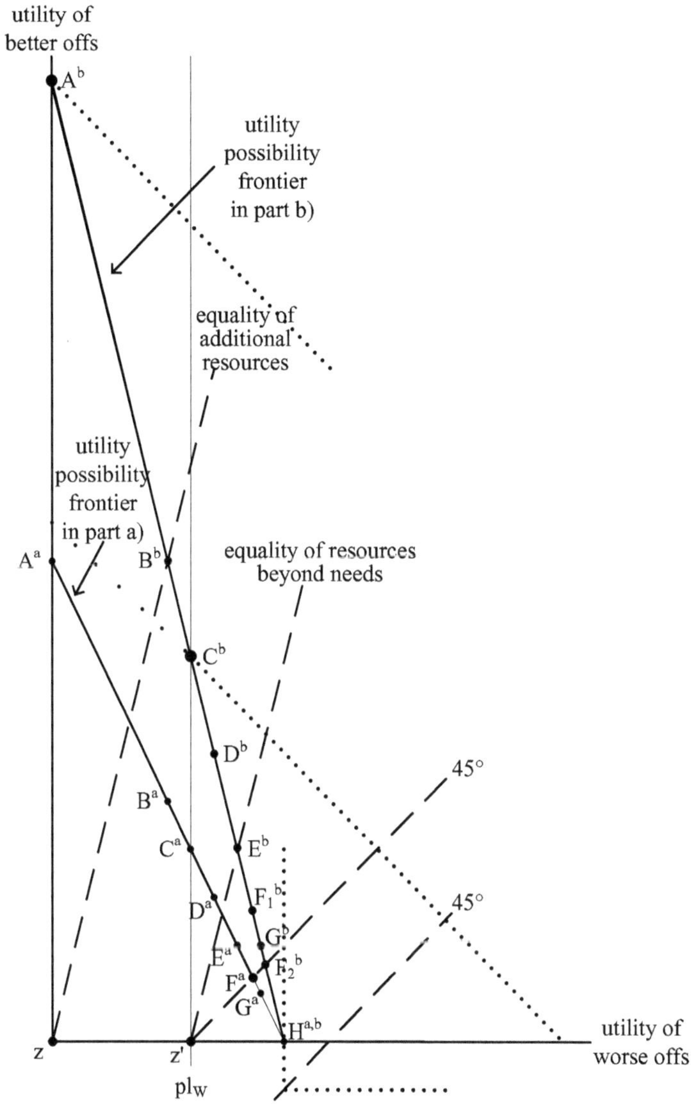


Figure 5.7: Truncated efficiency – Parts a) and b)

to the worse-off island provokes the same benefit for this group in both parts being regarded. In contrast, above point $H$ in part b) the better offs gain twice as much as in part a) from each unit of development aid.

A first comparison of resulting distributions on the two utility possibility frontiers already reveals that most allocation concepts demand paying the same amount of money to the worse offs in both parts being considered. Those respondents who have been called 'hard-nosed' utilitarians will certainly allocate again all resources to the better-off group, a solution reflected by point $A^b$. Also, the principles that demand equality of additional resources, either independently from the poverty line (point $B^b$) or above this level (point $E^b$), are located again on a subsidiary line running through points $z$ or $z'$, respectively. But now, due to the increased benefits of the project of the better-off group these lines are steeper than in part a). Furthermore, subjects who follow the idea of equalising overall utility retain to choose an allocation denoted by point $H^{a,b}$.

In situation 'Aid' the following distinction is possible: A participant who is willing to guarantee the same utility gain for both islands beyond fully regarding basic needs has two options. On the one hand, due to the increased benefits of the electricity project on island A, an equal gain – measured in number of households – is reached in part b) if the better-off group receives somewhat less and the worse-off group more money than in part a) (point $F_2^b$). Thus, both groups of recipients arrive at a higher utility level than before. Note that this change was rather prominent among our students in chapter 4. On the other hand, benefits can also be measured in percentage numbers of households on an island that are newly connected to the power supply system. But the total number of households on island A increases in correspondence to the decrease of costs for connecting a single household on that island. Thus, to help the same proportion of households on both islands, the same amount of money must be given to the worse-off island in parts a) and b). The corresponding point is $F_1^b$.

Before we finally come back to the idea of truncated efficiency, let us reconsider the case of trade-off preferences between equality and efficiency. It is obvious from Figure 5.7 that due to the steeper utility possibility frontier in part b), the tangential point of this line and a fixed band of indifference curves resulting from equation (5.3) will indicate a higher utility level for the better-off group than in part a). However, certainly this does not mean that better offs also receive a higher amount of the given resource. Moreover, it is not clear whether the utility gain of the worse offs will change and, furthermore, if it changes, whether the resulting level is higher or lower than before. It is likely that the answers to these questions depend on the degree of inequality aversion, $\tau$, in equation (5.3). To simply matters it is assumed that $\alpha = \beta = 1$. In Appendix 5.7, the following condition is proved for:

**Condition $\tau$:** Assume that preferences are represented by the isoelastic social welfare function given in equation (5.3) with $\alpha = \beta = 1$. If the utility possibility frontier gets steeper, then the utility level of the worse-off group declines (increases) if $\tau < 1$ ($\tau > 1$).

This result seems to be plausible. A smaller value for $\tau$ represents less inequality aversion and, therefore, more concern for the principle of efficiency. If the project of the better offs gets more beneficial, a respective external observer should be willing to invest more into this project and, consequently, less into the alternative program of the worse offs. In contrast, a social planner with a higher degree of inequality aversion ($\tau > 1$) would argue differently. If the project of the better offs becomes more beneficial, some money can be saved and invested into the project of the worse offs instead.

Let us reconsider the group of students in the third investigation, who changed their initially chosen allocation later on. Most of them wanted to pay more to island A so that one could have speculated that they switched between different allocation concepts. But this behaviour is not considered in the present chapter. A minority of respondents even gave less money to island A, but we have been unable to explain all of these choices in section 4.6.3 in chapter 4. Now, it has been demonstrated that both behaviours can perfectly be described by a SWF that allows for a certain degree of inequality aversion. Of course this finding does not hold for all choices observed. Nevertheless, besides those who immediately started with a compromise solution, several more subjects seem to have followed this explicit pluralistic conception of the principles of equality and efficiency. Thus, our results confirm the prominence of these preferences in favour of such a compromise in empirical investigations.

Interestingly, for the given isoelastic SWF in equation (5.3) a change for the case of $\tau = 1$ is not defined. Thus, although the direction of a change depends on the value of $\tau$, the amount that is distributed to the worse-off group will always change if the efficiency relation between the two projects is varied.[12] This result is different from most of the other ideas considered, because corresponding rules demand distributing the same amount to worse offs in all parts of the situation. Corresponding allocations are indicated by points $A, B, E, F$ and $H$. Nevertheless, it should be remembered that a single choice in accordance with these points could also be explained by an isoelastic SWF.

It must also be noted that the allocation concepts being considered in this chapter cannot explain why some of our students choose the same compromise solutions, like those reflected by points $D$ or $G$, in all parts of a given situation.

Finally, it has been shown that subjects who trade off efficiency and equality in the third questionnaire and attach more importance to the first principle will allocate less to the worse-off island in part b). But if they accept the

12 Of course, in the given situation this statement only holds between points $C$ and $H$.

poverty line, they should be constrained by this level and choose the allocation corresponding to point $C^b$. In view of the allocation concepts presented in this chapter, it is only these respondents who are responsible for the increased choice of this allocation which we in fact witnessed in our study. In situation 'Aid', but especially in situation 'Fuel', we observed a higher proportion of students who decided in accordance with truncated efficiency in parts b) and c) compared to the initial part a). From this viewpoint, it really represents a kind of truncated efficiency.

In this section, we have tried to identify different motives that may underlie choices of offered allocations. In the third questionnaire study, special attention was given to choices that are supposed to reflect truncated efficiency. Obviously, corresponding allocations are supported not only by utilitarians but also by subjects who trade off the principles of equality and efficiency or even truncated equality of additional resources. Moreover, it has been shown that these distributions become more attractive if responsibility or efficiency considerations are introduced. Overall, the trade-off preferences described are very general and could explain almost all choices. Nevertheless, it has also been revealed that at least for the applied isoelastic SWF the modifications mentioned necessarily lead to a change of the initial allocation. In conclusion, several distributions have been identified that could be motivated by equality concerns. Indeed, as shown in chapter 4, many of them have been observed in the third questionnaire study. Again, it should be noted that in the given setting some equality considerations could be separated from the needs principle.

## 5.6 Conclusions

It has been shown that graphical presentations of distributive justice problems and possible solutions can be a helpful tool to clarify the underlying structure and visualise inherent assumptions and restrictions. Clearly, graphs can only reveal certain aspects of complex situations. Moreover, strong restrictions to the underlying theoretical models are necessary to be able to force them into a simple drawing. Therefore, this approach cannot be a substitute for axiomatic descriptions that consider distribution principles and fully regard details of resulting allocation concepts. Furthermore, effects from different assumptions about the measurability of utilities have not been discussed.

However, only a few justice consider more than one out of the four identified allocation principles in a coherent conception, although currently the existence of these notions is greatly acknowledged. Nevertheless, we have tried to incorporate the effects of different allocation principles and resulting distribution rules into one single graphical presentation.

We started by presenting the most often discussed trade-off between the principles of equality and efficiency, which has also been considered in the first questionnaire. A distinction between aspects of needs and equality was not necessary yet, since both principles resulted in similar allocation proposals. As the graphs revealed again, the maximin equity criterion in the contexts presented made a clear statement in favour of one alternative, whereas distributions based on the efficiency principle are not unequivocal.

Furthermore, social indifference curves resulting from the isoelastic formulation of a social welfare function have been introduced in order to reflect preferences for trade-offs between the principles of equality and efficiency. They proved to be particularly useful to explain empirical outcomes which were initially difficult to understand. Nonetheless, Rawls's criticism on intuitionism, which underlies such trade-offs, has to be kept in mind. Indeed, many identified degrees of inequality aversion seem to be rather arbitrary, but they can regularly be observed in empirical studies.

Afterwards, aspects of responsibility have been considered. They can be interpreted as individual characteristics, which provoke different weights to individual utility levels. This effect is separated from the evaluation of the currently miserable situation of the worse offs. However, it can be shown that aspects of responsibility do not necessarily lead to a switch from one alternative to another in the second questionnaire study. One reason, which could also be deduced from the graphs, is the applied either-or structure of the decision problems. Also, positive aspects of risk-taking behaviour may lead to higher weights to utility levels of responsible individuals. Obviously, potential consequences of different aspects of responsibility should be the object of future empirical investigations.

The changes discussed in the third questionnaire study resulted in several modifications of the graphical presentation. Firstly, due to the option of splitting up the given resource in a continuous fashion, all points on the utility possibility frontier are feasible. Therefore, secondly, additional information on the course of this frontier had to be given. But probably the most important change, which has been inspired by several macro-justice studies, was the introduction of a poverty line that allows for the separation of the needs principle from some other equality concerns. In the graphs, the poverty line is represented by an additional constraint such that behaviours, which fulfil this restriction, can be identified and described. Indeed, several theoretical concepts predict the acceptance of the needs principle, and, thereby, the priority of this principle over efficiency or responsibility concerns.

Again, social indifference curves resulting from equality-efficiency trade-offs proved to be helpful to describe at least allocations above the poverty line. With the help of this preference structure some behaviours that seemed to be inconsistent could be rationalised without assuming a switch from one (combination of) principle(s) to another. Although almost all allocations may be explained by this SWF, behaviour must obey certain rules. Moreover, increased prominence of truncated efficiency can perfectly be presented by this preference structure if information on responsibility or efficiency is varied.

Certainly, there is plenty of room for future research on the relation between the identified allocation principles. The utilised graphs are one instrument to visualise underlying assumption and sources for conflicts between some criteria.

## 5.7 Appendix: Proof of Condition $\tau$

Suppose social welfare is evaluated by the isoelastic social welfare function

$$W = (u_w^{1-\tau} + u_b^{1-\tau})^{\frac{1}{1-\tau}}, \quad \tau \neq 1, \quad 0 \leq \tau < \infty, \tag{5.5}$$

where $W$ is associated with the utility levels $u$ of individuals $b$ and $w$, and $u_b > u_w$ always holds. Also, assume that $u_b \geq z_b$ and $u_w \geq z_w$ with $(z_b, z_w)$ representing the endowment point. Moreover, the value of $\tau$ reflects the level of inequality aversion. The utility possibility frontier is given by the linear relation

$$u_b = c - du_w, \quad c > z_b, d > 0. \tag{5.6}$$

In the initial case $I$ social welfare according to (5.5) is maximised subject to (5.6) if the marginal ratė of substitution between the two utility levels equals the slope of the utility possibility frontier. Thus, we have

$$(\frac{u_b}{u_w})^\tau = d. \tag{5.7}$$

Substituting from (5.6) into (5.7) and solving for $u_w$ yields the utility level of the worse-off person in the initial situation $I$:

$$u_w^I = \frac{c}{d + d^{\frac{1}{\tau}}}. \tag{5.8}$$

Now, consider the extended case $E$, where the utility possibility frontier is steeper but runs again through the initial point on the horizontal axis. Hence, the new line is given by

$$u_b = \gamma(c - du_w), \quad c > 0, d > 0, \gamma > 1. \tag{5.9}$$

In our contexts, $\gamma$ reflects the increased benefits of the alternative that supports the better offs in comparison to the project of the worse offs. As before, social welfare from (5.5) is maximised with respect to the new frontier in (5.9). The optimality condition reads

$$(\frac{u_b}{u_w})^\tau = \gamma d. \tag{5.10}$$

Substituting from (5.9) into (5.10) and solving again for $u_w$ gives the utility level of the worse-off individual in the extended situation $E$:

$$u_w^E = \frac{c}{(\gamma d)^{\frac{1}{\tau}}\gamma^{-1} + d}. \tag{5.11}$$

Now, we want to derive a condition for $\tau$ to ensure that $u_w^I > u_w^E$. Hence, with (5.8) and (5.11) we get

$$\frac{c}{d + d^{\frac{1}{\tau}}} > \frac{c}{(\gamma d)^{\frac{1}{\tau}}\gamma^{-1} + d}.$$

This can be rearranged to

$$d^{\frac{1}{\tau}} < (\gamma d)^{\frac{1}{\tau}}\gamma^{-1}$$

and reformulated to

$$\frac{1}{\tau}(\ln d) < \frac{1}{\tau}(\ln d\gamma) - (\ln \gamma).$$

Since we assumed $\gamma > 1$, it can be said that

$$\tau < \frac{(\ln \gamma d) - (\ln d)}{(ln\gamma)},$$

from which we finally derive $\tau < 1$.

# General Conclusions

Let us finally come back to the discoveries we have attributed to our young researcher at the very beginning of the present work. He or she had already realised that there not only exists a plurality of theories of distributive justice, but also a great heterogeneity of justice attitudes among laymen, which are revealed in numerous empirical investigations in all social science disciplines. Moreover, both corresponding streams of literature evolved almost completely disconnected from each other. Nevertheless, recently two important developments can be observed. On the one hand, modern theoretical conceptions are interpreted and distinguished with regard to their definition of the relationship between some well-accepted allocation principles. On the other hand, several researchers have started to carry out experiments and, particularly, questionnaire investigations that are inspired by theoretical arguments. The present work has been explicitly based on these two developments in the literature on distributive justice. Hence, after the presentation of our three survey studies and the explanation of their theoretical implications in the last chapter, we will conclude by summarising more general findings, which are considered to be important for future research.

To start with, from a very general point of view, the presentations of all the questionnaire investigations included three attributes. These are essential if the conclusions derived from the studies are to play a vital role in future theoretical and empirical research.

Firstly, the question has to be answered in what way results of an empirical investigation will be helpful for solving a previously identified conflict between theories of distributive justice. Surely, findings from such studies will be valuable if they are able to inform the theorist either about potential problems when putting a concept into practice or about possible biases. These may result from individual characteristics of the researcher or the process of developing the theoretical model. Nevertheless, throughout the present work we have assumed a third and more ambitious role of empirical studies. Although they cannot substitute for theoretical arguments, such investigations could play a constructive role in the process of model building. More specifically, they may help to evaluate the tenability of axioms that are suggested to be implemented in existing models. This procedure is required to identify a stable social equilibrium. However, the fact that the empirical investigation has to be theoretically grounded is a necessary precondition in order to claim relevance for this process. Therefore, at the outset of each chapter which presented a survey study, it was explained how the setting of the questionnaire originated in the existing theoretical literature.

Secondly, with respect to the previously described requirement of a theoretical foundation, the introduction of four allocation principles proved to be very helpful. Certainly, their application generally leads to simplified presentations of complex justice conceptions. However, as argued in chapters 1 and 5, several modern theories of distributive justice can be distinguished by these principles, including Rawls's priority of his difference principle, Walzer's (1983) conception of spheres of justice, or Fleurbaey's (1998) idea of equality of selected functionings. Here, the allocation principles regarded serve as a common ground for comparisons between different theoretical concepts. Nevertheless, they also constitute a central instrument to classify distribution conflicts, as they are described either with the help of hypothetical examples discussed by theorists or in empirical investigations. Hence, each presentation of questionnaire studies on distributive justice may benefit from describing the underlying allocation problem and the structure of the investigation in terms of these four allocation principles. In particular, the necessary connections between theoretical conceptions and the structure of hypothetical situations have been illustrated in chapters 2 to 4 of the present work.

However, even if the theoretical grounds are identified and the resulting empirical questions are formulated, thirdly, it is important to explain and rationalise the chosen empirical proceeding. At the end of chapter 1, we collected several reasons for our survey based approach and its realisation. Obviously, one should be well aware of all consequences of the chosen method. Questionnaire studies aiming at investigating justice attitudes are usually viewed to be the most appropriate way to mirror the spirit of the relevant social choice literature. Thus, in all of our questionnaires, different allocations reflected the acceptance or rejection of certain conflicting allocation principles. Moreover, in each chapter the implementation of the study has been described in detail. Certainly, the choice of both the applied method and the concrete implementation may have had some influence on the answers of respondents. Finally, several statistical tools accompanied all of our investigations. Certainly, these examinations could be carried out even further. However, they clearly permitted more valid statements compared to presentations of mere frequencies of different choices, which is still the more common approach in the corresponding empirical literature. Additionally, they allowed us to gain deeper insights into possible decision motives. Thus, modern empirical investigations should generally be subjected to more advanced statistical analysis.

So far, the appropriateness of the selected research method has been illustrated. Clearly, the previous explanations already represent one important aspect of the present work. However, there are several general findings that may also be useful for future research, especially in the field of empirical social choice.

As a first, and maybe most general result, we realised that trade-offs were much more likely in our studies than possibly expected. The switching behaviour observed in the first and second study but, particularly, the frequent choices of compromise solutions in the third investigation could be interpreted correspondingly. In chapter 5, we have already introduced some tools to present and interpret such trade-offs. Obviously, future axiomatic models in social choice theory should also allow for relationships between distinct allocation principles.

Moreover, similar to the great variety of different theoretical justice conceptions, we witnessed heterogeneity of justice attitudes among our subjects. This finding confirmed several other results reported in the empirical literature. Further research is obviously needed to determine conditions under which a greater agreement on a certain (set of) allocation principles among laymen could be reached.

The disagreement observed did not disappear in the third investigation, where several modifications were incorporated to promote the acceptance of truncated efficiency as a mixed conception. Nevertheless, some influential factors could already be identified. Besides clear effects from efficiency and responsibility modifications, the gender of a respondent had a remarkable influence on the acceptance of truncated efficiency, with men being more in favour of this conception. Also, it seemed to matter whether the allocation problem was described in a micro-justice or a macro-justice context.

Furthermore, in our literature review in chapter 4 it became apparent that especially the theoretical basis for truncated efficiency is rather weak. Therefore, respective future work should also focus more on this conception. In contrast to some other investigations, we have modelled the floor level as a poverty line instead of an arbitrary level stated by participants in the study. Consequently, we could explicitly control for the acceptance of the needs principle, which gained remarkable support. But this modelling is not only relevant for empirical investigations. Instead, it could also be incorporated in theoretical conceptions. Here, the cited paper by Tungodden (2000) serves as a promising starting point for describing this kind of mixed conceptions.

Only recently, the principle of responsibility has been established in the theoretical literature on distributive justice. In our second and third questionnaire study, additional aspects of responsibility were introduced on the side of worse-off people. Thus, the responsibility principle was allowed to moderate the trade-off between needs or equality and efficiency. Although this information about reasons for the existence of basic needs had a significant influence on decisions of participants, in general the acceptance of the needs principle seems to be of greater importance. Nevertheless, much more research on the impact of aspects of responsibility is necessary. Our studies point already to some relevant factors. For example, respondents seem to have reacted more often to additional aspects of responsibility if a continuous split of the given resource instead of an either-or decision was possible. Furthermore, this was also the case if behaviour was described as careless rather than risk-taking. Moreover, the idea of a delayed responsibility effect in chapter 4 showed both the significance of the needs principle and the 'punishment motive' for the support of the responsibility principle.

Another more general finding of the present work regards the influence of the gender of a decision maker on justice evaluations. Regularly, women were found to be more in favour of the equality and the needs principle, whereas men more frequently considered aspects of efficiency. Furthermore, in the third questionnaire study females more often supported compromise solutions and were also more in favour of punishing misbehaving individuals. However, we could observe that gender effects were regularly confounded by other factors, like the place of the investigation or the age of a respondent. For several reasons, our findings could be important for future research. Firstly, empirical researchers should take possible gender effects into account when they formulate their questionnaires, decide on the experimental setting or select their sample. Secondly, they should also routinely allow for gender biases when analysing their data. More generally, although the explanatory power of individual and questionnaire attributes for observed attitudes was found to be low, one should control for all available characteristics to obtain further insights into possible decision motives. Thirdly, we have already speculated that there could be gender-specific justice conceptions. Clearly, the development of this idea is still in its infancy, but it seems to be an avenue for future research.

Finally, in particular the literature review in chapter 2 with regard to the influence of gender has revealed that an interdisciplinary approach will be a fruitful way to better understand distribution behaviour and attitudes. This was also the case with respect to the empirical investigations on the acceptance of truncated efficiency from the fields of political science and social psychology, which have explicitly been theoretically grounded. In the general introduction, it was already remarked that, hopefully, the young researcher not only reads the relevant work in the field of economics, but also from other social science disciplines and philosophy. Unlike many researchers from some other areas in economics, social choice theorists are already used to considering the related work in neighbouring disciplines such as philosophy or political sciences. Nevertheless, several empirical researchers in adjacent subjects seem to be almost completely unaware of insights that their neighbours already possess with regard to related questions.

Probably the reader has already thought that the theoretical and empirical proceeding in the present work is only one possibility among several others. Indeed, the econometric analyses could be carried further, although the basic findings seem to be very stable. Certainly, the empirical realisation of the investigations may be modified and the trade-offs between allocation principles in the hypothetical situations could be formulated differently. From a theoretical point of view, the consideration of other (combinations of) allocation principles is certainly possible. Also, the graphs in chapter 5 are simplifications which may suggest more refined presentations. Furthermore, several other social welfare functions are also able to reflect trade-offs between different principles. However, on the one hand we have tried to give good reasons for the chosen approaches and always pointed towards several available alternatives. On the other hand, maybe you have already said: "their method is alright, but I would have done it differently". This is perfect. It would mean that our work has proved to be inspiring for other researchers and motivated them to at least consider doing research in the exciting field of empirical social choice.

# Bibliography

Agresti, Allan (2002). *Categorical Data Analysis.* Hoboken, New York: John Wiley & Sons.

Ai, Chunrong and Edward C. Norton (2003). "Interaction terms in logit and probit models." *Economics Letters* **80**, pp. 123-129.

Aiken, Leona S. and Stephen G. West (1991). *Multiple Regression: Testing and Interpreting Interactions.* Thousand Oaks, CA: Sage.

Alexander, Sidney S. (1974). "Social evaluation through national choice." *Quarterly Journal of Economics* **88**, pp. 597-624.

Allison, Paul D. (2002). *Missing Data.* Sage University Papers Series on Quantitative Applications in the Social Sciences 136. Thousand Oaks, CA: Sage.

Alves, Wayne and Peter Rossi (1978). "Who should get what? Fairness judgments of the distribution of earnings." *American Journal of Sociology* **84**, pp. 541-564.

Amiel, Yoram and Frank A. Cowell (2002). "Attitudes towards risk and inequality: A questionnaire-experimental approach." In: Fredrik Andersson and Håkan J. Holm (editors), *Experimental Economics: Financial Markets, Auctions and Decision Making.* Boston, Mass.: Kluwer Academic, pp. 85-115.

Amiel, Yoram, Frank A. Cowell and Wulf Gaertner (2009). "To be or not to be involved: A questionnaire-experimental view on Harsanyi's utilitarian ethics." *Social Choice and Welfare* **32**, pp. 299-316.

Amiel, Yoram, Frank A. Cowell, Liema Davidovitz and Avraham Polovin (2008). "Preference reversals and the analysis of income distributions." *Social Choice and Welfare* **30**, pp. 305-330.

Amiel, Yoram, Frank A. Cowell and Xavier Ramos (2007). "On the measurement of polarisation: A questionnaire study." IZA Discussion Paper No. 2686, Institute for the Study of Labor.

Anderson, Elizabeth (1999). "What is the point of equality?" *Ethics* **109**, pp. 287-337.

Andreoni, James and Lise Vesterlund (2001). "Which is the fair sex? Gender differences in altruism." *The Quarterly Journal of Economics* **116**, pp. 293-312.

Arneson, Richard J. (1989). "Equality and equal opportunity for welfare." *Philosophical Studies* **56**, pp. 77-93.

Arneson, Richard J. (1990). "Liberalism, distributive subjectivism, and equal opportunity for welfare." *Philosophy and Public Affairs* **19**, pp. 158-194.

Arneson, Richard J. (2004). "Luck egalitarianism interpreted and defended." *Philosophical Topics* **32**, pp. 1-20.

Atkinson, Anthony B. (1970). "On the measurement of inequality." *Journal of Economic Theory* **2**, pp. 244-263.

Atkinson, Anthony B. and Joseph E. Stiglitz (1987). *Lectures on Public Economics.* Singapore: McGraw-Hill.

Ball, Sheryl B. and Paula-Ann Cech (1996). "Subject pool choice and treatment affects in economic laboratory research." *Research in Experimental Economics* **6**, pp. 239-292.

Baltes-Götz, Bernhard (2006). *Logistische Regressionsanalyse mit SPSS.* Universitätsrechenzentrum Trier, AWS.SPSS.19. [Online] 28 July 2007. <http://www.uni-trier.de/urt/user/baltes/docs/logist/logist.pdf >.

Bar-Hillel, Maya and Menahem Yaari (1993). "Judgements of distributive justice." In: Barbara A. Mellers and Jonathan Baron (editors), *Psychological Perspectives on Justice.* Cambridge: Cambridge University Press, pp. 55-84.

Bentham, Jeremy (1776). *A Fragment on Government.* London: T. Payne. (Revised and edited by Jimmy H. Burns and Herbert L.A. Hart, 1977, London: Athlone Press.)

Berry, William D. (1999). "Testing for interaction in models with binary dependent variables." Manuscript, Department of Political Science, Florida State University.

Berry, Frances S. and William D. Berry (1991). "Specifying a model of state policy." *American Political Science Review* **85**, pp. 573-579.

Birnbacher, Dieter (2005). "Kommentar zu Gaertner/Schwettmann: Untersuchungen zur Einschätzung von Gerechtigkeit." *Analyse & Kritik* **27**, pp. 315-319.

Blackorby, Charles, David Donaldson and John A. Weymark (1984). “Social choice with interpersonal comparisons: A diagrammatic introduction.” *International Economic Review* **25**, pp. 327-356.

Bleichrodt, Han, Enrico Diecidue and John Quiggin (2004). “Equity weights in the allocation of health: The rank-dependent QALY model.” *Journal of Health Economics* **23**, pp. 157-171.

Bleichrodt, Han, Jason Doctor and Elly Stolk (2005). “A nonparametric elicitation of the equity-efficiency trade-off in cost-utility analysis.” *Journal of Health Economics* **24**, pp. 655-678.

Boarini, Romina, Geert Demuijnck, Christine le Clainche and Jérôme Wittwer (2006). “Moral intuitions about social inequalities and individual responsibility: A European comparison.” Manuscript.

Bolton, Gary E. and Axel Ockenfels (2000). “ERC: A theory of equity, reciprocity, and competition.” *American Economic Review* **90**, pp. 166-193.

Borooah, Vani K. (2002). *Logit and Probit: Ordered and Multinomial Models.* Sage University Papers Series on Quantitative Applications in the Social Sciences 07-138. Thousand Oaks, CA: Sage.

Bosmans, Kristof and Erik Schokkaert (2009). “Equality preference in the claims problem: A questionnaire study of cuts in earnings and pensions.” *Social Choice and Welfare.* Forthcoming.

Bossert, Walter (1995). “Redistribution mechanism based on individual characteristics.” *Mathematical Social Sciences* **29**, pp. 1-17.

Bossert, Walter (1998). “Comments on 'The empirical acceptance of compensation axioms'.” In: Jean-François Laslier, Marc Fleurbaey, Nicolas Gravel and Alain Trannoy (editors), *Freedom in Economics.* London: Routledge, pp. 282-284.

Bossert, Walter and Marc Fleurbaey (1996). “Redistribution and compensation.” *Social Choice and Welfare* **13**, pp. 343-355.

Boulding, Kenneth E. (1962). “Social justice in social dynamics.” In: Richard B. Brandt (editor), *Social Justice.* Englewood Cliffs, NJ: Prentice Hall, pp. 73-92.

Brickman, Philip, Robert Folger, Erica Goode and Yaacov Schul (1981). “Microjustice and macrojustice.” In: Melvin J. Lerner and Sally C. Lerner (editors), *The Justice Motive in Social Behavior.* New York: Plenum Press, pp. 173-202.

Brighouse, Harry (2001). "Can justice as fairness accommodate the disabled?" *Social Theory and Practice* **27**, pp. 537-560.

Buchanan, James M. (1976). "A Hobbesian interpretation of the Rawlsian difference principle." *Kyklos* **29**, pp. 5-25.

Camerer, Colin (2003). *Behavioral Game Theory: Experiments in Strategic Interaction.* Princeton: Princeton University Press.

Cappelen, Alexander W., Astri D. Hole, Erik Ø. Sørensen and Bertil Tungodden (2007). "The pluralism of fairness ideals: An experimental approach." *American Economic Review* **97**, pp. 818-827.

Cappelen, Alexander W., Erik Ø. Sørensen and Bertil Tungodden (2006). "Responsibility for what? Fairness and individual responsibility." NHH Discussion Paper 15/05.

Carter, John R. and Michael D. Irons (1991). "Are economists different, and if so, why?" *Journal of Economic Perspectives* **5**, pp. 171-177.

Clément, Valérie and Daniel Serra (2001). "Égalitarisme et responsabilité: Une investigation expérementale." *Revue d'Economie Politique* **111**, pp. 173-193.

Cohen, Gerald A. (1989). "On the currency of egalitarian justice." *Ethics* **99**, pp. 906-944.

Cohen, Gerald A. (1993). "Equality of what: Resources, capabilities and midfare." In: Martha Nusbaum and Amartya K. Sen (editors), *The Quality of Life.* Oxford: Clarendon Press.

Croson, Rachel and Nancy Buchan (1999). "Gender and culture: International experimental evidence from trust games." *American Economic Review, Papers and Proceedings* **89**, pp. 386-391.

Croson, Rachel and Uri Gneezy (2008). "Gender differences in preferences." *Journal of Economic Literature.* Forthcoming.

Dana, Jason, Roberto A. Weber and Jason Xi Kuang (2007). "Exploiting moral wiggle room: Experiments demonstrating an illusory preference for fairness." *Economic Theory.* **33**, pp. 67-80.

Davis, Martin (1983). "The effect of dispositional empathy on emotional reactions and helping: A multi-dimensional approach." *Journal of Personality* **51**, pp. 167-184.

Demuijnck, Geert and Christine Le Clainche (2007). "What we owe to persons with a disability: Theoretical disputes and shared intuitions." *Imprints. Journal of Egalitarian Theory and Practice.* **10**, pp. 37-68.

Deschamps, Robert and Louis Gevers (1978). "Leximin and utilitarian rules: A joint characterization." *Journal of Economic Theory* **17**, pp. 143-163.

Deutsch, Morton (1975). "Equity, equality and need: What determines which value will be used as the basis of distributive justice?" *Journal of Social Issues* **31**, pp. 137-149.

Devooght, Kurt (2003). *Essays on Responsibility-sensitive Egalitarianism and the Measurement of Income Inequality.* Ph.D. thesis, Leuven, K.U. Leuven, Faculteit Economische en toegepaste economische wetenschappen.

Dickinson, David L. and Jill Tiefenthaler (2002). "What is fair? Experimental evidence." *Southern Economic Journal* **69**, pp. 414-428.

Dworkin, Ronald (1981a). "What is equality? Part 1: Equality of welfare." *Philosophy and Public Affairs* **10**, pp. 185-246.

Dworkin, Ronald (1981b). "What is equality? Part 2: Equality of resources." *Philosophy and Public Affairs* **10**, pp. 283-345.

Eagly, Alice H. (1995). "The science and politics of comparing women and men." *American Psychologist* **50**, pp. 145-158.

Eckel, Cathrine C. and Philip J. Grossman (1996). "The relative price of fairness: Gender differences in a punishment game." *Journal of Economic Behavior and Organization* **30**, pp. 143-158.

Eckel, Cathrine C. and Philip J. Grossman (1998). "Are women less selfish than men? Evidence from dictator experiments." *The Economic Journal* **108**, pp. 726-735.

Eckel, Cathrine C. and Philip J. Grossman (2000). "Differences in the economic decisions of men and women: Experimental evidence." In: Charles Plott and Vernon L. Smith (editors), *Handbook of Results in Experimental Economics.* New York: North Holland. Forthcoming.

Eisenberg, Nancy and Randy Lennon (1983). "Sex differences in empathy and related capacities." *Psychological Bulletin* **94**, pp. 100-131.

Elster, Jon (1992). *Local Justice: How Institutions Allocate Scarce Goods and Necessary Burdens.* New York: Russell Sage Foundation.

Elster, Jon (1995). "The Empirical study of justice." In: David Miller and Michael Walzer (editors), *Pluralism, Justice and Equality.* Oxford: Oxford University Press, pp. 81-98.

Engle, Patrice L. (1990). "Intra-household allocation of resources: Perspectives from psychology." In: Beatrice L. Rogers and Nina P. Schlossman (editors), *Intra-household Resource Allocation*. Tokyo: United Nations University Press, pp. 63-79.

Faravelli, Marco (2005). "Looking for agreement: An experiment on distributive justice." Working Paper No. 92, Department of Economics, University of Milan-Bicocca.

Faravelli, Marco (2007). "How context matters: A survey based experiment on distributive justice." *Journal of Public Economics* **91**, pp. 1399-1422.

Farwell, Lisa and Bernard Weiner (1996). "Self-perceptions of fairness in individual and group contexts." *Personality and Social Psychology Bulletin* **22**, pp. 867-881.

Fehr, Ernst and Klaus M. Schmidt (1999). "A theory of fairness, competition, and cooperation." *Quarterly Journal of Economics* **114**, pp. 817-868.

Fleurbaey, Marc (1994). "On fair compensation." *Theory and Decision* **36**, pp. 277-307.

Fleurbaey, Marc (1995a). "Equality and responsibility." *European Economic Review* **39**, pp. 683-689.

Fleurbaey, Marc (1995b). "Equal opportunity or equal social outcome?" *Economics and Philosophy* **11**, pp. 25-55.

Fleurbaey, Marc (1998). "Equality among responsible individuals." In: Jean-François Laslier, Marc Fleurbaey, Nicolas Gravel and Alain Trannoy (editors), *Freedom in Economies: New Perspectives in Normative Ananlysis*. London, New York: Routledge, pp. 206-234.

Fleurbaey, Marc (2001). "Egalitarian opportunities." *Law and Philosophy* **20**, pp. 499-530.

Fleurbaey, Marc (2007). "Health, equity and social welfare." *Annales d'Economie et de Statistiques* **82**, pp. 24-62.

Fleurbaey, Marc (2008). *Fairness, Responsibility, and Welfare*. Oxford: Oxford University Press.

Fleurbaey, Marc and François Maniquet (2005). "Compensation and responsibility." In: Kenneth J. Arrow, Amartya K. Sen and Kotaro Suzumura (editors), *Handbook of Social Choice and Welfare*, Volume 2. Amsterdam: North-Holland. Forthcoming.

Foley, Duncan K. (1967). "Resource allocation and the public sector." *Yale Economic Essays* **7**, pp. 45-98.

Forsé, Michel and Maxime Parodi (2006). "Justice distributive: La hiérarchie des principes selon les Européens." *Revue de l'OFCE* **98**, pp. 213-244. Available in English as: "A hierarchy of principles: The European view of distributive justice."

Frey, Bruno S. and Stephan Meier (2005). "Selfish and Indoctrinated Economists?" *European Journal of Law and Economics* **19**, pp. 165-171.

Frohlich, Norman and Joe E. Oppenheimer (1989). "Participation, productivity and stability: Experiments on fair democratic income policy decisions." In: Mike Jackson (editor), *Operational Research and Social Sciences.* London: Plenum, pp. 195-200.

Frohlich, Norman and Joe E. Oppenheimer (1990). "Choosing justice in experimental democracies with production." *American Political Science Review* **84**, pp. 461-477.

Frohlich, Norman and Joe E. Oppenheimer (1992). *Choosing Justice: An Experimental Approach to Ethical Theory.* Berkeley, CA: University of California Press.

Frohlich, Norman, Joe E. Oppenheimer and Cheryl Eavey (1987a). "Choices of principles of distributive justice in experimental groups." *American Journal of Political Science* **31**, pp. 606-636.

Frohlich, Norman, Joe E. Oppenheimer and Cheryl Eavey (1987b). "Laboratory results on Rawls's distributive justice." *British Journal of Political Science* **17**, pp. 1-21.

Gaertner, Wulf (1992). "Distributive Judgments." In: Wulf Gaertner and Marlies Klemisch–Ahlert, *Social Choice and Bargaining Perspectives on Distributive Justice.* Heidelberg, Berlin, New York: Springer, pp. 17-59.

Gaertner, Wulf (1994). "Distributive justice: Theoretical foundations and empirical findings." *European Economic Review* **38**, pp. 711-720.

Gaertner, Wulf (2006). *A Primer in Social Choice Theory.* Oxford: Oxford University Press.

Gaertner, Wulf (2007). "Empirical social choice." LSE Philosophy Papers PP/03/07, Centre for Philosophy of Natural and Social Science, London School of Economics.

Gaertner, Wulf and Jochen Jungeilges (2002). "Evaluation via extended orderings: Empirical findings from Western and Eastern Europe." *Social Choice and Welfare* **19**, pp. 29-55.

Gaertner, Wulf, Jochen Jungeilges and Reinhard Neck (2001). "Cross-cultural equity evaluations: A questionnaire-experimental approach." *European Economic Review* **45**, pp. 953-963.

Gaertner, Wulf and Lars Schwettmann (2005). "Untersuchungen zur Einschätzung von Gerechtigkeit." *Analyse & Kritik* **27**, pp. 288-314.

Gaertner, Wulf and Lars Schwettmann (2007). "Equity, responsibility and the cultural dimension." *Economica* **74**, pp. 627-649.

Gamliel, Eyal and Eyal Peer (2006). "Positive versus negative framing affects justice judgments." *Social Justice Research* **19**, pp. 307-322.

Gilligan, Carol (1982). *In a Different Voice: Psychological Theory and Women's Development.* Cambridge, Mass.: Harvard University Press.

Göthlich, Stephan E. (2007). "Zum Umgang mit fehlenden Daten in großzahligen empirischen Erhebungen." In: Sönke Albers, Daniel Klapper, Udo Konradt, Achim Walter and Joachim Wolf (editors), *Methodik der empirischen Forschung.* 2nd edition. Wiesbaden: Gabler, pp. 119-134.

Green, Ronald M. (1976). "Health care and justice in contract theory perspective." In: Robert M. Veatch and Roy Branson (editors), *Ethics and Health Policy.* Cambridge: Ballinger Publishing, pp. 111-126.

Greene, William H. (2003). *Econometric Analysis.* 5th edition. Upper Saddle River, NJ: Prentice Hall.

Gyrd-Hansen, Dorte (2004). "Investigating the social value of health changes." *Journal of Health Economics* **23**, pp. 1101-1116.

Hammond, Peter J. (1976). "Equity, Arrow's conditions and Rawls' difference principle." *Econometrica* **44**, pp. 793-804.

Harsanyi, John C. (1953). "Cardinal utility in welfare economics and in the theory of risk-taking." *Journal of Political Economy* **61**, pp. 434-435.

Harsanyi, John C. (1955). "Cardinal welfare, individualistic ethics and interpersonal comparisons of utility." *Journal of Political Economy* **63**, pp. 309-321.

Harsanyi, John C. (1975). "Can the maximin principle serve as a basis for morality? A critique of John Rawls's theory." *The American Political Science Review* **69**, pp. 594-606.

Harsanyi, John C. (1977). *Rational Behavior and Bargaining Equilibrium in Games and Social Situations.* Cambridge: Cambridge University Press.

Harsanyi, John C. (1978). "Bayesian decision theory and utilitarian ethics." *American Economic Review, Papers and Proceedings* **68**, pp. 223-228.

Hayek, Friedrich A. von (1976). *Law, Legislation, and Liberty. Volume II: The Mirage of Social Justice.* London: Routledge and Kegan Paul.

Heckman, James J. (1976). "The common structure of statistical models of truncation, sample selection, and limited dependent variables and a simple estimator for such models." *Annals of Economic and Social Measurement* **5**, pp. 475-492.

Heckman, James J. (1979). "Sample selection bias as a specification error." *Econometrica* **47**, pp. 153-161.

Heider, Fritz (1958). *The Psychology of Interpersonal Relations.* New York, NY: John Wiley & Sons.

Heij, Christiaan, Paul de Boer, Philip Hans Franses, Teun Kloek and Herman K. van Dijk (2004). *Econometric Methods with Applications in Business and Economics.* Oxford: Oxford University Press.

Herne, Kaisa and Maria Suojanen (2004). "The role of information in choices over income distributions." *Journal of Conflict Resolution* **48**, pp. 173-193.

Hicks, John R. (1940). "The valuation of social income." *Economica* **7**, pp. 105-124.

Hochschild, Jennifer L. (1981). *What's Fair? American Beliefs about Distributive Justice.* Cambridge, Mass.: Harvard University Press.

Hutcheson, Francis (1725). *Inquiry into the Original of our Ideas of Beauty and Virtue.* London. (Revised and edited by Bernhard Fabian, 1971, Hildesheim: Olms.)

Jaccard, James (2001). *Interaction Effects in Logistic Regression.* Sage University Papers Series on Quantitative Applications in the Social Sciences 07-135. Thousand Oaks, CA: Sage.

Jaccard, James, Robert Turrisi and Choi K. Wan (1990). *Interaction Effects in Multiple Regression.* Sage University Papers Series on Quantitative Applications in the Social Sciences 07-72. Thousand Oaks, CA: Sage.

Jaffee, Sara and Janet Shibly Hyde (2000). "Gender differences in moral orientation: A meta-analysis." *Psychological Bulletin* **126**, pp. 703-726.

Jemmott, John B., III and Ruth Tebbets (1980). "Applying social cognition: A content analysis of the Bakke case." *Personality and Social Psychology Bulletin* **6**, pp. 30-36.

Jungeilges, Jochen and Theis Theisen (2005). "An econometric examination of equity judgements elicited through experiments." In Bina Agarwal and Alessandro Vercelli (editors), *Psychology, Rationality and Economic Behavior: Challenging Standard Assumptions.* Cambridge, UK: Palgrave.

Kalai, Ehud (1977). "Proportional solutions to bargaining situations: Interpersonal utility comparisons." *Econometrica* **45**, pp. 1623-1630.

Kalai, Ehud and Meir Smorodinsky (1975). "Other solutions to Nash's bargaining problem." *Econometrica* **43**, pp. 155-162.

Kaldor, Nicholas (1939). "Welfare propositions of economics and interpersonal comparisons of utility." *Economic Journal* **49**, pp. 549-551.

Kleinbaum, David G. and Mitchel Klein (2002). *Logistic Regression: A Self-Learning Text.* 2nd edition. New York: Springer.

Konow, James (2000). "Fair shares: Accountability and cognitive dissonance in allocation decisions." *American Economic Review* **90**, pp. 1072-1091.

Konow, James (2001). "Fair and square: The four sides of distributive justice." *Journal of Economic Behavior and Organization* **46**, pp. 137-164.

Konow, James (2003). "Which is the fairest one of all? A positive analysis of justice theories." *Journal of Economic Literature* **41**, pp. 1188-1239.

Konow, James (2005). "Blind spots: The effects of information and stakes on fairness bias and dispersion." *Social Justice Research* **18**, pp. 349-390.

Konow, James (2009). "Is fairness in the eye of the beholder? An impartial spectator analysis of justice." *Social Choice and Welfare.* Forthcoming.

Lee, Lung-Fei (1983). "Generalized econometric models with selectivity." *Econometrica* **51**, pp. 507-512.

Levitt, Steven D. and John A. List (2007). "What do laboratory experiments measuring social preferences reveal about the real world?" *Journal of Economic Perspectives* **21**, pp. 153-174.

Lévy-Garboua, Louis, Claude Meidinger and Benoît Rapoport (2004). "The formation of social preferences: Some lessons from psychology and biology." In: Louis-André Gérard-Varet, Serge-Christophe Kolm and Jean Mercier-Ythier (editors), *Handbook of the Economics of Reciprocity, Giving, and Altruism.* Amsterdam: Elsevier.

Lippert-Rasmussen, Kasper (2001). "Egalitarianism, option luck and responsibility." *Ethics* **111**, pp. 548-579.

Lissowski, Grzegorz, Tadeus Tyska and Wlodzimirz Okrasa (1991). "Principles of distributive justice." *Journal of Conflict Resolution* **35**, pp. 98-119.

Little, Roderick J.A. and Donald B. Rubin (2002). *Statistical Analysis With Missing Data.* 2nd edition. Hoboken: Wiley.

Mack, Joanna and Stewart Lansley (1985). *Poor Britain.* London: Allen & Unwin.

Major, Brenda and Kay Deaux (1982). "Individual differences in justice behavior." In: Jerald Greenberg and Ronald Cohen (editors), *Equity and Justice in Social Behavior.* New York: Academic Press, pp. 43-76.

Manski (2002). "Identification of decision rules in experiments on simple games of proposal and response." *European Economic Review* **46**, pp. 880-891.

Mellers, Barbara E. (1982). "Equity judgments: A revision of Aristotelian views." *Journal of Experimental Psychology* **111**, pp. 242-270.

Messick, David M. and Keith P. Sentis (1979). "Fairness and preference." *Journal of Experimental Social Psychology* **15**, pp. 418-434.

Michelbach, Philip A., John T. Scott, Richard E. Matland and Brian H. Bornstein (2003). "Doing Rawls justice: An experimental study of income distribution norms." *American Journal of Political Science* **47**, pp. 523-539.

Miller, David (1992). "Distributive justice: What the people think." *Ethics* **102**, pp. 555-593.

Miller, David (1994). "Review of justice: Interdisciplinary perspectives." *Social Justice Research* **7**, pp. 167-188.

Miller, David (1999). *Principles of Social Justice.* Cambridge, Mass.: Harvard University Press.

Mishan, E. J. (1977). "Economic criteria for intergenerational comparisons." *Futures: The Journal of Forecasting and Planning* **9**, pp. 383-404.

Mitchell, Gregory, Philip E. Tetlock, Barbara A. Mellers and Lisa D. Ordóñez (1993). "Judgments of social justice: Compromises between equality and efficiency." *Journal of Personality and Social Psychology* **65**, pp. 629-639.

Moore, B., Jr. (1978). *Injustice: The Social Bases of Obedience and Revolt.* White Plains, NY: M. E. Sharpe.

Moulin, Hervet (1995). *Cooperative Microeconomics.* Princeton: Princeton University Press.

Nagel, Thomas (1991). *Equality and Partiality.* Oxford: Oxford University Press.

Nagler, Jonathan (1994). "Scobit: An alternative estimator to probit and logit." *American Journal of Political Science* **38**, pp. 320-355.

Nash, John F. (1950). "The bargaining problem." *Econometrica* **18**, pp. 155-162.

Nozick, Robert (1974). *Anarchy, State, and Utopia.* New York: Basic Books.

Ordóñez, Lisa D. and Barbara A. Mellers (1993). "Trade-offs in fairness and preference judgments." In: Barbara A. Mellers and Jonathan Baron (editors), *Psychological Perspectives on Justice: Theory and Applications.* Cambridge: Cambridge University Press.

Østerdal, Lars P. (2005). "Axioms for health care resource allocation." *Journal of Health Economics* **24**, pp. 679-702.

Pharo, Patrick (2001). *Les Sens de la Justice, Essai de Sémantique Sociologique.* Paris: PUF.

Rabin, Matthew (1993). "Incorporating fairness into game theory and economics." *American Economic Review* **83**, pp. 1281-1302.

Raphael, David D. (1970). *Problems of Political Philosophy.* London: Macmillan.

Rawls, John (1971). *A Theory of Justice.* Cambridge, Mass.: Harvard University Press.

Rawls, John (1974a). "Some reasons for the maximin criterion." *American Economic Review, Papers and Proceedings* **64**, pp. 141-146.

Rawls, John (1974b). "A reply to Alexander and Musgrave." *Quarterly Journal of Economics* **87**, pp. 633-655.

Rawls, John (1982). "Social unity and primary goods." In: Amartya K. Sen and Bernard Williams (editors), *Utilitarianism and Beyond.* Cambridge: Cambridge University Press.

Rawls, John (1996). *Political Liberalism.* New York: Columbia University Press.

Regenwetter, Michel, Bernard N. Grofman, A.A.J. Marley and Ilia Tsetlin (2007). *Behavioral Social Choice: Probabilistic Models, Statistical Inference, and Applications.* Cambridge: Cambridge University Press.

Riphan, Regina T. and Oliver Serfling (2005). "Item non-response on income and wealth questions." *Empirical Economics* **30**, pp. 521-538.

Roemer, John E. (1993). "A pragmatic theory of responsibility for the egalitarian planner." *Philosophy and Public Affairs* **22**, pp. 146-166.

Roemer, John E. (1996). *Theories of Distributive Justice.* Cambridge, Mass.: Harvard University Press.

Rooney, Patrick M., Debra J. Mesch, William Chin and Kathryn S. Steinberg (2005). "The effects of race, gender, and survey methodologies on giving in the US." *Economics Letters* **86**, pp. 173-180.

Rubin, Donald B. (1976). "Inference and missing data." *Biometrika* **63**, pp. 581-592.

Rubinstein, Ariel (1999). "Experience from a course in game theory: Pre- and post-class problem sets as a didactic device." *Games and Economic Behavior* **28**, pp. 155-170.

Rubinstein, Ariel (2001). "A theorist's view of experiments." *European Economic Review* **45**, pp. 615-628.

Sabbagh, Clara (2001). "A taxonomy of normative and empirically oriented theories." *Social Justice Research* **14**, pp. 237-263.

Samuelson, Paul A. (1950). "Evaluation of real national income." *Oxford Economic Papers* **2**, pp. 1-29.

Schnell, Rainer, Paul B. Hill and Elke Esser (2005). *Methoden der empirischen Sozialforschung.* 7th edition. München, Wien: R. Oldenbourg Verlag.

Schokkaert, Erik (1999). "M. Tout-le-monde est 'post-welfariste': Opinions sur la justice redistributive." *Revue Economique* **50**, pp. 811-831. Available in English as: "Mr. Fairmind is post-welfarist: Opinions on distributive justice." Discussion Paper DPS 98.09. Catholic University of Leuven, Department of Economics.

Schokkaert, Erik and Bart Capéau (1991). "Interindividual differences in opinions about distributive justice." *Kyklos* **44**, pp. 325-345.

Schokkaert, Erik and Kurt Devooght (2003). "Responsibility-sensitive fair compensation in different cultures." *Social Choice and Welfare* **21**, pp. 207-242.

Schokkaert, Erik and Bert Overlaet (1989). "Moral intuitions and economic models of distributive justice." *Social Choice and Welfare* **6**, pp. 19-31.

Scitovsky, Tibor (1941). "A note on welfare propositions in economics." *Review of Economic Studies* **9**, pp. 77-88.

Scott, John T., Richard E. Matland, Philip A. Michelbach and Brian H. Bornstein (2001). "Just deserts: An experimental study of distributive justice norms." *American Journal of Political Science* **45**, pp. 749-767.

Sen, Amartya K. (1973). *On Economic Inequality.* Oxford: Clarendon Press.

Sen, Amartya K. (1977). "On weights and measures: Informational constraints in social welfare analysis." *Econometrica* **45**, pp. 1539-1572.

Sen, Amartya K. (1979). "The welfare basis of real income comparisons: A survey." *Journal of Economic Literature* **17**, pp. 1-45.

Sen, Amartya K. (1980). "Equality of what?" In: Sterling M. McMurrin (editor), *Tanner Lectures on Human Values.* Cambridge: Cambridge University Press.

Sen, Amartya K. (1984). *Resources, Values and Development.* Oxford: Blackwell.

Sen, Amartya K. (1985). *Commodities and Capabilities.* Amsterdam: North-Holland.

Sen, Amartya K. (1987). *On Ethics and Economics.* Oxford: Blackwell.

Sen, Amartya K. (1992). *Inequality Reexamined.* Oxford: Oxford University Press.

Sen, Amartya K. and Bernard Williams (editors) (1982). *Utilitarianism and Beyond.* Cambridge: Cambridge University Press.

Shapiro, Robert Y. and Harpreet Mahajan (1986). "Gender differences in policy preferences: A summary of trends from the 1960s to the 1980s." *Public Opinion Quarterly* **50**, pp. 42-61.

Siegel, Sidney and N. Jon Castellan, Jr. (1988). *Nonparametric Statistics for the Behavioral Sciences.* 2nd edition. New York: McGraw-Hill.

Skitka, Linda J. and Philip E. Tetlock (1992). "Allocating scarce resources: A contingency model of distributive justice." *Journal of Experimental Social Psychology* **28**, pp. 491-522.

Smart, J.J.C. and Bernard Williams (1973). *Utilitarianism: For and Against.* Cambridge: Cambridge University Press.

Stolzenberg, Ross M. and Daniel A. Relles (1997). "Tools for intuition about sample selection bias and its correction." *American Sociological Review* **62**, pp. 494-507.

Studenmund, Arnold H. (2001). *Using Econometrics: A Practical Guide.* 4th edition. Boston, Mass.: Addison Wesley Longman, Inc.

Temkin, Larry (1993). *Inequality.* Oxford: Oxford University Press.

Thomson, William and Hal R. Varian (1985). "Theories of justice based on symmetrie." In: Leonid Hurwicz, David Schmeidler and Hugo Sonnenschein (editors), *Social Goals and Social Organization: Essays in Memory of Elisha Pazner.* New York: Cambridge University Press.

Tinbergen, Jan (1946). *Redelijke Inkomensverdeling.* Haarlem: De Gulden Pers.

Törnblom, Kjell (1992). "The social psychology of distributive justice." In: Klaus R. Scherer (editor), *Justice: Interdisciplinary Perspectives.* Cambridge: Cambridge University Press.

Traub, Stefan, Christian Seidl, Ulrich Schmidt and Maria Vittoria Levati (2005). "Friedman, Harsanyi, Rawls, Boulding - or somebody else?" *Social Choice and Welfare* **24**, pp. 283-309.

Tungodden, Bertil (2000). "Egalitarianism: Is leximin the only option?" *Economics and Philosophy* **16**, pp. 229-245.

Tversky, Amos and Daniel Kahneman (1981). "The framing of decisions and the psychology of choice." *Science* **211**, pp. 453-458.

Vallentyne, Peter (2000). "Equality, efficiency, and the priority of the worse off." *Economics and Philosophy* **16**, pp. 1-19.

Wagstaff, Adam (1991). "QALYs and the equity-efficiency trade-off." *Journal of Health Economics* **10**, pp. 21-41.

Wagstaff, Adam (1993). "Erratum - QALYs and the equity-efficiency trade-off." *Journal of Health Economics* **12**, p. 237.

Walzer, Michael (1983). *Spheres of Justice: A Defense of Pluralism and Equality.* New York: Basic Books, Inc.

Williams, Alan and Richard Cookson (2000). "Equity in health." In: A.J. Culyer and J.P. Newhouse (editors), *Handbook of Health Economics.* Volume 1b. Amsterdam: Elsevier, pp. 1863-1910.

Winkelmann, Rainer and Stefan Boes (2006). *Analysis of Microdata.* Berlin, Heidelberg: Springer.

Yaari, Menachem and Maya Bar-Hillel (1984). "On dividing justly." *Social Choice and Welfare* **1**, pp. 1-24.

Young, Peyton H. (1994). *Equity: In Theory and Practice.* Princeton, NJ: Princeton University Press.

For the avoidance of doubt, input of the whole or any part of this publication into any generative artificial intelligence model, chatbot, program, software or technology is expressly prohibited without the prior written consent of the publisher.